SOMEONE
MUST DIE

(Preserving a People)

Befriending the hostile Nomadic
Yuquí of Central Bolivia

ALAN FOSTER

ISBN 978-1-0980-3977-6 (paperback)
ISBN 978-1-0980-3975-2 (digital)

Christian Faith Publishing, Inc.
832 Park Avenue
Meadville, PA 16335
www.christianfaithpublishing.com

Printed in the United States of America

Acknowledgments

I WISH TO THANK MY deceased father, Lester Foster, for the extensive journals and letters he preserved, which made the first portion of the book possible. I also want to thank departed fellow worker, Bob Garland, for the use I made of his description of the 1980 shootings. Thank you also to Phil Burns and to Steve Parker for use I made of materials they wrote or edited. And last, but not least, I want to thank those who read or edited my writings and offered their input on ways to improve upon them. May God receive the glory for what He accomplished through His servants!

Carland Loreen,

Thank you for all you and your family have done over the years to advance the Kingdom of God on earth.

With much love,
Alan and Vickie
9 April 2010

Preface

THIS IS THE TRUE STORY of the effort to preserve several small bands of the nomadic Yuquí (you-KEY) in central Bolivia from annihilation by settlers, loggers, hunters, trappers, cattlemen, and oilmen who were invading their territory. As missionaries, our concern goes beyond preserving the body, since man's eternal relationship with God is of the greatest importance. Much of the story is compiled from journals and letters written by my father, Les Foster, or from my journals, letters, and memories about our experiences, along with our many missionary colleagues, in befriending and helping the once hostile nomads settle down.

The majority of the names I use for the Yuquí portrayed in this book are pseudonyms used intentionally in this information age to protect the individuals and their descendants. In the early part of the book, the recreated dialogue technique has been used since very little actual dialogue was recorded, whereas in the latter portion, much of the dialogue was recorded or written down shortly after the incidents so is often the actual words spoken.

In writing this story, I have chosen to ignore many of the more revolting and brutal aspects of the Yuquí way of life that I witnessed while living among them as those would be of little positive value and would only serve to shock and horrify the reader. The way of their ancestors is in the distant past for the current generation of Yuquí, and many of them have no idea what their people were like back then.

The Yuquí will always have a warm place in my heart and memories. It is a privilege to have known them and to have been able to help them transition from the nomadic life to a more sedentary one.

Alan Foster

Prologue

THE HARSH SOUND OF AN arrow grating its way across a palm-wood bow put my senses on alert, and I found I had thrown myself to the ground to the right of where I had been walking. In the process, I had rotated 180 degrees and was looking down our back trail as my gun fired four quick shots in the direction of the attackers. Simultaneous with my reaction, I heard the thud as an arrow drove into Steve's body and the sound of air being violently expelled from him along with an agonized groan.

In my heightened sense of awareness, I took in the entire scene at a quick glance. Potbelly had a fully drawn bow with an eight-foot arrow and was trying to get a bead on Felix who was crouched over and turning to his right. With my gun still aimed down the back trail, I threw two quick shots closely over Potbelly. There had been no conscious thought to pull the trigger for my first four shots, but the next two shots were fired with an attitude.

We had done so much for these jungle dwellers, and now they were repaying our many kindnesses in this manner! My shots startled the attackers, causing them to scream with fright. Two of them dropped their bows and arrows, and all four fled. As quickly as the attack had begun, it was over.

Of the four attackers, the vision that was seared into my mind was that of Potbelly with the fully drawn bow as he tried to follow Felix's movement and get a shot at him. Fortunately, my two shots over his head and Felix's movement had caused that shot to miss.

We three missionaries had been leading the way down the trail on an aborted fishing expedition with nomads we were in the process of befriending. Felix had been leading the way, then Steve, then me, with the four jungle dwellers following us. We had interacted with them over the course of several years, hunted together in the jungle, and spent at least two nights camped with them in the jungle. Why, after almost sixty encounters with them, would they turn on us in this way? Why would they try to kill my two colleagues?

Steve lay on the ground where he had fallen. A bamboo bleeder-tipped arrow entering low on the right side of his back had driven itself all the way through his body, pierced the tip of the lung, and left the point of the arrow protruding from his chest. Steve's moaning broke the silence, and then his first words: "Pull it out, brother, it hurts."

While both men had been hit by bleeder-tipped arrows, Felix was only lightly wounded. An arrow had ricocheted off his left shoulder blade, causing a shallow wound. Meanwhile, Steve had an arrow point embedded in his body. The bleeder-tipped arrow had a bamboo tip shaped like a lance. The tip itself was two and a half inches wide and roughly eighteen inches long, and the cupped shape of the bamboo made a wide semicircular incision where it had entered his body. The tip was poking out the front of Steve's chest while the part that had been attached to the arrow shaft protruded from his back. While I knew he must be in terrible agony, I replied, "I can't pull it out, we need to leave it in to stop the bleeding."

Tin Miners Invade the Chapare

LAND OF GOLD AND FORTUNE! It was the early 1500s when into the land of the Incas came the Spanish Conquistadores, mounted on horses, wearing iron clothing and carrying the most modern weapons of their day. The empire of the Incas would soon succumb to the treachery and deceit of the invaders, and the populace of their empire would be enslaved while being greatly reduced in numbers by disease and maltreatment. Gold was king, and silver was his queen!

In Bolivia, it wasn't until 1953, after the revolution by the MNR (National Revolutionary Movement) that the peasant farmers once again received ownership of the vast tracts of land the Spanish conquerors had divided among themselves. Four hundred years of slavery for the descendants of the Incan empire! The brutality of the Spanish overlords had at last been overthrown by those who wanted to return the land to the people and nationalize the mines so their wealth could benefit the masses instead of a handful of wealthy descendants of the Spaniards. Although Bolivia received its independence from Spain in 1825, the landlords had continued to keep the vast masses of people enslaved and impoverished while becoming ultra-wealthy themselves.

Bolivia has been described by one writer as "a pauper on a king's throne," indicating that the country has vast exploitable wealth but very poor people. Bolivian natural resources include the world's largest known lithium deposit, tin, zinc, silver, gold, natural gas, oil, and over 230 other minerals, yet the vast majority of inhabitants were and are severely impoverished. Wealth is abundantly available but has not been properly managed.

Before WWII, tin was the principal export of Bolivia, and mining employed large numbers of people. After the war, as production plummeted, thousands of miners became unemployed. With the revolution of the early 1950s and the breaking up of large landholdings, the government opened up the eastern jungle area at the base of the Andes Mountains adjoining the Amazon basin and gave free land to unemployed miners.

What no one realized was that bands of hostile nomads, descendants of the Tupí-Guaraní tribe, were already living and roaming in that area. As their homeland was invaded by the unemployed miners, the situation was ripe for conflict.

The Chief Approaches Death

DEATH WAS NEAR, AND IT was clear that the elderly chief wouldn't last much longer. He had been going downhill now for months and no longer had the strength to travel through the forest with the band of nomads. His two oldest sons, Strong Arm and Big Chest, were worried. Their father had been a powerful leader and provider, and it would be necessary to send other spirits along to accompany him in death. Otherwise, his spirit might return and punish them after death.

Death of a high-class person in this group of jungle dwellers was always a difficult time. Among other things, someone must die to accompany the high-class person in death. This was necessary to keep him or her happy in the afterlife, and they would need servants such as they had been accustomed to in this life. Who knew what might be needed in the next life? The spirits of the dead who lived up in the sky must be kept happy.

Strong Arm and Big Chest knew their father had been one of the more powerful leaders of their small band, and it would be necessary to send more than one or two men to accompany him in death; several important adults must be sent along with him. It fell on Strong Arm and Big Chest to make that happen. Someone must die!

The two brothers headed off into the jungle, ostensibly to hunt, but in reality, to discuss the problem.

"What shall we do, younger brother?" began Strong Arm, once they were far enough away from camp. "Who shall we send along with dad in death?"

This was a tough problem made even more difficult by the knowledge that each man they killed would mean one less hunter and gatherer to provide for their small group. Eighty people had a very difficult time surviving off the land since they grew no crops and subsisted on what they could hunt with bow and arrow or gather from the forest. Life was already challenging enough without sacrificing several providers.

"I think we will need to send at least this many along to accompany father," suggested Big Chest to his older brother, holding up five fingers. "Dad has been no ordinary leader of the people."

Since their language had no counting system, fingers were necessary to indicate an accurate number. The discussion between the brothers continued as each realized they would need to kill multiple people in order to appease the spirit of their important father. Now the problem was how to kill that many without being injured or killed themselves by those they would need to execute. No one wanted to die, but everyone in the tribe would expect the brothers to honor the spirit of their father in this way. It was a time-honored custom, and no one wanted the spirit of the dead person to return and make their lives more difficult. His unappeased spirit would be living in the sky and could affect their everyday lives by keeping them from getting game in the hunt, sending sickness, or bringing storms that would fell tree limbs or trees on them. They all knew that appeasing the spirit of the great chief would be necessary. Otherwise, his spirit would make their lives unbearable.

After chatting for a time, the brothers split up, each going his separate way to hunt for meat, honey trees, fruit, and whatever else they could find to feed their families for another day. The conversation was on hold for now, but they would need to continue it before their father breathed his last.

The day continued, hot and humid, with buzzing insects tormenting all who lived in the tropical forest. Big Chest had gone off toward a nearby swamp to hunt. These isolated old river bends in the middle of the forest were a prime habitat for many types of animals. Maybe he would find a capybara grazing in the grasses along the edge or perhaps an alligator or caiman sunning itself. Any of these would be suitable to feed his family for a day or two. The capybara would be especially nice since it was one of the few jungle animals with a nice layer of fat under the skin. Fat meat was rare but delicious.

The capybara spent much time in the water, and the extra fat kept it warm, even in the cool water where it loved to repose. An alligator or caiman, on the other hand, was lean meat, but the small intestine was fatty and especially delicious when smoked over the fire. In fact, it was his favorite protein delicacy! Rarely did he share it with his children but occasionally gave his wife a portion as he had special feelings for her. He thought of her longingly. Even though she was his cousin, the tiny size of their jungle band dictated his marriage to her. Eligible partners were not abundant. She was a good partner and did her share in the relationship. Not only had she stripped and dried ambaibo tree bark to make rope for the hammock they slept in, but she also made his bowstring and her bark "skirt" out of the same material.

Big Chest continued making his way along the edge of the swamp, stopping frequently to listen to the many sounds of the jungle. It was a noisy place, but he had lived there all his life and could distinguish most of the sounds—raucous birds, squawking, whistling, or hooting; croaking frogs, the swish of a branch as a monkey jumped from one tree to the next, the mooing of the jaguar as it searched for a mate, the whistle of the tapir, the terrified cry of a peccary (type of javelina pig) as it fled from danger, the lion-like roar of the howler monkeys, the distinctive whistle of the capuchin monkey as it roamed together with the squirrel monkey, searching for fruit, or the cry of a young alligator for its mother. All of these and many more sounds were so familiar to Big Chest that he recognized them without realizing how familiar they were.

In front of him, an area of swamp grass had been flattened to a width of about two feet, extending from the border of the jungle out into the wetland. Danger! Evidently, a large anaconda lived in this bog and had slithered back into the water recently. He would need to be extra vigilant. A snake this size could swallow a man whole, not the end he wanted to contemplate for himself. He continued cautiously forward, knowing that at least there would be evidence of flattened grass or leaves if the snake were to come out of the swamp elsewhere. Even if he were to spot the snake, there was no sense killing it as people didn't eat snake, no matter how large it was. The best thing was to avoid it and continue looking for animals that could be eaten.

Further along, the grass became less dense, and he could see an area of open water. He advanced stealthily, watching and listening, trying not to startle any edible animal he might come upon. A rotting log lay, partly in and partly out of the water, and alongside of it, on the far side, he could see the fin of a large fish extending up out of the water. He wouldn't be able to shoot it from this side due to the log being in the way, so would have to make his way farther along the bank and shoot once he was on the other side of the log.

He eased back into the trees along the bank, worked his way forward another fifty paces, and then crept back out toward the open water of the swamp. Now he was on the other side of the log and could shoot the fish. Slowly raising his seven-and-a-half-foot bow, he threaded a barb-tipped arrow of the same length to the bowstring, sighted carefully down the shaft, aiming a few inches below and forward of the fish fin. There was a grating sound as the smooth bamboo arrow rasped its way across the palm-wood bow.

Thunk! The arrow impacted the fish, but instead of the arrow and fish taking flight out into the waters of the lake as he had anticipated, the arrow and fish stayed in the same location, although the fish was thrashing around on the arrow. The arrow point had passed through the fish and sank into the soft rotting log. At least he wouldn't have to wade out too far into the swamp to retrieve the fish as it was only about three feet from shore.

Looking around cautiously in case there was anything he had missed seeing, he eased his way up to where his arrow was embedded in the log. With the hard tip of his palm bow, he jabbed the head of the fish several times until it was unresponsive; then, carefully gripping the eighteen-inch-long hardened palm arrow tip, he worked it out of the log and brought the arrow and fish up on shore. He now had a nice catfish weighing about ten pounds and still had plenty of time to continue hunting. It was only midmorning.

Not wanting to carry ten pounds of fish for the rest of the day, he hung it on a tree branch about five feet off the ground. A jaguar might be able to reach it there, but most other animals wouldn't get it too easily. Ants and flying insects would doubtless find it there but wouldn't damage it too much.

Big Chest rested for a minute or two, had a few swallows of the great-tasting tannin-flavored swamp water, and then continued working his way around the swamp. He still hoped to find a tapir or a capybara, but at least he had food for his family's supper. It wasn't often he got a large fish this easily. Normally, he would have brought his slave with him to carry his game, get the fish he shot out of the water for him, and do any of the less desirable tasks, but since he had wanted to talk to Strong Arm in private, they had both left camp without their slaves. If he lost any arrows today, he would have to come back tomorrow with his slave and have him rescue the lost arrows, whether they were up in a tree, out in the swamp, or elsewhere. He wasn't about to risk his own life unnecessarily by climbing too high up a tree or venturing far out in a swamp where a large anaconda lived and hunted in order to retrieve an alligator or capybara.

Pondering on those issues got him to thinking more about his slave. He really needed his slave to bring in his firewood, keep his smoky fire going in the night to keep insects away, carry in the game, retrieve arrows, and many other useful chores. At the same time, he and Strong Arm needed to kill five men to accompany their father when he died. Would he have to kill his slave? Or were there others in the group who were more expendable? He hated the thought of not having a slave, but he didn't want to risk the wrath of his dead father's spirit. This could be a tough choice! Who could they kill? Who was the most expendable? Someone must die; or in this case, several people.

The sun continued to rise, nearing its midpoint in the sky, almost noon. By now, the turtles and alligators would be out, sunning themselves. Maybe he could find a nice alligator, although the thought of going into "Anaconda Swamp" to retrieve it didn't sound at all appealing. Even so, the need for food was compelling and often required taking great risks. If he saw an alligator, he would face whatever dangers necessary to kill it. Without food, there would be no survival, and it was unlikely his wife would offer him any special favors.

Soon Big Chest decided to move away from the swamp, circling out into the forest and working his way back toward where he had hung the fish. He might scare up other game farther from the edge of the swamp. After going a short distance, he stopped and stood still for a few moments, listening to the sounds of the jungle. Hearing nothing of importance, he began to whistle, imitating the sound capuchin monkeys make when they get separated from their troop. He began softly and, when there was no reply, continued calling but increased the volume of his whistle little by little. Nothing.

He moved on, stopping every few minutes to whistle for the capuchins. They were one of the more abundant animals in the woodlands and could be found almost daily. While he and his family enjoyed eating them, it was a lot of work getting these small creatures, so larger game was preferred. Often his arrow would miss the monkey and lodge high up in a tree or the arrow would miss and go far enough that finding it again could take a good bit of time. Even when his arrow penetrated a monkey, the arrow and monkey would often remain up in the tree, making it necessary to climb the tree and kill the wounded monkey in order to retrieve arrow and game.

Many times, a monkey that was transfixed by an arrow would begin gnawing on the arrow, damaging it to where much extra work was entailed in repairing it. Sometimes, on longer shots, the monkey would dodge the slow-moving arrow, causing a miss, even though he had aimed correctly. His preference was to hunt monkeys while his slave was along to handle the more dangerous aspects of retrieving the game or arrows. Even so, he would shoot monkeys if they made an appearance.

One fish would be a light supper for a family that lived principally on meat, and others in the tribe would be hoping he had found enough game to share with them. Living off the land by hunting and gathering was a grueling way to survive. Sharing with others when you had an abundance was important for survival of the band of nomads.

Not only was Big Chest attuned to the sounds of the forest, but there were many smells to which he had become accustomed—the "warm" body aroma of a tapir, the pungent scent of collared peccaries or white-lipped peccaries, the odor of monkey feces on the ground under the tree where they had spent the night, and many more. Occasionally, he would sniff the air, looking for any indication that might lead to additional food for his family and small band of jungle dwellers.

In the quiet of the jungle, a branch "swished" down and up. There was no breeze to make such a sound, so it was likely that an animal or a bird had jumped off the branch, making that noise. Big Chest once again began whistling softly for capuchin monkeys and this time received a response. He grinned with excitement and looked for a spot where he could stand with foliage camouflaging him so he wouldn't be readily seen from above by the monkeys. Once he was in place, he stood all his long arrows up vertically so he would be able to "load" and fire quickly.

Positioning his bow horizontally about shoulder height through the vegetation around him, such that he could quickly slide an arrow onto it and shoot upward, he continued calling softly to the capuchins. Whistler monkeys have a natural curiosity which, unfortunately for them, is a deadly trait with which to have been born.

As Big Chest whistled, shielding his mouth with cupped fingers in order to soften the volume as well as make it harder to tell where the whistle was coming from, the monkeys moved slowly in his direction, looking around for the monkeys that were calling to them. Occasionally, he would stop briefly while the monkeys moved closer and then call again, softer each time.

Soon he could see the whistlers approaching along with smaller squirrel monkeys. Eventually, a large capuchin was nearly overhead, searching diligently for whoever was calling to it. Big Chest launched his first arrow, impacting the torso of the large male capuchin with a loud thud. The injured male began screaming with pain and fear as other monkeys rushed over to see what had happened. None of them were yet aware of Big Chest who cautiously threaded a second arrow into his bow and sighted on the next largest capuchin he could see.

Whump! The arrow released and a second capuchin began calling out in pain. Big Chest grinned to himself. Two shots, two large monkeys. Things were looking good. There were aspects he enjoyed about jungle life, and a successful hunt was one of them. The troop of monkeys were looking around diligently, trying to spot the danger, and now many of them began fleeing away from the two injured monkeys. Not knowing where the danger lay, many of them ran through the trees directly above Big Chest. He carefully fitted a third arrow to his bow and watched for the best possible shot at the largest monkey he could see. There were no more capuchins visible, but a good-sized squirrel monkey momentarily perched directly above him, looking intently for the danger confronting the troop. The shot was too good not to take.

Big Chest's arrow impacted the yellow and black monkey in the chest, and it tumbled to the ground almost at his feet. It was so stunned, it hadn't even begun to cry out, so Big Chest speedily finished it off, knocking it on the head with a piece of tree branch. Fitting another arrow to his bow, he stood for a moment, waiting to see if another good shot would present itself, but the monkeys had fled. Now he would have to climb up and get the two wounded monkeys before heading home. The hunt had been successful, allowing him to go home and share game with his loved ones before beginning to repair his arrows for tomorrow's hunt. Hunting was a daily necessity, except for those rare occasions when they had an abundance of meat.

The Band Separates

Strong Arm coveted his brother's wife, Tame Pig, who was a beautiful woman and would have been his first choice of a marriage partner had she been old enough when he came of age to marry. However, his younger brother, Big Chest, had been the right age to marry Tame Pig when she came to womanhood, so she became his. That didn't stop Strong Arm from occasionally propositioning his brother's wife when Big Chest was out of camp hunting or whenever he happened to find himself alone with her.

Tame Pig with husband Chief Big Chest.

While he loved his wife, Little Tapir, he wasn't averse to a relationship with his brother's wife as well. From time to time, Big Chest's anger exploded against his older brother when he would return to camp and learn from Tame Pig that Strong Arm had once again propositioned her. Sharing meat with a woman was one way of letting her know he had an interest in her, and Strong Arm offered game to his brother's wife whenever he could do so without the knowledge of Little Tapir or Big Chest; although in a small band of nomads like theirs, it was impossible to keep such a secret.

Knowing that he offered game to Tame Pig didn't set well with his wife, Little Tapir, or with his brother, but it didn't stop Strong Arm from trying again and again. The months went by, and friction grew between the brothers. With their father dead, these two were the acknowledged leaders of their band of seventy-four people. When their father died, they had killed five grown men to accompany his spirit rather than risk retaliation by his spirit after death. He had been a powerful leader, and they knew his spirit had been watching to make sure he got the respect he deserved after death. He could still come back to impact their lives in many negative ways.

The two brothers were in constant competition with each other, seeing who could be the most successful at the hunt and who could ingratiate himself best with other members of the tribe. They were the two most important providers for the entire group, although a few other men also did their fair share.

After saying goodbye to Tame Pig, Big Chest picked up his bow and arrow and headed out on the day's hunt. Strong Arm lingered behind, ostensibly repairing arrows that were damaged during yesterday's hunt. Once his brother was gone, Strong Arm waited until Little Tapir along with a few other women went off to strip bark from the ambaibo trees along a nearby arroyo. Tame Pig was busy tending her children and didn't pay much attention to what was going on around her. She would have been smart to have gone with the other women but didn't realize that until Strong Arm approached and suggested that the two of them go out of camp together. She wanted no part of it, resisting his advances and letting him know in no uncertain terms that she wasn't interested.

Strong Arm was angry with her evasive tactics and, taking her by the arm, began dragging her out into the jungle where they could be alone. She fought back, and he began striking her with his hand, insisting she accompany him. Then he threw her to the ground, but she curled into a fetal position to protect herself, making it more challenging for him. He backed off for a moment, trying to decide what to do next, and she took the opportunity to rise to her feet and flee back toward the relative safety of the camp. She bolted, but he grabbed her once again and, as they fought, threw her, thinking she would go to the ground. Instead, she impacted the root system of a pachubilla palm tree.

The pachubilla is a tall slender palm rising as much as 200 feet into the air and is supported by a root system of many slim legs reaching up at a sixty-degree angle from the ground before attaching themselves to the trunk of the palm four or five feet up. Each leg of the root system is two to two and a half inches in diameter and covered with sharp squatty thorns about three-eighths of an inch long.

When Tame Pig's body struck the root system of the pachubilla palm, she screamed in agony as some of the thorn tips broke off in her body while others scratched or scraped their way down her arms, side, and back, opening cuts and assorted puncture wounds as she slid down. Strong Arm was terrified at how things had turned out. He knew his brother wouldn't take this assault on his wife lightly. Grabbing his bow and arrows, he fled to the jungle where he could spend the day hunting as he tried to decide how to deal with the situation when he had to face his younger brother. Maybe if he shot a tapir or other large game, he could give out generous portions of meat to appease all those he had offended.

Women and children who were near the camp heard Tame Pig's screams and came to her aid, doctoring her wounds, and ministering to her in her agony. Some of her wounds were almost like knife cuts where she had slid across thorns, others were puncture wounds, but all of them were extremely painful. With no modern analgesics or pain-deadening salves, it was a going to be a very bad day!

The hours passed too quickly for Strong Arm, and with the knowledge of the upcoming confrontation with his brother on his mind, he couldn't really focus on the hunt. Soon he would need to return to camp and face the wrath of his younger brother. It was then the thought came to him: Why not go back early and flee with his family? Maybe his younger brother was still out on the hunt, and he could gather Little Tapir and their children and leave, avoiding the confrontation until Big Chest had time to calm down.

He headed back to the camp, and as he neared, he slowed to approach stealthily, not wanting to get caught off guard if his brother had returned. He could hear murmured voices as well as the occasional groan from Tame Pig but no indication that Strong Arm was in camp, so he went on in. Soon he and his family had gathered their few belongings—bark hammock, cooking kettle, bow and arrows, ax and machete—and were on their way out of camp. Once they were out of hearing distance from the camp, Strong Arm stopped and instructed Little Tapir, "Go back to camp and look around as if you left something behind. If any of your friends ask what you're looking for, quietly tell them that if they would like to travel with us. They should talk to their husbands tonight and have them join us tomorrow or the next day at the grassy area where I recently shot a tapir. We don't want to travel alone."

He knew it might be many moons before his brother forgot about Tame Pig's injuries, or maybe that would never happen; better to be prepared to survive without the larger group. If a few families joined them, they could roam the forest with their own band. Once Little Tapir returned from the camp, they moved quickly, wanting to put distance between themselves and the larger group before nightfall.

For the next three days Strong Arm and Little Tapir lingered in the forest near the grassy area but far enough from it to not be easily located by his angry brother. Each day, Strong Arm hunted near their camp, keeping alert for other members of the band who might choose to join his family, and eventually, four other families who had decided to accompany them appeared. With five families and four slaves, the small group numbered twenty-seven people. Now they could move farther away from the main group of their people.

Over the next months, they worked their way south and east, eventually crossing the upper reaches of the Ichilo River, ending up between it and the Yapacaní River. It would be more than thirty years before they reunited with the group that had been led by Big Chest, and by then, both brothers would be dead.

Big Chest and his small band, in the meantime, worked their way north and west, crossing the upper reaches of the Chimoré River to begin roaming between it and the Chapare River. The two brothers would never see each other again, although the story of Tame Pig and the thorny pachubilla palm would be recounted many times over the next thirty years as she narrated the painful experience.

The Missionaries

Les and Lois Foster arrived in Bolivia in 1955 and, a few months later, were asked by their mission board to spend some time near the town of Todos Santos in the Chapare River region where the tin miners turned colonists were now living and farming. Another missionary was returning to the homeland for a few months to see friends and family; Les and Lois would live on her jungle farm and keep an eye on things while she was gone.

The town of Todos Santos boasted a grass airstrip adequate for a DC-3 aircraft, one of the surplus airplanes sold all over the world after World War II. The plane brought in passengers and cargo and departed with travelers and bales of odiferous cow hides destined for the tanneries of Cochabamba. Both cattle and hides were brought up the Chapare River on wooden river barges from cattle ranches many days downstream. The grass streets of the small frontier town were cratered with potholes, and cows, burros, ducks, and chickens roamed free. Pigs refreshed themselves in the mudholes around the main plaza, and the houses were mostly palm and bamboo structures roofed with dry, flammable, palm leaves.

Les and Lois Foster family at the Todos Santos airstrip with a DC-3 parked behind them.

Normally the town was quiet, with only five farm trucks and two tractors to disturb the silence. A rustic sawmill stood near the bank of the river where large rafts of logs arrived to be pulled up to the mill by tractor. The total population of the town, including surrounding farms and colonies, was estimated to be under 1,800 people.

The colonists in the surrounding farms were mostly Quechua Indians who had once formed part of the Inca Empire in the high Andes. The first of them had arrived in the area about thirty-five years earlier to clear farms in the jungle. Trails had been cut and the land surveyed, then the jungle was felled, crops were planted, and thatch-roofed houses were built.

The ambience was much like early settlements on the frontiers of the western United States. Each colony had its own political boss, mayor, and other leaders who were under the rule of the authorities in the town of Todos Santos. Todos Santos was in the section of El Chapare in the state of Cochabamba of which the city of Cochabamba is the capital.

Shortly after arriving in Todos Santos, Les began hearing from townspeople about a group of hostile nomads who were stealing from farmers a short ways upriver. "Another colonist has been shot! We need to kill the Indians!" stated Juan, one of the miners turned farmer who had come to town to buy supplies. "They steal our crops and our chickens. Then we have no food for our families."

"Does anyone speak the Indian's language?" asked Les.

"We don't know what tribe they might be, and it's too dangerous to go into the jungle and find them." Juan was one of the small-scale farmers living in the La Jota colony. His cash crop and that of all the other farmers was coca, the leaf from which cocaine is extracted. In addition to coca, some grew modest amounts of cacao as a cash crop, but most of the crops were for their own consumption. Plantains and manioc (a potato-like edible tuberous root) were the principal staples, while corn, rice, and papayas were other easy to grow and abundant crops. Various types of citrus fruit also grew in profusion and without much effort on the part of the farmers.

Les continued chatting with Juan. Although Les had only been in Bolivia for a few months, he was working hard to learn Spanish, and conversations were a helpful part of picking up the language. "Do you know how many Indians there are?" he questioned.

Juan didn't know the answer but offered the following: "We've seen some of their abandoned camps with fifteen to twenty fires. Maybe there are sixty people, although we don't know for sure. Maybe there are more, maybe less. They sure eat a lot, though. When they steal plantains, they sometimes take more than a hundred stalks, leaving us with nothing to eat. They also take our manioc, corn, and other crops. Then we can't feed our families."

Les and Lois spent the next two months keeping an eye on the Nueva Vida farm for Marge Day and adjusting to the novelty of life in the Bolivian jungle. Les relates the following in one of his early journals:

> As we lay side by side on the double bed, but in individual mosquito nets, the hair on the back of our necks stood up as we heard one of the most terrifying screams I've ever heard. Lois, shaking, turned to me and asked, "What was that?"
>
> I said, "I don't know, but it sounds like someone who has been lost in the jungle so long they have turned into a raving maniac."
>
> She replied, "Oh, Lester, don't say things like that when I'm already so scared. I can't sleep, and there are two thicknesses of mosquito netting between us."

The jungle is full of strange sounds at night, and biting, stinging insects abound both day and night. As Les lay there in his mosquito net, watching the bats fly around overhead, he thought to himself, "This is a real blessing having these bats to eat the insects that have been biting us so much." But then during the night, as he heard bats flapping around right outside his mosquito net, he came to the realization that not all of these were ordinary bats, but rather some were vampire bats, hovering, waiting for him to roll over against the net's side and give them a chance for a meal. The bats, who spent the night swooping through the house eating flying insects, also left manure all over the house, so the kitchen counter and tabletop had to be washed down before they could be safely used.

At the same time, during their time there at Nueva Vida, God generously supplied them with fish, wild ducks, and other jungle meats, so there was never a lack of protein in their diet. They had little responsibility and could spend time getting to know their new environment and asking questions from river travelers who stopped by. It was a time of adaption to the isolation of the jungle.

Les and Lois had been released from Spanish study in the city of Cochabamba about a month previously and then waited until their two oldest children were out of school before leaving for Todos Santos. Once they arrived in Todos Santos, it took two days to find a boat large enough to carry their family, supplies, and equipment down to Nueva Vida in the Yuracaré Indian territory. Upon arrival, they were abandoned to learn and adapt on their own as veteran missionary Marge Day left for the USA while her helper, Mateo, a young believer from the Trinitario tribe left to visit his family in another area of the jungle lowlands.

The only tame living things Marge and Mateo left behind were chickens, ducks, turkeys, and cats. The Foster family was now isolated in a place where they would be forced to use the limited amount of Spanish and Yuracaré they had been studying up until a few days ago.

It was a rare day that they didn't receive visitors, most of them Yuracarés traveling the Chapare River in their tiny dugout canoes. Often, as many as three families would show up in a single day, and the Fosters would use the opportunity to play Gospel records in the Yura language and, although limited in the language, talk to them of their personal need for a Savior. It was a wonderful feeling to be able to share God's Word with these people. One morning, three Yuracaré believers stopped in, and they all had a great time of Christian fellowship, even with their limited ability to communicate.

Suppertime came, and it was going to be a special meal tonight! In fact, it would be the first time the Foster family had enjoyed this delicacy. Not everyone had opportunity to eat monkey, but this would be the first of countless times the family would enjoy this animal, so plentiful in the Amazonian forests. It was delicious, something like squirrel, although each variety of monkey had its own unique flavor.

The day prior to eating monkey for the first time, Les had been on his way by trail to a small lagoon about half a mile upriver to see if there was a wild duck he could shoot. Hearing noise in a bamboo patch, he stopped to listen. The noise turned out to be a monkey coming down a bamboo stalk, causing it to rustle, but it ran off through the jungle before he had a chance to shoot. The next afternoon, he took a short walk out the jungle path that went from the house away from the river. He hadn't gone far when he came to a tree with a type of unknown red fruit and noticed that something had been eating them. The ground was covered with half-eaten ones.

Hearing a rustling noise, he looked up to see a monkey going through the trees. The monkey stopped, and Les fired. Suddenly the whole jungle came alive with monkeys scurrying through the trees, screaming at the top of their lungs. There were probably a hundred or more of them. They were just the right size to make one apiece for each family member.

Les was thrilled; he had thought that never in his life would he have a chance to hunt where game was so abundant, but now, here he was in a place where you could almost walk up and hit game on the head with a club.

Keeping an eye on Marge's two boats was another of Les' responsibilities, and each time it rained, the water levels in the Chapare River fluctuated wildly. One night, it rained heavily up in the Andean foothills, and the river level quickly rose eight feet; another eight feet, and it would have been up to the house.

Marge had warned him about the river, so he was expecting wild water level fluctuations; even so, Les had to keep a close eye on the boats. The boats, one a *chalupa* made of boards and the other a dugout canoe were kept at the edge of the river in front of the missionary camp. As the river rose or fell, Les had to either tie them in closer to shore or let out chain and push them out farther from shore so they wouldn't go aground and sink as the water fell.

One morning, he went out to look and found the stake where they were tied was well out into the river, underwater, so he put on his swimming trunks, waded out to where they were tied, untied them, and drove another stake farther up the bank, tying them higher. Since it was rainy season, he had to check the boats several times a day and during the night.

In other ways, the rainy season was a blessing. Initially, Les and his son, Alan, had been carrying a hundred gallons of river water a week for washing clothes and dishes, but once the rains began in earnest, they could set buckets, barrels, and other containers under the eaves of the house and catch nice clean rainwater. Marge's farm also had a hand-operated pitcher-pump, but the water pumped from the ground was "hard" water and not suitable for bathing and washing clothes.

There was no lack of insect life in the tropics, including numerous varieties of ants, so to protect foodstuff and other items that ants loved, Les had to tie strings or wires from the rafters and hang the bags of foodstuff from them. Around the strings and wires, he tied other strings soaked in kerosene so the ants, cockroaches, and other insects couldn't walk down the strings or wires. Even the fifty-gallon metal packing barrels in which flour and sugar were stored had to have kerosene-soaked string around them to keep the insect life from crawling up and into them. This system worked reasonably well.

The Fosters had also brought two slabs of bacon with them to help flavor their food, and as the bacon hung from the ceiling, it grew mold. Bacon was too valuable to toss, and with no refrigeration, Lois would scrape the mold from the bacon and go ahead and use it. With no store anywhere nearby, Lois also needed to bake bread twice a week using a folding portable oven over a camp stove.

Three insects made life especially miserable in the Bolivian tropics—the *ejeni*, the *polvorín*, and the *marijuí*. Of these no-see-ums, two of them were so tiny, they could go through mosquito netting or screen wire. The marijuí was the largest of the three and was a biting gnat about the size of a small flea. When you go out in the morning or on rainy days or in the evening, swarms of them land on you. Each bite leaves a tiny blood blister on the skin, and the bite itches much like a mosquito bite.

The *ejeni* and *polvorín* are also real pests but don't leave a blood blister. Unfortunately, the *ejeni* is active even on bright moonlit nights, and the only way to get any rest is to have a mosquito net with extremely fine netting or hide under the covers and swelter in the tropical heat.

Cockroaches are another abundant pest, ranging from the three-inch size down through many smaller varieties. Several of the larger varieties fly and, as they are attracted to light, will fly right at you or even land on you as you sit in your living area at night. The housing at Nueva Vida and in Todos Santos was not screened, so the Fosters most often climbed into their mosquito nets shortly after supper as it was impossible otherwise to keep the mosquitoes and other insects fought off.

Shortly after arriving in Nueva Vida, a report was received of a group of hostile nomads who were seen upriver from Todos Santos. These "savages" or "barbarians," as the local people called them, were killers and fourteen years prior when they came into the area, had killed a colonist, burned his thatch-roof house, and wounded other settlers who had moved down from the high Andes. Now that the nomads had returned to the area, the first thought of the farmers was to take a hunting party out and look for the "savages."

When they came upon the nomad encampment in the jungle, there were no men present, just women and children as the men were out hunting. The colonists, as the settlers called themselves, surrounded the camp and opened fire with their rifles and shotguns until all the nomads had fled, were killed, or captured. They weren't sure how many nomads they might have wounded but were sure they had killed one young woman; they also captured four young children and brought them into town.

After committing this atrocity, the colonists realized that the nomadic warriors would want revenge and were terrified of what might happen in the future. They also had four small Indian children in their possession and had no idea what to do with them. First, they approached a missionary couple, Bob and Joyce Wilhelmson, to see if they would take the children; however, under the circumstances of how the children were captured, it seemed to best to let the ones who had captured them take responsibility for them. Eventually, the children were taken in by four families in Todos Santos who cared for them, educated them, and raised them as their own. The children were too young to help anyone learn their language and, over time, integrated into the Spanish-speaking Bolivian culture.

As the missionary team pondered why God had allowed the killing and kidnappings, they began to realize that in many ways, the nomads and the farmers were similar. Neither of them knew the love of Christ, and their only thoughts were to protect themselves and get revenge for the atrocities being committed against them. Both sides were guilty of atrocities, and there would be many more before the nomads were eventually befriended. The farmers were avenging the killing that had happened fourteen years previously as well as a more recent shooting and were terrified of the nomads.

The nomads would now take revenge for the loss of their children and the killing of the young woman. Soon the missionary team was caught in the middle of an escalating crisis. Fortunately, the governmental authorities were far enough removed from the situation that they favored giving the missionaries an opportunity to attempt friendly contact with the unknown jungle dwellers, so they put out an order to the farmers and colonists not to shoot the nomads. While the desire of the government was to see the nomads peacefully settled, the missionaries' desire went beyond that; they aimed to reach these souls for Christ.

As Les wrote in his journal:

> Civilization alone means nothing for eternity. Many people are called civilized but will spend an eternity in hell. But the gain we want is to see these souls find eternal life in Christ. Pray much for a friendly contact with these nomads. We don't know yet what to call them...as no one knows what tribe they are from.

Initial speculation was that the nomads could be bands of the Sirionó tribe who roamed to the northeast, but there were several reasons to doubt that they were Sirionó. There was a woman in Todos Santos who was known as the "tame Sirionó." At the time the four children were captured, she tried to communicate with them, but they couldn't seem to understand her. She herself said that these were not her people but were of the Rubio (blond) tribe. She informed the missionaries that the nomad arrows were different from her people's arrows. Missionary Jean Dye, who knew a few phrases of Sirionó, also tried communicating with the captured children, but to no avail.

Les made a trip over to the Yapacaní River where another band of nomads had been attacking farmers, hunters, and loggers. While there, he talked with bilingual Sirionó who said that these were not their people but were Yuquí Indians. Carroll Tamplin of the World Gospel Mission, who was trying to befriend one of the nomadic bands, had bilingual Sirionó working with him. When he took them out into the jungle to see the abandoned nomad camps, the Sirionó called the nomads *Curuqua*, a Sirionó word which seemed to mean "a large hairy monster that roams the jungle just outside the Sirionó camps at night."

The Sirionó were afraid to leave their camps at night for fear of meeting the Curuqua. *Rubio*, which means blond in Spanish, had been used by some when referring to the nomads since several of the nomads who had been spotted were of a very light complexion, much lighter than the Sirionó.

Other evidence which pointed strongly toward the nomads not being Sirionó was their bows and arrows. A Sirionó man who worked with the Firestone family, missionaries from another mission, looked at a captured set of bow and arrows and said they definitely were not Sirionó. If anyone should know, he should as he had recently come out of the jungle himself and was still adjusting to life out of the forest. He made several comments regarding the arrows.

For one thing, he said that his people carved the barbs on the palmwood tip of the *chonta* arrows, whereas the nomads had "lashed" the barb on with fine string and beeswax. Also, the nomads feathered their arrows with a variety of feathers, including colorful macaw feathers, whereas the Sirionó only used black feathers. The bow also differed in that the Sirionó bow tapered much more at both ends than the nomad bow.

With all these distinctions, it appeared the nomads weren't Sirionó, Guarayo, or Guaraní, and little by little, to clarify and simplify, the missionaries and others began to refer to them as Yuquí (you-KEY).

Hunt for the Elusive Nomads Begins

Bob Wilhelmson and Les Foster were the beginning of the missionary team that would go into the jungle looking for the Yuquí with the hope of befriending them, but first they had to find them. With no detailed maps of the area, the best way to locate the Yuquí seemed to be to go to the farms where the Yuquí had stolen bananas and try to follow their trail from there to their camps. As nomads, they rarely stayed more than a few days in a given location, constantly moving as they looked for game, fruit, honey, and other foodstuff. Finding them would not be easy!

Bob and Les headed east from El Coni, one of the farming colonies along the Coni River. Even though rainy season was officially over, the men found the jungle quite wet and were constantly having to wade through water. Soon they came to an abandoned farm and saw where the nomads had taken bananas by twisting the stalks off the plants with their bare hands. As they went farther, they found that the jungle dwellers had used the very trail they were on and had apparently left the area heading for the bamboo fields of the Chimoré River. Possibly, they were heading out there to get more shafts for making arrows.

The colonists had told them that this is what happened fourteen years previously when the nomads came into the area. The last time they had been gone about thirty days before returning to burn a colonist's house, kill one farmer, and wound several others.

Bob and Les continued east along the trail toward the Chimoré River until they came to a place where the water became waist deep and then deeper still, so deep they couldn't have crossed without swimming, so they were forced to turn around and go back. They headed back toward the colony of El Coni to rest and wait for the water to recede.

The next two days were dry, with no rain, so they once again took off for the Chimoré River. When they reached the area of trail that had previously been impassable, they found they could wade through some parts and then located the limb of a fallen tree bridging the deepest part of the small stream or arroyo, so they walked across that to the other side. As they followed the trail, they could see the bare footprints of at least twenty nomads going toward the Chimoré River. Not only was the trail marked by bent and broken twigs as the nomads marked them, but Bob and Les could also see where some branches had been cut by the nomads, evidently using machetes stolen from the colonists.

Continuing along the trail, they came upon a tree the nomads had felled to harvest honey. In many places along the trail, they had to slow down as they waded through swampy areas, allowing the swarms of mosquitoes that were following to catch up to them, and joined by the ones already present, they would be engulfed by the buzzing, biting, bloodthirsty horde. More than once, they came to the bank of a deep jungle stream and were forced to leave the trail as they looked for a fallen log on which to cross. Clearly, the nomads, not being hampered by clothing, were able to wade across as long as the water was not too deep, and where they had been forced to cross on fallen logs or tree branches, there were long vertical poles shoved into the muddy bottom of the waterways to use as handholds while crossing.

The day was half-gone when Bob and Les finally ran out of time and turned back without having seen the Chimoré River or the nomads. Not having come equipped to spend the night, they decided it would be better to wait for the weather to clear and then take bedding, mosquito nets, and food and go prepared to spend several days at the Chimoré River, looking for signs of the nomads. Even for Bob and Les, new to the jungle as they were, they had found the nomads were leaving such a clear trail that they had hopes of encountering them. Whether finding them would result in a friendly contact, being shot and killed by fearful warriors or only a sighting remained to be seen. Bob and Les were well-aware that Satan desired to see these people destroyed without ever having an opportunity to hear of Christ and His love for them. He wouldn't give up his hold on them easily.

The two missionaries desperately longed to make a friendly contact with this group before they had a chance to make more arrows and return to the colonies to kill or be killed. Marge Day had already offered the bananas and other produce from her farm to be used to feed the nomads if and when a contact was made.

Occasionally, there were humorous incidents as Les relates in his journal:

> Yesterday afternoon Bob was writing to his wife Joyce and I was lying down as I've not been feeling well, when all of a sudden, I heard the farmer's dog barking and Bob jumped up and ran wildly into the tall grass yelling "*Tatú! Tatú.*" I jumped up and started pulling on my pants while yelling, "Bob, what's wrong?" He went charging off into the jungle still yelling "*Tatú, Tatú.*" I didn't know what it was all about, but my first thought was that he was trying to say the Sirionó word, "*Tatú chudeje,*" which we understood to mean, "Come." I thought maybe he had seen a nomad peering from the jungle near the house. I took off after him yelling, expecting to see a nomad in full flight. "Bob, what is it?" It wasn't until he fell into a hole full of water that he stopped long enough to tell me that he was chasing a *tatú* or armadillo as we call them, hoping to catch it for supper. Falling into the hole lost the race for him so we ended up with boiled rice and *charque* (salted dried meat) for supper again instead of delicious fried armadillo.

A few days later, word was received that the nomads had come out and stolen more crops about eleven miles upriver. Bob and Les made plans to head up that way but would need reinforcements, so they waited for Tommy Moreno and Bruce Porterfield to come down from Cochabamba and join them in their hunt for the elusive nomads.

Soon the quest began in earnest, but after almost three weeks of searching the area, the missionary team knew little more than they had in the beginning. The nomads were proving to be very elusive. Eventually, the missionaries found themselves back in La Jota, a colony farther inland than the El Coni colony, where the colonists were in a state of agitation and very much afraid. While the missionaries had been searching for the nomads farther to the southwest, they had come back into the area around the farms and ambushed two fishermen who were returning from the Chimoré River.

One fisherman was extremely fortunate in that the arrow destined for his back impacted the pack full of fish he was carrying and didn't penetrate through to him. Then, a week later, a woman who was washing clothes in a small stream flowing through La Jota was shot with five arrows. She died within minutes. The Yuquí had begun taking revenge for the loss of their children!

When the missionary team arrived in La Jota, the colonists were anxious to help them in any way possible, thinking it would give them additional protection to have the team in their colony. As the men told them of their plan to move over to the Chimoré River, right in the heart of Yuquí territory, and build a house from which to reach out to the nomads, the colonists began to grumble as they preferred the missionaries stay there in La Jota to protect them. After much talking by "the professional savage tamer," as the colonists called Bruce Porterfield, the colonists decided to help the team build a house on the banks of the Chimoré River, so the next morning, missionaries and farmers packed up, and the farmers helped carry the missionaries' supplies out to the Chimoré.

In three days, with some time off for fishing, a rustic, thatch-roofed house was completed, and the colonists headed back to their farms in La Jota. The missionary team was on their own, trusting God to bring about a friendly encounter with the nomads.

The next day, they headed out to look for trails made by the nomads and soon came upon a deserted camp where an estimated forty to sixty natives had camped. Following almost invisible trails consisting of small broken twigs, they came on another smaller camp about two hours downriver from the house. Searching more in that area, they soon found where several palms had been felled and the hearts, much like cabbage, had been used for food by the wandering tribespeople. There was also an abundance of snail shells and turtle shells in their camp, and it was obvious they had eaten the turtles. What the snail shells were for, they had no idea at the time but, in later years, would learn that the edges of the shells were broken off, and then the shells were used to scrape and smooth both the eighteen-inch long palm-wood arrow points and the seven to eight-foot long palm-wood bows. The trail led to the Chimoré River, but there was no evidence of them having crossed the river and no discernible trail moving away from the river on either side. Once again, the nomads had vanished!

Dick Strickler, a new missionary arrival, soon joined the team, and Paul Mason also came to help briefly as Tommy Moreno and Bruce Porterfield had to leave to continue their responsibilities elsewhere. The team was in constant flux as an assortment of missionaries helped for short periods and were then replaced by others. Dick and Les soon settled in as the only long-term members of the team.

An Amazing Provision

While based out of the thatch house on the Chimoré River, Les saw God's love and power demonstrated on his behalf. Les became very ill with a large inflamed boil on his upper leg and was unable to walk more than a few feet. His situation was deteriorating, and there was no way he could consider the five or six-hour hike to Todos Santos from where he would be able to get a flight to Cochabamba and medical help. Carrying him out would have been extremely challenging for his coworkers and likely have been a several-day effort, very difficult. The men were praying daily for Les' recovery, expecting the inflammation to begin healing itself, but it got worse and worse.

It was then that God, in His amazing way, unexpectedly sent a small "bubble" helicopter. An oil company was doing exploration in the area, and when the chopper flew over and saw the tiny clearing and thatch house on the bank of the Chimoré River, the pilot decided to land. He was on his way to Todos Santos but hadn't been there before and was unsure of the way, so landed to ask directions. He was an American and was happy to carry Les to town in return for directions! This was an amazing and unlikely event during an era when the

Oil company owned bubble helicopter landing in front of thatch missionary house at the Chimoré River.

Bolivian Amazon was still very undeveloped. The missionaries had no portable radios, and helicopters were rare—clearly a provision from God!

A few weeks went by with little progress, so the rest of the missionary team returned to the town of Todos Santos to rest, resupply, and spend time with their families. Dick Strickler, being single, opted to spend the time in La Jota, the most distant colony, where he could continue building friendships among the colonists and sharing God's Word with those who had started to show an interest.

Missionaries from other works in Bolivia had been coming and going, helping in the effort to locate the nomads, but with the retreat to town, most of them went back to their families and ministries in other parts of Bolivia. Wayne and Ruth Gill were living in Todos Santos, so Wayne began helping on the contact effort as needed. Dick Strickler, being out in La Jota, was alert to any activity by the nomads and soon sent one of the La Jota colonists into Todos Santos with a note requesting help.

About two weeks earlier, the bearer of the note had been going from El Coni to La Jota and came face-to-face with twenty naked nomads, all men and all carrying bows and arrows. They were about five yards into the jungle on the north side of the trail poking their arrows up in a tree, trying to knock down some fruit. He reported that he was only five yards from them before they saw him or he saw them. When they did see each other, the Yuquí let out a yell and ran farther into the jungle, although he could still hear them in there talking to one another. He had his rifle with him and could have shot two or three of them but didn't fire his gun.

The nomads were all armed with bows and arrows but, fortunately for him, they also chose not to shoot. As the missionaries thought through the situation, they realized they had passed through the same area where the nomads had been about the same time they were there. Had they been seen by the nomads? Had divine protection spared their lives? They would never know.

Two days later, Wayne, Dick, and Les went down to where the nomads had been seen by the colonist and cut a trail following their path as best they could and, about an hour into the jungle, came upon an abandoned Indian camp. With that, the number of camps they had seen so far that year was twenty-one, none of them with people in them. This was one of the newest camps, only one-day old as the ashes from their fires were still completely dry, and dew hadn't fallen on them yet. Clearly, the nomads were in the area and not that far away as this camp had been made long after the settler's encounter with them two weeks previously. The missionaries continued the search but found no other camps in the area.

On a Saturday, a few days later, Don Juan, one of the farmers at La Jota, came to see Les for an injection as he was sick with the flu. The colonists had learned that the missionaries had some medical training and could give shots, repair minor wounds, and perform other basic first aid for the colonists there at La Jota. Before coming to see Les that morning, Don Juan had walked with his wife and son as far as El Coni, heading to Todos Santos. Along the La Jota trail, he saw huge tiger tracks, so he kept watching to see where the jaguar had come out of the jungle and onto the trail. When he got down close to the Arroyo Magdalena, he saw bare footprints where one lone nomad had crossed the trail going from north to south and then going back again to the north. This was only a short way from where the twenty nomads had been seen.

The next day, Rolf Fostervold and Les left La Jota and went into town to get a room ready for Rolf's wife, Irene, who was to arrive in a few days. The two men decided to go to the Coni River, following a trail the nomads had made in that direction. They had hung gifts along that trail and thought this was a good opportunity to see if the nomads had found and taken the gifts. Les and Rolf were going along the trail quietly, as was their custom, and as they neared the Arroyo Magdalena, just before entering one of the abandoned nomad camps, they heard a low groaning. They stopped, and wanting to hear the sound better, Les took off the pith helmet he habitually wore in the jungle. He and Rolf knelt together there on the trail, putting on more insect repellent as they waited, silently listening.

For a full five minutes, they could hear a low humming or groaning but weren't sure whether the sound was human or a tiger (which sounds something like that too). Then they were startled to hear it clear its throat, very humanlike, before continuing to hum. For a full fifteen minutes, they knelt there together, praying and asking God for wisdom as to what to do. Could it be an old sick nomad left there to die as he or she was too old to keep up with the others? Or might it be one of them humming as they went about work in their camp?

The men decided to go on up the trail a little farther and see if they could better locate where the sound was coming from. Finally, after several minutes, Les called out in Spanish, "We are your friends. We have gifts for you. Come to see us." Les repeated this three times with no response from the noisemaker. Then he called out in Spanish, "We are going now but will come back in three days." Still no verbal response, but the humming stopped and didn't start up again.

Les and Rolf went on into Todos Santos where they helped Irene get settled in and, after a brief couple of days in town, headed out once again to their base at La Jota. They needed to make the next two weeks count as their children would soon be arriving from boarding school for several months of vacation, and they would need to spend a good portion of that time in town with their families.

* * * * *

Map of the area where the Yuquí contact effort began and where most of the confrontations between colonists and nomads occurred.

A few days later, Les and Rolf headed back out to the base at La Jota where Dick Strickler was keeping an eye on things. Dick didn't mind staying out there by himself as it meant he didn't need to make the lengthy hike to the Coni River and then the river trip to Todos Santos. It also gave him opportunity to visit the farms of the various colonists in La Jota and share God's Word with them. Many of the farmers were interested in learning more about God and His Word from the missionaries, and several came to faith through the witness of the missionaries.

One of the farmers who stopped by to visit the missionaries was Daniel, and on one of his visits, Les discussed the truths of God's Word with him. As Les wrote to Lois, "I'm pretty sure Don Daniel Yankee knows the Lord as his Savior now. I served him coffee yesterday morning and talked with him for about an hour."

With no radio communication, the principal way the missionary men kept in touch with their wives and coworkers in Todos Santos was by sending notes with farmers who went to town for supplies. Severino, one of the farmers, showed up one morning and asked if he could take any messages to town for them, so Les sent a note to Lois.

> It's been a busy week so far. Thursday, we hiked our trail to the Arroyo Magdalena and picked up the gift knives and machetes but left clothing and painted a white strip on the buckets that were already hanging there. We have decided to paint a white band around any gift that can be painted, and we have also painted a white band around our pith helmets. We are hoping that when the Yuquí see us, they will identify us as the gift givers and not shoot but rather desire a friendly encounter with us.

A few days later, they hiked out to the Chimoré River and then back in another trail, picking up most of the gifts. They didn't want to leave a large quantity of gifts out during the time they would be in town with their families. On that hike, they found fresh breaks marking a nomad trail about an hour from their camp, so it appeared the Yuquí were still in the area. As they headed home, they scared up a large collared peccary (javelina pig) but didn't shoot at it in case the Yuquí were nearby and might hear and be frightened by the shot. Nearing their camp, they stopped at the Arroyo Jota where the men bathed and washed out their sweat-soaked underclothing.

The next day, the men went out toward an old orange grove called El Naranjal. It was located in a high area of jungle and had once been a Franciscan mission to the Yura Indians. However, the priests had so much trouble with the nomads that they had abandoned the area decades previously, and the jungle had regrown almost to its original height. This seemed an ideal expanse of jungle, almost an open woodland with plenty of game, the kind of place where the nomads would doubtless spend a good bit of time, especially in the rainy season since it wouldn't flood. Two days later, the entire missionary team headed in to Todos Santos where they would spend time with their families and rest and recuperate from the arduous weeks in the jungle.

Occasionally, during the school vacation, the men made brief trips out to the La Jota area to see if there were any new signs of the Yuquí or if any of the gifts had been taken, but there was no evidence they had come into the area. No crops had been stolen from the farms of the colonists, and there had been no shootings, so the men planned a trip farther out to the Chimoré River, to the place where the nomads had crossed the river when they came into the area early in the year.

The trail the missionaries had made on a prior trip while following a nomad trail of bent twigs was now very overgrown in places, and the hike, which should have taken four hours, took seven. The team spent the night camped in a patch of bamboo on the bank of the river in the very spot where the natives had crossed the river and, the next day, trekked two hours upriver without their packs until they arrived at a place called Cerro Colorado, so called because of the red cliffs in the area.

After scouting here and there for recent signs of the nomads, it was time to head back to their camp farther down the river. All three men—Rolf, Les, and Dick—dreaded the arduous hike back down through the jungle to their camp, so they cut down a *pachuba* palm and used it to make a crude raft. While the raft was not large enough to support the men, they were able to place their clothing, machetes, and other gear on the raft and then float down the river, holding onto the sides of raft and letting it support their weight. Going back down to their camp like this took only thirty minutes compared to the two hours it had taken them to hike up earlier in the day. It was also a refreshing respite from the oppressive jungle heat! On this entire trip, the team found no indication that the Yuquí had left the area but were unable to ascertain where they might currently be roaming.

The next day, Rolf and Les headed into town for supplies, once again leaving Dick in La Jota. Another single missionary, Harold Rainey, was due to arrive on the next DC-3 flight from Cochabamba and would be joining the team. No sooner had Rolf and Les arrived in Todos Santos than they were informed that four hunters had seen fresh footprints and heard the jungle dwellers. Les and Rolf headed over to talk with the hunters and learned that this had taken place where the Arroyo Jota flowed into the Chimoré River. While the missionary team had been searching for signs of the nomads *up* the Chimoré, the nomads had gone *down* the river. Clearly it was not God's timing for an encounter between the two groups.

Once Harold arrived, the team got their gear together and headed back out to the La Jota colony, intending to follow the Arroyo Jota down to its mouth where the fresh footprints had so recently been seen. Two and a half hours from where they planned to spend the night, they began seeing fresh footprints of the nomads. The prints looked to be only a day old, and as they followed the prints deeper into the area where it appeared the nomads might be camping, the missionaries found a small palm leaf basket which looked as if it had been woven as a child's toy. It looked as if they were following not just a hunting party of nomads, but a band which included families.

No doubt, the main camp was located not too far away. The team spent the next two days camped nearby, searching the jungle each day for other indications of where the nomads might be camping. Eventually the missionaries found a heavily traveled trail leading from abandoned camp to abandoned camp, but soon it became too late to continue that day, even though they had just gone through an Indian camp that was very fresh. The team was forced to make their way back to their own temporary camp or risk being caught in the jungle in the dark with no lights, no mosquito nets, no food, and no weapons. They had established that the nomads were working their way back to the north so planned to continue in that direction the following day. Unfortunately, after four days and without encountering the nomads, they ran out of supplies and had to go back La Jota to stock up on provisions.

No sooner had they gotten to their base camp in La Jota than one of the colonists arrived in a state of great excitement to let them know that the nomads had been heard again between the colonies of La Jota and El Coni, but overnight, a cold south wind set in with heavy rain, and the missionaries were unable to get out into the jungle for several days. When eventually the weather improved and the missionaries went to check the trails where they had left gifts for the nomads, they found that five of the gifts had been taken. It appeared that a hunting party of nomads had come back through the La Jota area and taken two shirts and three cans with wire handles.

The nomads liked the one-gallon cans, which originally held CARE relief food products, to use as cooking pots over their campfires. Also, a gift machete was missing from one of the more isolated Yuquí camps. While friendly contact had not been made, the missionaries were encouraged that their gifts were being taken and expected that eventually this would result in friendship and an opportunity to learn this unknown language and tell these people of Jesus Christ. Wouldn't it be wonderful to see them represented in the bride of Christ! Revelation 5:9, "[a]nd they sang a new song, saying, "Thou hast redeemed us to God" (KJV).

With their children still on school vacation, the missionary team decided to go back into town, to Todos Santos, and spend some time with their families and share the exciting news with their families of the gifts having been taken.

While in town, Les also spent time with some of his many Bolivian friends and, one afternoon, was talking with Don Hilarión, the elder of the church in Todos Santos. Don Hilarión let Les know that he would come over to his house for a visit in the evening after he got off work at the sawmill he operated for one of the Italian families in town.

About 8:00 p.m., there were voices outside the door, and Les assumed Hilarión had arrived. There was a loud knock, and Les went to the door to find a colonist from Puerto Aurora standing there. The colonist had gone first to see Rolf, whose Spanish was limited, but was so agitated that Rolf had been unable to understand anything except that he was saying something about the "savages" coming out again. Les questioned the colonist, "Where were the nomads seen?"

"It was at the farm of Juan Chaillapa, at Puerto Aurora," was the reply, but then he went on to say, "A fellow by the name of Senón Aguilar was shot by the savages."

"Was he killed?" questioned Les.

The response was a quick: "No."

"So where is Senón? Does he need medical help?" asked Les.

"He's down at the river in a canoe," came the reply.

Les and Rolf grabbed their flashlights and headed for the bank of the Chapare River. Sure enough, there was Senón Aguilar, lying in the bottom of the dugout. Accompanying him were his wife and another man who, along with the informant, had paddled the canoe down the river, bringing the injured man for the limited medical help available in this jungle village.

The iron-hard chonta palm point of the arrow was still sticking out the right side of Senón's chest. Before leaving Puerto Aurora, other farmers had stood the man up next to a tree with the arrow abutting the tree and chopped off the seven-foot arrow shaft, leaving only the eighteen-inch barbed point embedded in the man. A blanket was brought from Foster's house, and the man was transferred to the blanket, which served as a stretcher to carry him up to the doctor's house.

The doctor was a German who had fled Europe after WWII and seemed to be hiding in the small village of Todos Santos. He kept a low profile and preferred not to practice his medical skills. The doctor was quick to say that there was no room for the man at his house but agreed to help remove the arrow if the missionaries could find another place to perform the procedure. The nearest place with the necessary space was Rolf and Irene Fostervold's small rented room, and they acquiesced readily, so the man was carried there for "surgery" on their bed.

Fortunately, another doctor was passing through town at the time with an antimalarial team that was getting ready to head downriver. So with the two doctors as surgeons, Lois and Irene acting as nurses, and Rolf and Les helping by holding the man down, the "operation" was performed, and the barbed arrow point removed. The doctors gently pushed and pulled, rotating the barbed arrow point until they were able to free the barb and draw out the arrow point. It had gone in two or three inches and hadn't penetrated the lung, but even so, once it was removed, air was sucked in and out of the wound as the farmer breathed.

He spent the next two days in bed at Rolf and Irene's house until the weekly DC-3 flight arrived from Cochabamba, and he and his wife were able to fly to the hospital and doctors there. There was no question that the arrow was one belonging to the nomads who had been terrorizing the colonies.

This was the first shooting the missionaries knew of since the woman washing clothes had been shot with five arrows in La Jota in April. It was now December. The missionaries were very concerned that their time to befriend the nomads was limited as the colonists had already threatened several times to go in with a commission like they had done two years previously and kill the nomads. They had only held back because the jungle dwellers had refrained from shooting or killing for eight months, and the missionaries had met with the colonists several times and talked them out of going but had convinced them to wait and give the missionaries a chance to make friendly contact.

With this new shooting, the colonists felt that more than just their crops were at risk and that the only way to protect their lives was to go in and slaughter the nomads before the hostiles killed them.

War between the colonists and the nomads might go on for many years as they slowly killed each other one by one, and eventually, the jungle people would be exterminated, although a similar number of farmers would likely be killed along the way. If the colonists were to go in with a commission, they would likely kill only a few of the nomads—the old, the young, or those unable to escape. Then next year, the warriors would be back to ambush the colonists one or two at a time along the jungle trails.

While the missionaries had not yet made contact with the jungle dwellers, their efforts seemed to be moving forward. The missionaries had established a "gift area" where they were regularly leaving gifts, and the nomads were picking them up. To this point in time, ten gifts had been accepted. These consisted of shirts, machetes, bananas, and gallon cans with wire handles which they used for carrying water, cooking, etc. The second bunch of gifts that were taken included bananas, which the colonists had been sure the nomads would not accept for fear of poison. After the second batch of gifts was taken, more offerings were put out, but now, with this new shooting, the missionary team was unable to go back and see if the latest items had been taken or not.

The colonists and the army were considering arming a commission to go and kill the nomads, and if the missionaries were in their houses in La Jota at that time, any Indians fleeing from the commission would run right through their area. The risk of them killing the missionaries or burning their palm-thatch houses and killing them as they fled the burning houses would be high. Also, if the missionaries were present, the nomads might identify them as part of the group that was shooting them and further contact attempts might be difficult or impossible.

After much prayer and discussion, the missionary team opted to stay in the town of Todos Santos until the issue of a commission had been settled. While it looked very much like a posse would be going in, the missionaries realized that one of the few positives was that if any older Yuquí were taken captive, they might help the missionaries learn the language, thus improving the odds of success in future contact efforts.

The missionary team was confident that God was in control and could use any situation that might arise to improve the chances of sharing the Gospel message with these people who had never had opportunity to hear it.

Another new twist in the ongoing situation was that another religious group had learned of the Yuquí and was doing what they could to have the Fosters and their coworkers removed from the area. The other group had much influence since one of them was the son of the local army colonel and had political pull. If some of the nomads were captured, it was likely the other religious group would be the ones to benefit. Les sent a letter to their prayer partners, asking them to pray about the deteriorating situation.

* * * * *

The year 1957 came to a close, and the new year began with good news: The colonist who had been shot, Senón Aguilar, was released from the hospital and had recovered nicely from his arrow wound. Considering the unsanitary conditions of his initial surgery and the lack of proper medical supplies, his survival and recovery was a miracle in itself.

The second item of good news was that the commission of colonists and soldiers decided not to go into the jungle and kill the nomads. Part of the reason for them coming to that decision may have been that the Yuquí fled the area after shooting Senón, and no one wanted to wander the jungle for weeks looking for a "needle in a haystack."

Likely, the Yuquí themselves realized they weren't safe in the area after the shooting and fled as they hadn't come to steal crops from any of the farms, although there was one report of bare footprints having been seen along the Chimoré River farther east. The missionaries hadn't been out to check the gifts for several weeks due to the threat of a commission, and now it was the middle of rainy season and all but impossible to get through the jungle.

Swamps and streams that could normally be waded across would have to be swum, and trails were too wet and muddy to hike since this was the peak of rainy season. Also, it was time for the annual mission conference, and a special linguistic conference was being held along with the regular field conference. The missionaries thought the value of the linguistic conference would make it well worth attending since once a friendly contact was made with the nomads, they would need linguistic skills in order to learn the language.

The conference was a time of refreshment and encouragement as they fellowshipped with coworkers in Cochabamba. Once the conference was over, most of the missionary children climbed onto the back of a farm truck and headed off through the Andean foothills to the boarding school of Tambo, near the town of Comarapa, an eight to ten-hour trip.

After the children left, it became apparent that Lois was ill, and when the doctor came to see her, he diagnosed yellow jaundice. Lois became very yellow, especially her eyes, and along with medicine, the doctor said she would need to spend at least four weeks in bed, resting. Les felt he should stay and minister to his sick wife, but two coworkers, Beulah Mason and Audrey Hoogshagen, insisted on caring for Lois in Cochabamba in order to free Les to rejoin the contact effort in the Todos Santos area.

Les was reluctant to leave his ailing wife, but most of his coworkers seemed to feel it more important for him to get back down to the jungle, so he, along with Dick Strickler and Harold Rainey, flew back to Todos Santos. The Fostervold family remained in Cochabamba to study Spanish, something they had missed out on when first arriving in Bolivia as they had been urgently needed at that time to help with the contact effort.

Now a new problem arose due to the heavy precipitation of the rainy season in the Andean foothills. The Chapare River had changed its course. Todos Santos, the uppermost port on the Chapare River and the missionary supply base, had lost a major source of its water as up near its headwaters, the river had cut through and was now dumping the bulk of its water into the Securé River, which ran into the Mamoré River, three days below Todos Santos. The only water now running past Todos Santos was that being contributed by the Coni River, which was only a very small portion of the water that had previously run past the town.

Now while the rainy season was at its peak and the Chapare River should be full of water, a person could wade across. The river was hardly navigable even by a small dugout canoe such as the missionaries used for their travels. Once dry season arrived, it would be impossible to travel by canoe, and the missionaries would be stranded in Todos Santos, unable to move supplies by river to their base in La Jota.

As the missionary team pondered this change, they realized they might need to consider a larger boat which they could load with gas and supplies for a longer period of time and then make the lengthy trip down the Chapare River to where the Ichilo River emptied into it, then up the Ichilo River to the mouth of the Chimoré River, and up this river to the area where the nomads roamed. It would be a five to seven-day trip one way, but it would allow them to transport their supplies by boat rather than carrying them on their backs. Also, once they arrived on the Chimoré, they could go up and down the river, penetrating the jungle at different places to look for signs of the Yuquí.

This would be advantageous as they wouldn't have to cut so much trail and could use the river for transportation from one gift trail to another. It would also mean they could be gone from town for longer periods of time, but the downside was that in an emergency, it would take a full week to motor back to Todos Santos if there was enough water. Todos Santos, while a small town, didn't offer much in the way of medical help. For that, you had to fly to the city of Cochabamba, and there was only the weekly DC-3, which flew when the weather cooperated.

Another advantage of a move to the Chimoré River was that the missionaries could draw the nomads eastward, away from the colonies, and toward the unpopulated area along the Chimoré River. If contact were made there, it would lessen the risk to the colonists who were farther west in La Jota, El Coni, and Puerto Aurora. Maybe the river changing its course was God speaking to the missionaries, letting them know it was time to consider a new and different plan of action!

As Les contemplated the situation, he wrote in his journal:

> It's a blessing to know that God controls everything and that nothing can touch His children except He permit it. "He rebukes the sea and makes it dry; He dries up all the rivers" (Nahum 1:4a, KJV). It's God who has done this (drying up the Chapare River). Our concern is but to know how He wants to work in our lives because of it.

Now the question was, had God partially dried up the Chapare River in order to guide the missionaries to a new plan?

While in the process of considering such a major change of strategy, Bob Wilhelmson, Harold Rainey, and Les went downriver thirty-five minutes to Marge Day's farm where she was opening a boarding school for children of the Yuracaré tribe. Marge was planning to bring boat loads of Yura children from the scattered farms along the Chapare River for short school sessions twice a year. After crops were planted and while waiting for harvest, she would have a school term, and then again, after crops were harvested, she would have another school term. She would need to travel the river four times a year, bringing children to school and taking them back to their farms, but she hoped to teach them the three R's—Reading, 'Riting, and 'Rithmetic.

This would help integrate them more into the fabric of Bolivian society and would give them the knowledge they needed to protect their families from the often-unscrupulous traders who traveled the river taking economic advantage of the uneducated Yuracaré. Once they understood math, they would know when a trader was trying to cheat them. The three missionary men were busy laying the floor of the new school for Yura children when they heard a boat and motor coming down the river.

The motorized canoe had hardly touched the sandbar in front of Marge's farm before Joe Snyder was out of it, running the 150 yards across the sand to the house. He had come from Todos Santos to let the men know that the Yuquí had come out at La Jota and shot another settler. Needless to say, Harold, along with Les and Lois, left immediately with Joe for town.

This new shooting had taken place at the same spot where the woman had been killed a year previously by the nomads. The wounded man, Bernavé Amurrio, was shot in the left shoulder as he and two others were clearing weeds from a patch of bananas. The following day, they brought him into town to Wayne Gill's house for medical attention. Marge, who was a trained nurse, dressed the wound, which did not appear serious, as the arrow was without a barb and hadn't penetrated too deeply.

The young man's father, Cirilo Amurrio, came to see Les and Lois and asked if they would go back to La Jota to live. "All of the colonists are frightened," began Cirilo, "And we would feel safer with you missionaries living near us." He went on to tell more about what was happening in the colony. "About ten days before my son was shot, as one of the colonists was out hunting near La Jota, he came upon a small animal dead with an arrow in it. The animal was freshly killed and had apparently been shot by the savages but had run away from them to die. A few days later, we went out to El Naranjal to hunt and to gather oranges from the old orange trees there. As we neared the Naranjal, we found fresh footprints of the savages."

Neither of these things were reported to the missionaries until after the shooting. Had they learned of these sightings earlier, they would immediately have gone back to La Jota to live and keep an eye on the gift trails.

The missionary team remained in town for a few more days, awaiting the arrival of a new outboard motor they had ordered when their plan had been to make the trip down the Chapare River and up the Ichilo River to the Chimoré River. Now, with this development, they would instead leave for La Jota as soon as the motor arrived.

The contact team was very reduced in numbers with Dick Strickler in Cochabamba recovering from surgery and from hepatitis. Only Harold, Les, and Lois were available to go to La Jota. The plan was to leave Lois alone in camp as Harold and Les took trips out into the area around El Naranjal, leaving gifts for the nomads and looking for signs of them. Any thought of going by boat over to the Chimoré River and seeking a contact there instead of trying to make a contact from the La Jota colony would need to be put on hold until the missionary team had more members.

It was encouraging to see God working in another way. The Bolivian Army colonel who had been opposing the missionaries in their work was replaced by a new colonel. In God's providence, the new colonel was a vibrant Christian, a born-again believer, and a very good preacher! His wife and nine children also arrived in Todos Santos along with the colonel, and the local church was overjoyed to find that he and his family were musically gifted. Their singing in the church and bold testimony in the community gave a real boost to the struggling church.

Colonel Domingo Medrano soon met the missionary team and showed interest in helping the contact effort in any way possible. One of the first steps he took was to approach the Bolivian government for permission to make an official order that regardless of what might happen, *no* commission would be allowed to go into the jungle and kill the nomads.

The missionaries were thrilled with this news as it would take pressure off them and would be an assurance that months and years of work couldn't be ruined in a single day by a commission going in and stirring up the Yuquí. The colonel also requested permission from his superiors to allow ten soldiers to go out to the farthest edge of the colonies and build houses and a clearing for the missionary team. This would allow the missionaries to live out there for longer periods of time and begin planting crops they could share with the nomads. Les was thrilled, as evident from his journal, "It's an encouragement to see these proofs that the God we serve is the God of the impossible."

Soon the contact team was once again living on the far eastern fringes of the La Jota colony, checking gift trails daily and looking for their first encounter with the nomads. Supplies began to run low, so Harold and Les headed to town, leaving Dick to interact with the colonists. Harold and Les shook Dick's hand, telling him goodbye. "We'll see you about Monday." Then they headed off to Todos Santos to meet Lois who was coming in by plane from Cochabamba where she had gone to be with the children during their midterm school vacation and had pictures taken for their new passports.

Harold and Les hiked as far as Lobo Rancho, near Puerto Aurora, where they had left their canoe and motor on the last trip out to La Jota. They found the Coni River even lower than it had been when they came up the last time. The lack of water then had meant they had to get out of the canoe numerous times and push it across shallow places. Going down would be easier in some ways as they would have momentum and could just slide over some spots they could hardly cross going up. They got into the canoe, started the motor up, and headed off downriver at slow speed.

On the entire trip, they only had to get out of the canoe to push about eight times where the water was too shallow to get through. On the other hand, where the water was deep, there were countless snags, entire trees with jagged roots sticking out of the water and out of sight under the water, with the river roaring through the more congested places like rapids. In one such place, Harold and Les had just come through a narrow, very swift place between two groups of snags and needed to make a sharp right turn to get around another group of snags. While making the turn, the propeller lost its grip in the water, and Les lost control of the canoe.

Before he could get control, he saw they were going to hit the snags broadside on the left side of the canoe. Harold was sitting on that side, so Les yelled to him to get his arm or leg out and catch hold of the snag to help break the hard impact. Les yelled, "Catch us! Harold, don't let us hit!" Over the noise of the motor, Harold misunderstood and, thinking the river to be shallow, jumped out of the canoe and into water over his head. At that very instant, the crash came, and he missed being crushed between a sharp tree root protruding from the water and the canoe by only inches.

Later in the trip, while going down over the lower set of rapids just above where the Caracota River dumps into the Chapare River, Les hit the rapids just a little too far to the left of where he usually went through and found the canoe heading for a group of snags dead ahead. He realized that if he tried to turn the boat to get around them, he would only get partly turned by the time they got to the snags, thus hitting them broadside, which would be more dangerous, and the boat would undoubtedly tip, take in water, and possibly capsize. The best thing to do was head straight for the snags and hope to go between them.

Les yelled, "Pray, Harold!" Then he gunned the outboard. The canoe hit with such speed that it didn't even slow down but shot right through the blockade, scraping both sides of the canoe. Harold and Les both breathed a big sigh, and Harold grinned from ear to ear, but then the grin became a look of fright. Les glanced ahead again and saw another huge snag directly in their path. He cut the canoe to the right and missed it by inches, two inches to be exact. Had they hit it or gone around the other side of it, they would have run headlong into a completely impassable group of twisted snags with the water roaring through them.

Once again, Les breathed a sigh of relief and, looking heavenward, said a silent, "Thank you!" So often, it seemed that when they came to places in the rivers where they just couldn't see a way through, where it looked as if the logjams ran from one bank to the other, God seemed to open a way, and the canoe would go shooting through, although often scraping either side of the canoe.

While in town, Harold and Les learned that Colonel Medrano had received permission to send a few soldiers out to help build two houses and a small clearing for the missionaries at the easternmost fringe of the La Jota colony. Some of the colonists also volunteered to help as did a few of the Christians from the church in Todos Santos. At the same time, a report was received that signs of the nomads had been seen along the Chimoré River about sixteen kilometers northeast of La Jota. The missionary team made a quick trip down into that area, leaving gifts along trails that the nomads seemed to frequent as well as hanging gifts in abandoned Yuquí camps they encountered along the way.

Once the new missionary outpost was complete, the team hoped to plant corn, manioc, and bananas to attract the nomads, so in preparation, they began cutting the straightest possible trails out into the jungle in several directions from the site of their proposed base, leaving gifts along the trails, anticipating that the nomads would follow the trails to the missionary camp. The missionaries also noticed that for the most part, the nomads were following the same migratory trails they had used in previous years and camping in many of the same spots, so the team placed gifts in abandoned camps and other locations where the nomads were likely to appear in the next few weeks, while at the same time recognizing that God would need to prepare the nomads' hearts for a friendly encounter. Les sent out another prayer bulletin to their prayer partners worldwide, reminding them to "not grow weary in prayer."

About this time, a colonist came to the missionary team in La Jota bringing a note from Joyce Wilhelmson in Todos Santos. She had come across the army secretary in town and, since he knew she was one of the missionaries, asked, "Señora, did you hear about the man who was shot?"

This was news to Joyce, so she listened carefully as he related the story. "A man, his wife, and their little baby went out to the Chimoré River on Monday to fish. Yesterday as they were coming back to town without having caught any fish, they were confronted by a large group of savages, so they ran like mad down the path. They ran as fast as they could go, of course, and when they figured they had out-distanced the savages, they slowed to a walk to rest a little. With this, the savages appeared ahead of them on the path and started shooting arrows. They got the man with two arrows, but he and his wife either pulled them out or cut them off and they took off running again. Once again when they slowed down a bit, the savages were ahead of them on the trail and shot some more arrows, one of them with a bamboo lance point."

Later, Joyce had a conversation with the uncle of the wounded man to see if she could verify the information. According to the uncle, after being shot, the wounded man motioned with his machete across his neck, trying to make the nomads understand that he'd kill them. Upon seeing this, the jungle dwellers made lots of noise and clapped their hands as if making fun of him. The man was wounded badly enough that he couldn't go farther, the uncle reported, so his wife finally left him and went to look for help. She hiked on down the trail to an Army farm where a man by the name of Don Pedro was working and asked him for help. The two of them went on into town to ask the colonel for help, but as they couldn't find him, the colonel's secretary sent soldiers out to bring in the wounded man.

They headed right out, but it began getting dark before they reached him, and they got "cold feet" so went back to town without him, leaving him to survive the night as best he could. The next morning, the soldiers went out again and this time found the man with three arrow wounds. Even so, he was slowly making his way down the path toward town. They got the man to town shortly before the weekly flight from Cochabamba, so he was loaded on the plane and sent to the city for medical care. This was by order of Colonel Medrano who told his secretary, "Arrange for the man to go on the flight. I think the missionaries will be willing to pay for his ticket."

A few weeks later, the missionary team consisting of Les and Lois along with Harold Rainey and Dick Strickler were contentedly living in their two new houses in La Jota that had been built with the help of the soldiers, colonists, and others. Often the men would leave Lois alone in camp while going out to check gift trails and replace any gifts that had gone missing.

Frequently, the missionaries would eat the noon meal together, the two single men joining Les and Lois. Lois did the cooking over a campfire in the tin-roofed shed attached to the back of her house, and the basic food she prepared was not too much of a chore. They all found they enjoyed the smoky flavor of the food cooked over the open fire. While Lois prepared the meal, the men would sit around the table and discuss the contact effort and how they could encourage the Yuquí to lose their fear and come to the missionary camp.

Also, while waiting, the men would set the table, and Dick would take one of the "clean" handkerchiefs he had washed in the creek and use it to wipe the mold off his bread before eating it. After a few days, Les noticed that Dick was not just wiping mold from his own bread but that he was using the handkerchief to wipe the bread for all of them. Les mentioned to him that he considered using a handkerchief to wipe the moldy bread to be unsanitary, but Dick responded, "It's a *clean* handkerchief!"

Les replied, "If *you* get *your* handkerchiefs clean by handwashing them in the creek, you are the only one of us who does."

They argued back and forth for a minute or two and then let the subject drop. A few days later, Dick once again washed his clothing by hand in the creek and, shortly afterward, came to talk to Les. "Les, I want to apologize for wiping the moldy bread with a handkerchief. Until I washed clothes today, I hadn't really realized how hard it is to get clothing, and especially handkerchiefs, clean by hand." Needless to say, they never used handkerchiefs to wipe bread again!

Late one afternoon, after the men arrived back in camp from checking the gift trails, something seemed to be bothering Puppy, their German Shepherd mix. Puppy ran to the edge of the jungle and then back and forth along the edge, barking. Les went over toward the dog to call him back, and it was then the missionaries began to hear the whistling of the nomads as they signaled one another while passing through the jungle a stone's throw away from the missionary houses. They were just within the jungle, west of the Foster house going from north to south. They were close enough that Les and Lois could smell them.

This may sound impossible, but at almost every report of the jungle dwellers, the person reporting had made a similar comment, "A smell similar to wild pig." The following day, the missionaries could hear them felling trees about 200 yards south of their houses, using axes which, no doubt, were stolen from colonists. Four days later, a colonist came by the missionary base to report that the nomads had been seen in the sector southwest of the missionary camp. This seemed an especially dangerous zone to pass through, as the Yuquí had shot three people in this area in the recent past. Evidently, they were on their way to steal bananas from the farms in that area when farmers who were out hunting chanced upon them. According to the farmers, they had remembered the missionary advice and turned around and left without firing at the nomads.

The next day, the missionaries went down the gift trail to the south of their houses and left additional gifts, hoping to draw the Yuquí to their camp. Then, the following day, they went deeper into the area where the nomads had last been reported, the Naranjal area.

The Naranjal, or Orange Grove, was an old grove of orange trees which had grown up with the surrounding jungle for the last fifty years or more. It had been the site of a Franciscan mission to the Yuracaré Indian tribe, and was located about two miles southeast of the missionary camp on the banks of the Arroyo Jota. It was abandoned after yearly attacks by the nomads caused most of the Yuracaré tribe to move farther north, eventually settling along the Chapare River.

As the team neared El Naranjal, they discovered that the nomads had found and taken the gifts, so the gifts were replaced with fresh ones the missionaries were carrying. The hope of the team was that by now, the Yuquí were beginning to identify the white-banded gifts with the white-banded pith helmets and the two houses on the banks of the Little Jota Arroyo.

* * * * *

Now that the missionaries had a base with two thatch houses and gift trails leading to that base, one of the never-ending problems was getting supplies to the base. It meant either leaving the base abandoned while they were gone or leaving one man alone to guard the base. Leaving a man alone was risky since if the nomads were to follow the trails into the camp, they could easily overwhelm him, killing or kidnapping him. Each supply trip required three or more days away from the base and a trip to and from Todos Santos.

First was the several-hour hike to the Coni River, then a trip by motorized canoe down the Coni and Chapare Rivers as well as time in town preparing the supplies while spending time with their families. The return trip was more exhausting since the supplies had to be carried on their backs from the Coni River to their base at La Jota. Usually, several trips between the Coni River and their base were required before all the supplies were safely on-site. Many of these trips were done before dawn or late at night so they could be in camp during the day when the nomads might show up.

After months of prayer concerning the supply problem, finally in mid-November, Dick and Les were in town and went to see Mr. Marshall of the Royal Dutch Shell petroleum company, which was doing exploration in the area. "Is there any possibility of renting a helicopter for about an hour to fly supplies out to La Jota?" queried Les.

Mr. Marshall, whose workers occasionally had frightening close encounters with the nomads was happy to oblige. "We would love to help you, but we will be moving our base of operations out of Todos Santos on Saturday, so any flights would need to be made before that."

It was a Monday, and at the time, there was no area large enough to land a helicopter at the La Jota base. The missionaries would have to enlarge their clearing by about 400 percent and only had four days to accomplish that. Early the next morning, Dick and Les left for La Jota by canoe and trail, making the trip in record time. On their way through the La Jota colony, they stopped and talked with as many of the colonists as they could readily find, most of whom agreed to talk to fellow farmers and then go out to help the missionaries enlarge their clearing. The farmers were pleased to have a chance to earn some cash money, which was always in short supply for pioneers trying to survive off the land. Also, once the nomads had been befriended, the colonists would feel safe to invest more labor into their farms, making them more profitable and improving their lives. The colonists were glad to have this opportunity to help.

That very afternoon, many workers showed up to begin enlarging the clearing, and the following morning, leaving Harold in charge of the workforce who were clearing a landing strip, Dick and Les made the trip back to town to get the supplies ready. They prepared about 1,600 pounds of cargo, which included not only foodstuff but gasoline and a small generator to power the radio which they hoped to have soon. Once the supplies were ready, Les and Dick headed out to the Todos Santos airstrip, where Royal Dutch Shell had their base, but were told they would have to come back on Thursday afternoon as the bubble helicopters were very busy. This turned out to be a God-orchestrated delay as they later learned that the clearing in La Jota was not ready, and Harold was praying the helicopter wouldn't arrive until Thursday afternoon or later. Had the helicopter gone on Thursday morning, it would have been a wasted trip.

Finally, around 4:20 p.m., on Thursday afternoon, Les left by helicopter for La Jota, making the five-hour trip in five minutes. The initial trip was to reconnoiter, and after the pilot pronounced the clearing adequate for cargo flights, he headed back to Todos Santos and began ferrying the provisions. He was able to make four more trips on Thursday afternoon and three trips the next morning to finish up. Royal Shell graciously refused payment, a great blessing to the missionary team! With grateful hearts, the missionaries thanked God for this help and rejoiced that they wouldn't need to make so many supply trips to Todos Santos in the near future.

Dick and Les were still in town and didn't arrive back in La Jota until midafternoon on Friday. On the way in, they discovered the gift about 200 yards from their house was missing. Going on into camp, they picked up some fresh gifts and went out to not only replace the missing one, but to hang additional gifts closer to the house.

Les and Dick had no sooner arrived back at their houses when they heard two rifle shots, and minutes later, the son of their nearest neighbor arrived in a panic. "The savages shot my dad" the terrified boy exclaimed.

"Did you see the nomads?" questioned Les.

"No, but my brother and I shot the rifle twice in the air to scare the savages away," he added.

Dick Strickler using lance-tip arrow point to indicate where the arrow struck José.

Les and Dick jogged down the trail, following the frightened young man the short distance to his house. They found that the bamboo-tipped arrow had struck low, down on the left shoulder blade, and the bone had stopped the arrow from penetrating. Had it not been for the arrow hitting the bone, the angle was such that it would undoubtedly have pierced his heart and lung. When the arrow struck the bone, the shank broke, and the man himself reached around and pulled the bamboo tip of the arrow out of his back. The missionaries not only treated the wound but also gave him an anti-tetanus shot and followed up over the next few days with injections of penicillin. Fortunately, his wound didn't appear to be too serious, but it was a close call.

Dick stayed at the man's house a little longer than Les, no doubt taking this opportunity to talk to him again about his spiritual condition while Les headed down the trail alone back to their houses. As Les walked along, he could hear the nomads back in the jungle, whistling as they signaled one another. Les, realizing the danger he might be in, yelled out the only Sirionó phrase he could remember, hoping it was similar enough to their language that they might understand him. "Don't run away!" Then he yelled in Spanish, "I am your friend. I have a machete to give to you."

The machete was the only gift-like object he was carrying, so that would have to do. The whistling stopped, and he passed on down the trail, unmolested. Did they recognize him as one of those who had been giving them gifts? Or had God chosen to restrain them from shooting?

The next morning, the missionaries stayed in their clearing, looking down the gift trails every few minutes to see if the jungle people had returned to take any more gifts. About 11:00 a.m. the gifts were still there, but at 11:45 a.m., when they looked again, some of the gifts were missing.

As the men went down the trail with more gifts, including a stalk of bananas, Lois and the Foster children stayed in the clearing close to the house, watching and listening. The children had come to spend their school vacation with their parents on the jungle base. When the men arrived back, Lois and the children reported that while the men were gone, they could hear the nomads around the clearing, signaling each other by whistling. Les began to wonder, "Was it a wise decision bringing my children out here for their vacation?"

He and Lois had prayed much about the decision, but now second thoughts were creeping in. In fact, months later, one of the mission leaders wrote, asking him about that decision. He replied:

> When our children arrived in Todos Santos from Cochabamba for their school vacation, Lois and I came into town to meet them. We had been praying for weeks about whether God would have us take them out to La Jota to live during their vacation or not. We knew the danger of the nomads. It was one thing that Lois and I put our lives in a place of danger, but it was another thing to put our children in that same place. I prayed much that if it was against God's will that our children go to La Jota to live, He

would stop us in some way. The children arrived, and we began making preparations to leave for La Jota. All along, I was watching for signs from the Lord that would indicate they were not to go. But no signs came.

The day arrived for us to leave by canoe for El Coni and then by land to La Jota. As we were going upriver in the canoe, I sat at the outboard motor in the back of the canoe. Lois sat across from me. In front of us sat the three children, one in front of the other. I remember looking at Anna and remembering different little incidents in her life that had given us joy and happiness as parents. I thought of her now, trusting her parents that they were doing what was right, and would protect her and be a help to her. She didn't fully understand the danger we were taking her into. What if the nomads came out and attacked our little clearing? I wouldn't shoot them to protect my family. Each member of my family is born again and would go to be with the Lord should the nomads kill them. On the other hand, should I kill one of the nomads they would burn in hell for eternity, and their blood would be upon my hands. I remember thinking, "Will Anna ever return to Todos Santos?"

Then I looked at little Beverly. She was so happy being home. She didn't enjoy school very much anyway. And Bev is one who loves to play. In La Jota I built a swing for her, and she spent hours swinging in it, singing at the top of her voice. I remember looking at her and wondering if the nomads would kidnap her and carry her away, possibly to rape and mistreat her. Tears came to my eyes, and I wondered what I was doing here and how I got into this spot of danger.

Then as I looked at Alan I wondered if he would ever return to school at Tambo, or if his body would rot in the soil of La Jota.

As the thought cycle continued depression deepened. I thought of the "normal" families back home and how they go to church and worship God and live in nice houses and have the security of a civilization where laws rules. How did I ever get into this situation?

It was then that the words of Jesus to Peter, "Get thee behind me Satan," directed to the author of these thoughts came to me. I prayed that God would keep me from falling prey to Satan in his attempt to get me to turn back because of the danger. At that time my thoughts turned to better things, and I no longer worried about the fate of my family.

The real victory in this incident came at the end of the school vacation when the children returned to Todos Santos on their way back to boarding school. As a family, talking over this vacation and comparing it to other vacations, we all agreed that this had been the happiest time we had ever had together as a family!

Lois and I had been concerned because there would be nothing for the children to do in La Jota. They could take no toys with them, as we were carrying everything, pressed for weight, and needed to take food. But once there Alan spent most of his time fishing in the little stream that ran by our house. Anna and Beverly had their own little fire and cooked the fish Alan caught. Beverly enjoyed the swing I put up for her and Anna helped Lois cook meals over the campfire. Even staying in the small clearing didn't seem to bother them.

Over the next couple of days, there were no indications that the nomads had returned, no gifts taken, no whistling, so the men went to check the gift trail to the Naranjal. All the gifts along the trail had been taken. The missionaries normally placed a stick about six feet high in the middle of the trail, hanging the gift on that and attaching a long white streamer of torn-up bedsheets so the gifts would be easy to spot from a distance. As the missionaries walked the trail to the Naranjal, they chuckled to see that the nomads had cut many more sticks and planted them along the trail, evidently hoping the gift-givers would leave many more gifts.

Taking the hint, the team left gifts on all the sticks. One of the sticks was a forked stick with three limbs, one of them pointing south. From the one pointing south, the missionaries could see breaks where the people had gone through the jungle in that direction. Many gifts were hung by the men, including three burlap bags, three paring knives, two small mirrors, three large plastic combs (bright colored), two one-gallon cans with wire handles, two T-shirts, and a stalk of bananas. All of these were items that had been previously taken by the nomads, so the missionaries were confident the Yuquí were finding them useful.

The trail was two and a half kilometers long, and the team left sixteen new gifts along it, averaging one about every 150 meters. The trail had many long straight stretches, so most of the time, a gift could be seen from any point on the trail, and the trail led to the missionaries' clearing and houses. The nomads could follow a trail of gifts right to the missionary clearing!

Due to the shootings, little by little, the La Jota colonists were abandoning their farms and moving to town, occasionally going back out to harvest their coca leaves, a little manioc, and assorted other food items. With the bulk of their bananas and manioc being stolen by the nomads, the farmers were struggling to feed their families. Some of them approached the missionary team and asked them to pay for the stolen crops. Les, Harold, and Dick went to meet with a small group of colonists, expecting a demand for a significant amount of money. They were surprised when the colonists requested only about one-tenth of what the missionaries expected, about twenty dollars total! The missionaries happily paid the modest amount, and the last of the La Jota colonists left for town.

Several of the farmers whose houses were nearest to the missionary camp told them to make free use of anything they left behind—flattened barrels which were used for roofing small sheds, a few boards, and other odds and ends—and told them to help themselves to any of their crops. Suddenly, the missionaries had all the fresh papaya, citrus fruit, and other assorted products they could consume. These fruits were not something the nomads had learned to eat.

It took several days for the colonists to carry their more important belongings out to the Coni River and then to town by canoe. The day before the last load was scheduled to be carried out, Jorge Herbas and his father were on their way back to the La Jota colony after carrying a load of belongings to Coni River.

As they neared the La Jota colony, only about 400 meters out, they heard the jungle people talking on the south side of the trail. Jorge turned that way and saw a large group of warriors, and at almost the same instant, an arrow flew by, very narrowly missing Jorge and lodging in a tree beside him. He fired two shots "up in the air" to scare the warriors away, and they left in such a rush that one of them dropped his seven-foot bow and three arrows, each six and a half to seven feet long, some of them with barbed palm tips.

Jorge reported that he shot into the air, and while the missionaries wondered if that was true, they said nothing to Jorge but questioned among themselves, "Would a jungle warrior leave his bow and arrows behind if he were not badly wounded or killed?" At least with the La Jota colonists moving out, this type of incident should quickly become a thing of the past, and friendship with the nomads might soon become a reality for the missionaries.

In fact, the very afternoon the colonists finished pulling out, the nomads came down one of the trails close to the missionaries' houses and took two more gifts. One was a gallon can with a wire handle and white strip of paint around it, just like most of the gifts were marked. The other gift taken especially thrilled the missionaries. It was a basket woven of palm leaves by the nomads themselves and left

behind when they were surprised while stealing manioc
at one of the Bolivian farms.
The missionaries had found
three such baskets and filled
the largest one with corn
and bananas, hanging it on a
pole in a trail 180 yards from
the house. It was put out on
Sunday, and they planned
to leave it for one week and
then replace the contents if it

Les Foster with a Yuquí
palm-leaf backpack

hadn't been taken. On Friday, the basket disappeared with the contents no doubt still in edible condition.

Even though the nomads had been close to the missionary camp
several times and, at times, almost surrounding it, judging from the
whistling, voices, chanting, etc., the missionaries had yet to see them.
Several nights, Lois was awakened as she heard them singing, chanting, or wailing in the jungle nearby. It was clear they were camped
extremely close by, and without doubt, the missionaries would be
able to locate the camp and walk into it, but they felt it would be
presumptive on their part to try that at present. There was too much
anger in the nomads' hearts against the ones who had stolen their
children, and they had no way of knowing the missionaries hadn't
taken part in that atrocity.

The team was confident God was working in the nomads'
hearts, preparing them to show themselves on the gift trails or to
follow one of the trails to the edge of the missionary camp. For the
jungle dwellers to camp so close by seemed evidence that they didn't
fear the missionaries too much.

Now that the colonists had moved to town, the missionaries
continued busily improving their encampment in the jungle as well
as checking gift trails daily and replacing gifts as they disappeared.
They were well-aware that each trip down a trail was an opportunity
for the nomads to show themselves in friendship or send arrows in
their direction, yet each missionary had committed their life into

God's hands, knowing that the God who protected Daniel in the lion's den also desired the nomads to hear of His Son, the Redeemer, and could protect them from the dangers of the jungle.

Harold and Les hiked into the La Jota colony to pick up a few sheets of flattened out fifty-gallon fuel barrels some of the colonists used for fireproof roofs on their cooking sheds. Les was building a generator shed a short distance from his house and wanted the metal sheets for roofing the building. The nearest farm belonged to José Cárdenas, and when the men arrived there, they found the nomads had burned down his house, his kitchen, and the chicken house behind the kitchen. With no buildings left standing, the site looked barren. The conflagration was recent, within the last two days as rain had not yet fallen on the ashes and some of the larger pieces of wood were still smoldering.

The first thought to come to Les was, "José and the other colonists will be so infuriated when they learn of this that they will want a commission to come in and kill the Yuquí."

Dick, on the other hand when he heard about it, commented, "Maybe this is God's way of keeping José from coming back out and living here again. We've already paid him for his crops, but he's sure to want to come back and harvest his coca leaves. With no house, he may not be tempted to come." Since José and his sons had "shot in the air," as they phrased it, or more likely, as the missionaries suspected, "shot at" the jungle people, this "housewarming" could also be construed as a going away present for him from the nomads.

Two days later, Dick, Harold, and Les went back into the abandoned colony of La Jota to pick up more flattened out barrels. Les' son, Alan, went along to help carry back papaya, winter squash, avocados, and other produce. Three trips were required, one in the morning and two in the afternoon. On the last trip, they found a rickety wooden cart with squeaky wooden wheels, loaded it with flattened barrels, and pulled the noisy contraption along the trail.

During an earlier trip, the fellows had heard the nomads chopping down trees in the jungle to the south of Juan's house, so they knew the squeaky cart would be heard, clearly identifying their location to the warriors. As they made their way back to the missionary camp, they needed to cross a small stream where the cart had to be unloaded and the contents carried across a log bridging the stream and then reloaded onto the cart once it had been pulled through the stream.

During the crossing, Les realized that he had left a piece of board behind, so he sent Alan to retrieve it while the men were reloading the cart. With the nomads in the vicinity, Alan wasn't happy about being sent alone back down the slippery trail for a piece of board, thinking as he went of all the shootings that had taken place, of the farmer's child who had been kidnapped, and the many other dangers the jungle posed.

Knowing that with the farmers gone the Yuquí could now roam freely in the La Jota area, the men decided it would be good to go into the colony often, carrying gift cans, bags, machetes, etc., with the hope of meeting them and offering gifts from their own hands. They were confident that God was in the process of softening the nomads' hearts and preparing them for a soon-to-be-realized friendly contact.

When word reached town that José's buildings had been burned by the nomads, many of the colonists who had been cooperating with the missionaries and giving them time to make friendly contact with the nomads turned against them. The leader of one of the nearby colonies went to Cochabamba with the intent of obtaining rifles and ammunition so a commission of farmers could go into the jungle and annihilate the nomads. By the time the missionaries learned of this, twenty rifles had already been procured, and the leader was expected back within two weeks to lead the commission on its deadly mission.

The missionaries sent out letters and radio communications to prayer partners, asking them to pray that God would protect all involved—the nomads, the colonists, and the missionary team. The missionaries were especially concerned since on this occasion, it seemed that a greater number of farmers had joined together for this purpose and were more determined than ever to eliminate the danger from hostile nomads. As Les wrote to his prayer partners, "We believe the answer is Christ who alone is able to change the hearts of these nomads and cause them to become useful citizens of Bolivia and friendly, helpful neighbors to the colonists."

Over the next few weeks, the nomads continued to destroy the farmers' houses one by one. Erasmo's house was still warm with a little smoke rising when the missionaries came upon it; at Severino's house site, the ashes were already cold, and it appeared to have been burned the previous day; Naira's house and kitchen were a raging inferno, and the men couldn't get close to them because of the heat. It appeared the nomads had just been there, and the house had been burning for less than an hour. There were *achiote* (*urucú*) pods scattered around, and it looked like the nomads had spent time smearing the red coloring on their bodies as they fired the house and gloated in their victory over the colonists. It had only taken moments for them to destroy the labor of many months.

The Dummy

HERBERT WAS A DUMMY, AND I mean a real dummy. Not just your average non-intelligent dummy, but as dumb as they come dummy. He just stood there, rain or shine, in the middle of a trail carved on a heading of 205 degrees through the western portion of the Bolivian Amazon. The nice thing about Herbert was that he was fulfilling the purpose for which he was created, not like so many people who spend their lives living with little or no purpose or living for the wrong purpose.

One of the dummies used to offer gifts to the Yuquí.'

Herbert had no idea that the surrounding jungle and even the trail he stood on were fraught with dangers, not the least of which were the hostile nomads who occasionally roamed through the area. Dangers abounded there where Herbert calmly stood. The creek nearby harbored large caimans, the South American cousin of the crocodile, as well as anacondas large enough to easily swallow him. Jaguars could often be heard at night, mooing in the moonlight, much like a cow.

And the insects! Clouds of mosquitoes, several types of blood-sucking no-see-ums, numerous assortments of horseflies and deerflies, inch-long stinging ants, and more. And then there were the snakes, many varieties, which included several deadly types, not least among them the English Bushmaster (Lachesis muta), one of the largest poisonous snakes in South America whose venom is a potent brew of nerve-attacking, tissue-attacking, and blood-attacking varieties; not a snake with which you would want to have an encounter. I never saw a small one. They were always six feet long with fangs an inch and a quarter long, and they gave way for no man, woman, or child.

You would think Herbert would have been smarter than that, standing there, hour by hour, day after day, night after night; but he was just a dummy with no understanding of the true purpose of his existence. With all that standing around, Herbert began to put on a little weight around the middle, and his shoulders began to sag from the tropical moisture. And then one day, the unexpected happened; a nomad warrior stealthily approached Herbert, took the gallon can with wire handle from Herbert's hand, and began to dismantle poor Herbert.

First to come off was his purple straw hat, then his head, a twenty-five-pound-size cloth sugar sack stuffed with corn husks; and next the shirt came off, and then the trousers and his tennis shoes. Soon Herbert had been reduced to a few pieces of cloth which were hauled off into the forest by the wandering warrior.

Even in "death," Herbert would be useful; soon the warrior's wife would unravel the clothing Herbert had been wearing and use the thread to create useful items—a new bowstring for her husband, new ropes for the cord hammock, or possibly a new cord baby sling for carrying her infant.

Herbert was greatly appreciated in his new home, but he was no longer recognizable as the dummy who had stood so faithfully on the trail. He had fulfilled his purpose, holding out gifts to the hostile nomads and beginning to plant in their minds the possibility that someone in the wider world cared about them.

With Herbert gone, his brother, George, took his place standing about 180 yards from the Foster house on a trail which led back to the house and allowed Les and Lois to keep an eye on George as he stood there, holding a gift can with wire handle, a machete, and a can of sweetened condensed milk. To make it easier for the nomads to access the can of condensed milk, Les had punctured a hole in the top and then resealed it with beeswax covered with adhesive tape. He was confident that once the people tasted sweetened condensed milk, they would want more of that. Who wouldn't!

Within three days, George went missing and. Even though Les and Lois had been watching the trail closely, they never saw the nomads as they sneaked out of the jungle around noon and took him. Later in the afternoon, Les, Dick Strickler, and Harold Rainey went out the gift trail and found that all the gifts they had hung along the trail had been taken. Replacing the gifts with fresh ones, they also placed a new dummy, Jonathan, 180 yards down the trail.

Jonathan stood faithfully in place, holding out gifts for four days before relinquishing his task and being replaced by his "brother," Daniel. The missionaries had found an abandoned palm-leaf backpack woven by the nomads, and Daniel contentedly wore it on his back filled with a gift of corn for the jungle people.

Each day, Les, Dick, and Harold would go out one or more of the gift trails and as the gifts continued to disappear, the missionaries put out additional offerings. On some of those trips, they found fresh evidence of the nomads, manioc peelings, corn husks, banana stalks, plantain peelings, sugarcane, feathers, fresh dung, prints from bare feet, etc. Most of the foodstuff had been stolen from the small farms belonging to the colonists who had farmed the area during the past few years.

As the dummies continued to disappear, the missionaries' hopes for friendly contact began to soar. Surely if the nomads were antagonistic toward them, they could have shown that by shooting one of the dummies full of arrows or slashing it to pieces with a machete. Instead, they kept returning to accept the proffered gifts, leaving the missionaries to wonder if it was time to consider approaching a Yuquí camp in the jungle. The Foster children headed back to boarding school, leaving their parents along with Dick and Harold to continue reaching out to the Yuquí.

The day after dummy Daniel had been put into place on the "generator" trail, the missionary team happened to be standing near the generator shed. It was 2:45 p.m. when Lois glanced down the trail. "They're taking Daniel's head," she exclaimed. Les looked down the trail, and sure enough, several of the nomads were there, taking gifts from Daniel as they dismembered him.

Les moved toward the gift trail leading toward Daniel, and taking hold of a gift can located there, he held it up, yelling in Sirionó, "Don't run away!"

With that, a warrior who was about fifty yards closer to the missionaries than the dummy came out of hiding from beside the trail, looked at Les, and then turned around and ran straight down the trail toward Daniel.

The warrior was about five feet nine inches tall with a muscular chest and arms. He had a "bowl type" haircut and was painted red from head to toe with coloring from the seeds of the *achiote* (*urucú*) plant. The nomad took a knife from one of the gift poles and then ran on down to take Daniel's head.

Les hurriedly picked up three more gift items and, along with Harold and Dick, began slowly making their way down the trail, calling out in both Spanish and Sirionó to the warrior while holding out gifts for him, but he quickly vanished into the jungle alongside the trail.

The whole incident happened so quickly, it was almost like a dream, and Les expressed it in a letter to friends:

> I just felt like running down there and throwing my arms around that warrior and hugging him when I saw him. I was so glad to see him. But before we could get down there, he had disappeared. They are so afraid of all…men because of earlier treatment. We are going to have to show them over and over that we don't shoot nor are we going to hurt them in any way.

Three weeks went by, but the nomads didn't return. Contact had seemed so imminent, but now it looked like the Yuquí had moved on. Saturday, midafternoon, Dick went over to Les' house with the news that some of the gifts on the north trail, which led away from his and Harold's house, were missing. The men immediately gathered up two gift cans with wire handles, two paring knives, and a ball of fine string, suitable for tying feathers onto arrows, and headed out the gift trail, hanging the gifts strategically along a 500-meter stretch of trail, the portion they could see from the house. Then they went down the south gift trail to where Daniel the dummy still stood, although with a replaced head.

Having stood in the rain and weather for over three weeks, Daniel was in pretty bad shape to greet a group of nomads, so the missionaries "retired" him and, in his place, left a small can of sugar, a machete, a gift can, and a basket filled with corn. It was a basket the nomads had abandoned while stealing from the colonist's farms. By 6:40 p.m., the missionaries could hear the nomads chanting in the jungle to the west of their encampment. It was too late for the nomads to travel any distance that day; evidently, they were camped nearby.

* * * * *

Sunday! Day of rest! But there would be no rest for the missionary team! There were things that needed to be done. The men headed into the La Jota colony to see if the nomads who had been around the previous day were a large group or just a few scouts checking to see if the produce of the colony was ready for harvest. Very little had been taken from the farms, and there were many more crops ripe for harvest. No doubt the "spies" who had been around yesterday had gone to bring back a larger group.

Two *tembe* palm trees had an abundance of ripe fruit, so the missionaries headed back to their houses for an axe and then returned to the colony to chop the trees down and gather the fruit for cooking and eating. Tembe is a type of peach palm that grows in a thick cluster, kind of like a banana plant, and puts out multiple stems. It needs to be boiled for about thirty minutes before being eaten and has a delicious, oily, squash-textured flesh.

Monday came, and around noon, Dick went over to tell Les and Lois that he could no longer see the gifts on the north trail. Dinner was cooking, but it could wait. The men picked up a few gifts, then went along the half-mile stretch of trail, finding some of the gifts missing, so they replaced them. As a special treat, they hung a can of candy and sugar at the end of the trail along with a gift can on one side of it and a paring knife on the other side. Then they returned home and ate lunch.

After lunch, Les went back over to Dick and Harold's house to talk with them about going into the colony of La Jota to see if the nomads might have taken gifts as they passed through, and maybe the missionaries could encounter them there. They decided to leave at once, following the north trail to where it crossed a trail made by the nomads, and then following the Yuquí trail into La Jota. Doing this, they might come across the nomads as they were coming out of La Jota loaded with produce.

The three men went the half-kilometer to where the can of sugar and candy had been placed ninety minutes earlier and found it missing. Evidently, some of the nomads were still nearby, so it might be better to remain in the clearing, replace gifts as they were taken, keep an eye on the gift trails, and call to the elusive jungle people if they came out onto the trail to take gifts. The men returned to their clearing, got another can of sugar and a ball of fine string, and took them out to hang on a stick 500 meters from their clearing, then returned home to wait and watch for the Yuquí. Dick and Harold took turns watching the north gift trail while Les and Lois kept an eye on the south trail.

It was four o'clock when Les looked down the trail, and what a surprise! The trail was alive with people, or at least that was his first impression. About fifty yards from the clearing was a boy, twelve to fourteen years old, but with a muscular manly build. Fifty yards farther down the trail was what appeared to be a woman, and at the 180-yard gifts, there were two men or a man and his grown son. Les ran to the first gift, a gallon can with wire handle and a white strip painted around it, grabbed it and, holding it out toward the nomads, yelled in Spanish, "We are friends!"

There was a mad scramble as they ducked back into the jungle on the west side of the trail. Les refrained from yelling, and soon their curiosity got the best of them, and he saw heads bobbing in and out of the jungle as they looked down the trail toward him to see what he was doing. He stood there, waving the gift can toward them while calling softly to Lois to bring more gifts to him.

Harold was looking over from his house to see what was happening, so Les motioned that he should join him. By the time Harold and Dick arrived on the scene, the nomads had disappeared back into the jungle. Harold, Dick, and Les each took gifts in hand and, holding them up in the air, walked down to where the nomads had been a few moments earlier. The men could still hear them talking among themselves back in the jungle a little way but didn't see them again.

After putting new gifts on the poles in the trail, the missionaries returned to their clearing. Once the excitement in the missionary camp abated, they realized they had only seen four people—a boy, two men, and a woman—not the abundance of people they had at first thought.

The two men that Les and Lois had seen both were around five feet nine inches in height with powerful chests and arms. No doubt, these had been developed from pulling the seven-foot bows they used. Les had one of their bows and several arrows the colonists had given him but was unable with all his strength to pull the bow back far enough to shoot an arrow effectively. Many of the missionaries and colonists had tried drawing the bow, but few were able as it required well-developed chest and arm muscles. At least one of the nomads seemed to have his hair cut in a "bowl" style, and none of them were wearing any clothing at all.

This time as before, when missionaries had seen them, they were covered from head to foot with *achiote* (*urucú*) paint. Achiote is a pod with bright red-orange seeds, which when mixed with water, makes a "war paint" they use to cover their entire bodies.

The missionary team was encouraged by this close encounter with the jungle dwellers as it seemed their fear was lessening, and they had stayed in sight a little longer than the previous time.

Over the next few days, the nomads came out on the trail in plain sight of the missionaries three different times. One of the times, there were about a dozen of them, and as the missionaries waved gifts at them, they stayed in sight on the trail for several minutes, waving their arms, dancing up and down, and yelling. One of the times, when the missionaries went down to replace gifts that had been taken, they found that the nomads had left a palm leaf basket at the end of the trail where they had taken gifts. Whether they were leaving the basket as a gift or hinting they wanted it filled with more corn such as the missionaries had previously left in such baskets was unclear. Either way, the missionary team felt that progress was being made and less fear was being shown.

Another day dawned, and now it was midmorning. As was his custom, Dick looked down the north trail and was surprised to spot a larger group of nomads than they had previously seen. Dick headed over to get Les, and the two men, accompanied by Harold, all hoisted gifts and walked out toward the nomads. This time, there were about a dozen of them, all of them painted from head to toe with *urucú* as before, but this time they were carrying bows and arrows. For the next three minutes, they stayed right in the trail, watching as the missionaries waved gifts at them.

They in turn waved their arms in the air and danced around in the trail, shouting at the missionaries. Les tried dancing around just like they did and waved his arms at them while still holding the gifts. As the missionaries slowly edged their way down the trail, planning to either offer the gifts to the people or replace them on the poles, the nomads moved off the trail and hid in the fringes of the jungle. Halfway down the trail, gifts were missing, so the missionaries replaced those and then returned to their clearing for a bunch of ripe eating bananas, a ball of large twine, and a paring knife. They carried these items to the end of the trail where the nomads had been only minutes before and replaced those missing gifts as well.

While the men were replacing the gifts, some of the nomads had gone through the jungle over to the south trail and removed the gifts from that trail, so the missionaries went over and placed a stalk of bananas, can of sugar, machete, and ball of fine string on that trail.

As the missionaries would place gifts along one trail, the nomads would remove the gifts from the other trail, kind of like a game!

Eventually, the Yuquí showed up back on the north trail where the missionaries were standing, holding out gifts they hoped to hand personally to the jungle dwellers. For two or three minutes, the nomads stood there, watching, but as the missionaries slowly moved forward, the Yuquí faded into the forest and disappeared.

For the next two weeks, the game continued. Gifts would be taken and replaced. Occasionally, one or more of the nomads would be spotted, but any time the missionaries tried to get closer in order to hand gifts to the people, they would slink back into the jungle, not reappearing until the missionaries moved farther back.

The missionaries tried various things, hoping to end the stalemate. The men removed their shirts, thinking the naked nomads might better identify with them if they weren't hidden under clothing. They tried playing a tape recorder with music, hoping they would be fascinated by the sound and come closer. Corn seemed to be one of the preferred items, so the missionaries began putting out more baskets and bags of corn.

Finally, one afternoon, the largest man they had yet seen came out onto the trail. The sun shining through his long shaggy hair gave a red cast to it. Once again, the missionaries took off their shirts and tried approaching closer, but the nomads vanished. At one point, they saw an Indian bow thrust out of the foliage beside the trail, hook one of the gifts, and draw it back into the forest. The missionaries went down and replaced all the missing gifts, and soon, eight nomads came out and retrieved them. The missionaries were trying to leave the gifts closer and closer to the house, but occasionally, nomads who were watching would step out of the woods and motion that they should put the gifts farther down the trail. Clearly, they didn't want to be drawn in too close.

A few days later, the big man showed up again. This time, he stood in the middle of the others and at the front. He was a huge giant of a man and danced, jumping up and down, and waving his arms more enthusiastically than the others. It appeared he might be the chief. This group didn't seem nearly as afraid of the missionaries as others who had been coming to take gifts. Whereas the others had always been quick to duck back into the jungle if the missionaries approached too closely, this group seemed bolder and not as fearful.

It looked as if progress was being made in breaking down the fear the nomads had of the missionaries, and although growth of trust was slow, it was apparent. Whereas early on the Yuquí had run wildly into the jungle at first glance, within a few visits, they were staying on the trail for several minutes with the missionaries only 300 yards away. Eventually, they stayed on the trail for an unbelievable time of twenty-seven minutes. On this visit, they were only one hundred yards away, and men, women, and children stayed in the trail for an hour and ten minutes. Fear was being replaced by curiosity. No one from the outside world had been friendly to them before. Who were these unusual people who shared useful items with them?

The missionaries decided to push harder for a face-to-face encounter. They tied up bunches of corn, about six ears to a bunch, and left them in plain view of the trails but in the missionary clearing. Corn seemed to be a preferred gift and maybe would be desirable enough for them to brave close proximity to the missionaries. After the missionaries placed corn in their clearing, they headed down the trail to hang additional bunches on poles in the trail. As they were doing this, some of the nomads came out of the jungle about 200 yards down the trail from the houses. The missionaries held the corn up to them, and they held their arms up, just like the missionaries were doing.

An interesting observation the missionaries had made during these encounters was that they could hold anything up in the air *above* their heads, and the nomads would stay on the trail, but if the men held it out *toward* them, they would run off into the jungle. They seemed to have a fear of something being pointed at them, and it was no wonder since on numerous occasions, the colonists had pointed guns at them and hurt or killed them.

As Dick, Lois, and Les advanced toward them, carrying corn, they stayed in the trail until the missionaries were within fifty yards before ducking off the trail to the safety of the jungle foliage. The missionaries continued down the trail, carrying the corn in their hands held high over their heads. They knew the nomad warriors were in the jungle around them but couldn't see them. After hanging corn on the gift poles, the missionaries turned and went back to their clearing.

It was mid to late afternoon before the nomads worked up enough courage to come out and get the corn that was only fifty yards from the missionary clearing, although the missionaries didn't see this happen. Once the corn was gone, Dick, Lois, and Les went back down and hung a new gift can with corn in it, then came back almost to the house, although staying on the trail to watch. In a couple of minutes, a man peeked out of the jungle, then stepped boldly into view to retrieve the can and corn. Once again, the missionaries headed down to hang a fresh bunch of corn but decided to move the gift a little closer to their clearing.

Les pulled up the stick with the corn on it and carried it about twenty yards closer to the clearing, then stopped. As he went to push the stick into the ground, he unconsciously made a grunting sound while pushing. There was a mad scramble about ten yards west of the trail as six or eight nomads who were hiding there ran wildly away through the jungle. *Poor timid people!* thought Les. As Les, Dick, and Lois headed back to the clearing, he commented, "After that, it will probably take them some time to work up their courage to return."

Not so! Within two minutes, the nomads could be seen peeking out of the jungle again, although now they were 100 yards from the clearing. There were ten or more people, although not all of them were visible at the same time. One was a little potbellied boy about three years old, and there was also a small girl who appeared to be four or five years old. There were four boys or girls between eight and fourteen years old and a man who might have been the father of a portion of the group. A couple of teenagers completed the group.

For the next hour and ten minutes, they remained on the trail. They would wave their arms, and the missionaries would wave theirs. Les would do jumping and arm waving much as he had done in his army air force calisthenics training, and the nomads would imitate him, doing the same thing. Then the nomads would do side bends, so the missionaries would do side bends. When Les jumped up and down and danced around, they would follow suit.

Soon Les began to feel exhausted as if he'd been through an army obstacle course. From time to time, Les would try to advance toward them, but as he approached, they would duck off the trail. Finally, Les took his shirt off and found they would let him advance a little farther without running, but eventually, they would flee to the safety of the forest. Then Les decided to remove his trousers, leaving on only his undershorts and shoes. Now they let him advance to within fifty yards of them before running to the safety of the jungle. Each time he returned to the missionary clearing, the group would come right back out onto the trail again.

The nomads were repeating one motion over and over again. It almost appeared as if they were beckoning the missionaries to come closer. They would lift their whole forearm and then wave their hand past their ear. As they repeated this motion over and over, Les took it as a cue to advance toward them, but as he approached, they would always run. Finally, Lois realized what was going on. They were imitating Lois brushing away the mosquitoes that were flying around her ears. They "mocked" everything the missionaries did, and the missionaries "mocked" everything they did; it was just part of the game.

It was clear that little by little, fear was breaking down, but with no language in common, how were they to communicate?

Occasionally, when the children would imitate the crazy things the missionaries did, they appeared to be overcome by bashfulness and would put both hands up in front of their faces and giggle. Through all this time, the nomads were jabbering among themselves, but the missionaries couldn't hear clearly enough to pick up individual words or meaning.

It was close to noon the next day when Dick ambled over to the Foster house to let Les know that he could no longer see gifts on the north trail. The gifts on the south trail leading into the jungle from the Foster's house were still visible, so no doubt, the nomads would show up there at any moment. The men headed toward the north trail but then stopped and had a short time of prayer, asking God to watch over them and to bring about a friendly close-up encounter with the nomads. As they were praying, Lois called over to them, "I see them on the south trail."

The men had been heading for the north trail but came running back to see four natives about 125 yards down the trail from the edge of the clearing. They had already removed the gifts, so Dick, Harold, and Les went down and replaced them. Two warriors stood in the trail, holding their bows and arrows. One of the men conspicuously threw his bow down in the trail as if to say he wouldn't use it. As the fellows headed down to replace the gifts, the warrior picked up his bow and joined his companion as they ran off the trail and hid.

The missionaries had retreated less than fifty yards when the warriors came back out and took the basket of ripe plantains the men had just left for them. The plantains were in a basket that had been woven and abandoned by the nomads. While the warriors were taking the gift, Les yelled at them in various languages—Sirionó, Spanish, Yuracaré, and English, and the warriors yelled back. Neither understood what the other said!

The missionaries had a brief discussion and decided they would have Les go down alone with the next gifts. This seemed to help as the warriors would let him get within twenty to twenty-five yards of them before they would run away. Then, while they were back in the jungle, they would continue talking to Les, and he would do his best to imitate them and yell the same thing back. When Les replaced the gift, he moved only about twenty yards away and stayed there as the jungle people came back out and took the gifts. While their fear was not gone, it was receding daily. No doubt, true hand to hand giving of gifts was imminent.

Soon the warriors planted a stick in the trail and began wiggling it back and forth while jabbering to Les. Pointing at the corn hanging in the missionary clearing, they made it clear they wanted the gift corn brought to their stick and didn't want to approach the clearing to get it. "Jabber, jabber, jabber, jabber!" They continued telling Les to bring the gifts down there where they were; they didn't want to get nearer to the clearing.

Les advanced toward them, but they ran off into the jungle a little way. He replaced the gift, and they came right back as soon as he had gotten back twenty yards or so. The three people who were on the trail were men, but it appeared to the missionaries that there was also a little girl visible at times. They all continued to jabber, jabber, jabber at Les, and he did his best to repeat the same thing back to them. They got the most disgusted look on their faces, and the oldest fellow, overcome by Les' ignorance, stomped off into the jungle, only to return in a minute or two.

After an hour of "conversation," the closest things to words Les had heard was *watai, barai, ari, chori*, and a few other little things. It sounded like their jabbering's were full of the "*ch*" sound. Dick was exhilarated to have captured a few words and phrases and later that evening dug out some Sirionó and Guarayo word lists to see if any of the words or sounds they had heard that day made sense but found nothing that matched his lists.

Early the next morning, Les turned off the generator after talking by radio to the mission supply man in the city of Santa Cruz and then went over to strategize with Dick and Harold. Heading back to his house at 8:30 a.m., he looked down the south trail and saw at least twelve men accompanied by children and women. The group was already within twenty yards of the missionary clearing, and when they saw Les, they started crying and begging for food as they advanced, pointing to the bunches of corn hanging in the clearing and indicating that he should bring the corn to them there on the trail.

Les decided to try some of the language he had heard the previous day, so he shook one of the sticks with corn in the missionary clearing and yelled, "*Ari Ari!*" He had no idea if that made any sense or what it might mean, but after a short conversation among themselves, the group advanced toward the missionary clearing. There was an axe hanging right at the edge of the clearing, an exceptionally valuable gift, but they stopped short of it and wouldn't come closer.

Les carried some corn over and placed it on the same stick with the axe, then backed away toward the clearing. They came a little nearer, again yelling and motioning for Les to bring the corn closer to them. He yelled back, "No, no, no" and beckoned them toward the clearing. Finally, the warriors laid down their bows and arrows and came down to the very edge of the missionary clearing. Lois, Dick, and Harold stayed back so as not to scare them while Les, by himself, edged up closer until he was able to hand one old man some corn and a gift can. There were seventeen or eighteen nomads. All the men had shaggy shoulder-length hair, and two or three of the more mature men had a few chin whiskers, not quite a light beard.

The women wore their hair plucked or shaven halfway back on their foreheads, somewhat like a man with a receding hairline over half of his head. The children seemed to have "bowl" style haircuts, but not all of them. One of the younger women wore a "dress" made of woven bark fiber of some kind. It was almost like a burlap bag with both ends cut out but of a coarser weave. The other women wore no clothing but were naked, just as the men and children. The jungle men wore nothing at all, not so much as an armband, G-string, or anything; unless, that is, you counted a few feathers glued into their hair with beeswax.

While Les stood there, conversing with them, they kept saying, "Wa'aru, Wa'aru (ua eru = those bring)" while pointing at the manioc patch. Les pantomimed that the manioc was still very small and not ready to dig and eat. They seemed to understand that and then asked about the other bunches of corn hanging around the clearing. As one would ask about a bunch of corn, Les would walk over, bring it back, and give it to them. They would cry and cry and thank him and then ask for more. They kept saying "Tanima" and sometimes "Tanima aru." At the same time, they would make a motion of feeding themselves. It seemed they were hungry and asking for food.

Les called to Dick who came over with pencil and paper to try and write down some of the words they were hearing. The nomads had no problem with Dick joining them until he pulled a pen out of his pocket to write. When they saw the pen, they all turned and ran. Les held up his hand and yelled "Chori! Chori!" And they turned around and came back. One old woman wanted Dick's pen, so Les suggested to Dick that he put the pen away and try a pencil instead. Harold now joined the group, bringing more corn for them, and they asked for more yet.

Wanting to get Lois in on the action, Les called to her to bring out some sugar. Right away, they saw that she was a woman, and one of the native women wanted to take her away into the jungle with them. "Lois, I think you better return to the house," commented Les. Lois promptly did so, remarking later that she had been "shaking in her boots" when she got that close to them.

Having seen Lois, several of the young men wanted her to go with them, but Les diverted their attention by pouring sugar into his hand, then licking it and smacking his lips. This looked good, so they all stuck out their hands, and he poured a little sugar in each one. They licked it up, smiled, and laughed and said, "*Tapi! Tapi!*"

The gifts and foodstuff were going fast, and Les was trying to hold off as much as he could between gift-giving in order to keep the people around longer and to make the gifts last. They pointed to Lois, back at the house, and said, "*Mamara toto.*" Then they began motioning to bring more sugar out. Right about then, it started to rain a little bit, and one of the native women started to cry and pull on Les' clothing, pointing up at the rain as if to say that she wanted some clothing to keep her from getting wet. Les went over to his house, leaving Dick and Harold alone with the people while he gathered up several old T-shirts and other clothing they had been saving as gifts and took those down and passed them out among the group.

As each item of clothing was handed to them, they would smell the item before accepting it. Later, Les wrote, "The nomads did *not* smell like wild pigs as had been reported. They smelled just like fresh bacon. My mouth really watered while I was with them." They smelled of smoke from always being around the smoky fires over which they cooked and which reduced the insect population in their camps.

Les tended to sweat profusely in the hot, humid tropics, and one thing the nomads kept doing was to take their hands, wipe the sweat off his chest, and as they did so, say, "*Chö na*,"* by which they seemed to mean that he sweated a lot.

One of the warriors made a strange sound, something like, "*Aaaauuu, Aaaauuu, Aaaauuuu!*" throwing his head back as he did it and then saying something Les didn't understand, pointed to the missionary clearing. This happened repeatedly, and finally it became clear to Les that he was trying to imitate a rooster crowing and saying that he wanted a chicken.

The missionaries had a small flock of birds but didn't plan on giving those out on the first contact. The natives continued to ask for items, and when the missionaries refused, they didn't become out of sorts but would just ask for something else. Sugar was doled out slowly, probably about one and a half pounds of sugar total that first day in lots of about three tablespoons worth at a time in a tin can. Each time they would ask for more, and Les would bring out a little more. Eventually, it seemed that this first contact, with its strange stresses, had gone on long enough, so the missionaries let them know they had nothing more to give at the moment.

It seemed that the word for yes was *ai*, and when the nomads wanted the missionaries to repeat something they had said, they would say, much like we do in English, "*Huh.*" Eventually, Les pointed to the sun in the east, motioned to indicate it moving across the sky to the west, and tried to get across to them to come back later in the afternoon. As the missionaries headed back to their houses, the nomads whistled at them and waved goodbye while heading off into the jungle. The whistle was one steady whistle, air being sucked in, making a diphthong going from a rather low note to a higher one.

As the nomads moved off into the forest, the missionaries could hear them talking and chopping down trees. A few of them lingered on the trail for about a half an hour, and each time the missionaries would look out, they would advance a little as if to ask if it was time for the next feeding. The missionaries were busy writing down the assorted words and phrases they had picked up, and Dick was dili-

---

* Yuquí words are indicated in italics. The umlaut found over vowels (ä, ë, ï, ö, ü) indicates a nasal vowel.

gently comparing them to their word lists to see if they could attach meaning to any of it. Little if any of it made sense, although they were pretty confident that *ai* meant yes. One small word after that much time with the nomads!

The nomads appeared a little later the next morning while Les was getting ready to shave. He was holding a hot wet washcloth to his face when he looked out of the house and saw a man peeking from the jungle. Shaving could wait until later. Stepping out of the house, Les began calling, "*Tanima! Tanima!*" while holding up corn.

As he went back into the house, Dick and Harold arrived, and in a few moments, Dick said, "I can see several of them down the trail."

Les looked out and saw seven men with bows and arrows coming toward the camp. As they got within fifty yards of the clearing, the men dropped their bows and arrows and came on to the edge of the clearing.

Les headed over that way with corn as they waited nervously for him. Planting a stick in the trail there where they stood, one of them pointed to it and said to Les, "*Atu ua!* (meaning, "Leave them there!")"

Les went a couple steps farther, held his ground, and said without knowing what it meant, "*Atu ua! Atu ua!*"

Seeing that they were very uneasy, he put the corn on the ground and backed up a few steps. They came forward and picked up the corn. In all, they spent an hour with the missionaries who were able to capture many more words and a few phrases, although they were unsure what most of it meant. Twice, when the Fosters' dog barked, they became frightened and ran, but Les laughed at them, and they would stop, turn around, laugh, and come back. They kept saying they wanted food by pointing at their mouths and saying "*Tapi, tapi.*" Sometimes it seemed as if they put a "*Tatu*" or "*Tata*" on the end, which seemed to give emphasis.

The missionaries' ears were beginning to get attuned to the sounds of the language, and they noticed many nasalized vowels, which they hadn't discerned in earlier contacts. There was also a *cho* in which the "o" was a nasal, and then there was one word, *Taiu,* which sounded as if the *aiu* was nasalized.

Once, when Les was returning from the house with sugar, he thought he would try the low whistle and beckoning sign the nomads had used with the missionaries the day before. He stopped part way down the trail, beckoning and whistling as they had. They all started doing the same thing, then Les laughed, and they joined in as he went on down the trail to them. They were being helpful, repeating words and phrases over and over when the missionaries didn't understand them right away. They were also showing some manners and grace, which the missionaries hadn't expected.

Dick lost his pencil, and when Les got his out to give to Dick, one of the nomads reached over to take it from Dick. Les gently took hold of his hand and shook his head. Immediately, the nomad drew his hand back with no sign of resentment and started talking about something else. In both contacts, Les had been wearing his wristwatch, and so far, none of them had shown any interest in it or asked for it.

A little later, Les once again took sugar down to them, and as he began pouring it onto the wide leaf which the fellow held out to use as a plate, some of the sugar spilled off. Les said, "Ooooooo (going up the scale)," just as they did when things weren't going as they wished. Then he reached over beside the trail and plucked a larger leaf, a *patujú* leaf, wider and shaped much like a miniature banana leaf to put the sugar on. He happened to get a leaf with an old, dry, uninhabited hornet's nest on the underside of it. Les had been stung two days before by a hornet, and his face had been swollen both times the nomads had come to see the missionaries.

Les took the opportunity to point at the hornet's nest and then at his face. One of the natives rubbed Les' face and said something in a sympathetic tone of voice, which Dick was able to get down on paper. While they weren't sure of the meanings, every word, phrase, and sound would be helpful as they worked at deciphering this unknown tongue.

Eventually, the group of natives took their leave, likely to go hunting, and the missionaries had a three-hour respite. Les went to finish shaving, but by 12:40 p.m., as the rain let up, he looked down the trail and saw seven or eight warriors and boys with bows and arrows almost at the edge of the clearing. They were the same ones who had visited the missionaries in the morning. No doubt, they were on their way back from hunting and had stopped by to see if they could talk the missionaries out of a few chickens.

Les picked up some corn, and they stood patiently waiting as he carried it out to them. They laid their bows and arrows down and seemed unafraid. They only visited for about twenty minutes, long enough for Dick to jot down a few more words. Several of them acted as if they were cold and seemed to be asking for clothing, so Les headed back to the house and brought out an old pair of pants. Not much clothing for eight individuals, but the pants were all he had available to give away. The weather had turned cold, and with the wetness and the nomad's lack of clothing, no doubt they wanted to get to their camp and sit close by their campfires. They kept pointing at the sky and saying something like, "*Cuidadicho! Cuidadicho!*" before starting off down the trail.

As the missionaries headed toward their houses, the natives called them back to the edge of the clearing and handed Les a palm-leaf basket, pointing to Lois and saying, "*Mamaruche.*" The missionaries had begun to wonder if the word *Mamaru* meant woman as they had heard it several times in that connection. Les carried the basket to Lois as the nomads watched, standing in the trail to see how she would respond to this gift. Les warned her, "Don't act too enthusiastic over it" as it seemed some of the men were still showing too much interest in her.

During that twenty-minute contact, the nomads had also again asked for chickens by pointing at the chickens, throwing their heads back, and making an "*Aaauuu, Aaauuu, Aaauuu*" sound, probably the closest they could come to a rooster crowing.

They seemed to be in a real hurry to leave, which was a surprise to the missionaries as usually they had been the ones to break off the contact, but in about fifteen or twenty minutes, the missionaries began to understand the reason for their haste. A very heavy south wind and cold, cold rain hit the first of the year. Later, as the cold rain poured down, the missionary team could hear the nomads out in the jungle to the southwest, crying and yelling. It seemed they were camped close by within hearing distance.

Two days later, contact resumed, and that day, the nomads came to visit the missionaries twice, first at 10:30 in the morning and later at 12:50 in the afternoon. The 10:30 group consisted of twenty visitors, counting women and children. One of the four women was wearing a short bark skirt, which she used as a baby sling. The bark skirt was like a bag with both ends cut out, and the baby was pushed down into the upper edge of the bag, thus hanging by its mother's side.

The cold rain made for a miserable time as the entire group, missionaries included, was out in the weather. The missionaries encouraged them to leave and come back later, but the nomads insisted on staying. The missionaries tried going back to their houses to sit down low behind the half-wall encircling the house, thinking the natives would give up and leave, going back to their shelters and warm fires. Instead, the nomads approached nearer and nearer to the house, calling to the missionaries to come out.

They remained in the missionary clearing for almost fifty minutes and accepted gifts of corn, sugar, and a chicken. They also wanted the dog, but the missionaries suspected he would be killed and eaten, so they didn't let them have Puppy. When the nomads finally left, they could hear them whistling and calling to one another out in the forest for quite some time.

The 12:50 p.m. group arrived, whistling and calling to the missionaries just as they were sitting down for dinner. Leaving dinner to get cold, the missionaries headed back out to entertain the Yuquí for thirty minutes, getting some new words, and giving them sugar and corn. On the earlier visit of the day, the missionaries had given a machete as a gift. Now this group asked for a machete, so Les returned to the house and brought one out, making signs that he would like to trade it for an arrow.

The nomads talked it over among themselves and seemed to conclude that it would be too dangerous for Les to have an arrow. They felt his chest and seemed to try to tell him that he might hurt himself with it. One older woman wanted the dress Lois was wearing. Lois was wearing slacks and a blouse under her dress as protection against the abundant insects, so she took off her dress in plain sight of the natives, and Les carried it down to the woman. She was overjoyed to get such a fine piece of clothing. It wasn't long before the group left, no doubt anxious to get back to their warm fires, and this time, they didn't stay around and whistle so much.

The language barrier was just one of many problems the missionaries were facing. Supplies were another major complication. It was a five-hour trip by trail and river to the town of Todos Santos, so it usually took three days to make a supply trip, and then all the supplies had to be carried the last two hours from the port at Puerto Aurora. The missionary team was small, only four people—Les and Lois, Dick Strickler, and Harold Rainey. The risk was already high for such a small group when facing twenty or more warriors who might quickly become hostile if they didn't get their way, and to reduce the missionary team by sending someone to town for supplies would only add to the danger for those few who were left behind.

For four days, the nomads had come out once or twice a day, but on the fifth day, they didn't show up. Was this an opportunity to make a quick trip to town for supplies? The missionaries decided to wait two more days, and if the jungle dwellers hadn't made an appearance, Les and Lois would go into town for supplies.

Day seven arrived with no sign of the nomads, so early in the morning, Les and Lois headed down the trail toward the port. They only made it into the colony of La Jota, where they found a freshly woven palm-leaf basket full of achiote and bananas lying in the trail and an arrow on the ground beside it. They stopped, and Les picked up the arrow to inspect it and then laid it back down. As he laid the arrow down, Puppy, who had gone over to the north side of the trail, scared some nomads who had been hiding there, watching.

Les and Lois realized that the Yuquí could come to their camp for a visit at any time, so after leaving a gift can with some sugar on the basket, they headed back home.

Two days later, the nomads still had not made an appearance at the missionary camp, so once again, Les and Lois headed to town for supplies. The afternoon they arrived in town, Les began gathering supplies, anxious to return to their base in La Jota as quickly as possible. The next morning, he went over to a local store owned by

Emilio Bottega, one of the Italian immigrants in town, and used his radio receiver to listen in on the mission radio broadcast in case Dick and Harold had anything to report from the contact base. The news was not good!

Harold reported that the very day Les and Lois went into town, the nomads showed up around noon. With the Fosters not there, the natives went right into their house and began stealing items. The ceiling of the house was composed of palm boards, and the Fosters slept up there on thin mats under mosquito nets. The nomads went upstairs and down, taking whatever tickled their fancy. Harold and Dick did their best to stop them, but the nomads became violent and started wrestling with them. Harold commented, "Les, it's urgent that you get back out here."

Within ninety minutes, Les and Lois had the canoe loaded and were heading up the Chapare River for Puerto Aurora. By 2:00 p.m., they had arrived home and learned that the nomads had just left fifteen minutes previously. During this contact, the nomads had once again come into the Foster house, and what they hadn't stolen, they had broken open to see if it was edible or of any use to them. The house was a disaster zone!

Also, during this contact, they had been asking for Lois in such a way that Dick and Harold were quite concerned. Les was also troubled. Up until now, the nomads had stayed at the edge of the clearing a short distance from the house, and he had felt that Lois was safe in the house. Now that the Yuquí had come into the house twice, it seemed evident they would march right into the house when they returned.

One of the natives, whom the missionaries had begun calling Wide Eyes among themselves, had shown excessive interest in Lois on the first contact. What if the nomads were to show up right now? What, if anything, would Les be able to do to protect Lois?

As Les relates in a letter:

> My first thought was, *I'll tell Lois to hide in the mosquito net upstairs*, thinking maybe they wouldn't see her in there. Then I thought,

How foolish! They would surely see her in there, and she would not even have my help if she was upstairs in the mosquito net and I was downstairs with the bulk of the nomads.

After further thought, Les went over to Dick and Harold's house to discuss the situation with them. All three men agreed that Lois should go right back into town. Exhausted as they were, Les, Lois, and Puppy headed off down the trail toward Puerto Aurora and the town of Todos Santos. As they left their clearing, going along the trail to the east of their house, they could hear the nomads in the woods, hunting the missionaries' chickens. Les and Lois were both praying silently, "God, please keep us from meeting the nomads."

God was pleased to answer their prayers, and it was a relief to them both when they finally arrived at the Lobo Rancho trail, not far from the port where their canoe was tied.

Normally, when Les and Lois would go along the jungle trails together, Les would lead with Lois following along behind, as Les relates:

> Sometimes I would be hiking along not thinking of her and then would look back to see her 50 to 100 yards behind me, as she was unable to keep up with my normal hiking pace. But this time as we left La Jota with the nomads all around us Lois was right on my heels even though I was walking much faster than I normally hiked! At times it felt like she was going to walk up the back of my legs!

While in town, Les took the opportunity to send a radiogram to mission leadership in Cochabamba, letting them know that help was desperately needed. Were there a few missionary men who could be spared from other locations to help for a time on the contact?

Two days later, Les headed back out to La Jota and found that while he was gone, the nomads had come out again, wrestled with

Dick and Harold, and mistreated both men badly; as a result, Dick had a sprained ankle. The treatment they had received was severe enough that at times, both men had feared for their lives.

It was several days after Les' return before the Yuquí again paid the missionaries a visit. In the meantime, Rolf Fostervold and Jim Ostewig had arrived from Cochabamba, ready to put their lives at risk in the effort to get the Gospel message to the jungle dwellers. Two days after Rolf and Jim joined the team in La Jota, the nomads showed up at the missionary base.

Not knowing how the jungle dwellers might respond to new and unknown faces, the missionaries had decided that when the nomads returned, Rolf and Jim would hide in Les' house until Dick, Harold, and Les were interacting with the people, then they would call the new men out one at a time to meet the nomads.

When the nomads showed up, they came in by way of the north trail, and when they saw Les was back, they smiled, laughed, and came running to him, greeting him by wiping the sweat from his chest and back. One of the more powerful warriors went over to Les, handing him his bow and arrow and told him to show them how high he could shoot the arrow. Les already knew how difficult these bows were to draw but also realized this could have a significant bearing on their respect for him. He prayed silently, "God, give me strength for Your glory" before fitting the arrow to the bow, pulling it all the way back and releasing the arrow.

It must've been an impressive shot, because it went way up, and the whole group of nomads, about twenty-five in all, let out with "*Ah! Ah!*" Then a larger fellow, with an even more impressive bow went over and told Les to try his.

Once again, Les breathed a silent prayer as he accepted the bow and demonstrated his temporary, God-given prowess. Again, God undertook! The people seemed impressed, and it appeared they had accepted Les as one of their own. Unfortunately, now they wanted Les to shoot almost every bow in the group, but compared to the first two, the rest of them proved not to be a challenge.

Chickens became the new topic of conversation as they asked Les if there were any chickens left. By now, he knew the word for yes, so responded, "*Ai*." Handing him a bow and arrow, they had him lead them on a hunt for the rest of the much-reduced flock of twenty-five chickens. Soon, all the birds had been accounted for, and any hope the missionaries had of eggs in their diet was history.

While hunting chickens, the group ended up over near the Foster's house, and the nomads spotted Rolf and Jim before they had been "officially" introduced. Both men came out with their arms in the air as they had earlier been instructed by their colleagues. None of the Yuquí seemed surprised to see them, and they were greeted with pinches on the breast and around the waist and sounds of "*Oo! Oo!*" The men seemed to have been accepted by the jungle people.

Now the group wanted the missionaries to pull their trousers down so they could see clearly whether they were men or women, so one by one, the missionaries had to pull down their pants and let them see the evidence. Satisfied that they were all men, they went over to Dick and Harold's house where the nomads insisted on sharing stolen bananas with the missionaries, feeding them until everyone was full.

The chief then asked the men if they wanted wives. Of course, they knew that Les had a wife so they didn't make that an issue with him. Jim also was able to adequately communicate with them that he wasn't interested, so the men took Jim and Les back over to the Foster's house, leaving the women alone with Rolf, Dick, and Harold.

The women were very forward with the men, propositioning them repeatedly with no interest shown by the missionaries. Soon the women began to get upset with the three missionaries and yelled something over to one of the nomad warriors. Several of the more muscular men went over and caught Dick and Harold as they tried to escape from the women, wrestling with them and trying to throw them to the ground. Les and Jim were being restrained by the rest of the warriors from going to the aid of Dick and Harold until finally, Harold started yelling to Les, "Rolf needs you!"

Les pushed his way by the restraining men and went over to help Rolf. A half-dozen women were all intent on having their way with Rolf, and he was yelling for help. When Les arrived on the scene, the women moved away, freeing Rolf, and everyone went back over to the Foster's house.

Les had noticed that often, the people would sit around, delousing one another and combing each other's hair with a jungle pod that had spikes on it, kind of like a hair brush, so to help diffuse the somewhat tense mood, Les pulled out his pocket comb and began to comb the hair of several of the nomads. They liked that very much, and as the mood lightened, one of the younger men began telling Les a story of hunting a bird.

For almost ten minutes, he imitated the bird, its motions, the sounds it made, and how it moved from location to location as he hunted it. He continued by going through the motions of fitting an arrow to his bow, sneaking up on the bird, and letting the arrow fly. He showed how it hit the bird and the bird fell dead. He then asked Les to bring the dog back out so he could shoot and eat it. There was little doubt they would have followed through with that idea as they had already shot and eaten the Fosters' house cat. Puppy was fortunate they had taken him to town when Lois had gone in.

It wasn't long until the jungle dwellers became hungry and one of them brought out a large piece of wild pig that had been roasted over an open fire and passed it around. They shared it with everyone, including the missionaries. Now that they were content once again, the women remembered Rolf. The chief's daughter sat up on the table with Rolf and started stroking his face and trying to sit almost on his lap. He gently pushed her away, and the chief became irate, pushing Rolf back against the wall and trying to choke him. A little later, they tried to choke Dick and Harold also.

The nomads liked to wrestle very much and, when doing so with the missionaries, could get very rough with them. The wrestling was not playful but was a method of showing hierarchy among men in the group.

The nomads were also enthralled when Les or Jim would sing for them and would ask them to come over and sing, but when Dick or Harold began to sing, they started beating on them and told them to stop. They seemed to have very little use for Dick and Harold and appeared to look down on old age and physical weakness, which both Dick and Harold displayed.

Initially, they didn't try to force their women on Les as they did with the others, but that all changed when some of the warriors took Les aside from his companions and painted him with the bright red-orange *urucú* (achiote) paint. After the nomads painted Les up to look like one of them, one young woman went over to him, put her arms around him, and looked up into his face with her eyes sparkling. Les looked down at her and smiled but then ignored her as he went on talking with the rest of the Yuquí, and she didn't persist.

More and more, it seemed the missionaries were being treated with a lack of respect and with physical abuse. All their foodstuff and supplies had been stolen, broken open, or ruined by the natives, so it didn't seem wise to leave a small group of missionaries in La Jota while others went to town for supplies. Consequently, once the nomads had disappeared for the day, the whole group of missionaries headed into town to meet a new missionary arrival, Bud Garmo, who was coming to lend a hand. While in town, they would also pick up supplies and have a short break from the stress of interacting with the Yuquí.

Bud was a large, heavyset man, so they anticipated the nomads would show more respect for him. He was also an accomplished soloist, and chances were, they would enjoy his singing.

The day after Bud arrived by DC-3 from Cochabamba, the team left for La Jota, not knowing what to expect. Would their houses have been burned down in their absence? Would there be anything left of the base and belongings? When they arrived at their camp, it was almost dark, but the moon was bright and they had flashlights. They found that the worst, or very nearly so, had happened. The nomads had taken an axe to the radio transmitter and receiver, tape recorder, gasoline barrel, volt ohm meter, and about everything else. Very likely, they had been looking for food as for them, it seemed to be the most important thing.

Seeing the destruction, the team decided to just leave gifts they had brought for the nomads on the table in Foster's house, load up some of the more valuable equipment, and head for town again.

After gathering up the equipment they planned to take, they left right away for town, arriving back in Todos Santos around midnight.

Three days later, they headed for La Jota again, this time not even bothering to take blankets as the nomads had been stealing clothing, blankets, jungle hammocks, and anything else they found useful.

It was midmorning four days later that a group of fifteen Yuquí showed up. They immediately began asking for more "*Tapi, tapi* (sweets)" and also asked about the children that had been stolen from them at the time of the commission three years previously. The missionaries acted as if they had no knowledge of the missing children or of the incident the nomads were recounting. With that, the people began asking for more food, and Les told them he would go and get them some more.

The missionaries picked up their empty backpacks and headed in toward the colony of El Coni with the Yuquí following along. Every few hundred feet, the nomads would bring the march to a halt and once again ask if the missionaries were going to bring back more food. After assuring them that was their plan, the people would say, "Let's go," and away the procession would march again. Then they would stop again, and a bunch of them would gather around Les to blow on his chest and cool him off while an old woman would paint him with some more *urucú* before the march continued.

This went on for two or three kilometers until eventually, the nomads tired of it and left the missionaries to continue on their own.

It was difficult to know what to do next as the missionary team couldn't live in La Jota with no food, no mosquito nets, no blankets, and no gifts for the nomads. There was no way to keep their belongings from being taken. The Yuquí had become aggressive to the point where their demands were impossible, and they took anything they wanted. Also, the missionary team was once again reduced in numbers as Rolf needed to return to Cochabamba, and Bud was ill and had to return to the city. This left just four missionary men to interact with the entire band of violent nomads.

Jim, Harold, Dick, and Les gathered up some gifts and headed back out to La Jota, arriving late in the afternoon and spending the night in miserable conditions, although at least they had a roof over their heads. Very early the next morning, leaving the gifts in Les' house, they headed back to town before any nomads showed up. As they walked the trail back toward the river, they began seeing foot-prints of the jungle people about halfway between the La Jota and El Coni colonies, evidence that the Yuquí had come looking for the missionaries.

After a few days in town, Jim, Dick, Harold, and Les once again loaded their packs with sweets and other gifts and headed out to the La Jota base with the hope of encountering the nomads and having some interaction with them. As Les commented in a letter:

> We plan to take more gifts of sweets, make one contact and then come back to town. We can hardly stay longer, for when the nomads come out, they carry away everything we have there, and we then have nothing to eat.

In the same letter, he also commented:

> As you can see there are many challenges involved. We need your prayers. Even though we are unable to stay out there in our houses, because of not having a way to protect our things, and we are unable to stay with the nomads in their camp because of moral issues, yet we are not beat down by the enemy.

He continued, confident that God had a plan for these people to hear the Gospel message.

* * * * *

It was a time of discouragement. So much effort had gone into making face-to-face contact with the Yuquí, and the initial contact had gone well enough, but after the natives lost their fear of the missionaries, violence had escalated to where being with them was impossible. Instead of the contacts becoming easier and friendlier, they became more of a trial. On one of the contacts, upon the advice of another missionary, Les had worn a pistol in a holster, thinking it might command more respect from the nomads. This proved to be the wrong thing to do as the day before had been a Bolivian holiday during which much dynamite was exploded in celebration.

The nomads were able to hear this dynamite exploding from twenty-four kilometers away, and when they came to see the missionaries the next day, they were very nervous. It appeared they thought the dynamite to be the guns of the colonists and that they were entering the jungle to kill them. Les tried to calm them down but to little avail. They wanted to take his pistol, but for fear of them hurting one another with it, he didn't want to give it to them. Finally, as the chief and a few others kept Les occupied in talk, one of the nomads cut the holster from his belt, and the pistol fell to the floor.

Jim Ostewig grabbed the pistol and held it behind him to protect them from getting it, but the chief quickly grabbed Jim and, along with another nomad, began to choke him. Jim said later he thought that was the end of him. Les could do nothing to help him as one of the warriors was holding him back. Jim passed the pistol to Harold while the nomads were trying to get it, so the warriors were also threatening to shoot an arrow into Harold.

After they finally got the pistol, one of them left the house with it. The rest began to calm down to where the missionaries were able to sit around and talk with them. It was 3:30 p.m. before the missionaries were finally allowed to leave, so they arrived back in Todos Santos late in the evening, after dark.

After waiting two days, the missionaries once again headed out to La Jota with gifts for the Yuquí, planning to arrive in La Jota late at night and leave early the next morning. They also planned to look around for the pistol, Jim's watch which had been forcibly taken, as well as any mosquito nets, clothing, backpacks, or other items the nomads might not have kept. When the missionaries arrived at Les' house, they were greatly surprised to see the pistol there in plain sight on the table. It hadn't even been removed from the holster. The missionaries wondered if the Yuquí even knew what it was as whenever the colonists shot at them, they used rifles, and none of the colonists carried pistols.

The missionaries once again left gifts on the table and headed back to town early the next morning before the Yuquí showed up.

Four days later, the missionary team went back to La Jota with the hope of interacting with the nomads. Leaving their equipment in the colony of El Coni, they went on to La Jota, carrying only gifts for the jungle people. They found the Yuquí had once again come to their houses and taken the gifts that had been left for them. The missionaries spent the whole day there, but the nomads didn't show up, so the team left more gifts and then headed back to El Coni to spend the night.

The following day, they hiked back out to La Jota, arriving around 11:00 a.m., and found that the Yuquí had already been there and taken the gifts which had been left for them the day before. It was encouraging that they were still in the area, and the missionaries were optimistic they might have opportunity to interact with them, hopefully in a positive way. Lighting a fire, the missionaries sat around, cooking a gallon of *hualusa* (a potato-like root) for dinner. While they were cooking, Jim looked up and saw a group of nomads coming down the trail. It was the chief, his wife, their two older sons, and two other young men.

The missionaries welcomed them, and the entire party sat around the fire until dinner was ready. Jim then began pulling cooked *hualusa* from the can and passing it to Les to peel, after which he would hand pieces around to the nomads.

Within half an hour more, Yuquí showed up, and everyone went out to meet the new arrivals and to hear of the hunt they had been on. About this time, Les remembered fresh tiger tracks he'd seen that morning down by the Little Jota Creek which flowed by the house, so he took the group down there and showed them the tracks. One of the warriors, with his bow ready, made a perfect imitation of a tiger call, trying to call it in, but of course, the tiger was far enough away by then that they received no response.

Then one of the warriors handed a bow and two arrows to Les and told him to shoot some fish for them as that was how they most often fished, although sometimes they also fished using poison. Les indicated to them that they should wait as he would be right back. He had a small line and hook hidden up at the house, so he retrieved those and brought them to the bank of the arroyo. The nomads watched with interest as he caught a grasshopper, placed it on the hook, and dropped it into the water. They laughed and joked at him trying to catch a fish in that way.

Les was silently praying as he fished, "Lord, help them to see that we can be useful to them. Build the relationship so we can learn their language and tell them of You."

It wasn't long until a nice though modest fish took the bait. The chief's wife thought that was great and went up to the house to get some burning brands from the fire. Using the glowing sticks, she stoked up a small fire near the creek and began roasting the fish as Les caught them.

Soon he had pulled in six fish, two of them piranha, the man-eating variety. The nomads were very careful in handling these fish, holding them by the tail and then dropping them into the fire whole—scales, intestines, and all—to roast.

Finally, after about three and a half hours with the Yuquí, in the best and friendliest contact to date, the missionaries left for the El Coni colony, accompanied by the nomads for about one third of the way. By now, it was late afternoon, and the missionaries knew they wouldn't arrive before dark if they didn't hurry, so they ran down the trail with the Yuquí, arm in arm.

When they reached the spot where the nomad trail turned off to the north, they stopped while the missionaries continued along the colonist's trail. Each time, the missionaries looked back, they could still see the jungle people standing there, whistling at them, waving and shouting in friendship. During this excellent contact, the nomads over and over asked for assurance that the missionaries would return. It appeared that the prayers of God's people were being answered in a positive way!

Les was excited at the progress, and his mind was already thinking ahead to when they might be able to hunt together with the nomads, using guns to supply a greater abundance of meat for them, spending nights with them in their jungle camp, and mastering the language to where the Gospel message could be shared with them. At the same time, he realized they had a long way to go and wrote the following to his prayer partners:

> They seem much friendlier toward us, but don't think for a minute that your prayers are not still urgently needed! We still face many, many, problems. To mention a few prayer needs: there is always the need for prayer concerning the nomads wanting to give each of us wives. This problem must be solved before we will be able to stay overnight with them in their camp. Then there is the need of a way to guard our equipment and food from their continual theft. Then there is the need to learn their language so we can get across to them the most important reason we want to be their friends. We know according to God's Word that some of these will be in the bride of Christ. Pray that progress in the work may be fast so that no more of these souls will face eternity without hearing of the Savior.

The mood on the contacts varied greatly. The excellent contact they had just enjoyed was definitely the exception as most of the contacts were heavy with tension. One minute the nomads would be laughing and joking with the missionaries, while the next minute, they might be lobbing arrows just over their heads as they walked the trail together or choking a missionary until he was in danger of passing out. Even so, the nomads clearly had greater esteem for Les than for any of his coworkers and seemed to accept him as the missionary chief, treating him with greater respect.

Dick and Harold were both physically exhausted, so they flew out to Cochabamba for medical checkups and a couple weeks' rest. Les' heart had been bothering him, so he planned to go see a doctor after they returned and would also spend some time with Lois and the children while they were on vacation from boarding school. With Harold and Dick leaving, Don Hay, Paul Mason, and Bruce Porterfield flew in on the same plane that took them out. The new men would assist on the contact effort for a few weeks.

Bruce had some contact experience, having helped years earlier in the effort to befriend a tribe in another part of Bolivia, so he could offer valuable insight that others on the team didn't have.

The same afternoon the new men arrived, they climbed into a canoe with Les, and the team started off up the Chapare River on their way to La Jota. They were hardly out of sight of town around the first bend of the river when a cold south wind with rain blew in, so they turned around and went back to Todos Santos. The storm took two days to pass, and around noon on the third day, they headed back up the river, spending the night in the El Coni colony where they would leave their equipment while they went on to La Jota.

The following morning, they left for La Jota, carrying sugar, sweetened condensed milk, corn, and a live chicken for the nomads. Although the mosquitoes were plentiful and voracious, the men wore no shirts and carried nothing in their pockets as they knew the nomads would steal everything they took with them.

Soon they entered the colony of La Jota, and up ahead, they could see smoke rising from a burning house. As they walked by, they saw it was Don Severino's thatch kitchen shelter. It was clear the fire had been started within the last two hours, and the missionaries began to wonder what they would find when they got to their own houses. If they had also been burned, should they turn right around and head back to town? What kind of mood were the nomads in? Would it be safe to stay? Their first thought was that they should probably turn right around and go back to town.

Before arriving at their clearing, the decision was made for them as they met the nomads who had set up camp on the trail and were busy helping themselves to sweet potatoes from one of the farms.

Their fire was right in the middle of the trail, and they were using it to cook the sweet potatoes, roasting them in the coals. The missionaries were pleased to see that the whole group was not there, only the chief and his party of about fifteen people. When the Yuquí first saw strangers coming down the trail, they fled, but as the missionaries whistled and yelled the words, "*Tapi! Tapi!*" which they took to mean sugar, the nomads realized it was their friends and came back to see the missionary team.

Soon the two groups were greeting and interacting with one another, rubbing one another's chests and hair and jabbering at one another. They didn't seem in the least surprised to see three new faces, nor did they seem to miss the three old ones. They asked if the missionaries wanted to go on to their houses, and everyone seemed good with that decision. The missionary men helped pick up and carry baskets full of *urucú*, bananas, and sweet potatoes, and off the party headed, down the trail to the missionary clearing.

After talking and playing together for a few minutes, they wanted the men to catch some fish. Hooks and line were one of the few items the missionaries had brought along other than gifts, and soon they were busy fishing in the Little Jota Arroyo which ran by the missionary's houses. The fish weren't biting too well there, so after some discussion, they decided to go out to the Big Jota Arroyo about two kilometers away. The chief and five others accompanied the missionaries to the Big Jota Arroyo while the others stayed at the missionary houses, cooking a portion of the stolen produce.

Fishing was exceptionally poor, so after an hour, they all returned to the Foster's house and found boiled sweet potatoes awaiting them for lunch. The missionary team sat around, talking with the people until about 2:00 p.m., and then headed back for Todos Santos, arriving at dusk. This had also been one of the better contacts to date, although once, when one of the Yuquí wanted Don to go over to a certain place to fish and Don didn't move quickly enough to please him, the nomad threw a heavy, jagged piece of bark at Don and cut his head a little. Several times, one of the warriors fitted an arrow to his bow and aimed it at Paul but didn't shoot. Even at this point, the contacts could be ended very quickly by a short fuse, a quick temper. Only God could prevent such a tragedy.

Encouraged by how the contact had gone, three days later, the missionaries took off again for El Coni, staying overnight there and going on to La Jota the next morning. The air was fresh after a cold rainy storm that had moved through, so the morning they left town, the missionaries purchased five kilograms of freshly butchered beef to carry along. Knowing how much the nomads valued meat, the missionaries were confident the jungle dwellers would be especially welcoming when they showed up with such a nice gift.

Once again, when they neared La Jota, they found the nomads camped right on the main trail, but this time, even though it was still the chief's group, some of the people who had been with him the previous time were missing, and in their places were new ones. Right away, the missionaries could sense that the natives were in a foul mood. Even so, when they saw the men coming from about one hundred yards away, they whistled for them to advance.

They had only taken a few steps when one of the new arrivals, a fellow the missionaries had taken to calling Toughy among themselves, put up his hand for them to stop. They stopped until he whistled again for them to come on. Les took the meat out of the bag in which he had been carrying it and handed it to the chief. The chief's wife smelled it and made a comment, indicating that it was old and smelled funny. It was likely they had never tried beef before, and the odor was slightly different from the tapir they were accustomed to eating.

With the cool weather, the meat was still fresh, but she didn't think so. Angrily, she threw the meat down on the ground in front of Les!

Others of them were more welcoming to the missionaries, standing there, rubbing their white skin, their hair, their sweaty chests, and backs for a short time, but then, when it came time to go on down the trail, they insisted that the missionaries carry all the gifts, plus the manioc, bananas, and everything heavy as they headed on down to the missionary clearing. The nomads walked along as if they had just acquired a new group of slaves. Les thought, *I don't really mind being a slave to these people if through that they might come to hear the Gospel.*

But the treatment was very different from any of the other contacts and showed a very superior attitude on the part of the nomads. Equality was more what the missionaries had in mind.

Paul was carrying a camera, and occasionally, the nomads would take the camera from him by force. Whenever this happened, the missionaries would all register their displeasure, and the nomads would give the camera back. Also, Bruce was wearing a shirt, partly to see if they would let him keep the shirt this time or insist on him removing it and giving it to them. Over the course of the contact, Paul was able to take four pictures when he wasn't being observed too closely. These would be the first pictures they had been able to take of the nomads.

The missionaries had decided to try something new on this contact; variety seemed to help ease the tenseness that threatened to be ever-present. They planned to teach or at least show the nomads how to plant field corn. All the missionaries, except Bruce, went into the Foster's house while Bruce remained nearby outside, clearing a small plot in which to plant corn. In the meantime, Don and Les, who had retrieved the chunk of beef and brought it along, started cutting up the meat and preparing to cook it at the insistence of some of the nomads. They also sent Paul to the arroyo to bring water for cooking and drinking.

Once the meat was over the fire, cooking, Les went outside with one of the nomads to demonstrate how to plant corn. Les took a pointed stick, poked a hole about an inch deep, and dropped in three kernels of corn. Soon he had four hills of corn planted and planned to continue planting more. At this point, Toughy came out and saw what Les was doing. Angrily, he insisted that Les go back and dig up the dozen kernels he had put in the ground and let Les know that he wasn't to throw perfectly good food away like that. That stopped the planting for a time, but later on, Bruce went out to plant corn in front of them and was able to talk Toughy into helping plant it. It was thrilling to see Toughy, the chief, and Bruce all out there, planting corn together!

Again the warriors decided the missionaries should show their prowess with bow and arrow. After the missionaries had shot arrows several times, Toughy threaded an arrow to his bow, pointed it at Paul, and let go, missing Paul by only about a foot. It was an intentional miss but showed his perverted sense of humor. A short time later, Toughy threw half a can of water on Paul, then looked over at Les and threw the other half on him.

Les got up and stomped out like he was mad, and then informed them, "No more *tapi tapi* (something you suck from fingers, i.e. sugar, honey)!" and acted as if he were going home. Some of them went over soothingly, took hold of Les, brought him back into the house, sat him down, and began to wipe the water off and make over him. Les thought the situation was improving and that they would calm down a little, but a few minutes later, Toughy began choking Bruce. When Les intervened to get the choking stopped, Toughy swung around and hit Les in the eye, nearly giving him a black eye.

In Toughy's defense, years later, the missionaries learned that his young daughter was one of the children stolen when the commission of colonists fired into the nomad camp years earlier, killing the young woman and kidnapping four children. For all Toughy knew, these missionaries could have been part of that posse. Toughy never saw his daughter again and didn't know that a caring family had taken her in, given her an education, and treated her as one of their own.

With maltreatment escalating, the missionaries realized it was time to leave, so they began indicating that they were leaving and would come back another day. The chief was anxious they remain, explaining that there was another group hunting somewhere in the direction of the Naranjal and that he wanted the missionaries to wait until they got back.

Finally, Toughy, the chief, and a few others started down the missionary trail toward El Naranjal, forcing the missionaries to accompany them. Every few feet, they would stop and have the missionaries yell for the other group, calling out something that sounded much like, "Jeremiah, Jeremiah."

The missionaries would humor them by yelling, "Jeremiah, Jeremiah," and then point at the sun, indicating they needed to arrive home before dark, but the nomads continued to push them farther on down the trail.

Soon they reached a point in the trail where many gifts had been left by the missionaries and taken repeatedly by the Yuquí before the initial contacts. Les and his coworkers stopped at one of the gift poles and began acting out the way in which the nomads would peer from the forest, dart out, grab the gifts, and run back to the safety of the foliage. The nomads got so engrossed in the play acting, they stopped insisting the missionaries accompany them farther.

On the way back to the clearing, rough play started up again as they began choking Don, but eventually, they all made it safely back to the clearing. Once there, Bruce began trying to get the idea across to them that he would like them to give him a bow and an arrow and that he would bring them a machete in return. It soon became obvious that the nomads were interpreting Bruce's request as a desire to go hunting with them; the idea of trading seemed to be a foreign concept.

As the missionaries left the clearing, a good-sized group of nomads accompanied them as far as the Arroyo Magdalena and then parted from them as the missionaries continued unaccompanied to the El Coni colony. As they had walked along the trail together to the Magdalena, several of the warriors had handed their bows and arrows to the missionaries to carry, and every little way, they would stop and tell about killing one thing or another along the trail.

In one spot, they had killed a bunch of quail; in another, they had wounded a wild pig and had to run it down. In another place, they had shot at the colonists. In one spot, they told of three men passing and how the chief stood in ambush, ready to shoot them. The missionaries wondered if the three men had been Dick, Harold, and Les but thought it better not to ask that question until the distant future when friendship might be less precarious.

Once the Yuquí stopped and indicated there were wild pigs ahead. One of them handed Les an arrow to fit to the bow he was carrying, but as he picked up the arrow, it cracked. They took it away and gave him another arrow. The cracked arrow was handed to Paul to carry. Not knowing it was cracked, he fit it to the bow he carried, and the arrow broke. The chief, his wife, and one of their sons blew their tops! They pulled on the camera around Paul's neck, pushed him and, in general, mistreated him. Soon after this, when they came to a log bridging a stream, the chief tried to push Paul into the water. This would have been bad in more ways than one as Paul had the film with the pictures of the nomads on it, and it would have gotten wet. Continuing down the trail, they mistreated one after another of the missionaries.

For part of the way, they were shooting arrows ahead of the missionaries who were leading the way down the trail. Les was the first one in the line, and every few feet, an arrow would come lobbing too closely over his head, landing in the trail just in front of him. He would turn around to see who was shooting them but couldn't tell which warrior thought this was fun. Les walked along, thinking to himself, *If I stumble and fall, I'll probably end up with an arrow in the back of my head.* All in all, it was one of the worst contacts to date.

Once back in Todos Santos, the team spent much time discussing the contacts to this point. They were struggling to understand how the nomads could act so good one time and then so bad the next. Dick spoke up, "They've become far too demanding. I think we should wait about two weeks before going back out again. Maybe that will help bring them to a place where they realize we don't have to stay out there and accept the things they are doing to us."

The others were quick to agree. "Maybe going without the sweets, machetes, knives, and other gifts for a while will make them realize they could miss out on all the goodies," commented Harold.

The missionaries spent the next two weeks in town, hoping that a "cooling off" period might cause the Yuquí to appreciate them more and be seen as a protest against the way they had been treated.

About this time, Les shared the following in a letter to prayer partners:

> One thing I forgot to mention. I had always heard how the nomads would blow their nose and then wipe it in their hair. Before I'd wondered if this was true or not. But now I know.

The nomads seem to all have runny noses right now and they truly do blow it in their hands and then wipe it in their hair. Great gobs of slime were wiped into their hair over and over the last time we were with them. Once one of the women blew her nose into her hand and held it out to me to look at. I just told the Lord, "I know Your grace is sufficient!" He was merciful and she ended up wiping it into her own hair instead of in mine. The same woman had a baby. Once she milked herself into her hand and held it out for me to lick up. I kindly told her to give it to her baby, which she did, thanks to God. I write these things, not to be gross, but that you may know exactly what we are facing down here. I know God has been preparing my heart for a long time for this contact and I have perfect peace in Him throughout all of these things, but we really need your prayers for grace and wisdom.

Incidents like this were also useful in putting names on people, and after this, among themselves, the missionaries referred to this lady as Milk Shake Girl. Of course, that wasn't her given name but helped the missionaries identify her in their discussions.

During the two-week hiatus, Les, Lois, and Bruce headed up to the city of Cochabamba by road on the back of a farm truck carrying produce. The men who had remained behind in Todos Santos planned to go into La Jota at night by flashlight from time to time during their absence and leave gifts but not actually make contact. The plan was derailed before it began. The same afternoon that Les and Lois arrived in Cochabamba, they got a call from the government radio service that Les needed to come to their office and talk by radio to Bob Wilhelmson in Todos Santos. The communication was done by government radio operators in Morse code and was not good news.

As Les noted in a letter, "Well, the worst or very nearly so has happened." Bob let Les know that the nomads had come into the El

Coni colony, one of the few times they had come so far into the more developed area, and had stolen a child from one of the colonists. Bob asserted, "Les, we think you should come back immediately as the colonists are 'up in arms' and demanding immediate action by the military authorities to rescue the boy. Don't wait for the weekly plane but get on a truck and head back tonight if possible."

This was Friday, and the airline usually flew on Saturday, so Les went from the radio office directly to the airline office and got reservations for Saturday's flight as that should get him to Todos Santos quicker than a truck. Later in the evening, he called the airline to get information as to what time the flight would go and found the flight had been canceled until Monday. Les kissed Lois goodbye, grabbed his travel bag, and headed downtown to see if he could get a truck. None were leaving until the next morning, so he went back to the mission guesthouse for the night.

The next morning, Les was back down at the marketplace, bright and early, and was able to get on a truck heading to Villa Tunari. Eighteen hours later, at two in the morning, he arrived in Villa Tunari, crossed the Espiritu Santo River, where he found a truck headed to the San Mateo River. The truck left him there, and he crossed the river by dugout canoe and waited and watched for a truck to take him the last thirty kilometers to Todos Santos, finally arriving around 3:00 p.m., having made a dangerous, grueling, and exhausting thirty-one-hour trip over one of the world's deadliest roads along the high peaks of the Andes, a straight-line distance of only seventy miles!

Bright and early the next morning, Don Hay and Les installed the outboard onto the dugout canoe and headed up the river to El Coni colony to talk with the colonists. The first few farmers they met with didn't seem as riled as the missionaries had heard or expected but did let them know that a meeting of the El Coni colonists and others from nearby colonies was planned in two days on June 3. The missionaries were welcome to attend that meeting. They were also told the story of the kidnapping in greater detail.

The wife of one of the colonists had been walking along the main trail between El Coni and Puerto Aurora carrying a baby with her five-year-old son walking by her side. As they passed the junction where the trail leaves El Coni for La Jota, the nomads were there, waiting in ambush. First, they shot a shower of arrows in front of her and behind her, and it appeared they were not wanting to kill her but just to get her to run so that they could catch the little boy. She screamed and ran. They shot other arrows at leg level, trying to trip her. One of the arrows hit and stuck in her dress, penetrating her leg about a quarter of an inch. It was a chonta palm-tipped arrow with a barb.

As the woman ran, the warriors caught the boy and carried him away. A group of armed colonists assembled a little later and followed footprints down the main trail to La Jota, the trail the nomads had used, but couldn't overtake them.

The missionaries arrived at the June 3rd meeting with no idea of what might be planned. The political boss of the colonies had a long paper prepared in which, at the top of his voice and with much beating on the table, etc., he accused the missionaries of many things as he read his diatribe to the eighty or ninety persons there. He began by angrily attacking the missionaries, "You've been working for three and a half years on this contact and have in no way benefited us, the colonists. You've never reported to the colonists what you are doing out there, how many savages there are, or how many tools such as machetes, axes, and knives you have given to the savages. It's your fault these things are happening. The savages are using the tools you give them to make more bows and arrows to kill more of us."

The colonists were so riled up that defending themselves or the Yuquí would only have made matters worse, so the missionaries said nothing and were asked no questions. The minds of the colonists were already made up. While it was true that the missionaries had been giving tools to the nomads, they had already been stealing those items from the farmers houses and, in at least one of the early shootings, it appeared that they had shot one of the farmers in order to steal his axe. Reminding the colonists of these truths would only inflame the situation, so the missionaries kept quiet. A few extra tools in the hands of the nomads would make little difference.

Soon the rhetoric began to rewrite the past as one of leaders took the floor. "Three years ago, we found four children abandoned by the savages. We graciously and lovingly rescued them, protecting them from wild animals and death in the forest. We found good homes for them in town, and now they steal one of our children." The mood was grim, but the missionaries were not asked to contribute their thoughts, and it was probably better that way. Even refuting this untruth would have only inflamed the irate farmers.

The way the meeting ended, after much anti-evangelical speaking by many of the leaders and colonists was with their demand that the missionaries accomplish three points within thirty days. Those points were:

1. Have the nomads return the boy who was stolen;
2. Bring a delegation of two of the "savages" to the junction where the La Jota trail meets the El Coni trail and have them meet with the colonists to make peace. Bring an interpreter to the meeting (in the town of Todos Santos, there was a man who claimed to know the language of the nomads, but each time the missionaries learned new words and tried them on him, he had no idea what they meant; even so, the colonists were convinced he knew the language, and he was willing, if paid enough, to pose as interpreter);
3. That the missionaries bring a delegation of several "savages" to the colony at El Coni to meet all the colonists assembled together and show the "savages" how many and how powerful the colonists are.

The threat was made that if these points were not fulfilled within thirty days, the colonists would go in fully armed, not with rifles only, but also with automatic weapons to kill once and for all every one of the nomads. The political boss had already talked with political leadership in the departmental capital of Cochabamba and read a letter from them, giving the colonists permission to form a commission and go in.

Les wrote:

> I feel about as helpless as I've ever felt in
> my life. Unless God's children pray in a special
> way and God undertakes to answer those prayers
> these poor nomads will be killed to the last man.
> I believe the colonists can and will do it!

The injustice of it all weighed heavily on the missionaries, especially after all the physical abuse and mental stress they had endured
trying to befriend and settle the Yuquí. In another letter, he wrote:

> This is a terrible injustice to the nomads
> who have been robbed of their children by the
> colonists, shot and killed by the colonists, and
> when they fight back, are now threatened with
> annihilation. But here on the frontier the gun
> speaks louder than the law.

After the meeting, the missionaries went on to La Jota, leaving
more gifts for the Yuquí, and then spent the night in El Coni before
returning to Todos Santos to share the results of the meeting with
their coworkers.

* * * * *

Communication with the Yuquí remained the most challenging obstacle. The missionaries had no clear and easy way of helping
them understand the feelings of the colonists and how big and powerful the outside world was. While the missionaries knew the farmers
had the manpower and weapons to annihilate the jungle dwellers,
the nomads were convinced of their own superiority. When the missionaries suggested to them that the farmers might shoot them, they
laughed and pantomimed how they would shoot the farmers in the
eye! If only someone could be found who knew the language or a
closely related language.

Once again, the missionaries began putting out the word by radio to missionaries from other missions around Bolivia to see if there was a bilingual native speaker of Sirionó, Guarayo, Guaraní, or another closely related language who might be willing to come and attempt to communicate with the nomads on their behalf. If they could only convince the Yuquí of the strength of the colonists and to stop shooting, the work should be able to move ahead.

So far, based on words the missionaries had gathered, it appeared that Sirionó was the closest related language. It was thought that a Sirionó might be able to make himself understood to the nomads. The team would be willing to fly such a person to Todos Santos and pay a good wage if he was willing to go with them to meet the nomads and try to get across to them what the colonists intended to do and convince them that the farmers had the capacity to carry out their threats.

As they awaited a response from the scattered missionary community, the men continued their treks into their now abandoned La Jota base, leaving gifts. Occasionally, they would arrive by flashlight late at night, spend the night, and leave very early in the morning, whereas at other times they would spend the day waiting at the Fosters' house, hoping for an opportunity to interact with the nomads. On those occasions, when they spent the day, they would hide their blankets, backpacks, and foodstuff in various locations around the clearing. They never hid it all together as they hoped not to lose it all to the nomads.

On one such occasion, Les left the other men at the house and went into the El Coni colony to pick up additional gifts and supplies they were storing there. While he was gone, the Yuquí showed up, aggressive and demanding, insisting the men accompany them out the north trail. By now, the natives were used to Dick scribbling on paper with his pencil, so they didn't hinder him as he left a note for Les. Judging by the attitude of the nomads, he thought it might be the last note he ever wrote.

Les,
　　If you don't find us around the Yuquí have probably taken us out the north trail with them.

Your blanket and pack and some of our things are hidden in the regrowth east and a little south of the outhouse about halfway to the arroyo under some *patujú* leaves. Some of our canned foods and salt are hidden under the brush pile east of the house.

Five days later, a group of colonists came to the missionaries and insisted on accompanying them to La Jota to meet the nomads. "We want to meet the savages and become friends with them," insisted Juan, one of the men who had abandoned his farm and whose house had been burned. The mindset of the colonists was that they would be able to talk to the Yuquí and reason with them. Surely the nomads understood Quechua or Spanish!

"You'll blame me if the nomads get angry with you and kill you," responded Les. "How are you going to talk with them? You don't know their language, nor do we, so we can't interpret for you."

Juan was insistent, believing the missionaries didn't want the Yuquí to meet and interact with him or his colleagues. "We won't hold you or your mission responsible. We want to meet the nomads. We want to talk to them and convince them to stop shooting and stealing."

After further discussion, it was agreed that a formal, legal document would be drawn up in town and signed by both parties, the missionaries, and the colonists, absolving the missionaries of any responsibility for what might occur. I include the translated document:

We, the colonists who have signed below from the Colonia Fiscal of Todos Santos, adults, farmers, neighbors and capable ones, DECLARE: That, of our own and spontaneous will we have decided to accompany Lester Foster, Leader of the Mission, in the exploration he is doing looking for the savages in the forests of the "La Jota" region, without any obligation; therefore, any misfortune, or damage that we might suffer in our persons will be on our own account and our own risk, in no way will it be the responsibility of Mr. Lester Foster or the Mission whatever might happen.

As a record of this DECLARATION, we subscribe signing below those of us who know how (to write) and placing our digital print (those of us who don't know how to write), with the help of the Señor Judge of the Parish of this location, in Todos Santos del Chapare on this 30th day of the month of June nineteen hundred and fifty-nine years.

Signatures or fingerprints were included at the bottom of the agreement.

Meanwhile, Bruce Porterfield had gone to the capital city of La Paz to talk with governmental authorities about the ongoing war between nomads and colonists. They responded by sending a radiogram to the leaders of the colonies, asking that they give the missionaries three months' time before proceeding with their commission. The missionaries doubted very much whether this arrangement would be acceptable to the colonists, and it was doubtful it would work for the missionaries. They had been working under continual threats of a commission and short-term deadlines during so much of the time they had been trying to befriend the hostile Yuquí that they were afraid to invest too much in the work for fear that after a few months, the colonists would go into the jungle and stir up the Yuquí to where it was impossible to continue in that area, and the effort would have to be moved to a more distant location. It would really be preferable to draw the nomads away from the colonies by coming in from the east rather than the west, but that approach had its own problems.

The colonists sent word to the missionary team that they would like to meet with them and made it clear this was to be *absolutely the last meeting*. They wanted a guarantee that the nomads would be peacefully settled within two to three months or the missionaries needed to move out of the area and the colonists would do their best to annihilate "the savages," as they called them.

During these weeks of waiting for the commission to either happen or not happen, the missionary team had not been idle. Their request for a Sirionó or Guarayo translator had brought results. Carroll Tamplin of the World Gospel Mission had flown over with his son, Jonathan, the WGM pilot, and brought along a young Sirionó man. This group accompanied the missionary team into La Jota and made contact with a handful of the Yuquí. The Sirionó translator was also conversant in the related Guarayo language and what little he could understand while attempting to converse with the nomads was from his knowledge of Guarayo, not Sirionó.

This was an encouraging step forward, and after the contact, the missionaries began searching again, but this time for a Guarayo interpreter. Eventually, a willing Guarayo Christian was found and went into the jungle several times with the missionary team, but no contact was made with the nomads during those trips.

Les was convinced there were two reasons they were no longer encountering the Yuquí. In the first place, it was now dry season, and traditionally, that was when the nomads made their annual move to the north, a low and swampy area they could only access during that time of year. It was a great place to hunt alligators, capybara, tapir, and other large animals when the water was low and the animals abundant as they congregated near the water. In a few months, when the rains began, the nomads would come back to the south and begin devouring the farmers' crops again.

Secondly, Les believed there was a spiritual reason. Back when the colonists had given them the three points to complete within thirty days, he had fully intended to go in, meet with the nomads, and try to get across to them the ultimatum by the colonists that if they wouldn't give up the boy, the colonists would go in and kill them.

Les was pretty sure of the reaction of the Yuquí if he was able to get this across to them. The native warriors had no true or accurate idea of the magnitude of the outside world and, in their worldview, were convinced they were the predominant group of people. Once before, when Les tried to encourage them not to go into the El Coni colony because the colonists would shoot them with their guns, their response was extreme anger. One of the nomad warriors showed Les his barbed arrow and explained that the colonists better be careful, because his arrows had barbs on them, "and when they go in, they don't come out!"

Les was convinced now that God hadn't wanted him to give this message to the Yuquí since it might have triggered more shootings, some of those possibly of the missionaries themselves.

* * * * *

By now, thanks to friendships with Americans in one of the oil companies who were searching for new reserves, the missionaries had been able to obtain aerial photographs of some of the area where the nomads roamed. The photographs included parts of the Chimoré River. The missionaries had begun to think that if they could set up a base over there, they could draw the nomads away from the colonies, not into them. According to the aerial maps, one spot looked to be high jungle and might be suitable for a base. While the Yuquí were off to the north, it might be wise to make a trip over there and see if it was a good place to build a farm. If they could plant bananas, manioc, and corn, maybe they could draw the nomads over there and see them settled beyond the colonies while they learned their language and helped them settle down.

A permanent move to the Chimoré River would mean going by river instead of by land so as to come in from the east and not the west. It was important to draw the nomads away from the colonies so that they could not kill and be killed. This would mean a trip down the Chapare River, up the Ichilo River, and then up the Chimoré River, a one-way trip of five to seven days minimum. Once a spot had been located, the missionaries would need to hire Bolivian laborers to come in and help them build houses and clear a large area for planting. Ideally, this would need to be done during the dry season while the nomads were away to the north.

Now, with the Yuquí out of the area, a preliminary exploratory trip could be safely made, entering the area from the west, so Les Foster, Dick Strickler, and Hudson Birkett—who had recently arrived from England and was helping on a temporary basis—along with Pascual, the young Guarayo Indian who would try to communicate with the nomads if they were to run into them, headed up to El Coni, leaving the canoe there and then hiking on out to La Jota for the night. The next day, the team followed the nomad trail north from the missionary clearing and continued in that direction until they estimated, using the aerial maps, that they were due west of where they wanted to come out on the Chimoré River.

They headed east, cutting trail with their machetes through jungle that became more and more impenetrable. Soon they were only advancing a few feet at a time before having to rest. Finally, stymied by the dense vegetation, they came to a complete halt and stopped to discuss the situation. It seemed like it would be better to go back to La Jota and follow the trail from there to where they had once had a house on the bank of the Chimoré River. From there, they could make a raft and float north down the river to where they wanted to go.

Early the next morning, they hoisted their packs and started off for the Chimoré River, arriving about 11:00 a.m. A raft of palm logs proved unsuitable, not floating well enough to carry the men, and there was no balsa in the area. Nothing seemed to work for a raft, so after eating lunch, they headed off, hiking north along the bank, following the flow of the river. By late afternoon, they found themselves at the bottom end of a large sandbar where they made two small shelters of bamboo leaves to spend the night.

The next morning, they followed the river as it made a long curve at the bottom of which was another sandbar. To keep going north, they would need to cross the river and walk the sandbar on the east bank. As Dick and Hudson waited on the west bank, Pascual and Les swam the wide swift river, carrying axe and machete to cut a couple of balsa trees they had spotted on the east bank. Their intent was to make a raft and take it across to ferry the supplies and the other two fellows across.

As the two men moved from cutting the first balsa tree into position to cut the second, Pascual was almost bitten by a four-foot-long English bushmaster snake, the deadly Lachesis muta. It struck with such ferocity, and its reach was so far, that Les couldn't get close enough to kill it with a machete. Finally, he cut a long piece of bamboo and was able to beat the snake until it was stunned, then he approached closer and was able to kill it with a machete. Had Pascual been bitten by this poisonous snake so far from medical help, his odds of survival would have been miniscule. Once again, God had protected them from the serpent!

Nicholas Montenegro holding a six-foot-long dead bushmaster. He had stepped over the sleeping snake before noticing it and killing it and was quite shaken by the experience.

Halfway down the next sandbar, a flock of terns, a seagull-like bird, attacked the men, diving at them and crying out angrily as they walked along. Pascual was quick to realize that the terns were nesting nearby, so they all began watching closely as they walked and soon gathered eighteen eggs, which were a welcome addition to their soup pot that evening.

By the time they reached the lower end of the tern sandbar, it was time to camp for the night. Once again, bamboo-leaf shelters were constructed, soup was boiled over the campfire, and the team discussed the accomplishments of the day and what tomorrow might bring. Later, as they sat on logs around the campfire after supper, they began hearing pounding in the jungle on the west bank of the river; it sounded like someone pounding one piece of firewood against another to break it up. Since it was coming from across the river in an area where no one but the nomads roamed, they wondered if it could be them.

The next morning, stepping out of their shelters, they found a trail where a large alligator had walked across the sand only fifteen feet from where Hudson had been sleeping. For a new missionary just arrived in Bolivia, Hudson was having quite the adjustment. After a quick breakfast of oatmeal with powdered milk and sugar, the team decided to hide their equipment in a bamboo patch before continuing their northerly heading. They didn't plan to go much farther north and expected to be back at this campsite before nightfall. After all this effort, when they finally reached the site they had come to check out, they found it wouldn't be suitable for making a farm so, by noon, were back at the previous night's camp to eat lunch.

After lunch, they packed up, hiked back up the sandbar, and crossed the river again on their raft with Dick and Hudson sitting on the raft while Pascual and Les swam alongside, propelling the craft. By late afternoon, they arrived at the lower end of the sandbar where their first shelters had been built and where they intended to once again spend the night. Dick and Hudson went on up to the shelters to start a fire for cooking supper while Pascual and Les remained behind to fish for a few minutes. Soon they caught a pair of small fish to use as bait that night, so about five minutes after Dick and Hudson had gone on ahead, Pascual and Les followed them up the sandbar.

As they walked along, they looked down to see tiger tracks right in the fresh footprints of the other fellows. The tiger must've been lying at the edge of the jungle while the fellows walked by; then after they passed, it likely came down, smelled their footprints, and continued down the sandbar. Upon seeing or hearing Les and Pascual coming upriver, no doubt it stepped back into the jungle's edge to let them pass. They had no guns with them since they didn't want to pose a threat to the nomads if they encountered them, so they could have been easy prey for a tiger. Fighting a tiger with only a machete didn't seem like the best idea but would have been their only option.

They were quick to thank God for "clouding the tiger's understanding" as Les phrased it in a letter. Early the next morning, along with the usual sounds of ducks, wild turkeys, and monkeys, they could hear the low moan of a tiger nearby on their side of the river and the answer of another from the other side of the river.

They got on the trail quite early, since they were anxious to get home, and arrived in "civilization" late that afternoon. They had seen enough to realize that there were no suitable sites on the upper portion of the Chimoré River for making a farm. Eventually, they would need to go back and check farther down the river. They thought maybe they would have a better idea soon as to what the future held as the next day, they would be meeting with the colonists.

The following day, heavy rain and blowing wind arrived from the south. The temperature plummeted, and the meeting with the colonists was called off but rescheduled for three days later. When the meeting was finally held, the missionaries were encouraged and wrote a lengthy report to prayer partners as to the amazing way God had worked. I will leave much of this in Les' words:

> Yesterday we had what was announced by the colonist's as "our last meeting" with them. Ever since the beginning of the contact effort three and a half years ago, we've been under pressure by the colonists. We haven't been able to move freely nor do what we've wanted to do or thought was right, because the colonists continually pressured us to do one thing or another. We've had one ultimatum after another, one deadline after another to meet. This has both hindered the work and caused the colonists to say that we don't keep our word. At the meeting of June 3 this year, we were given three points to complete within 30 days and because we did not do those three things within the 30 days, we were called liars. Some of the colonists were ready to bypass us and go in once and for all to kill

the nomads. If we could not guarantee certain things, such as: replace everything stolen by the "savages," get the boy back, etc. etc., they would listen to us no more, and this was absolutely the last chance.

Our plans were to leave this area, and with the experience we had gained here try to befriend a different band of this same tribe in another area far away from settlements. After the colonists had their say, they turned the meeting over to us to hear what we had to say. I unfolded a large map of Bolivia and showed them the La Jota area where this small group of Yuquí roam, then I told them of other bands, which we are confident are of the same tribe, roaming in other areas. There is a group down the Chapare River near the mouth; a group just below Puerto Grether on the Ichilo River; a group on the headwaters of the Chore River; a group on the Yapacaní River; and then the group that the Tamplins are trying to contact on the Palometillas River. These are only the *known* bands, the groups that are near enough to civilization to be seen and heard about.

I told the colonists that not only did they want this to be the last meeting with us, but that we also wanted this to be our last meeting with them. This was their last chance. If they chose war with the nomads, it wouldn't just be a little fight but would go on for years and years. Their children would still be being shot and having to defend themselves. Even if the colonists went into the jungle now and killed every nomad in this group, which was unlikely, in a few years another group of these nomads would likely move into this area and they would have the same fight all over again.

Their choice was either an endless war or let us go ahead *completely* unmolested. If they chose peace, they would need to give us liberty to work for an unlimited amount of time. Otherwise, we could not continue here in this area

The meeting went on for several hours. The colonists tried to get every concession they could. They tried to get us to promise to replace anything stolen by the nomads. I told them we couldn't do this because we ourselves have no promise of continued money coming down from the States and couldn't offer a promise of payments we might not have the money to make. They also wanted us to guarantee that the nomads wouldn't shoot another colonist. Obviously, we couldn't promise this either.

After much talk, many questions by them and much wisdom and grace supplied by God, the meeting ended by their choosing peace under our terms. The way things stand now, we have complete liberty to work without their threatening us in any way, and without their giving us any more deadlines to meet. There is only one limitation and that is the thing that we want to advertise for real prayer support! We are completely free to work _unless_ there is another person shot by the nomads. If a shooting occurs that will be the end for us and without even calling another meeting, a commission will go in and we will need to pull out. This is the only limitation. Please ask and believe God to keep the nomads from shooting another person.

I believe this is the greatest victory the contact effort has ever had with the colonists. I believe the door is open like it has never been before. We can expect great things from God.

The colonists plan to return to their farms in La Jota, while we desire to move to El Naranjal, the site of the abandoned Franciscan mission, and set up a base there. It is farther from the colonies so we should be able to draw the nomads away from the farms. We want to build a house with a wall of seasoned palm logs. Then we plan to put heavy plank doors on it. World Gospel Mission's pilot, Jonathan Tamplin has said that if we can find a place to build an airstrip, they will serve us with their airplane. We have several missionaries who would like to join our team and help make all this a reality.

The nomads seem to have made their annual move down into the lowlands north of La Jota to hunt and fish, so we don't expect them back in the area for about three months. If we can hire men from town and from the colonies, we should have time to build a fortified house and possibly a crude airstrip before they return. We haven't seen the nomads for two months now, but the last contact in June was a friendly one and we believe they left on good terms with us. We are optimistic about the future.

Within two weeks, the missionary team had signed a contract with the colonists to clear a site in El Naranjal for an airstrip and strong house, and with the promise of cash income, the colonists were anxious to get to work. They were also motivated since they wanted to finish the work and be out of the area before the "savages" came back for rainy season. Within a month, the necessary jungle had been felled and was drying so it could be cleared by burning. There was no heavy equipment this far out into the jungle, so all the work had to be done manually.

Three weeks after the jungle had been felled, it was dry enough that the contractors were able to burn the downed trees and undergrowth, and the heavy work of removing stumps from the airstrip site began. As Les, Lois, and Dick walked from their old houses at La Jota out toward the Naranjal to see how the work was progressing, they could hear the explosion of dynamite being used to blow out stumps on the new airstrip two kilometers away. Eight of the colonial leaders had been engaged as contractors, and they had hired crews, so there were twenty-eight or more men working much of the time.

The bulk of them were dynamiting and digging stumps or doing earthwork for the airstrip, while the rest started building two missionary houses. One house would have a corrugated aluminum roof and a walled-in room of hard palm logs with a heavy plank door. It could be locked so that gifts and other missionary belongings could be stored there to avoid theft by the nomads. The other house would be much like the houses used by the colonists, a palm leaf roof supported by six upright palm logs, and mostly open to the environment.

The Naranjal's location, two kilometers farther into the jungle than the outlying colony of La Jota, made it a preferred place for interacting with the nomads, although it was still too close to the colonies to be ideal. If the nomads could be settled in that location, there was enough high ground surrounding the airstrip to plant a large farm and provide for the nomads without them needing to raid the farms of the colonists. The missionaries were praying fervently that the next set of contacts would be successful and lasting and wrote to their prayer partners to intercede with God for such a reality.

Pascual, the young Guarayo Indian man who was still helping the missionaries, went over the word lists the missionaries had gathered from the nomads and found that many of the words were similar to his language. If he was willing to continue helping when the Yuquí returned, it might speed up the effort to learn the language.

Over the course of the earlier contacts, the missionaries had been identifying the nomads with English names they could use when talking among themselves. The chief's name seemed to be Papai, but among themselves, the missionaries referred to him as Chief.

From the beginning, he had been one of the friendlier ones, with a kind face, and seemed to have a tender heart. They hoped he remained in power or at least that a more belligerent individual would not gain power. Toughy had been one of the most aggressive of the nomads, choking various missionaries, throwing them to the ground, shooting arrows near them, and threatening in other ways. By now, from things Toughy had described to them, they were sure he was the father of at least one of the children stolen by the commission almost four years previously. This could explain his belligerence.

Roughneck and Wide Eyes had originally been antagonistic, but their actions and attitudes had improved greatly. Witch Doctor had at first been hostile but seemed to be warming up to the missionaries. Then there was Milk Shake Girl, so named for reasons I mentioned earlier.

By mid-November, most of the colonists had finished working on the new mission base at El Naranjal and gone back to their farms, some to rebuild houses the nomads had previously burned, others to harvest or plant. The airstrip was not yet usable, but the missionaries planned to spend their days improving it as well as checking gift trails while they waited for the nomads to reappear. Les had gone into Todos Santos to pick up additional supplies and take them out to the Naranjal. Now he was ready to go back out and join the other men at the new base.

The day before he was to leave for El Naranjal, a farmer from La Jota arrived in town and came by Les' house. "The savages are back. One of the young men saw them," stated the colonist.

As Les heard more, he wondered if the nomads really were back. The eighteen-year-old who had reported seeing them was known for his overactive imagination, so it was likely fear had motivated his report. Even so, Les was glad he wouldn't be making the trip through the jungle by himself, later writing, "I rejoiced that *God* was with me so I didn't have to take the trip through the jungle to our new camp alone."

Early the next morning, Les loaded up the canoe and headed up the Chapare and Coni Rivers. As he came abreast of Carajota Creek, a boy waved him over to the bank. "Señor, could you please take me, my mother, and a couple of small packages up to El Coni colony?"

Les always liked to help people out if possible, so he agreed to wait while the boy went and got his mother and the packages. "He and his mother" turned out to be another canoe tied alongside of Les'—ten people, eight dogs, sixteen or seventeen burlap bags full of assorted items, plus what looked like most of the cooking utensils for the whole group. Pulling all the extra weight upriver with one small outboard motor, Les arrived much later at El Coni than he had planned but with peace and joy filling his heart, knowing that he was walking in God's plan.

It was still not quite noon, so he decided to go on to Chincherel Creek to eat his lunch. Twenty minutes from the Chincherel, he came upon the trail that had prompted reports of the nomads being back in the area. Sure enough, it looked like it could be them.

Les dropped his pack to the ground to scout up and down the trail which ran from north to south across the east-west colonist trail he was on. There were many bent over small branches of saplings along the trail, just the way the nomads mark their travels through the jungle. Going on, Les soon approached Magdalena Creek and heard voices ahead of him around a bend in the trail. He stopped and listened closely to see if he could tell what language they were speaking. It sounded like Quechua, so he proceeded, expecting it to be colonists. Sure enough, it was a man and a boy resting there on their way to Todos Santos from La Jota.

As they conversed, they explained, "We are the last ones leaving La Jota. All the colonists have left on account of the savages. They've come back and begun stealing our crops again."

"Would you be so kind as to take a note to town for my wife?" Les inquired.

The colonists were happy to do that for him, so he wrote a brief note, letting Lois know of the new developments.

As Les left the two farmers, he suggested to them, "As you go through the colonies on your way to town, make sure you let anyone you see know that the nomads are back in the area."

Striding on down the trail, Les made it to La Jota in good time and found that the nomads had left a freshly woven palm basket right in the trail. He pressed on through the vacant colony and past the charred remains of his old house, which he had burned when the missionary team moved to El Naranjal as they didn't want the Yuquí to continue to look for them there. Then he went on to El Naranjal.

Dick and Harold were there when he arrived as well as three colonists who were finishing up the last of the work they had been contracted to do. "The nomads have returned, and everyone has moved out of the La Jota colony," Les announced to the workers. "It would be good if you three leave very early in the morning or by flashlight at night. That way, you can avoid an encounter with the nomads," he recommended.

The work had gone well, and it looked like the airstrip might be operational by the end of the week. The pilot would need to check it out by flying over it and, if he concluded it was adequate, try a test landing with no cargo. After that, they could have him fly in steel barrels, a radio and generator, and all the other items they would need to keep the contact effort going. The barrels would be used to store supplies under lock and key in the strong house. Much had been accomplished in a short time, and now their preparations were almost complete. They were nearly ready for contact with the Yuquí to resume.

Nine days later, a Shell Oil Company helicopter flying over the town of Todos Santos dropped a note randomly into a lady's yard. She picked up the note and saw that it was addressed to Lois Foster, so she sent one of her children over to deliver the note. It was from Les. The helicopter pilot had seen the new airstrip at El Naranjal and landed to see who had built an airstrip in the middle of nowhere. As he would be flying near Todos Santos on the way to his destination, he was happy to drop a note in town, although he didn't want to take the time to land and ask around for Lois.

"Dear Lois," began the note, "the nomads showed up this morning for the first time here at El Naranjal. They were with us for about two and a half hours. It was the same group as before, ones we know. There were eighteen of them, and they acted much the same as in the past. Let everyone know to be praying for us."

The following day, Jonathan Tamplin was due to fly in and test the airstrip. He took two passengers with him on that first flight and landed with no difficulty. Taking off, however, proved to be more problematic. Near the end of the airstrip was a mound that appeared to be where one of the Franciscan mission buildings had once stood. When the airstrip was made, the old building site had not been adequately leveled and was noticeably higher than the rest of the strip. As Jonathan neared the end of the modest runway on takeoff, it began to appear that the runway would be too short for the amount of weight aboard—two men and a boy—and the plane would end up in the stumps and trees off the end of the runway.

As this realization dawned on him, the small Cessna hit the mound and bounced into the air, clearing the stumps and trees with minimal margin. Once they were safely airborne, he breathed a sigh of relief before turning to Norm Hurst and Alan Foster to comment, "I'm not too sure we would have made it without the bounce from the mound." Until the airstrip could be improved and extended, he would limit takeoff to himself, the pilot, and one other person.

The next day, the radio was flown in along with other equipment, but it was three days before the missionaries could get it set up as each day the nomads came to visit. The third day, Saturday, Les finally got in touch by radio with Lois in Todos Santos. He had news to report, and it wasn't all encouraging. "the Chief wanted to wrestle with me, but I knew things could get rough and out of hand quickly, so I showed disgust like they do when they don't approve of something, and that stopped the wrestling." He went on to report news that was of greater concern. "One of the warriors drew an arrow and pointed it at Harold, and it appeared he might really shoot him. I began yelling, 'No! No! No!' and made motions not to, and at that point, others of the nomads bawled their companion out and told him not to do that."

Lois was encouraged to hear that the nomads were beginning to pay attention when asked not to do something but concerned with the violence that lay just under the surface. Les also reported that the nomads were being more patient and helpful in trying to communicate with the missionaries, repeating words for them and correcting them as they mispronounced words. Day after stressful day, the contacts continued with the missionaries, never knowing what kind of mood the nomads would be in when they came to visit. Some contacts were friendly and enjoyable, others were tense.

One of the more enjoyable contacts was when the chief, began telling hunting stories. Their stories were always entertaining as they pantomimed much of the action and used many sound effects. Even without understanding the words, the stories could be somewhat understood. As this story began, the missionaries weren't initially sure if the chief was describing animals they had shot or if it had been humans. He indicated that there had been three and that the warriors had shot three arrows.

An early encounter with the nomads at El Naranjal. From left, Dick Strickler, Chuck Johnson, Hudson Birkett, Chief Big Chest, Harold Rainey, Chief's wife (Tame Pig), unknown nomad, Les Foster, Big Tummy.

The arrows had gone in about eight inches, which he showed by pushing the point of his arrow between his fingers that far. He said that the shooting took place somewhere north of the missionary camp and then went on to act out how one of them was hit in the chest on the right side and was only wounded and escaped through the jungle by crawling after he fell.

Many times before, the chief and other men had related and acted out hunting trips they had been on, how they shot this kind of bird or that kind of animal, so this wasn't new; yet somehow, it seemed different. That afternoon, Les related the story over the radio to the mission supply man in Cochabamba.

A few days later, Rollie Hoogshagen, the supply man, came on the radio, excited by an article in the newspaper. It told of three hunters who were hunting down north, almost thirty kilometers from the missionary base. As they were in the jungle near where the

Chapare River flows into the Mamoré River, they came upon a group of nomads. There was an exchange of shooting, and two of the hunters were killed outright. The third escaped with an arrow in him by crawling through the jungle.

This matched the chief's story, making it very clear that these were the warriors who had done the shooting.

Three weeks later, another significant event occurred with long-term consequences! The morning of December 26, 1959, Les was on the radio with the World Gospel Mission pilot, Jonathan Tamplin, and asked him to fly a load of supplies from Todos Santos to El Naranjal. On the first flight, he would take Lois Foster as well as Joan Birkett, whose husband was currently helping on the contact, to the Naranjal where they would stay for about half an hour while Jonathan shuttled in a load of supplies. The ladies could spend the time visiting with their husbands and then go back to Todos Santos on the last flight.

That morning, the nomads showed up early, and as Jonathan's plane arrived, they were still there interacting with the missionary team. It was their first time being there for the arrival of an airplane, and being frightened, they ran into the edge of the jungle to watch. With a contact in progress, it was decided that it was too dangerous for Lois and Joan to stay there as planned, so Lois got out of the plane just long enough to wave at the nomads in the edge of the jungle, even though she couldn't see them. They knew her from the first five contacts in La Jota and would often ask about her.

Lois and Joan had made a cherry pie as a special treat for the men and as they hadn't been able to eat since breakfast because of the nomads being there with them; and it being now 2:00 p.m., as the plane was taking off, the men cut the pie and began to eat it. Before they were through eating, the nomads began to whistle and come out of the jungle. The men had hardly gulped down the pie before the nomads arrived. As they became aware that the missionaries had eaten and not shared the food with them, they became enraged. The pie crumbs around the missionary's mouths were clear evidence, but they also had Les open his mouth so they could see the small pieces of pie stuck to his teeth. It made them so irate that the missionaries had eaten and not shared with them that Toughy, one of the stockier and less friendly of the warriors, began jabbing Chuck Johnson, who was helping out at the time, with an arrow. In all, he poked and threw his arrow at Chuck five times, each time a little harder.

Chuck put up his hands to protect himself and received puncture wounds to the hands and chest. The last two wounds drew a significant flow of blood. Toughy had broken his bow earlier in the day while showing how high he could shoot an arrow, otherwise he might have shot Chuck. Les yelled at Harold Rainey who was hiding inside the strong room to start up the generator. The nomads had never been exposed closely to this type of noise and fled when the noisy motor started. They had no idea what type of monster might lurk in the strong room. It's anybody's guess how much further the situation might have deteriorated had the generator noise not scared the Yuquí away.

With these developments, it had become too dangerous to remain in contact with the nomads, so when Jonathan arrived with the load of cargo, they asked him instead to evacuate the team and as much equipment as possible to Todos Santos. He made nine more flights and was able to pull all the men and the majority of the equipment out.

Four years of effort and twenty-three contacts wiped out in a few tragic moments, and all over an unshared cherry pie! What did the future hold for the missionaries? For the nomads? For the colonists? Could Les go in by himself and try to live and roam with the nomads until he had enough language to convince them to settle peacefully? They seemed to have a greater respect for him than for his missionary coworkers. Could he could travel with them, carrying his shotgun, and providing abundant meat for the group, thus making himself invaluable to them?

This was just one of the many thoughts and ideas that went through his mind as he and the team discussed the future. They were also concerned that if they abandoned the effort, the colonists would proceed with a commission and decimate the band of nomads. The only positive aspect of that might be an opportunity to work with a captive nomad and learn the language before making another effort to befriend those who survived the posse.

Six weeks went by, and the Fosters along with their coworkers continued in Todos Santos, unsure what to do next. It was Sunday, and in fifteen minutes, they would be heading up to the evening church service. All that changed when a colonist showed up at their door, breathing hard after his dash up from the river. "The savages have shot José Panoso," panted the man. "We've brought him to town. He's down at the river in a canoe."

José had been paddling up the Coni River from the port where the missionaries normally left their canoe on their trips to La Jota. It was five o'clock in the afternoon, and as he customarily did, José was going a short way upstream to fish. As he went along, passing a place where the jungle was especially thick, the warriors had set an ambush. Three arrows came flying simultaneously out of the thicket, but two of them missed him. The third hit him in the left side of his back. It was a bamboo-tipped arrow, similar to a lance, and went in very deep, possibly hitting a rib in the front. He pulled the arrow tip out right away, leaving an open gaping wound which bled freely.

Bringing him into town had taken two men two hours paddling in a dugout canoe, and now José was in a state of shock and very weak and pale from loss of blood. The missionaries helped carry him to the house of a friend of his while Les ran home for his limited medical kit while sending his son, Alan, dashing to the church to get Marge Day, a missionary nurse who happened to be in town.

José was writhing in great pain, so the first thing Les did was give him a shot of morphine to ease his misery. By the time he had accomplished that, Marge arrived, but José was very restless, rolling from side to side. His heart function was erratic and his pulse was weakening. Marge doubted he would last much longer, so she sent Alan running around town to the various houses that stocked a few medications to see if any of them had a heart stimulant they could inject. Meanwhile, Marge dressed the wound and kept a close check on his pulse, which continued getting weaker and weaker.

Soon, twelve-year-old Alan arrived back carrying a precious vial of stimulant, but by now, José was near death. As a last desperate measure, Marge gave him the injection but hadn't even finished the shot when he died. It was 9:20 p.m. Later, when the situation was discussed with doctors in the city, their comment was, "If José had left the arrow point in rather than pulling it out, it would have slowed the bleeding and he might have survived the shooting." Alan was impressed with their analysis and made a mental note to follow that advice if he was ever in a similar situation.

The next morning, Les was summoned to the police station where an angry group of colonists were assembled. They were looking for legal grounds to blame the missionaries for the shooting. Never mind that colonists had been getting shot long before the missionaries first arrived in Todos Santos. The angry farmers started out by asking, "Did you promise to meet the savages yesterday in La Jota?" They thought maybe the nomads had come to the river, thinking they would find the missionaries coming out to see them. Then they asked, "When you pulled out of El Naranjal in December, why didn't you give us permission to go in and kill the savages?"

The truth was that after the missionaries pulled out of El Naranjal, they had met with the leaders of the colonists to let them know they had evacuated and gave them freedom to do what they wanted as they had abandoned the contact effort for now. A few of the leaders grudgingly admitted that they had been informed, but obviously they hadn't mentioned that to the rest of the colonists. In the end, the meeting failed to blame the missionary team for the shooting. At the same time, the farmers began organizing a commission for the following week, giving time for one of the ranking colonial leaders to make a trip to Cochabamba for guns and ammunition. They also promised that if they captured any of the nomads, they would turn them over to the missionaries to help them learn the language.

"*Mañana, mañana*"—everything is "tomorrow" in the lowlands of Bolivia, and this was born out again when it took a full month for the commission to be assembled. Getting arms and ammunition took time, but once all was in place, the posse was well-armed with submachine guns and rifles. Part of the reason it had taken so long to prepare the incursion into nomad territory was that it had been put together in secret. A government order had been sent to the authorities in Todos Santos, forbidding the colonists to shoot the nomads.

Very few people were aware of it when the commission finally headed into the jungle where the posse followed nomad trails day after day, until finally, they came upon the site where the forest dwellers were currently camped. The encounter was made early in the morning and found most of the Yuquí still in their camp. One of the pet monkeys the nomads kept sounded the first warning, followed by an old lady who yelled the alarm to the warriors who were still in their palm shelters. When the old lady cried out, the leader of the colonists shot and killed her. As the warriors came running out one of them, either the chief, Wide Eyes, or Toughy—according to the description given by the farmers—was shot and killed by another colonist. How many others were shot and killed was not disclosed to the missionaries as the colonists who participated in the raid had been sworn to secrecy. It was clear that rumors were inaccurate as some indicated that the rest of the nomads escaped, whereas others specified that all the children were killed as well as the majority of the adults.

The colonists destroyed all the bows and arrows that had been abandoned as the nomads fled and brought back the machetes, axes, and kettles from the camp, so even though some of the nomads may have escaped, they would struggle to survive with few bows and arrows and a limited number of tools for making new weapons. With no weapons, hunting would be especially difficult, and they would be eating a lot of palm cabbage until they could get rearmed. Once they returned to the colonies to steal crops, they would no doubt be very vengeful!

As Les wrote:

> I am unable to express the feeling of sorrow we have in the contacts ending in this way. We had hoped there would be none or very few killed and that the colonists would bring back captives from whom we could learn the language. But the colonists took no captives, nor did they intend

to take captives. They say they want to kill every
individual in this group! We pray God will cause
the rest of the nomads to escape so far that it will
be impossible for the colonists to find them.

It was clear to the missionary team that it would no longer be
possible to attempt a contact from the western side of the area where
the colonies were located near the Coni River. Instead, it would be
necessary to go in from the east in order to draw the surviving nomads
away from the colonies toward the Chimoré River. They decided to
spend the next three months familiarizing themselves with that area
and getting an idea of where and how to proceed.

To get over to that area by boat was a five to seven-day trip one
way, so it would be time-consuming and require many supplies, both
gasoline for the outboard and food for several weeks. The exploratory
trip would require a boat ride down the Chapare River and then up
the Ichilo River. They planned to go as far as Puerto Grether, stopping at any small farms or villages along the river as they tried to
determine where different groups of the nomads might be roaming
and what time of year signs of them were typically seen in the different areas. They were sure that several bands of nomads existed as
there had been confirmed sightings in areas that were separated by
wide deep rivers that the nomads would not normally cross. They
would also go up the Chimoré River to see if there was a suitable
location to set up a base and a large farm where they could provide
for the nomads without a need for them to go into the colonies to
raid and kill or be killed.

Most of the missionaries on the team had been in Bolivia for five
or more years without a break, so they planned to first return to the
homeland for a year, see extended family, visit partnering churches,
and share their vision for reaching the nomads with the Gospel. They
would need to accomplish all of the survey work before their children
finished their school year in three months.

The Continuing Saga of the Yuquí

WHILE DICK STRICKLER AND THE Foster family were in the United States for a year, visiting family and reporting on the Yuquí contact effort to churches and individuals who had been partnering with them through prayer and finances, the conflict in the Bolivian Amazon continued. Late in 1960, another colonist, Erasmo García, was killed by the Yuquí, and the story was not a pretty one.

Erasmo had come to realize that farming in La Jota was a perilous venture and decided to sell his farm, abandoning the labor of many years. While taking a prospective buyer to see the farm, the two men were attacked by nomad warriors, and Erasmo was killed. The other man escaped but with an arrow pinning his arm to his body. When a posse went searching for Erasmo, they found that the "savages," as they referred to the Yuquí, had shot him through the heart, cut off his head, and then punctured his body full of arrow holes. The message to the colonists was clear: "Send commissions to kill our women and children, and this is how we will respond!"

After the shooting, the nomads fled the area, and it would be eight months until they were heard from again, shortly after the Fosters arrived back in Bolivia.

Meanwhile, over in the El Púlpito area of Bolivia, far to the east of Todos Santos where Carroll Tamplin of World Gospel Mission was trying to befriend a different band of the Yuquí, the hostiles attacked and killed one of Carroll's workers. Previously, they had wounded one of his helpers, so their mission organization decided he should abandon the contact effort. Carroll and his wife, Doris, were returning Stateside due to health issues, and it was unknown if they would come back to Bolivia. Carroll wrote Les to let him know that he was welcome to begin a contact effort in the El Púlpito area if and when he was able.

While in the United States, Les had visited some of the mission training centers and shared with the students the need for more team members in the effort to befriend the Yuquí. Several families responded, and among those who eventually came to help in the work were Bob and Shirley Smith and Bob and Mary Garland. The Smiths were one of the first to respond and, in a letter to Les, wrote the following: "[t]he Garland family, two children; Bob Garland is quite good in learning language, and his wife is the top linguist here this term, she is really sharp."

That was exciting news as the team really needed a linguist. Dick Strickler had been doing his best to meet that need and had the brain for it but had difficulty hearing the sounds.

By late June, the Fosters were back in Todos Santos, although getting there had been another opportunity to fully trust God. The road to the jungle lowlands was not being properly maintained and was in such poor condition that many vehicles were plunging off the treacherous Andean mountain road into the abyss, often thousands of feet down. On the other hand, the airline was having financial issues, so to conserve fuel while flying, once they had cleared the mountains, the pilots would routinely turn off one engine for the descent with the hope that it could be restarted in flight when needed. In a letter to a friend, Les asked, "How would you like to fly over the jungle with only one engine in a heavily loaded DC-3?"

Almost immediately after their arrival in Todos Santos, reports started to come in again about the nomads being heard or seen. The first report was from Yuracaré Indian students at Marge Day's school nine kilometers down the Chapare River from Todos Santos. The students heard whistling across the Chapare River from the school and a baby crying. It could only have been the Yuquí as no one else inhabited that area of jungle. Two weeks later, a young man was coming upriver, trying to make it to town before dark, but when he saw he wouldn't make it, he stopped at a farm just downriver from town but on the side of the river where the nomads roamed.

The farmer whose house he spent the night at told him he had gone into the jungle to the east about 500 meters and came upon a trail recently made by the nomads who were heading south. The same day the young man brought this report to town, fishermen coming back from the Chimoré River also reported that on their way out to the Chimoré, they had seen a trail that looked like two or three "savages" had gone from north to south, but on their back from the Chimoré, in the same place, they reported that "a whole herd of savages" had crossed the fishing trail going south.

Ten days later, three men from Todos Santos decided to go to the Chimoré River to fish. Because the Chimoré was unpopulated, it was not unusual to catch fish weighing well over one hundred pounds, so it was a popular fishing destination. They had only gone about halfway between the Chapare River on which Todos Santos is located and the Chimoré River when they began to hear strange whistles coming from three sides of them. A swamp lay on the fourth side. Fear gripped them as they realized the nomads had them trapped.

They couldn't go back to the Chapare River the way they had come, because the warriors might have set an ambush along the trail. The only thing they might be able to do to save their lives was launch out through the alligator-infested swamp. They managed to escape through the swamp and arrived safely back in town late that afternoon.

The Houseboat

THE MISSIONARY TEAM HAD A new strategy in mind. Instead of attempting friendship from El Naranjal or La Jota, which were too close to the colonies, they were going to have a large, wooden, flat-bottom boat built, a barge, the same type the local merchants used to travel the river. The missionaries would use the houseboat as a floating base which would allow them to travel to the Chimoré River, fully supplied, and remain there for several months at a time as they attempted to draw the Yuquí away from the inhabited area around the colonies. Also, since it appeared the nomads didn't know how to swim or use boats, the missionaries could moor their houseboat on the far side of the Chimoré River while using a small aluminum boat a church in Colorado had donated to cross the Chimoré and interact with the nomads. They would be much better able to control theft and violence on the part of the Yuquí. Now, while waiting for the new team members to arrive, they needed to have the large boat built.

A letter soon arrived from Bob Garland, introducing his family to the contact team:

> [a] short letter to introduce ourselves to you. I'm 30 years old and my wife Mary, is 26. We have two children, a girl, Lorraine, who is four and a boy Mark, two and a half years. My wife and I have a definite burden to work with those who have never heard the Gospel and would consider it a real privilege to work among the Yuquí.

They needed to finish their missionary training and trust God for financial and prayer partners but desired to join the team as soon as they were able. A total of five families or single missionaries had expressed a desire to become part of the team, although not all of them panned out.

In the meantime, Dick Strickler and Les were planning a trip down the Chapare and Ichilo Rivers to purchase lumber for building the houseboat. Not all the necessary funds had yet come in, but they had enough money to get started and were trusting God to supply what was lacking as it was needed. It was a big project which they anticipated would take several months, but by then, the new families should have arrived, and they would have the necessary personnel. A boat that was currently being finished for another missionary had taken almost five months to complete, and the new families were due to arrive in five months, so the timing seemed like it might be just about right.

Rainy season with its torrential rains came to an end, and as dry season came on, it seemed that the Yuquí had gone back north once again, leaving the area around the colonies. There were no new sightings or encounters with the nomads, but Les and Dick knew that in four months, when the rains recommenced, the nomads would come back to higher ground where they could enjoy the farmers' crops. If they could get the launch finished quickly, maybe they could be over on the Chimoré River by the last part of the next rainy season and begin luring the Yuquí away from the colonies.

Les had brought a kerosene-operated refrigerator back from the USA, and Lois was thrilled to at last be able to keep perishable items without them spoiling quickly. Whereas in the past, meat had to be used up within a day or two, now it would keep for up to a week in the fridge, which meant that Les wouldn't have to spend as much time hunting and fishing once they were out on the Chimoré River. The refrigerator would go on the boat with them, but first the boat had to be built, which would mean at least one trip downriver.

Now the holdup was dry season; there wasn't enough water in the Chapare River to make the trip down to the sawmill, so they needed rain in the Andean foothills to raise the water level sufficiently for their trip. Once they purchased the wood, they would need more rain so the boat could bring the wood up to Todos Santos where Don Mario Bottega, an Italian immigrant, would oversee construction. He was the town's premier boat builder!

The boat was to be a flat-bottom barge of mahogany wood with a light-weight superstructure of cedar wood. Mahogany would last ten years in the water. It would take about a week to build the hull, then it could be launched into the Chapare River and the superstructure added. At the very top would be a pilot house for good visibility in identifying snags and sandbars in order to avoid them. The *pontón*, as this type of boat was called, would be forty-three feet long and nine feet eight inches wide. It would have a shallow draft of three to four feet for navigating the treacherous jungle rivers.

One of the next things they would need was a diesel engine to power the pontón. It was a time of discouragement for the team as they waited in vain for well over a month for the water level in the river to rise. Their desire had been for a quick completion of the boat, but with inadequate water levels, a shortage of funds, and the need for a diesel engine, it looked as if they wouldn't be ready to move ahead on the contact effort when the new coworkers arrived from the homeland.

During this period of delay in Todos Santos, Les and Lois continued reaching out to the local people, helping with medical needs, assisting in work projects, and telling people about their need for a Savior but saw little response to their witness. This along with untrue rumors about them and their children added to their discouragement. It didn't help that they received a letter from their principal funding church, letting them know that funds were depleted and they would be receiving less income each month until more money was available in the church missionary fund.

Through this time, Les spent much time in God's Word and read encouraging books by Christian authors. As he read, God encouraged his heart, such that he wrote in a letter:

> God gave me this thought through a book
> I recently read, "In *His* strength, ever rising up
> within us, we are able to do as much as those
> who are dowered with the greatest mental and
> natural gifts, and we escape the temptation to

vainglory and pride by which they are beset." I came to realize that God has not called me to be a great orator, not in Spanish, nor in English, but rather has saved me the temptation to be proud of my ability and given me the privilege of trusting Him to use me to reach the Yuquí tribe for Christ, which someone who is a great orator might not want to waste their abilities on.

He faced and accepted the fact that God had gifted him uniquely, and language ability was not one of those gifts! His heart was in befriending and evangelizing the Yuquí!

After seven weeks of waiting with anticipation for water levels to rise in the Chapare River, it finally happened, and they were able to head off downriver to purchase mahogany for the hull of the pontón. As they traveled down the Chapare and Ichilo Rivers on a boat with no refrigeration and where no stores existed to purchase supplies, once again God provided meat as needed. Les wrote:

> It seemed that God supplied so much game that it got to where I'd sit on deck and watch as it went by because we had more than we could use. Wild black ducks were abundant, as were alligator and wild turkeys (about the size of a chicken).

At night, when the boat would stop for the night, they would take the aluminum boat out and, with a flashlight, spot alligator's eyes along the shore, then paddle over and shoot them if they needed the meat. Les wrote, "Alligator is much like lobster meat."

While no large financial gifts were received for the boat and motor, it seemed that God was supplying just enough to keep the project moving forward. They had enough money to buy the lumber, pay the expenses of the two trips to get the wood, and pay the two men who went along to help load and unload the lumber. The money ran out when they needed nails to start building, but Dick dipped into his personal funds and bought nails.

Don Mario, who was building the boat, agreed to accept a seven and a half horsepower outboard motor as part of the payment, so little by little, the venture crept forward. Many people in Todos Santos called the nomads the *Chori*, a corruption of the name of the Chore River where at least one band of Yuquí roamed, so the missionaries decided to name their pontón *El Chori*. They would paint the entire boat a light-blue with a white stripe horizontally around the roof below the pilot house. That way, they hoped the Yuquí would identify the boat with the white striped gifts they had given them in La Jota and El Naranjal.

On one of the trips to get lumber life almost ended for Les. I'll let him recount the story in his own words:

> The firing pin of the .22 rifle clicked on an empty chamber. There in the water ahead of Bob Wilhelmson's launch a wounded duck paddled as I stood on the roof of the boat with no more shells. I rushed to the ladder leading down to the front deck and started down facing forward, away from the ladder. As I started down the heel of my boot caught on a rung of the ladder and the next thing I knew I was falling headfirst into the Mamoré River right in front of the boat. I came up expecting to be able to gulp a breath of air but got only water. Because of the forward motion the boat was now above me. Hearing the engine running, my first thought was to swim to one side of the boat before the propeller passed by. The weight of my clothing, boots, and the rifle I still held in my hand hindered swimming to where I was barely able to reach the starboard side just before the propeller passed by. When I surfaced the boat was out of reach, so I yelled and treaded water waiting for them to see me and turn the big lumbering boat around. It took a long time for the boat to make the turn, so I

swam the 20 yards to shore to wait for it. While under the boat I remember thinking of the Yuquí Indians yet unreached with the good news of Christ who died for them and feeling that God would somehow see me through. Just a few days before Lois and I had been thinking and talking about (Hebrews 1:14, AMPC1) "Are not the angels all ministering spirits (servants) sent out in the service (of God for the assistance) of those who are to inherit salvation?" and wondering how many times God, by His angels might have protected us from death. Even though, while under the boat I was unable to get the gulp of air I so badly needed, yet I felt a new strength sustaining me until I finally did come up. Thank God for setting His angels to watch over us!

The first trip to pick up mahogany took three weeks due to shallow water in the Chapare River, but the second trip only took eight days and a few days later the launch was finally under construction. And for those who might be wondering, "Yes, he did get the wounded duck!"

Once they were back in town, they learned that the Yuquí had once again come into the area and began stealing bananas from the farmers. There was nothing they could do about that except pray that the launch would be completed sooner than expected so they could initiate the contact effort from the Chimoré River. So far, there were no shootings to report. They would continue to share the Gospel and build friendships in Todos Santos while they awaited the completion of the launch.

One exciting thing that happened during the waiting period had to do with a friendship they had made about eighteen months previously. Álvaro (pseudonym) was a young man of fifteen who, along with his father, had recently moved from Trinidad to Todos Santos, rented the room next door to the Fosters, and boarded with their landlady. In Trinidad, capital of the Beni department of Bolivia, they had attended church but seemed to have little understanding of God's Word and what it meant to be "born again."

Álvaro spent much time with the Fosters, especially when their children were on vacation from boarding school and attended church with them from time to time. Les had hired Álvaro and his father to assist in building the airstrip at El Naranjal and had helped them with medical issues from time to time. During those eighteen months, Álvaro hadn't seen and understood his need for the new birth. One day, Les was talking with him and commented, "I'm so sad that you won't be in heaven with me since you've never accepted Jesus as your Savior."

Álvaro, who was now living about half a mile away, thought this over for a few days and then came back to see Les, letting him know, "I'm thinking much about what you said to me."

Six days later, Álvaro came to visit again and wanted to talk. Up to this point, he had seemed convinced that God would accept him if he was good enough, was nice to people, and could please God. On this visit, Les explained again that "according to the Bible, we are all sinners and not able to help ourselves because of our sin natures. Because we are sinners, we must die for our sin and be eternally separated from God. There is nothing we can do!" Then Les explained to him that Christ, God's Son, came down, and when they were getting ready to nail Álvaro to the cross to die for his sin, Jesus said, "I'll take Álvaro's place, I'll die for him. Let him go free!"

At that point, Álvaro commented, "Now I understand. Christ is my substitute. He died in my place." That night Álvaro placed his trust in Christ!

Three weeks later, Don Juan Herbas' two sons were going east along the trail toward La Jota. About a quarter of the way between El Coni and La Jota, as they approached an old bridge, three arrows came flying at them from an ambush on the other side of the small stream. Fortunately, the arrows missed their marks, and the boys were able to escape without being hurt. The bridge seemed to be a favorite spot for ambush by the Yuquí, since after the boy had been kidnapped three years before, Les and the team had found an ambush in this same spot.

With these near misses, talk was revived of a commission going into the jungle to kill the Yuquí. The missionaries were excluded from those meetings, but a friend reported to them of a meeting he attended in the local army post where not only the leaders of the colonies but also the army commander was in favor of putting together a posse and going after the nomads. Sadly, the town's priest was one of the more vocal supporters, suggesting they use bombs to "kill off the savages who are stealing food from the poor colonists."

A month later, the nomads came into the Puerto Aurora colony and raided the farms, carrying off many bananas and much manioc. Their well-beaten exit trail indicated the entire band was once again in the area and served to fan the flames of desire among the colonists to exterminate these troublesome thieves.

Rainy season had begun in December, drawing the Yuquí back to the higher ground around the colonies. December also freed Les and Lois' children from boarding school for a month, so they headed to Cochabamba to be with their kids, have medical checkups, do back-to-school shopping, and purchase materials to continue building and equipping the houseboat.

Early in January, Les received a letter from Carroll Tamplin, who commented, "I'm still having trouble with my voice box. The doctor says it got cracked when the Yuquí choked me."

Les wrote back, "So sorry to hear that! One of the things I did while in Denver two years ago was to take a course in judo and jujitsu, and among other things, they taught us two very easy ways to escape from someone who is choking you."

The Denver police department had graciously allowed Les to take their training after he described the violent treatment the missionaries had received at the hands of the Yuquí.

Progress on the launch was agonizingly slow. The boat was being built out in the open, and now that rainy season was underway, construction was slowed. The wooden hull had to be dry for caulking or the tar wouldn't stick properly. Then a pipe to house the propeller driveshaft needed to be installed before the hull could be turned right side up and launched into the river where the superstructure would be added.

Some of the metal parts were being machined at a shop in Cochabamba which added to the delays as there was only one flight a week to Todos Santos, and often it was canceled due to rain or lack of sufficient cargo and passengers. Occasionally, machined parts didn't work correctly and had to be returned to Cochabamba to be re-machined and returned to Todos Santos.

Delay after delay, and now the new missionaries were beginning to arrive in Bolivia, anxious to join the team and head for the Chimoré River. For that to happen, the houseboat needed to be completed and make some test trips up and down the river. Once they left Todos Santos for the Chimoré, there would be no machine shops or highly trained mechanics; they would be on their own in the middle of nowhere, having left the last town of significance behind.

The original plan had been to have the pontón ready by January, but with all the delays, they were now optimistic that by June, it should be ready; but they still hadn't found a diesel engine to install, and a clutch, propeller, and other assorted hardware would be needed. By mid-February, the boat was in the water, and the superstructure was being built.

While waiting for the launch to be completed, Les and Lois made a trip to the El Coni colony to visit the colonists who had helped them in so many ways while they were based there in their attempt to befriend the Yuquí. They took along a generator as well as movie and slide projectors so they could show movies and slides of the Yuquí in the schoolhouse. They stayed for two nights, sleeping in jungle hammocks, and showed the pictures twice. Several of the colonists who had gone in on the commission came to see the pictures and commented, "There is no doubt it was Toughy whom we killed."

Les had two real good pictures of Toughy who had been one of the most violent of the Yuquí, and Les later wrote, "We may find the nomads more cooperative with Toughy out of the way."

Living in a frontier town made for many interesting experiences, and while waiting for the completion of the launch, they had a few. A tiger and its mate began coming into town at night to kill pigs, so two men set a gun trap on one of the trails used by the tigers and managed to kill one of them. Les and Lois went up to take pictures of the dead tiger, and while they were there, the people commented, "We can still hear its mate calling out in the jungle nightly." Even the streets of the town were dangerous.

The town was dangerous for other reasons as well. Boats often arrived, carrying cattle from ranches far downriver. When commercial boatmen stopped at the ranches to buy cattle, the ranchers would go out, round them up, and load them aboard the boats to be shipped upriver to Todos Santos and then trucked on to Cochabamba. When the barges arrived in Todos Santos, the wild cattle were unloaded and tied in pairs, head-to-head, facing each other. This way, a wild cow couldn't easily attack a person on the street as the two cows would try to go in different directions.

Occasionally, a pair of cows would manage to break free from one another, and the individual cows were a deadly menace on the muddy grass town streets. One evening, Les and Lois were on their way to church when they encountered a lone wild cow. Les turned and ran, expecting Lois to follow, but when he looked back, there was Lois, swinging her folded umbrella at the charging cow. Her yell and the swinging umbrella caused the cow to veer, missing both Les and Lois, but came very near to goring another young fellow as it continued its trajectory across the town square.

Another Sunday night, as they passed the police station on their way to church by flashlight, the beam of Les' light fell upon a small alligator lying in the trail right in front of them. Keeping the beam in its eye, Les carefully reached down and caught it by the neck. He kept the alligator, which was later identified as a caiman (South American cousin to the crocodile) so his children could have it as a pet when they came home on their school vacation. When the children came home, they didn't keep the small caiman long as it had teeth like needles and was very aggressive, so eventually, against the advice of the locals, they released it into the river.

By now, the Fosters had been back in Bolivia for a full year and were eager to have the boat completed and be out trying once again to befriend the nomads. They weren't alone in this desire as two of the new families had arrived and were also anxious to move forward. Not having faced the brutality and sadism of the earlier contacts, two of the new men asked, "Why don't we just abandon the boat project, walk into the jungle, and make contact with the Yuquí?"

Dick and Les, having experienced the highs and lows of the previous contacts, answered, "If we contact them in this area, we will have signed their death warrants. We will end up drawing them back to the colonies where they will ambush colonists, provoking them to form a posse that will go into the jungle and wipe out the Yuquí."

All the missionaries wanted the work to move forward quickly, but past experience dictated that a new approach was imperative.

All of them struggled to understand the delays as they knew God wanted the Good News of His Son preached to the Yuquí, but they were confident God was doing something in their own hearts and in the hearts of the nomads to prepare them for future friendly encounters with the missionary team.

The newly arrived Smith family kept busy studying Spanish, three hours of conversation each morning and a one-hour grammar class in the afternoon. Initially, they were using a young Christian man for conversation, but when he had to leave to help his father on their farm, they found a young lady who was not a believer to help with conversation.

At first, the girl rebelled at having to read the Bible and tried her best *not* to understand what she was reading. But a person can't read the Bible for an hour each day without having an effect of some kind take place in their life. Slowly, she became less belligerent toward God's word, and finally, she even looked forward to reading it. Verse after verse in the Bible began to reach her heart. She would stop and ask questions, and the missionaries would explain to her what the verses meant. One morning, she was reading 2 Corinthians 11 (KJV) and stopped after reading verse 14, "Satan himself is transformed into an angel of light."

"What does that mean?" she questioned.

As she continued reading other verses and the missionaries answered her questions, she began to understand God's way of salvation and accepted Christ as her Savior. While the missionary team was chomping at the bit to move forward with the contact effort, God was drawing people to Himself through their witness in Todos

Santos. Time was *not* being wasted! As Les wrote, "We want to be used by God each day wherever we are."

Soon the children came home for the summer, and the families were in Todos Santos along with some school friends who were visiting for a few days. Alan and two of his friends were down at the waterfront, watching one of the commercial barges arrive from downriver. It was always a thrilling time when a boat arrived and much of the town turned out to see the excitement. Cattle and hides would be unloaded along with merchandise coming up from Brazil.

Shortly after the barge landed and tied up, the captain came ashore and, seeing Alan there, called him over. "I have a message for your dad. The savages have been stealing bananas from Francisco Blanco's farm. He asked me to let your dad know."

"Thank you so much. I'll be sure and let him know," replied Alan. Alan and his two teenage school friends, Paul and Tim Wyma, hurried up to the house to give Les the message.

At 6:00 a.m. the next morning, the three boys, along with Bob Smith, Dick Strickler, and Les were on their way downriver to talk to Francisco. They arrived at Frank's at 9:15 a.m., and he took them right over to his banana plantation on the eastern side of the river to show them where some twenty stalks of bananas had been stolen on Saturday. The boys stayed in the boat while the adults went into the plantation with Frank.

Sure enough, there was a wide well-beaten trail leading from the plantation into the jungle. The men followed the trail two hundred feet into the forest and found where the nomads had stopped to pull the "hands" of bananas off the stalks, leaving bare stalks behind. After returning to the plantation where Frank awaited them, he led them around the banana patch, showing the different plants where the nomads had taken bananas. As they worked their way north into another section of the plantation, they began seeing fresher looking breaks on the plants, and Frank commented that these hadn't been gone on Sunday when he found the others missing. Appearances led them to believe these had been taken the previous afternoon.

Frank suggested, "I think the savages are camped on a high belt of jungle which runs north and south about halfway to the Chimoré

River from my farm." He and his brother Orlando were woodsmen, hunters, and trappers, very knowledgeable in the jungle. "My brother and I are going to follow the savage trail and see if we can find their camp," he told Les.

Knowing these men were professing Christians, Les advised, "That's a very risky and dangerous thing to do, so be sure and pray much about it before you consider doing that."

The new additions to the missionary team had once again begun to question why they had been encouraged to rush to Bolivia, only to find that nothing was moving forward on the contact effort. Their understanding had been that the holdup was lack of personnel. Now they were here and discovered the boat was not ready and wondered if they had been misled. Les, on the other hand, had fully expected the boat to be ready by the time the new workers arrived and had done his best to make that happen, but the delays were out of his control.

In his journal, Les wrote, "I must certainly agree with them. I had no idea the launch would be the hold up."

Once again, the new men talked to Les and Dick about dropping the idea of a houseboat and going out to La Jota or El Naranjal to make a contact. Dick and Les, on the other hand, felt they would gain absolutely nothing and that such an action would lead to the murder of many more of the Yuquí and colonists.

In a letter addressing Les' concern, Bruce Porterfield wrote, "When you're dealing with killers, you can afford to go slow."

Bruce had been on some of the earlier contacts and shared the same concerns as Les and Dick. During this time, Les happened to randomly pick up a pamphlet to read. It was titled "Going Slow With God" and explained that what God wants in us is not a lot of feverish activity, but rather to come to that place of complete rest and trust in God where He fills us with peace and we began to see:

> [g]limpses into God's perfection, insight into wonderful truths, quiet unfolding of daily opportunities, gentle checks of the Holy Spirit upon our decisions or words, sweet and secret

promptings to do certain things, the quiet solv-
ing of hard problems and mental articulations of
special words of strength, which we have often
missed because we took our ear from God's telephone a little too quickly, or ran past the angle of
vision, or wasted time by asking questions, or got
in a feverish state of anxiety, or attempted to take
God's work into our own hands.

God, in His perfect timing, put this pamphlet in front of Les
just when he needed the encouragement!

Les was confident that God was using the waiting period to
change the hearts of the nomads from what they had been like on
the previous contacts to where they would value and respect the missionaries on the next set of contacts. Only God knew how much time
would be required to accomplish this work in the hearts of the Yuquí.
Les wrote:

The only way we can be sure it is *His* time
with the contact is to *wait on* Him. If a door
seems as closed as this one, I want to pray it open
and not break it open with physical activity! I
trust that we will very soon be able to continue
the contact, but I *want it to be God's time!*

The barge was coming along nicely but still lacked an engine.
Once again, God had a plan in mind. During one of the mission
radio schedules, Les learned of a D2 Caterpillar engine for sale in the
capital city of La Paz. The engine belonged to the Lutheran Mission
and was being offered for one thousand dollars, an excellent price!
The engine came from a Caterpillar that had been wrecked beyond
repair when it crashed into a ravine. Les wrote a letter to prayer partners, telling the story.

What a mess! There lay the tractor at the
bottom of the ravine in water almost up to the

oil pan! Up on the rim of the ravine was a "pale-faced" student driver, who a few minutes before had been enjoying the pleasure of a sneak ride on the farm tractor while the missionary was away in town buying supplies. He was a Quechua Indian boy, but now as he lay where the tractor had thrown him in its wild plunge down the bank, he was so scared he probably couldn't even have told you his name. It was so much fun until he got to looking at where he had been instead of where he was going. Then there was that terrible bucking like being thrown from a horse, before he found himself laying against the bush that saved him from going over the ridge into the gully below.

As the missionaries went down to inspect the wreckage after taking care of the driver, they found that the tractor had landed on its treads. The heavy springs had taken the shock of the crash thereby protecting the engine. But the rest of the machine was beyond repair.

After days of hard work, they finally managed to get the engine out of the ravine and loaded onto a truck to haul it to La Paz, the capital of Bolivia, which was not too many miles away. There they took it to a diesel shop for a complete overhaul. No doubt they wondered why God would let a thing like that happen. But God in his foresight already had another chore for that engine. "Old Michi" (Old Cat, Michi being the Quechua word for 'cat'), as we call our newly acquired Caterpillar engine, was destined to become the motivation power for the launch "El Chori."

I heard of this engine two months ago and we in the Yuquí tribal work spent much time praying about the possibility of a trip to La Paz to see about buying it. I found the engine was just what we need, but with a few parts missing. We plan to order the missing parts for it from the States. The launch is nearly complete, and the engine is at the airfield ready to be shipped down to Todos Santos on the next plane.

Les wrote to a friend in Denver, describing the finished pontón:

The houseboat.

Our launch is 49' 1" long and 10' 9" wide. On top of the roof is the pilothouse which is the width of the boat and 21 feet long. From water level to the top of the pilothouse is 15 feet high. Across the back of the boat we have a bathroom, generator room, and shower room. The first small window on the front right (starboard) side of the launch is the four-foot by five-foot radio room walled with acoustic boards to deaden sound so the radio can be used even when the 42-horse-power diesel engine is in operation. Then comes bedroom space for the crew, kitchen area, and behind that the engine compartment. Beyond that is the dressing room for the shower. A shower is needed because of the dangers of going into the rivers which we'll be traveling. There are many stingrays, electric eels, alligators, anacondas, and man-eating piranha fish. The generator will be used to power the radio. The pilothouse has a half wall partly for protection against arrows and partly to keep out the rain. The launch is built so we can shut it up tight against attack by the nomads. The hull is constructed of two and a half-inch thick mahogany boards and the super-structure of light-weight cedar wood.

The Lutheran Mission was delighted to be able to sell the D2 engine to such a good cause and dropped the price to $800, throwing in the clutch at no additional cost. Les had priced a similar engine in the States, new for $1,500, so he knew they were getting a bargain! The engine and transmission weighed in at 2,165 pounds and would have to be shipped either by air or by truck to Todos Santos.

While Les was in Cochabamba having a machine shop do modifications on the engine and clutch assembly, he had several opportunities to show slides of the earlier contacts with the Yuquí in Bolivian churches and enlist more prayer support. One of those churches was being pastored by Colonel Domingo Medrano who had been so helpful while in charge of the army post in Todos Santos.

Before Les could return to Todos Santos with the engine, Dick Strickler called him by radio from Todos Santos with an urgent message. "Some of the Yuracaré were out in the jungle across the Chapare River from Marge Day's school hunting near some lagoons and came across a group of Yuquí. Five arrows were shot at the Yuras, and Cristóbal Blanco, brother to Francisco and Orlando, was hit by an arrow but is not in serious condition. His brothers commented that they fired a rifle in the air and scared the nomads away."

After that report, Dick also learned that a few days earlier, other Yura hunters had been out near the Chimoré River where they came upon a nomad camp that was in use, although no people were present. They reported that there were cooking pots, empty cans, and bows and arrows in it. There was also a human skull painted orange with achiote there in the camp.

Two weeks later, the story about Cristóbal's shooting began to change. His condition was deteriorating, and a week after he was shot, his brothers took him to Nueva Vida to see Nurse Margarita, Marge Day. She was able to treat him for several days and got the bleeding stopped. While he was there, Marge learned a more accurate version of what had really happened. Cristóbal had been with a group of ten or more Yura men, women, and children who had decided to try and make a friendly contact with the Yuquí. They went to the Chimoré River and found an active nomad camp, but there was no one in the camp.

As they left the camp and started off through the jungle, one of the women in their group encountered one of the Yuquí women. Both women screamed, bringing men from both parties running on the double. That's when the nomads shot at least five arrows, one of them narrowly missing a Yura boy and another impacting Cristóbal. Cristóbal admitted to Marge, "After I was wounded, I shot at the savages with my rifle, and one of the savages screamed like he was hit."

After Cristóbal was shot, the director of the Yura government-operated mission, about an hour downriver from Marge Day's farm, canoed up to Todos Santos, looking for guns, ammunition, and men to form a posse and accompany the Yuras on a trip into the jungle to find and kill the nomads. Once again, Les sent a letter to prayer partners, asking them to pray that the Yuquí might be preserved to hear the Gospel message and even before partners in distant lands received the request. God answered.

Les wrote:

> God has once again undertaken in protecting the Yuquí. The director of the Yura mission came to town and gathered up twenty rifles, planning to take a posse into the jungle and kill the nomads. When the police chief heard about it, he came and asked me to take him down to the Yura settlement in our aluminum boat so

he could verify this report. When he discovered it to be true, he gave orders that the posse *not* go in until permission was received from the authorities in Cochabamba, the departmental seat. Then, as we left and headed upriver, once we were out of hearing of the Yuras, the police chief told me to have our mission representative in Cochabamba go to the authorities and asked them not to allow the commission to go in. This I did. The police chief also sent a radiogram to the authorities asking them not to issue the permission. This is a real answer to prayer. The fact that God is causing the highest authority in Todos Santos to take it on himself to do this is incredible. This man has the power of life and death here, and he has taken the side of the nomads! Praise God!

The following day, the police chief came back at Les' house to make sure he had communicated with the mission representative in Cochabamba. Les assured him he had done so. The chief enthusiastically commented, "Fine! Fine! We've received nothing yet, but a radiogram came for the director of the Yura settlement, and I read it. It told him *not* to send in a commission."

The next day, the chief of police came back to see Les again and informed him, "I have received orders both from the mayor and the police commander in Cochabamba telling me to direct the Yuras and their leader *not* to form the commission."

Les wrote, "I really believe that God is giving the Yuquí another opportunity to hear the Gospel. We pray they may accept us this time and cooperate with us in every way. Praise God for His power to accomplish that which He wills!"

Now it became even more evident that friendship with the Yuquí would have to be attempted from the Chimoré River as the Bolivian Army had taken over the clearing in La Jota where the missionary team had their first encounters with the nomads. Returning there was no longer an option. The forty-five soldiers who were based at La Jota were busy clearing land and planting crops while awaiting an additional one hundred troops who were to arrive any day.

New roads being built into the area would bring additional colonists and lessen the area in which the nomads could roam. Rumor had it that the soldiers in La Jota were "ready to do battle with the savages if they go back up that way again." At the moment, the Yuquí were roaming farther north, in the area where Cristóbal had been shot, but rainy season was due in a month or two, and typically, that was when they would come back into the area where the soldiers were now based. This was a recipe for disaster!

The engine had yet to be installed in the houseboat, so it would still take weeks or months until the missionaries could be on their way to the Chimoré to renew the contact effort. The delays were a cause of impatience with some on the missionary team, but there wasn't much Les could do to speed the progress. He wrote to a friend:

> It seems like everything is *Mañana! Mañana! Mañana!* We were told that we couldn't load the engine into the launch until high water came. Then two days ago we had a real good rise in the river. But when I asked if we would be able to put the engine in the contractor said, "No, we must wait until I get back from my trip to Brazil." How long would that be? Possibly a month! So, it looks like our "big moment" is still "tomorrow." If it isn't one thing holding us up it's something else. It took five months to get the lumber and start building the launch; now it has been almost a year since the launch was put into the river with the hull completed, but we weren't able to find an engine. Now we have the engine and it's a trip to Brazil causing delay! I do believe God is in this and that He is allowing the delays so we don't get back into contact with the nomads until He has prepared their hearts.

Five weeks later, the engine was finally installed in El Chori, and a new set of problems arose. Adapting a D2 Caterpillar engine for use in a river barge proved to be a bigger challenge than any of them had anticipated. Without going into detail, they had magneto problems, clutch issues, propeller difficulties, fuel system challenges—the list could go on and on as they tried to "get the bugs worked out," as Les phrased it. Some of the issues were minor, whereas others were major enough that parts had to be sent to Cochabamba to be machined and then returned to Todos Santos, each of them causing a time-consuming delay.

Six weeks went by as they worked on the challenges of the propulsion system for the launch, and during that time, they saw God working to spare the Yuquí. It was the height of rainy season when normally the nomads would have come into the La Jota area, not knowing that three detachments of soldiers were waiting to attack and kill them. Signs of the Yuquí were seen farther north, near the mouth of the Chimoré River, but so far, they had stayed out of the "killing zone."

The nomads were also reported to be stealing bananas from the Yura farms to the north, and once again, there was talk of a commission following their trails and killing them. The area was far enough from major settlements that there was no follow up, just talk. The director of the Yuracaré settlement downriver stopped by Les' house while in town to let Les know that he had convinced the Yura not to go looking for the nomads as the missionary boat was just about ready, and they would be leaving very soon to look for the Yuquí.

Dry Season Delays Departure

EVENTUALLY, THE HOUSEBOAT EL CHORI was completed, loaded with supplies, foodstuff, and personal effects, ready for a two-month trip over to the Chimoré River to try and renew contact with the nomads. It had taken two years to reach this point, far longer than anyone had anticipated, but now dry season had set in, so they would need to wait for rain upriver and a rise in water level to be able to leave Todos Santos. Lois had planned to travel with the men on the launch, but now the children were on school vacation, so she would stay in town with the two girls while sixteen-year-old Alan would accompany the men on the boat. Alan would have the task of baking bread for the men, keeping them supplied with that staple.

Dry season lived up to its name as the missionary team waited in Todos Santos for sufficient water to head down the Chapare River. Three months went by, but the water level remained low. Les' spiritual son, Álvaro, was doing his year of obligatory military service in Todos Santos, and the commandant sent him, along with five other soldiers and one civilian, out to hunt and fish along the Chimoré River, hoping they could get meat to feed the soldiers in town. The seven men hiked from Todos Santos to the Chimoré, planning to be back in about five days. Hunting and fishing were poor, so they stayed an extra day and were loaded down with fish as they started back to town.

They had only walked three kilometers when it began to "rain" arrows. They started to run, but as quickly as the nomads could fit more arrows to their bows, another volley of arrows would rain down on them, then another, and another. The poor soldiers had only two ancient army rifles among them plus a single-shot .22 caliber rifle Les had loaned Álvaro for hunting turkeys. The corporal had one of the rifles but panicked and couldn't get the rifle off safety. The other soldier with a rifle managed to get his off safety and fired.

The nomads briefly backed off, but soon, arrows started flying again. A bamboo-tipped arrow struck the lone civilian in the back below the right shoulder blade, going in at a steep angle, which kept the eighteen-inch length of the arrow tip from penetrating the chest cavity. Another arrow hit one of the soldiers in the pack on his back. Fortunately, the arrow impacted the five-gallon cooking oil can full of fish he was carrying, and while the force of the arrow knocked him down, he wasn't wounded.

One of the soldiers was very nearsighted and had no glasses. All through the attack and confusion, he kept asking, "What's going on? What's going on? What's going on?"

Les had given Álvaro twenty-three shells for the little .22 caliber rifle, but in the confusion, while trying to get the bottle open, it broke, and he lost all but five shells which happened to land in his pocket. As the soldiers reached a small stream where they had to cross single file on a log, Álvaro shot the five .22 caliber shells into the air, hoping to keep the nomads at bay while the soldiers crossed over.

The soldier who was hit in the pack and knocked down was a young man from La Jota. While living in La Jota, Harold Rainey had Bible studies with him and his brothers, and he had accepted Christ but later drifted away from God and was running with a bad crowd. After his close brush with death, he told the missionaries, "I'm going to live closer to God." His father had also come to faith while the missionaries had been working in La Jota.

Les had been visiting with Don Trifón and said to him, "I wouldn't walk these jungle trails if I didn't know Christ as my Savior. It's just too dangerous! At any minute, a person might get an arrow in his back and be in eternity without another chance to accept Christ."

That conversation helped Don Trifón see his need for a Savior. He later died, not from an arrow, but from tuberculosis, which was prevalent among the ex-miners. The wounded civilian was brought to Les for treatment, and after filling the wound with sulfa powder, Les closed it with butterfly stitches. A doctor later followed up with additional treatment.

Two days later, word came through the mission office in Santa Cruz that a soldier had been shot by nomads on the upper Ichilo River at the small village of Puerto Grether. This was a different group of nomads as there were several rivers that would need to be crossed to get to this area, and the nomads rarely crossed major rivers. Leroy Lindahl, World Gospel Mission pilot, flew in to Todos Santos in a Cessna 180 and took Les and Bob Garland over to Puerto Grether to talk with the army commander there and see what they could learn. On the way, they used the opportunity to fly along the Chimoré River and look for smoke that might indicate where the Yuquí in that area might be camped. It was midday with no smoke visible at that hour. They had wanted an earlier flight when smoke might have been visible, but rain delayed the flight.

After leaving the Chimoré River, they made a right turn to the southeast and followed the Ichilo River. Three bends up, they spotted a new airstrip being built by a wealthy sugar magnate who wanted a place to get away from the city for hunting and fishing. Two curves farther up the river, they flew over the tiny village of Puerto Villaroel, some ten houses huddled between yet another airstrip and a bend in the river. An oil refinery had been established here in the middle of nowhere for refining crude oil and shipping the refined products down river to the eastern portion of Bolivia. The missionaries were hoping to use the airstrip in this hamlet for supply flights once they began working along the Chimoré River. There was no road in or out of the village.

As they flew from Puerto Villaroel to Puerto Grether, they saw only one very isolated farm along the entire sixty-five-kilometer stretch of the Ichilo River. Puerto Grether consisted of a small airstrip paralleling the bank of the river with a single row of houses nestled behind it. The total population was sixty people while the army base consisted of a few mud huts. As the missionaries exited the Cessna, they were greeted by half the people in town who, on hearing of the reason for their visit, took them to see the army officer in charge. Dense jungle came right up to the edge of town, and the commandant explained that a group of soldiers had been clearing jungle to plant additional crops just a stone's throw from his house when two arrows came flying at one of the soldiers, one of which hit him in the back.

There was a rutted, muddy, dirt track leading out of the village to the city of Santa Cruz, and the man had been transported down this road on a farm truck to the city for treatment. The arrows had also been taken to town, so they weren't available to see. The commandant was able to give a good description of the arrows, one of which was feathered with an eagle feather. It wasn't often the nomads came this far south, and the consensus in town was that this was a small hunting party who had come from the Rio Víbora area, ten kilometers to the north. The Rio Víbora dumped into the Ichilo River about six river bends below Puerto Grether and was notorious not only for the nomads who roamed that area, but also for the abundance of electric eels in that river.

The small Cessna flew the men back from Puerto Grether to Todos Santos, and later, Les wrote:

> As we flew along looking down at the jungle, rivers, lakes, swamps, and streams that all look so peaceful and friendly from the air, it gave me a feeling that we were flying over the area that God has given us to occupy for Christ. It was good to get out there and hear of all the groups of nomads still roaming in this large area. It's a challenge we eagerly face.

Later, as the team discussed the opportunities, they realized they had heard of at least six groups of nomads in the area. How could they most effectively find and befriend these people before encroaching oilmen, hunters, farmers, and loggers killed them all off? Could they leave gifts in one area, then go to another location, leaving gifts there, and then go to a third area and leave gifts there, going back to check each area until they found gifts missing, and then center their efforts there? Was there any way to speed up the process?

They were still stuck in Todos Santos, waiting for the river to rise, but they weren't idle. People here also needed to hear of Christ and His free gift of salvation. One week, the missionary team went house to house, passing out Pocket Testament League Gospels of John. They passed out 255 of the booklets. When colonists in the surrounding area heard of the free books, others came to town and requested copies. One farmer showed up and asked Les for a booklet. "What booklet are you wanting?"

"The free book of Saint Anthony," came the reply.

Les was apologetic, "I'm sorry, it was the Book of Saint John we were giving out, but we have no more at the moment. Would you like a Gospel of Matthew?"

"I already have that one," the disappointed farmer let him know.

The clutch for the launch was still giving issues, so the decision was made to take it back to Cochabamba and have a replacement bearing installed. With the lack of water in the river, they couldn't leave for the Chimoré, so why not improve the boat and avoid mechanical issues later when they might be in a remote location?

Les boarded a farm truck for the dangerous trip to Cochabamba. Shortly after passing the summit of the road, some 15,840 feet up, another truck came up behind the one he was traveling on. The other vehicle was impatient to pass and honked repeatedly to let them know. The unpaved road was one lane only with occasional wide spots for a truck to pull over and let another go by, but at the time, they were in a very narrow stretch of road.

In a kilometer or so, there was a pullout, and the impatient truck hurried to pass and was soon out of sight around a bend as he rushed on his way. As the truck Les was on came around the same bend, there sat the impatient truck crossways in the road with his front wheels just a few feet from going over a cliff, which would have plunged it 1,000 feet or more down to the bottom of a chasm. The steering tie-rod had broken, and the driver lost control.

He was already out of the truck, looking very frightened. Ten or twelve passengers were still climbing out when the truck Les was on pulled up and stopped behind them. Les always carried Gospel tracts in Spanish. Pulling out a handful of tracts entitled "God's Simple Plan of Salvation" he headed for the people who had nearly lost their lives. He gave a tract to the driver first and commented, "Thanks to

God you aren't in eternity at this moment. You might want to read this brochure before you go any further."

Then Les went on and handed out tracts to the rest of the passengers. After pushing the truck back to where it wasn't blocking the road, the passengers re-boarded the truck Les was traveling on and headed on their way. From his spot on the back of the truck, he looked behind and saw some of the passengers from the other truck reading their tracts. Les wrote:

> I can't help but feel that God permitted the clutch bearing to burn out in order to have me there just at the right time to get the Gospel to those people whom I'd never seen before and may never see again this side of eternity.

On the Move at Last

EVENTUALLY, THE LAUNCH WAS OPERABLE, and rains raised the river level to where the missionary team was able to depart Todos Santos for the Chimoré River. Once they arrived, Les wrote:

> It almost seems like a dream! Here we are on the Ichilo River only a few curves above the mouth of the Chimoré River. This is what we have been working toward for these many months, to get back into position to start making contacts again with the Yuquí tribe.

It had taken two and a half years for this accomplishment to take place, far longer than any of the missionary team had ever imagined. They had done their best to speed things along, but clearly God had His reasons for allowing the delays.

When they had departed Todos Santos in *El Chori* eight days before, they were riding just behind a crest of high water that had passed during the night and knew they would soon catch up to the peak and have to tie up and wait, or the water ahead of them would be insufficient. Dick Strickler was navigating, following their progress on the map; Bob Smith was engineer, sitting by the diesel engine to make speed changes when signaled by the pilot; Bob Garland was sailor and deckhand, while Les piloted the boat, and Lois assisted in the pilot house and cooked meals for the men.

After the second day of travel, they had to tie up early and wait for the water to catch up as they had gotten so far ahead of the flood crest that they were striking too many sandbars. The following day, they continued on, arriving at the mouth of the Chapare River where they made a sharp right turn into the Ichilo River. Now they were headed southeast, making slow progress as they inched their way up this much larger river against the flow of water coming down from the Andean foothills. Even so, they were overjoyed to be out of the "trap" of Todos Santos.

The second day on the Ichilo River, they met a canoe with a hunting party and stopped to ask if they had seen any signs of the nomads. The hunters reported that four curves upriver, there was a small stream up which they had seen fresh signs of the Yuquí. Arriving at the stream, the missionaries unloaded the small aluminum boat from the roof of the launch and, using their outboard motor, went up the stream looking for trails coming down to the water's edge, indicating that the nomads had been camped nearby. There were three likely spots, but each proved to have been made either by tapir or by Bolivian hunters as they came into the area to hunt tigers and alligators.

The next day, they came upon another stream on the west bank of the Ichilo River and went up it in the aluminum boat, looking for trails coming to the water's edge. As they went into this stream, they found the current running with them instead of against them, which meant the Ichilo River was flooding back into the jungle. They went for a full hour, and eventually, the small stream exited into a big beautiful lake two miles long and half a mile wide. In the marshy areas, huge flocks of ducks fed.

Wild turkeys flew from tree to tree above the vine-covered high jungle. Ferns and little grassy glades gave the jungle a fairy-tale look. What a beautiful lake! This would be an ideal place for the nomads to hunt and might be a good place to bring them when establishing a farm and mission station. They motored slowly along one side of the lake, looking for trails down to the water and then came back along the other side. All three men saw it at once! There was a narrow trail and a tree limb whose bark had been stripped off. They stopped to investigate further. It appeared to have been a Yuracaré Indian hunting party as there was a tiger trap like the nationals make. It was built of heavy palm logs held up by a pole hooked to a trigger. As the tiger grabs the meat bait, the weight of

250 pounds or more of logs falls on him and he is crushed. The three men followed the trail a short distance into the jungle and found a campsite but no evidence that the nomads had been in the area.

Seven days after leaving Todos Santos, the missionary team arrived at Puerto Yuca. This new grass airstrip had been built by a wealthy businessman from Santa Cruz. He owned the San Aurelio sugar refinery and had the airstrip and base built as a retreat where he could come to fish and hunt from time to time. He had also built a very nice wooden, screened-in house as well as rustic housing for a caretaker. His large banana plantation might be of help in providing bananas once contact was made with the Yuquí. Also, as the nearest airstrip to the Chimoré River, it would be useful when the missionaries needed to transport supplies or personnel in or out. They had been planning to use the airstrip at Puerto Villaroel, farther upriver, but when they went to see that airstrip, they found it to be overgrown and no longer operable. God had given them an airstrip much closer than they had anticipated.

The day after they arrived at Puerto Yuca was Sunday, and one of the ladies living there showed up at the launch first thing in the morning. She wanted Lois to come and have a Sunday school lesson with her children. Lois was happy to oblige and followed the woman up to the few houses but was back at the launch in just a few minutes. "Honey, there are several young men up there, and they would also like to be taught."

Les followed her up to the houses and began conversing with some of the young men. There were twenty-eight workers on-site, finishing up the houses, airstrip, and plantation. As Les met with them, he found one young man who was a believer but admitted he had been timid about witnessing to his fellow workers. Les took the opportunity to give a fifteen-minute Bible message to those who were interested and then followed up by explaining as simply as he could God's plan of salvation.

When Les finished speaking, the young, "timid" believer asked, "Would you mind if I clarify one part of what you said?" He spoke for about an hour, after which Les invited those who might be interested in trusting in Christ to speak with him individually. Three of those present accepted the Lord as their Savior. The angels in heaven were rejoicing that day, as were the missionaries!

Christmas 1963

IT WAS CHRISTMAS SEASON AND the children would have a month-long vacation from boarding school. The launch was moored on the east bank of the Chimoré River, and the missionary men had begun cutting trails westward from the river into the belts of jungle where the Yuquí roamed, hanging gifts with long white streamers for them. There wasn't room on the houseboat for all the families, so the wives and children would stay in Todos Santos over the holidays while the men continued the contact effort on the Chimoré.

There was one exception. Alan would fly to Puerto Yuca when Lois flew out and would travel with the men on the boat. Living on a houseboat was wonderful for a sixteen-year-old as it meant he could have a fishing line in the water 24/7, and oh, the glory of fishing in virgin waters! Fish that were larger than he! Hunting was also fabulous—turkeys, ducks, monkeys, and much, much more!

The launch was moored four bends up the Chimoré River from its mouth on the east side of the river. Daily, the men crossed over and cut trail westward from the other bank while Alan and one man stayed on the boat to keep an eye on it and to fix meals. The team had no aerial photos or maps of this area, so they would cut westward only to run into an old lagoon or a dense patch of jungle that was impassable. After eight hours of cutting with a machete, they could walk the freshly cut trail in sixteen minutes.

When they hit a swamp or lagoon, they sometimes tried climbing a tree to see which way to go, but it was impossible to get high enough above the surrounding foliage to see anything. One day, they picked up an old trail with a few machete cuts along it but weren't sure if it had been made by Bolivian hunters or by the nomads. It petered out quickly and was of no help.

On one supply trip over to Puerto Yuca, they met Don Ramón Gutierrez, the owner and sugar refinery magnate. By this time, he had constructed a very comfortable screened-in house with electric generator, two-way radio, several boats, and other amenities. He had plans to invite the president of Bolivia, Señor Victor Paz Estenssoro, out for a visit, and with his friendships, it was likely that would happen.

Don Ramón graciously offered the use of his airstrip to the missionary team and assured them they were welcome not only to the bananas on his plantation at no charge but could also freely take banana bulbs (rhizomes) to start their own plantation. He also invited them to stay in his nice house if it was unused when they came on supply runs. He was not only generous with the missionaries but appreciative of what they were doing.

For two weeks, the team had been cutting trail, daily hoping to come across Yuquí camps or trails. But each day, they ran into impassable swamps blocking their way. Finally, they circled around to the south, and after crossing a low, rather swampy area, hit a vein of high open jungle, which they followed for two days before again coming into a low tangle of vines and a swamp. Circling farther to the west and south, they were able to skirt the swamp and came on a very low animal trail, a tapir trail going into the swamp.

As they followed this trail, cutting as necessary with their machetes, they came out of the swamp onto a grassy spot leading into a vein of high vine-covered jungle on the other side of the swamp. Coming out of the grassy spot, they found where a tree had been felled, making a bridge to cross the water on one side of the swamp. Someone had been here at some time! They walked across the tree-bridge and found themselves in the middle of an old nomad camp!

This was the first Yuquí camp they had found since moving to the Chimoré River. There was great excitement as they hung a gift for the nomads in the camp.

Moving beyond the camp, they went a mile farther, following a nomad trail consisting of a broken twig here and there when suddenly they were brought up short by shouts in the distance. They stopped, listening, thinking it might be the nomads coming back along their trail. But as they waited, the shouts seemed to get farther and farther away until they receded into silence. After following the Yuquí trail a short distance farther, they headed back to the river where they had left the little aluminum boat.

When the men arrived back at the river, they learned what the shouting had been. While they had been combing the forest, the river had suddenly risen and endangered the aluminum boat. It had gotten caught under a tree limb and was gradually being forced down into the water as the river rose, thus being in imminent danger of sinking. Bob Garland and Alan had been watching the aluminum boat through field glasses from the launch and could see this happening, so finally, Bob donned his swimming trunks and a life vest and went upriver, cutting his way along the bank with a machete. At last he felt he was far enough upstream to start swimming across. But as he swam out into the terrible current of the flooding river, he was swept far downstream. He called upon God for strength to make it to the other bank and finally made it to the other side far down river. Then he had to find his way, with no machete, slowly through the thick vine-tangled jungle back upriver to where the aluminum boat was tied.

When he finally reached the boat, he found the river was within an inch of going over the side and sinking it. He was able to get the boat out from under the limb and retied it in a safe place and then followed his coworker's trail into the jungle, looking for them. He reached the end of their cut trail and found nothing further as they had followed a compass heading that morning and hadn't left much of a trail. He stood there and yelled and yelled, which is what the other men heard and thought might be the nomads calling. Finally, he gave up and went back to the river and the boat to wait.

Meanwhile, Alan was alone on the launch, watching monstrous trees go charging down the turbulent river, hoping that one of them didn't snag the launch and sweep him and it away.

Daily, the small band of intrepid missionaries continued exploring the jungle to the west, hoping to find Yuquí camps or trails they regularly used. Sometimes they were able to use the aluminum boat to follow small streams inland before leaving the boat and proceeding on foot. They had heard, from Bolivian hunters, of a lake the nomads frequented as they hunted and fished, so they followed a small stream they believed to be the drainage for the lake. After going a short distance into the stream, they found it too shallow to proceed, and it wasn't wide enough to turn the boat around, so Les put the outboard motor into reverse and backed his way slowly out of the waterway.

As he neared the mouth of the stream, the outboard motor hit something that felt like a log, but it was no log; an eight-foot-long alligator came shooting out of the water, ran across the bank for a short distance, and then dove back into the water.

A few days later, the water level had risen substantially, so the men followed the same stream inland. This time, they were able to proceed for an hour before coming to a place where bamboo leaves had been tied up, creating a blockage across the stream. This looked suspiciously like an ambush such as the nomads were known to set. They would block a stream or trail, and when a person came to a halt, the warriors would be waiting to shoot arrows into them. The men didn't linger at the blockage.

Meat was not in short supply. Alan, Les' son, kept a line in the water day and night and caught an abundance of fish. He was quite pleased when he pulled out a thirty-seven-pound red-tailed Amazon catfish, his largest fish to date. When the men were not on the trail, they would also hunt on the east side of the river where the nomads didn't roam. Four types of wild turkeys and three types of wild duck were plentiful.

Other animals included two types of peccaries (javelina pigs), capybara (the world's largest rodent), and many types of monkeys, parrots, and other animals and birds. The men killed a large

Alan with seventy-pound red-tailed Amazon catfish he caught.

tortoise, and after taking the meat to eat, Les put the shell on an ant's nest near the riverbank so the ants would clean off the fragments of meat, and it could be used as a decorative flowerpot.

During the night, Yogi, the Fosters' dog, began to bark, and there was a loud splash in the river. Les shone a light out the boat window but could see nothing; however, in the morning, the turtle shell was gone, and a set of alligator tracks could be seen leading from where the shell had been, back into the river.

* * * * *

Les stood on the front deck of the houseboat, watching the steam rise from the river and filter its way into the dense jungle wall on either bank of the river. It was hard to imagine that it was only three days until Christmas. You could hardly ask for a less Christmas-like atmosphere—the hot, humid jungle and a temperature hovering near one hundred degrees. But the true Christmas spirit was easily captured as he thought of Jesus who was born for one reason—to die for him that he might live. What a message of hope!

He was anxious to share that message with the Yuquí. How much longer would it be until friendship would be established and they could learn the language well enough to share the message of the Savior?

The Christmas holidays were ending, and Alan would be heading back to boarding school after the most thrilling school vacation he had ever had. Spending a month on the *El Chori* launch while Dick Strickler, Bob Smith, Bob Garland, and Les Foster spent days cutting trails into the jungle, looking for the Yuquí Indians, had been exhilarating. None of his classmates had such a unique vacation.

Now it was Friday, and classes were to resume on Monday. He climbed into the small aluminum boat for the first leg of the trip back to school, the river trip to Puerto Yuca. A Bolivian Air Force Cessna would be flying Alan and his dad out to Santa Cruz from where Alan would take a bus on to Tambo, the mission boarding school. Bob Garland was also going along to see his family.

The Cessna could haul three passengers. The men climbed in and fastened their seat belts, looking forward to climbing to a cooler altitude and away from the ever-present biting insects. The starter ground as the pilot cranked the engine, and the first sign of trouble greeted them. A stream of black smoke came drifting from the cowling as the engine came to life, and wind from the propeller fanned the smoke into roaring flames. The men and Alan exited the aircraft, grabbed their suitcases, and ran to the edge of the airstrip, expecting the airplane to explode in a cloud of gasoline-fed flames. The pilot cut the ignition, shut off the engine, climbed out of the airplane, and began throwing rags and water on the engine. After a few heart-stopping moments, the fire was under control. Thankfully, it had been confined to the engine compartment, consuming wiring and flammable parts around the engine.

The airplane survived but would need considerable work before it was once again airworthy. The men would need to spend the night at Puerto Yuca. The following day, another small plane arrived, bringing an air force mechanic to look at the damaged plane, and Alan was able to fly out. Les and Bob had to wait for a later flight. Everyone agreed that a fire on the ground was preferable to what could have happened had they been airborne at the time.

* * * * *

A new year arrived, and Les and Lois Foster along with Bob Garland, flew back to Puerto Yuca. Before heading on to the Chimoré River, they made the short river trip up to Puerto Villaroel to collect banana bulbs for planting. These would be the beginning of the plantation with which they hoped to feed the nomads and keep them away from the colonies.

Bananas grow quickly in the tropics, and within twelve months, these plants should be producing and sending up many new shoots. Once they arrived back on the Chimoré, several days of clearing jungle was necessary before the bananas could be planted. Between the rows of banana plants, the men also planted Cuban field corn. They already knew that the Yuquí loved corn, and they could utilize the cleared area to grow a crop of corn while the bananas grew to maturity. Their "gift farm" was planted; now they needed to wait for it to produce.

They had chosen a site along one of the nomad trails leading to an old abandoned camp they had found a month before. They also left gifts in the abandoned camp, in the cleared farm area, and on the west bank of the Chimoré River where the trail ended. The launch was moored on the east bank directly across from the gift trail where they could keep an eye on it with binoculars. At any minute of any day, the Yuquí could find the gift trail in the jungle, follow it to the river's edge, and contact might be resumed.

While waiting, the missionaries cut several hunting trails on their side, the east side of the river. Not only did they need meat, but once contact was made with the Yuquí, they wanted to become an invaluable asset to the nomads by providing them with meat. Since meat was the most important item in the nomad's diet, they felt they would be better accepted by the Yuquí if they were able to help them in their search for food. Especially with the hungry nomads, there was truth to the statement, "The way to a man's heart is through his stomach!"

They would need to keep the Yuquí in the area over the long-term if they were to master the language and calm the angry warriors. Feeding them would be the best way to accomplish that.

By the end of January, supplies were running dangerously low, and due to the quantity needed, having supplies flown in was not an option. Since this was the height of rainy season, it was a good time to take the launch back to Todos Santos and pick up three-months' worth of food and fuel. The first two days of travel were downriver and very pleasant since the hordes of mosquitoes couldn't fly as fast as the boat was moving; but by the third day, as they headed up the Chapare River, the mosquitoes once again found the boat.

Lois hid in the radio room, the only room on the boat screened to keep insects out, while the men were all busy keeping the house-boat running, so they had to face the insect horde.

Once they arrived in Todos Santos, Dick would remain to keep an eye on the boat while Bob headed to Tambo, the boarding school, to see his wife and family. Mary was teaching there while Bob was in the jungle. Les and Lois would go to Cochabamba to purchase supplies and bring them back to Todos Santos, after which they would all head back to the Chimoré River contact site. They hoped that by the time they arrived back, the corn would be almost mature.

Six weeks later, the team arrived back on the Chimoré River and right away faced a measure of disappointment. While they were gone, their farm clearing had flooded to a depth of two feet, and all the corn had been killed. Other areas of nearby jungle had been underwater, even deeper, five or six feet. Clearly, this was not a good location to settle with the Yuquí.

Two months previously, Les had written to a friend who worked with one of the oil companies that had done exploration in the area to see if he could help get aerial photos of the area. The earlier photos the missionaries had obtained didn't include this area. The photos could be useful in establishing where the higher belts of jungle were. He was still waiting for a reply.

In the meantime, with flood levels clearly visible on the trees, the men would go up and down the river, looking for a higher area that either hadn't flooded or had only been a few inches under water.

Their first trip took them about two and a half hours upriver by aluminum boat. As they headed back down to the launch, their seven and a half horsepower Johnson outboard motor started running slower and slower and finally, with a rattling sound, cut out altogether. Les removed the plugs and looked into the cylinders to see if he could tell what was wrong. In the top piston, there was a lot of melted aluminum and aluminum filings. It was clear that the motor needed major repair!

Fortunately, they were upriver from the houseboat, not down, so they were able to paddle their way back, arriving just before dark. They were thankful to not be spending the night on the riverbank in the dark with no flashlights. But now they had no way to go up and down the river, looking for high ground and keeping an eye on their gift trails. The next morning, Les was on the radio, ordering a new outboard motor. Sadly, it would take two or three months to have one sent down from the States!

Rainy season was drawing to an end, so the risks of taking the houseboat up the Chimoré River and getting stranded there for months was too great. Now when they most needed the outboard motor, they no longer had it.

As Les once again considered the many obstacles they had faced over the last three years, God led him to Psalm 55:22, which he read in the Amplified Old Testament,* a birthday gift from his wife.

"Cast your burden on the Lord [releasing the weight of it] and He will sustain you; He will never allow the [consistently] righteous to be moved (made to slip, fall or fail)."

Releasing the weight of it—that is what stood out as he realized that God was trying to teach him to give his burdens, even the burdens of the work, over to Him, then release the weight of it and let God do the worrying about it. So after praying and doing this, Les dropped the weight and decided to write letters instead of worrying.

It had only been two months since Les had written to Jack Chavez about the need for aerial photographs, so Les was pleasantly surprised when Bruce Porterfield called by radio to let him know that a parcel of "photo maps" had arrived in Cochabamba. "We'll get these to you the next time we do an airdrop of mail," Bruce offered.

Since Les was in the jungle with no immediate way to send letters out, Bruce continued, "I'll let Jack know how grateful we are to him for his help and give him a little update on the contact effort."

"Thanks for taking care of that, Bruce. I don't know what we'd do without you there to help us," Les responded.

With few other options, the team decided to trust God to provide water when needed and took the houseboat up the Chimoré River. They planned to stay up there for a month and hope that dry season didn't cause them to get stranded up there. Once in place, they could paddle the aluminum boat across the river and keep an eye on the gift trail near their farm as well as cut trails into other nearby areas.

---

* 1 Scripture quotations taken from the Amplified® Bible (AMPC), Copyright © 1954, 1958, 1962, 1964, 1965, 1987 by The Lockman Foundation Used by permission. www.Lockman.org

It was risky, but they were anxious to encounter the nomads. Bob Smith was having health issues related to the tropical conditions and felt that he would need to leave the team and find a more temperate climate in which to work, so the team was also praying about a replacement for him.

The launch was moored eight hours up from the mouth of the Chimoré River on the east bank of the river. On the west bank, the men had cut an eight-kilometer-long trail in a northwesterly direction to a site that seemed to be frequented by the nomads. There was an abandoned campsite, several trails, a palm from which the heart had been cut and eaten, and a place where palm fruit had been gathered. Judging from the degree of green left in the palm leaves, the men estimated the nomads had been in the area as recently as three weeks previously.

If the Yuquí didn't show up in the next three weeks, the missionaries would need to leave the area while the river was still navigable and would be gone for at least six weeks until they could get a new outboard motor, resupply, and make the return trip. By then, the nomads would likely have gone north to the low swampy area they seemed to frequent during the dry season.

A recent radio report suggested the nomads were currently in an area about sixteen kilometers to the northwest of the missionary base. That gave cause for some optimism as the missionary gift trail headed that direction and went almost half the distance. The Yuquí could easily stumble across the trail on one of their daily hunting trips and would doubtless recognize the gifts as the handiwork of the missionary team and be desirous of coming for other useful items.

Les wrote to a friend:

> Wow is it hot today! Today tops all the days for the last few weeks. I see the clouds beginning to gather around the Andes mountains, so maybe we'll get a cooling rain. As I sit here at the typewriter the sweat runs down my arms and drips off my elbows, making little puddles on the floor on both sides of the chair.

When the missionaries weren't checking gift trails, writing letters, or doing boat maintenance, often they would go hunting. Les was thrilled when he shot his first collared peccary and wrote:

> I got my first wild boar here on the Chimoré day before yesterday. It was a 50-pound package of clicking teeth and clawing hoofs. Last Saturday Lois and I took a walk out through the jungle to check some steel traps I had set out some days before. Each day I went out and checked them in the morning and again in the afternoon. This time Lois went along. We went past a mound of freshly dug dirt that had come from an animal's den. On our way out, we saw there were no tracks in this dirt but on the way back an hour later there were fresh wild pig tracks on the mound. I left Lois there with the shotgun and turned to go out and bring the traps in with the idea of setting them here on the mound instead of out where they had been on a little trail. I had gone only about 30 yards when a pig grunted loudly and ran away into the jungle. He had been right near the trail watching us, but I didn't see him until he ran and didn't get a shot at him.
>
> On Tuesday I went out into the same area with my shotgun loaded with number 5B shot shell. I sat down and waited quietly for half an hour. About then I heard an animal eating over to my left, but the jungle was so dense in that direction that I couldn't see what it was. I continued to sit silently, waiting in case it wandered into my line of vision. Sure enough, in about two minutes here came this wild boar out from behind a clump of trees and vines. I pulled the gun up and let him have it in the head. He was about 15 or 20 yards from me. He went down

onto his haunches and started viciously clacking his teeth while looking around to see from which side his enemy was coming. I jumped up, reloaded with the first shell I could lay my hands on, which turned out to be a number four shot (for turkeys, monkeys, partridge, and other small game) but this stunned him to where he no longer wanted to fight, but rather turned to run. I fumbled in my shirt pocket and this time grabbed a number two shot shell and laid his skull open with this shot. The three shots had been so close together and were heard at the launch, that they triggered the fellows into action. Three shots in rapid succession is our signal either that we are being attacked by the nomads or that we have been bitten by a snake, or some other extreme danger is confronting us.

As I came along the trail carrying the boar back toward the launch, I met Bob Smith running wide-eyed down the trail with shotgun in hand. He had heard the shots, but Bob Garland was downriver on the sandbar looking for alligators, so Bob Smith had come in alone to help me. Along the way, as he was thinking of all kinds of things that he might run into (he didn't know yet why I had shot three times) he walked past a group of monkeys. They began to yell, and about scared the liver out of him! He thought that he himself was being attacked by nomads. He was very relieved when he met me on the trail and found that the three shots had only come from normal hunting and not from an emergency. It's incidents like this that keep life interesting!

The next day, after a time of prayer on the front deck of the launch, the three men climbed into the aluminum boat and paddled across the river. Tying the boat to a bamboo stalk, they set out into the jungle on a northwesterly heading. Les led the way with compass in one hand and machete in the other, cutting a minimal trail through the thick undergrowth. Bob Garland came along behind Les, widening the trail slightly and making a blaze mark on one side of each tree as he passed. Dick Strickler followed him, blazing the other side of each tree and cleaning up the trail a little more. Another typical day in the search for the nomads.

A Yura Indian hunting party had told the men that each time they went to a lagoon in this area to hunt tigers, they came across footprints of the nomads. The missionaries calculated that from their launch they could make a trail to the lagoon in five days of cutting. Two hours in, they came upon a stream where they felled a tree as a bridge on which to cross. On the far side of the stream, the jungle was a little more open, and they were able to advance more quickly. At lunchtime, they stopped for a rest, opened two cans of spam, and divided the meat three ways and then, for dessert, had a handful of raisins each. By late afternoon, they entered a low, swampy area, and as cutting grew more difficult, they decided to call it a day and begin afresh the following morning. They had been cutting for eight painful hours but found that it took only eight minutes to walk back to the river.

Six more days of trail cutting found them at last in the area where the nomads roamed. They had been cutting trail along the edge of a swamp on their left, when suddenly, they were brought up short by the sight of freshly cut palm leaves. As they looked closely at the palm tree, they could see that the heart had been cut out for eating. From there, they followed the bent twigs marking the nomad trail and soon came upon a campsite that was only a week old.

Farther along, they found a clump of palm trees where the nomads had gathered fruit. There was still unripe fruit on some of the palms, which led the men to believe that the Yuquí would be back to retrieve the fruit once it had time to ripen. The trek back to the Chimoré River was eight kilometers, and the missionaries left gifts in the nomad camp as well as along the trail leading back to the river. At the river's edge, they hung a gallon can with wire handle and a white streamer on it so it would show up better.

They were confident the nomads would know who had left these gifts for them and would follow the trail to the river. The only question was, would the missionaries still be there waiting for them? The missionary team needed to leave the area within two weeks or risk being trapped for months by low water with no way in or out. They had no outboard motor, and it was too far from the mouth of the Chimoré to park the launch there and paddle up the river to check the gifts.

A month later, they arrived in Todos Santos without having seen the Yuquí. Now they needed to await the arrival of a new outboard motor, gather supplies, spend some time with their families, and recuperate from the grueling rigors of jungle life. They also welcomed the opportunity to study the aerial photos. The airdrop had never happened, so now they could view the photos and see if there was a better location along the Chimoré River to set up a more permanent camp once the Yuquí began visiting them.

Les laid the photos out on the floor and perused the areas where they had been cutting trail. Although one important photo was missing, they could see that had they begun their first trail 500 meters downriver from where they did, they would have missed the big swamp and would have come across the main north-south nomad trail on their first attempt. So much extra work had been entailed by not having the photos earlier.

Three months went by quickly as the team spent time with their families. Les and Alan made an eight-day trip with the launch down and back up the Chapare River, helping Marge Day take the Yura children home after their school term. Then there were general repairs to do on the houseboat as well as a top to bottom cleaning along with a new coat of light-blue paint to preserve the wood.

Alan assisted his father as they built a new bedroom in the pilot house of the launch to accommodate the couple who would be taking Bob and Shirley Smith's place in the work. It was the nicest room on the launch with large airy windows on all four sides and high enough up to catch cooling breezes much of the time.

Now the children would head back to boarding school while their parents purchased supplies and prepared for the next trip to the

Chimoré River. River levels were low, as it was the height of the dry season, but the missionary team wanted to be ready any time rain in the foothills caused a suitable rise in the water level. Once they arrived at the Chimoré, they would need to moor the launch near the mouth of the Chimoré on the Ichilo River and use the aluminum boat with outboard motor to travel up to the site where they had left gifts.

It would be three or four months until the rains once again allowed them to take the launch up the Chimoré River. Now there would be two women on the houseboat as Mildred Presson was accompanying her husband, Bill. Bob Garland, Les and Lois Foster, and Dick Strickler completed the team.

Before the missionaries left Cochabamba, Dick Strickler, who was living on the launch and keeping an eye on things, called by radio to report that unseasonal rains in the foothills had raised river levels to within six feet of the top of the bank. It would take a few days for the water to recede, so odds were there would still be adequate water if the team could get to Todos Santos within the next week. Truckers arriving from Todos Santos reported that there had also been unusual amounts of snowfall in the high Andes, so it was likely the melting snow would maintain water levels in the Chapare River until the team was ready to depart from Todos Santos.

Within two days, eight barrels of fuel, diesel, and gasoline, along with 1,700 pounds of other supplies, had been loaded on a truck for Todos Santos. As Les chatted with truckers and passengers who had recently arrived from the jungle lowlands, he was astonished at what he heard. Due to heavy snowfall and the lack of road equipment, the one-day trip had taken five to six days. Farm trucks loaded with passengers had been caught unprepared at elevations of 15,000 to 17,000 feet for several days.

Now the missionaries would be riding that same road with their cargo, the only way for them to get it to Todos Santos. Delaying until the mountain weather improved could mean missing the high water in the river. Six days later, they had the necessary paperwork from the Captain of the Port of Todos Santos and were headed down the Chapare River, bound for the mouth of the Chimoré.

While there was a little more water in the rivers than usual in dry season due to melting snow in the mountains, there wasn't enough to risk moving the houseboat up the Chimoré River and getting trapped there. The boat was moored within sight of the river mouth, and the women were left on the houseboat while the three men made trips in the aluminum boat up the river, camping on a beach there for several days at a time. The first five-day trip was to weed the banana plantation and check the gift trails. A cold south storm blew in, and the entire trip was a miserable time of being wet and cold.

Bedding was soaked by gusting rainstorms and impossible to get dry. Several of the gifts were missing, but it wasn't clear whether they had been taken by Bolivian hunters or by the nomads. More and more Bolivian hunters were coming into the area as game was abundant, and they were willing to risk a deadly encounter with the nomads for the premium price tiger and alligator hides were currently bringing.

When the men arrived back at the houseboat, they learned that a group of Bolivian hunters had stopped by in their absence and reported signs of the nomads in the area where they had been hunting and trapping. Two days later, the men headed up the Chimoré River once again to look over the section of jungle the hunters had mentioned as well as an area they had taken to calling "number four gift trail." They had left three gifts on that trail seven months before and hadn't been back since.

As they walked the overgrown trail, they found that someone had been using it. There were bent twigs along the trail, the way the nomads broke branches to mark their trails. The trail had a beaten-down look to it as if it had been used quite a bit. Then, about half an hour from the river, they found where a palm tree had been felled by axe and the heart taken out. Farther on, two bee trees had been tapped, one having been felled by axe, and a short way beyond that, a small ambaibo tree had been stripped of bark. The nomads used ambaibo bark for making their bowstrings, hammock ropes, and women's skirts.

Going farther yet, they found still other palm hearts cut out and one more bee tree that had been felled by axe. Arriving at the gift site, the gifts were missing! While the evidence seemed to point predominately toward the nomads having been in the area, it could also have been national tiger hunters. Who had taken the missing gifts? Leaving more gifts along the trail, the men headed back out to the river and the aluminum boat, stopping once more along the way to check the gifts in their banana plantation.

When the men weren't checking gift trails, extending them, or cutting new ones, they continued clearing jungle and planting additional crops as a drawing card for the Yuquí. The men had found a higher section of jungle farther up the Chimoré River, so in addition to the original banana patch, they made a new clearing and planted manioc and more bananas. The farm clearing was about three kilometers from the river where it was less likely to be discovered by national hunters and was very close to an abandoned nomad camp where they were likely to come across it.

Christmas 1964

THE CHRISTMAS SEASON HAD ARRIVED yet again, and the missionary children would be out of school for a month. The houseboat was nearly out of supplies, so it was decided that the children would fly into Puerto Yuca and accompany the missionary team on the houseboat as it made the trip back to Todos Santos to resupply. The houseboat was moored at Puerto Yuca, awaiting the chartered plane that was to bring the children, but rainy season seemed to have begun, and the flight was delayed for a few days.

Eventually, the flight arrived, and the week-long trip to Todos Santos got underway. From time to time, along the way, the boat was moored as the travelers stopped to try out good-looking fishing spots, pick up ducks they had shot, or walk on uninhabited beaches. The record fish on this trip was a seventy-one-pound red-tailed Amazon, abundant in the Ichilo River.

After spending Christmas together in Cochabamba, the Foster family went their separate ways once again. Early in January, the children headed off to boarding school. Anna and Alan would be finishing their last semester of high school before returning to the homeland to adapt to life there. Les, Lois, and their team members were all having medical checkups, shopping, and preparing to head back to Todos Santos. As they purchased supplies, they also bought sheets of corrugated aluminum roofing. They were planning to make a clearing in the jungle and build houses of native materials roofed with aluminum. That way, the families could live on the contact site, and they could begin bringing in supplies by air to Puerto Yuca, rather than living on the launch and having to make lengthy resupply trips to Todos Santos. Bill and Mildred Presson would be delayed in returning since Mildred would be having surgery, so the team would once again be shorthanded.

By mid-February, the houseboat was once again moored up the Chimoré River, and the men had begun checking the gift trails. The trail leading to the manioc patch and beyond was well beaten down, and there were many broken twigs along the trail, but no machete cuts. When the missionaries arrived at the abandoned nomad camp, ten minutes' walk from the river, they found the gift missing. Due to the river's proximity, Les thought it likely that national tiger hunters had taken the gift.

As they continued inland, they found the trail beyond the camp also very beaten down by heavy use, but it wasn't until they came across a small, woven, palm-leaf basket lying right in the trail that their excitement began to rise. As they went on, they found the gift at the manioc patch missing as well as another gift thirty-five minutes farther into the jungle. By now, the trail was beginning to look much less traveled, but as they pressed on, they arrived at the log bridge they had made by falling a tree across the stream and found the gift there was also missing.

They paused to rest for a few minutes before crossing the bridge and, once across, saw what looked like a trail coming in along the stream from the west. Les commented to his two companions, "Maybe on our way back, we can check out that trail. It looks like it could have been made by the nomads."

On they went, stopping eventually to eat lunch and ask God to give them some definite sign which would indicate whether it was national hunters or the nomads who had taken the gifts. They were nearing a large lake where they knew the nomads came often to hunt and fish, and there, one hundred yards short of the end of the trail was the sign they were looking for. Sticking vertically in the middle of the trail was a six-foot-long Yuquí arrow! Praise God! What an answer!

Now the question was, "What did this mean?" Were the Yuquí warning the missionaries away from their territory, letting them know they didn't want friendship? Or were they letting the missionaries know that it was them, not nationals?

Les pulled the arrow out of the trail and inspected it. It was an old one that had been broken and then repaired. He had seen others like it that the nomads were still using. But why leave it behind? The missionaries continued to the end of the trail and, as expected, found the last gift missing. They took the time to hang a gallon can with wire handle as a fresh gift and then turned around, heading back to the launch, taking the arrow with them.

Upriver from the houseboat about 800 meters and on the other side, or the west side of the Chimoré, was a grassy glade which the missionaries called the Meadow. One of their gift trails came out there, and they could check the gift near the river's edge when they passed by in the aluminum boat. Seventeen days after finding the arrow in the trail, they went by the Meadow in the boat, looking closely to see if the gift was still in place. Neither Bob nor Les saw it, so they stopped, tied the boat, and went up the bank to take a closer look. Sure enough, the gift was gone.

After standing there, yelling and whistling for a minute or two in case the Yuquí were nearby and getting no reply, they hung a small, dead alligator on the gift pole and then went into the jungle to the nearest abandoned camp to replace the gifts there as well. Along the trail were fresh bare footprints leading to the river and back to the camp. Some of the prints were skid marks like someone would make if they slipped while running. Had they just scared the nomads away?

As they moved on toward the camp, they found very fresh *motacú* palm fruit skins and seeds tossed along the trail. There were also peelings from other unknown fruit along the trail. When they arrived back at the river, they added a gift can, hanging it from the nose of the alligator. They were confident that renewed contact with the nomads was imminent.

The next day dawned with a light cold rain. The temperature had plunged overnight from the high nineties down into the upper seventies, and the morning was chilly. Even so, the men went up to the Meadow only to find the alligator and gift can still in place, although the alligator had either fallen down or been knocked down by a predator. They dragged it farther out into the Meadow, leaving it there for the omnipresent vultures. After replacing the CARE can with an empty KLIM powdered milk can for greater visibility from the river, they headed back to the houseboat.

Midafternoon they returned to check on the gifts. All of them were missing and there were footprints and other evidence that the nomads had once again come to the Meadow. The men followed the trail to the abandoned camp, replacing all the gifts along the way.

Fishing was good in the late afternoon, and Bob pulled in a real nice red-tail Amazon weighing roughly fifty pounds. With the cool weather, the fish should keep fine, so the men planned to take it up to the Meadow as a gift for the Yuquí the next morning.

The rainy season was nearing its end; even so, rain fell most of the following day. With the Yuquí in the area, the men were not about to let rain prevent an encounter with the nomads, so they set up a tarp shelter on the beach across the river from the Meadow where they could keep an eye on the gifts, which now included the large fish, a cloth bag, and a haircomb. They took turns watching the gifts and surrounding jungle closely using binoculars, but the only activity was vultures who came to feed on the fish and alligator.

For the next five days, the men followed a similar routine—hunt on their side of the river for thirty or forty minutes before heading up to the beach across from the Meadow. Much of the game they shot was taken to be hung as gifts along with a small kettle of hominy which they soaked overnight and boiled up first thing in the morning.

Each day that the meat gifts were not taken, they were added to the growing discard pile for the vultures to gorge on and would be evidence to the Yuquí that the missionaries were good hunters and could help provide them with meat. When no Yuquí showed up over the next several days, the missionaries began to think and hope that this had been a small group of nomads who had gone to bring a larger group now that they knew the missionaries were in the area and where to find them.

Supper was over, and Dick was washing dishes and cleaning up the kitchen as Bob, Mary, Bethany, Lois, Yogi, and Les climbed into the aluminum boat to make the short trip upriver to check the gifts. It was the perfect time of day for a boat trip to cool off and enjoy the fresh air. As they went by the Meadow, they looked closely but couldn't see the gifts, so Les stopped at the beach and let everyone off except for Bob, and then Les and Bob crossed to the Meadow to investigate more closely.

Sure enough, not only had the nomads been there, but it looked as if they had spent the afternoon waiting for the missionaries. Piles of pacai fruit shells and motacú palm fruit husks and seeds littered the ground. The grass was very beaten down. There was also a stomped down area in the fringe of the jungle that looked as if someone had watched from hiding, possibly from ambush. The nomads had also found the remains, bones, and hide of the many animals the missionaries had discarded. It was evident that a large group of people had waited for the missionaries for a lengthy period of time.

The next morning, March 11, 1965, Bob and Les went out hunting for about thirty minutes on the trail behind their camp, and it wasn't long before Les shot a *melero* (*tayra*—an omnivorous animal from the weasel family). It was the only game they found in that short period of time, but they took it along with a comb, a white cotton sugar sack, and a can of hominy, and hung it all from the gift poles before going over to set up tarps on the beach and watch for the elusive nomads.

It was 10:05 a.m. when Dark Joven (young man) and Witchy, both of them slaves, showed themselves. Les and Bob yelled across to them, and soon, more people filed cautiously out into the meadow. The warriors were carrying bows and arrows as they called across to the missionaries. The wide meadow furnished good visibility, and the missionaries made a point to land their small boat at the riverbank near the middle of the grassy area, far from the tree line, then climbed to the top of the riverbank.

Early encounter with the Yuquí across from where the houseboat was moored on the Chimoré River.

The nomads, who had hidden themselves in the fringe of the jungle as the missionaries crossed the river, now began edging out into the Meadow. Witchy came first, then seven men and boys in all, most carrying weapons. Once they were within touching distance, the missionaries handed them a machete and two gift cans. The chief was in the group along with Toughy, Witchy, Dark Joven, his younger brother, Freddy, Iroquois, and another younger man.

After ten minutes, the missionaries indicated they were going back across to the beach for food. The team's lunch consisted of fried fish and sweetened drink, which they brought back over and shared with the nomads. One more nomad had shown up while they were across the river for a total of eight. For the next fifteen minutes, they talked, pantomiming, using guns to kill meat such as peccaries. The nomads loved that talk and encouraged the missionaries to go get meat and return later.

While the jungle offered abundant meat, it often took many hours of hunting to find it, and larger game such as peccaries weren't encountered all that often. Finding a pig quickly would be unusual, but God was gracious, and twenty minutes after Les and Bob went their separate ways on the hunting trails behind the missionary camp, Bob shot a collared peccary. They knew that God was providing in order to cement their relationship with the Yuquí.

Bob and Les carried the peccary back to the launch and, along with Lois, Mary, and little Bethany Garland, headed up the river to the beach across from the Meadow. The women would stay on the beach from where Lois would shoot movies of the next encounter with the nomads. Yogi, the dog, stayed behind to guard the houseboat. The Yuquí were waiting patiently in the Meadow to see what the men had shot and were pleased to see the pig. The missionaries had also brought a shotgun along, leaving it in the aluminum boat when they carried the peccary up. Les pantomimed how Bob shot the pig and then pulled out an empty shotgun shell, explaining how this had made the holes in the pig.

They visited for twenty minutes before indicating they needed to take the women and child back to the houseboat and then left after explaining they would come back when the sun was about halfway down in the western sky. Toughy had an ugly looking boil, and the missionaries planned to take medicine and see if he would allow them to treat it in the afternoon. When the nomads saw Les inspecting Toughy's boil, several others began showing him scars from healed boils they had endured. Only once during the contact had a couple of the young men begun to roughhouse, picking on Dick. Les was quick to show his displeasure, and other nomads told the young men to stop. The missionaries were determined that these contacts not disintegrate into the violence that had occurred five years previously.

The next morning, when the missionaries arrived on the beach across from the Meadow, they found a small group of Bolivian national hunters camped there. After the missionaries explained to them about the hostile nomads directly across the river, the hunters loaded up their canoe and paddled away down the river. It was mid-morning, and now that the hunters had departed, the Yuquí made their appearance. The group of twelve included women and children. The team had soaked a large aluminum kettle of dried field corn overnight and then boiled it first thing in the morning, so they brought the hominy to share with the nomads as well as a string of small freshly caught catfish.

The two groups spent some four hours together, eating hominy and two types of jungle fruit the nomads had brought along. Dick was busy with pencil and paper, doing his best to capture words and phrases. After a time, one of the Yuquí went back into the edge of the forest and soon reemerged carrying a very dented gift can. He wanted to know if the missionaries could straighten it out for him. Les pantomimed that he would need to take it to his big boat, the houseboat, to do that, and the Yuquí acquiesced.

The men headed back to the launch to repair the can and, once they were finished, took time to boil rice in it and add milk and sugar to the cooked rice. Mary had just finished baking cookies, so they took those along too. Mary accompanied the men back upriver but stayed on the beach while the men took the can of rice over to the Yuquí. They had brought a few sample cookies for the nomads and let them know that Mary had more cookies with her on the beach if anyone wanted to go over and accept cookies from her. It appeared they understood what the missionaries were suggesting, but none of them showed any desire to get in the small aluminum boat and cross the river. A few cookies were definitely not worth the risk involved.

Seeing the repaired can encouraged the nomads, and soon Iroquois disappeared for a few moments before emerging from the jungle with an ancient machete with no handle. He also brought a stone and wanted Les to sharpen the machete. This was Bob's specialty, sharpening knives, machetes, and axes, so Bob went down to the river's edge, wet the stone, and worked on the machete. It was so dull that the men asked the owner if they could take it to the launch and sharpen it there. That way, they could also make a new handle for it at the same time.

Bob, Mary, and Dick remained on the beach across from the Meadow while Les made a trip to the launch to sharpen the machete and craft a nice wooden handle for it. Once he was finished, he came back, picked up Bob and Dick, and went back across to interact with the Yuquí. After a time of whistling, jabbering, and pantomiming stories, Bob returned to the beach, picked up Mary, and brought her over to join the group. Once she arrived in the Meadow, she handed the can of cookies to Bob who took them over and presented them to the chief's wife.

After another fifteen minutes or so, the missionaries indicated they were going back to their big boat but would be back very soon. The encounter with the nomads had been going well enough that the missionaries had decided to bring Bob and Mary's young daughter, Bethany, as well as Lois Foster to interact with the Yuquí. They were convinced that if they trusted the nomads with their families, the Yuquí would reciprocate, bringing their women and children to interact with the missionary team. Trust builds trust!

When they returned to the Meadow, the women and Bethany initially stayed in the aluminum boat while the men went up to where the Yuquí stood. The nomads looked at Bob and said, "*Yiti tu eru* (Bring the child!)." While Bob didn't understand the words, it was obvious they were enchanted by his small blonde daughter, so he went down and brought Bethany up to join the group, and a short time later, Dick went down to tend the boat while Mary and Lois also joined the group up on the bank, sitting on the ground with some of the nomad women.

Although there was much jabbering going on, neither group had much idea what the other was saying. The chief and his wife were especially fascinated by Bethany, inspecting her teeth, and wanted Bob to drop her diaper so they could see if she was a boy or a girl. She wasn't so sure about all these strangers and began crying, so Bob didn't lower her diaper.

The encounter continued until the nomads began to get more assertive, wanting to see the missionary women's breasts, so the team decided they had stayed long enough for now. They were able to distract the nomads from that idea and only remained a few minutes longer before leaving with what appeared to be very good rapport while indicating to the Yuquí that they would come back the next day.

At one point during the contact, Witchy came out of the jungle, carrying his bow and arrows. Bob and Les quickly jumped up, registering disapproval, and the chief and others made him lay the weapons down. Les insisted that the bow and arrows be taken away, which Witchy did, after which he came over, sat down, and muttered indignantly under his breath throughout the rest of the contact.

The following day, contact once again began midmorning. This time, the three missionary men went up to the meadow without their wives or Bethany, taking a quail they had shot as well as fishing line and some palm fruit as bait. The forty-five-minute contact went well, and the chief brought out a very dull axe for the missionaries to take to the launch and sharpen. Bob had taken a camera along and was able to get a few good pictures of the Yuquí. A new Yuquí woman had come out and wanted to see little blonde Bethany, so the men went back to the launch to sharpen the axe and to bring Lois, Mary, and Bethany for a visit with the nomads.

Truly, trust does build trust! Once Lois, Mary, and Bethany arrived at the Meadow, several other Yuquí came out of the forest. Now there were five men, six women, and eleven children, including an eight-month-old baby who was still nursing. To this point, the missionaries had counted twenty-six Yuquí, although not all had come out on any one contact. The cameras didn't seem to be a problem, and both Les and Bob took close-up pictures freely.

From left: Bob Garland, Bethany Garland, Lois Foster, Toughy, Yuquí woman and child.

The Yuquí men began bringing more and more machetes to sharpen and put new handles on and another axe to sharpen. It wasn't long before the missionaries had a quantity of these and pantomimed they would need to go to the launch to work on them, indicating to the nomads that they would return when the sun was halfway down in the western sky. This gave the missionary team time to have lunch and fix the tools, so it was after 3:00 p.m. when the missionaries finally returned to the Meadow and found only the Chief, Iroquois, Toughy, and Freddy there.

Early that morning, Les had shot an alligator, which escaped wounded into the river. Now, as the missionaries were leaving for the Meadow, the alligator crawled out of the river to die. Les shot and killed it and took it along for the chief who seemed pleased to get it. He wanted to see where it had been shot and was impressed when he saw the bullet wound in the head. A little after 4:00 p.m., they seemed to get restless and indicated to the missionaries they should leave and come back the next day.

Bob and Les left at first light the next morning to go down river and see if there were any bananas ready in their original plantation. They were barely out of sight of the houseboat before they spotted a large flock of ducks on a beach. Les was running the outboard, and Bob was shooting as they chased the ducks around the river, ending up with six. Instead of continuing on for bananas, they went back to the houseboat and dropped off one duck for themselves, picked up Dick, and headed up to the Meadow.

A small group of nomads was waiting, consisting of the chief, his wife, Iroquois, Witchy, and Toughy's wife and two daughters. They communicated that Toughy was upriver chopping down a bee tree. A few other women were back in the shade of the jungle, tending children since the sun was terribly hot! Dick took some pictures and was busy writing down words. The nomads indicated to the missionaries that they should take off their shoes so they could see their feet. They had never seen such wrinkled, white, delicate feet and found them amusing. Theirs were brown and leathery with many cracks.

Soon the chief brought out another old dull axe that needed sharpened, and Iroquois brought a cooking can with holes punched in it that needed repaired. Around noon, the missionaries pantomimed that they were leaving and would be back midafternoon.

The afternoon group consisted of the chief, his wife, Witchy, Iroquois, and Toughy's wife and some children. They came out of the jungle, carrying palm leaves for shade. They jabbered as they sharpened the end of each palm branch before stabbing it into the silty soil, creating a rudimentary shelter for themselves and the missionaries. Even with the shade, the afternoon sun was sweltering hot, and after a short time, the missionaries suggested going into the edge of the jungle with them for shade.

The nomads had a small campfire in the jungle, and as they sat around the fire, eating wild papaya and talking, the missionaries watched as the nomads stripped the innards out of the ducks, wrapped them in leaves, and placed them in the coals to cook. Since the missionaries had shot the ducks using a shotgun, the holes in the birds were quite small compared to the hole an arrow would make. Now the Yuquí hunters wanted the missionaries to show them where one of the birds had been shot as it wasn't obvious to them. Les and Iroquois looked carefully at the duck and eventually found the hole where the tiny lead shot had entered, killing the bird. Bob suggested, "Maybe we should open a shotgun shell and show them the lead shot."

As Les began doing this, they seemed greatly disturbed, so he stopped and threw the shell a few feet away to show he meant no harm. They still seemed concerned, so Bob picked up the shell and threw it into the river as they watched. This seemed to satisfy them.

The talk now turned to bananas and manioc, and the nomads got the idea across to the missionaries that they should clear a farm area and plant crops alongside the Meadow. The entire time together was relaxed, and Les was able to snap twenty close-up photographs. When it was time to leave, the chief handed them a dull axe with no handle and asked them to repair it overnight and return it the following day. This gave assurance that the Yuquí didn't plan to leave the area yet.

Overnight, Les caught an eighteen-pound shovelnose catfish, which would be a perfect gift for the next day. After cleaning it, he carefully wrapped the innards to take along since he had observed that the nomads also prized that portion of the fish or game. When the men arrived at the Meadow, Roughneck and one of his children came out to meet them along with others. This was the first time they had seen Roughneck since the contacts at the Naranjal. His little boy was very afraid of

Shovelnose catfish (paleta) on left and pacú sunfish on right. Displayed by men in the town of Todos Santos.

the strange clothed men and cried a lot until his father picked him up and carried him.

The entire party went, almost at once, down the trail to the manioc patch where the nomads sat around as some of the missionaries worked at weeding and others transplanted papaya plants that had sprung up where seeds had been dropped. Roughneck had brought honey along and shared it with Les. The chief was very pleased with his newly sharpened axe and tried it out by felling several small trees along the trail.

Roughneck also shared motacú palm fruit with both Les and Bob after peeling it for them. The Yuquí soon brought out a machete, two axes, and a sugar pot for repair or sharpening, and after visiting for three hours, the missionaries let the people know that they would go back to the houseboat to sharpen the tools but would return later in the day. As the team left, the nomads remained at the manioc patch where they were contentedly cooking and eating.

It was 2:30 p.m. before the missionaries went back to the Meadow, this time accompanied by their wives and Bethany. Roughneck, White Joven (young man), a new woman with children, along with Iroquois and another woman with several children completed the group. Les asked about the chief, and they explained that he was out getting honey. There seemed to be some uncertainty in the air, and the missionaries sensed a need for caution, so initially, only Les went up the bank. The Yuquí wanted the rest of the missionaries to come up also, but Les indicated that the women were afraid.

The group of Yuquí moved away from the edge of the jungle out into the open area of the Meadow, creating a less threatening environment, and with that, the rest of the missionary team came up the bank, leaving only Dick in the boat "riding shotgun." If the situation deteriorated too badly, he would fire the shotgun in the air to frighten the nomads away.

As the initial distrust wore off, everyone began to relax. Roughneck was fascinated by little blonde Bethany and made over her a lot. White Joven began showing an interest in Lois, but when he reached over to touch her, Les stopped him. Later he forgot himself and once again got too close to her, but this time Roughneck pulled him back and then made a point of showing the missionaries how much of a beard White Joven had. The few scraggly chin whiskers seemed to be a point of pride to him for some reason.

On each contact, the missionaries had been making a note of the people they saw and had now counted thirty-one different individuals. Where possible, they had created English or Spanish names to use as they discussed the Yuquí among themselves. After ninety minutes of interaction with the nomads, the missionary team let them know they were heading back to the houseboat. Roughneck handed Les another machete to sharpen and put a new handle on, and the team headed home.

Over the next three days, contacts with the nomads continued, and from time to time, a new face would make an appearance. Soon the missionaries had identified thirty-nine Yuquí. Each morning before heading up to the Meadow, Les and Bob would go hunting behind their camp, hoping to have meat to take along and share with the people. One morning, it was a razor-billed curassow, another morning an agouti (a reddish rodent similar to a very large rabbit). Other types of curassow or guan were abundant, and the missionaries took many of those to share with the nomads.

Another part of the daily routine was collecting axes, machetes, cooking pots or cans, cups, and other utensils to repair or sharpen. It seemed the Yuquí were well-provided with these items, many of which they had received as gifts from the missionaries while others had been stolen from the colonists.

The Yuquí continued to show interest in having a farm of their own, so on one contact, the missionaries began clearing undergrowth with their machetes while Roughneck and one of the other young nomads felled a few trees by axe. That didn't last long, and after an hour of work, most of the Yuquí stood and watched as Bob and Les continued working on the clearing. Lunchtime came, and the missionaries left for the houseboat, promising to bring their wives and Bethany in the afternoon.

Physical touch was a big part of Yuquí life. Entire families slept in a single hammock, and from birth, children were held and handled constantly by parents, other adults, and siblings. Touch was a constant, and as they grew closer to the missionaries, they expressed their friendship with much physical closeness, fondling and touching. Much of the time, when they were sitting around together, the nomads would be using their fingers to go through one another's hair, looking for lice and removing them.

They seemed surprised to find that the missionaries didn't have lice. Most Americans seem to have a hard time with the physical touching, and while the missionaries were wanting to become close friends with the Yuquí, they also knew that there had to be clear boundaries. Even on the earlier contacts, the Yuquí women had aggressively pursued the missionary men, and now the Yuquí men were beginning to show an excessive interest in the missionary wives.

On the contact that afternoon, White Joven rested against Les a lot, not in any "bad" way, more in a way which showed acceptance and friendship. On the other hand, several times, either White Joven or Roughneck reached out to touch Lois, and Les had to let them know that this was not acceptable. White Joven was acting cocky and proud, and his attitude was such that the missionaries were concerned the situation could get out of hand. Toughy also eyed both Lois and Mary and asked for them.

Roughneck and White Joven became a little rough with Bethany. All in all, the missionaries decided it would be wise not to take their wives or Bethany back to interact with the people for a few days. There was a nice-looking younger nomad woman who mostly stayed back in the edge of the jungle throughout one of the contacts, but when she did come out, she tried to pull Lois' blouse down. Similar things continued to occur, so the missionaries decided it would be wise to head back to the houseboat before the situation deteriorated too much.

Due to the aggressive behavior, the next day, the missionaries decided to limit their time with the Yuquí to one contact. Even that started badly. Bob had shot an agouti and planned to give it to the chief, but when they arrived at the Meadow, White Joven tried to forcefully take the rodent from Bob. Les had to intervene, insisting that it was for the chief. Once it was clear it belonged to the chief, the chief handed it to White Joven and had him singe it in the campfire, burning the hair off, much as we would use scalding water to clean the hair off a pig.

Soon the nomad warriors began asking the men to bring Bethany and the missionary women up, but Les pantomimed, acting out how some of the men had treated the women the previous day. The chief rebuked White Joven who sulked for a time but then calmed down and was very cooperative for the rest of the contact. It seemed to be working well keeping the houseboat on the far side of the river and making contact on this side as the missionaries had a measure of control and things didn't quickly get out of hand as they had at the Naranjal.

The chief was anxious to have a farm of his own and suggested going to the edge of the Meadow to continue clearing land. Once the group got into the fringe of the jungle, they found Favorite Joven, whom they hadn't seen since the contacts five years previously. His wife was with him as well as a child the missionaries hadn't seen before. With this, they had now seen forty-three Yuquí.

Favorite Joven, an especially pleasant young man with one "lazy" eye, was cooking peach palm fruit (*tembe*) and occasionally tossed cooked fruit over to Les to eat. When Les tried to go over to Favorite Joven, he was told by the chief not to approach. Instead, the chief went over, got a handful of cooked fruit, and brought it to Les, indicating that he should take it home for his wife.

The tembe fruit is about the size of an English walnut, although some varieties are larger, and is typically red, orange, or yellow in color when ripe and has a hard seed, slightly larger than a pea in the center. It can't be eaten raw but must be boiled for a lengthy period of time before eating. The flavor is something like squash but not at all sweet. It is rich in oil and very nourishing. Most varieties of peach palm trees are covered with long slender black thorns, and since the trees tend to be tall, the Yuquí normally chop them down to harvest the fruit. The wood is often used for bows, and the heart or base of the young tender leaves is also excellent eating and quite sweet.

Les Foster, Bob Garland, and Roughneck. Since the Yuquí liked to be painted with red coloring, Les painted Roughneck with his name.

Once, while working on the clearing, Les cut a small palm and, removing the heart, gave half of it to Roughneck to eat. Later in the day, Roughneck went out and brought in a much larger palm heart, sharing a large portion of it with Les. Roughneck was a willing worker and felled several trees by axe as the missionaries continued clearing with machetes.

The hour-long contact went well, and the missionaries headed home, carrying more axes and machetes to sharpen and on which to put new handles. During the contact, one of the nomads found an empty used shotgun shell on the ground. Without bending over, he picked it up with his toes, transferred it to his hand, and examined it. Les explained that they had shot a razor-billed curassow with it, and the nomad appeared pleased to hear that. The contact had gone well, and the nomads seemed to be showing more and more respect to the missionaries.

The daily tensions related to interaction with the Yuquí was "working" on all the missionaries, and Les wrote, "All of us, except Dick, woke up grumpy this morning." He went on to say, "But thanks to the Lord, there were no harsh words between us today."

One minute, a contact could be going well, while moments later, the missionaries would wonder if they would survive the next few minutes. The team carried "smoke grenades," and one of their plans was to set off the smoke grenades if attacked and try to escape in the confusion by diving into the river. Praise God, they never had to implement that plan!

Now that things seemed to be going well on the contacts, the men decided it was safe to take Bethany and the wives along once again. They really wanted the women to be able to interact with their counterparts, thus bonding the two groups in friendship. They took a guan, some fish, a kettle of hominy, as well as cake and cookies. The cookies had been a real hit right from the first time they were introduced.

On the previous contact, Favorite Joven had shown an interest in seeing the little blonde girl, but he wasn't in the group awaiting the missionaries. The group was smaller than usual, possibly because they could see a weather front approaching, and sure enough, right as the missionaries landed at the Meadow, a cold south wind with rain arrived, and everyone was quickly soaked as they walked to the shelter and campfire in the edge of the jungle.

The Yuquí hastily cut additional palm branches, enlarging the shelter. With the missionary women having accompanied the men, it wasn't long before the nomads began "talking nasty," as Les phrased it, and wanted the women to undress. The wet cold weather was a good excuse to keep the contact short, and the missionaries left before the situation got out of hand.

Since the launch was moored 800 meters downriver, the missionaries thought it would be good to encourage the nomads to begin meeting the missionaries in the jungle directly across the river from the houseboat. They did their best to explain this to the Yuquí, and as the missionaries headed home, they left Bob on the beach to try and draw the people downriver. They didn't seem to get the idea.

After nine straight days of daily interaction with the nomads, it wasn't too surprising when none of the Yuquí showed up the following day. Bob and Les had shot another razor-billed curassow and a guan and took those up to the Meadow, built a fire, and started the birds roasting while working on enlarging the clearing. When none of the Yuquí showed up, Bob and Les also began cutting a trail following the river down toward where the houseboat was moored. By 1:00 p.m., it seemed obvious there would be no contact that day, so the two men headed home, taking the curassow but leaving the guan and a pile of feathers so the nomads could see they had been there. The missionaries were thrilled to have had seventeen contacts with forty-three nomads over an eight-day period. Things were looking up!

The only warriors they hadn't seen from the previous contacts were Wide Eyes and another young man. It seemed like the commission had not killed as many of the Yuquí as they claimed. Since Toughy was in the current group, they could only assume that it was Wide Eyes who was killed by the posse, not Toughy, as commission members had stated. They looked similar enough to be brothers and likely were.

Les was thrilled with the progress and confident that God had worked in the hearts of the nomads during the five-year hiatus, writing:

> I certainly feel that prayer has changed things. This time they are like different people. There

is none of the choking and fighting with us. No demanding and pushing us around. Once when one got a little too grabby and rough, I complained to the others in the group and he got a dressing down that has kept him acting very sweet since then. They continue to come out to us without bows and arrows, while we all carry our pistols. We also carry our machetes, which they have not tried to steal. Thank you for your faithfulness in prayer!

There were no encounters or signs of the nomads for the next eight days, and the missionaries used the time to enlarge both the clearing at the Meadow as well as the clearing on their side of the river where they planned to eventually build houses. They also finished the trail leading from the Meadow down to within sight of the launch and left a white gift bag hanging across from the launch so they could easily tell if any of the Yuquí had stopped by. Les had kept a count of tools repaired for the nomads and totaled it up—eleven axes sharpened, seven machetes sharpened, and an assortment of other items repaired for a total of twenty-six items they had fixed for the Yuquí.

On the recent contacts, the missionaries had found that when they would begin singing, the nomads would start beating the ground and chanting, and it appeared they equated singing with drunken parties. The missionaries stopped singing with them as it seemed to cause a certain agitation.

The afternoon of the ninth day with no visitors, Les, Bob, and Dick went up to the Meadow and found the gift can missing. There were fresh footprints but no people. The men went on over to where they were making the farm clearing and found a bow and two arrows leaning against a fern, so they decided to wait for the owner to return. Thirty minutes later, they heard whistling and calling, and soon, White Joven came into view. As the men called, whistled, and raised their arms, a larger group emerged from the forest. There was the chief and his wife, Favorite Joven and his wife, White Joven and his wife, Freddy, a young girl child, and a baby.

Once again, the missionaries encouraged them to accompany them down river to where they could see the houseboat. It took much cajoling and persuasion, but eventually, they began following the trail the missionaries had cut paralleling the river. Every so often, the group would stop and ask the missionaries if they would be shot. Each time they were reassured, and the trek continued.

At times, the group would stop and wait for the women and children to catch up. At one point, to warn them, Les pointed at a hornet's nest and said, "*Cua, cua*" (danger, danger). Initially, the nomads didn't understand the danger he was pointing to and turned to run back up the trail, but Les was able to point out the hornet's nest to some of them, and they calmed down and continued down the trail.

Finally, they reached the spot across the river from where the launch was moored and pointed out the houseboat to them. Some of them stayed there with Bob while Les went back up to the Meadow to get the aluminum boat and bring it down, first stopping by the launch to pick up gifts, a gift can, a large piece of fresh catfish, and some cookies. Over the next thirty minutes, they made two additional trips across the river for gifts, bringing a bowstring, more cookies, and some burlap bags. The Yuquí women were quick to open the bottom end of the bags and turn them into skirts such as they wore to support their babies when carrying them. Eventually, the party split up after agreeing to meet across from the launch the following day.

Bright and early the next morning, nomads began to appear in the gift clearing across the river from the boat. Les and Bob had already left to go hunting, and by the time they returned, the Yuquí had vanished. Even so, Les and Bob went across and hiked the seventeen-minute trail to the Meadow where they worked on the farm clearing for an hour before heading home for lunch. Still, no nomads had returned, so Les and Bob went back to the Meadow to work, smoking the guan over the campfire in case the nomads returned. It was three days before they saw them again.

By now, Bob and Mary had collected a short initial list of words. Bob was an excellent mimic, at times doing so well at repeating phrases back to the nomads that they seemed to think he could speak their language. During the years the contact had been inactive, Dick had studied the Guaraní language and was finding his understanding of that to be helpful as they tried to pick up Yuquí. Les had very little language ability, but the nomads seemed to look on him as the missionary chief, paying more attention to him than to the other missionaries. Language continued to be a top priority, and with no language in common learning, Yuquí was a tedious process.

It had been four days since the missionaries had encountered the Yuquí, so they were pleased when they saw them again. The four-day intermission had been a welcome respite as they needed a break after the many hours they had spent with the nomads. There was never a dull moment while with the Yuquí, and there were plenty of tense times.

Bob was out hunting when the nomads appeared across from the houseboat, so Dick headed out the hunting trail to call him as Les installed the outboard motor on the aluminum boat. It took thirty minutes for the missionaries to get ready, and by that time, the nomads had gone up to the Meadow, so the team joined them there. The chief was anxious to expand the clearing and was busy felling trees with his axe as the missionaries cut the lighter brush with their machetes. Three new Yuquí came out that day, a young man they called Witch Doctor's Son and two children. They had now seen forty-six members of the nomad band, although only seventeen of them had come out on this contact.

The new ones wanted to meet the missionary wives and especially little blonde Bethany, so the team motored back to the houseboat to bring the women up and allowed them to get in on the action. A minor incident occurred when the chief took Bob's hunting knife and sent one of the nomads into the jungle with it. The missionaries put up such a fuss that the chief quickly sent another man to bring it back. Later, one of the women pulled a button off Bethany's blouse and passed it over to the chief. Her own people were quick to give her a "dressing down," and the chief handed the button back to Bob.

White Joven's wife spent much of the time they were together stroking Lois' hair, seemingly impressed by how silky and smooth it was. Their hair was matted and coarse and appeared to never have been washed. One of the young women was nearing womanhood, and they asked for a bag she could use as a baby sling. Soon the chief brought out a machete to be sharpened, and someone else wanted one re-sharpened that had been sharpened a few days previously, so the missionary team headed back to the houseboat to eat lunch, sharpen tools, and cook some rice with milk and sugar for the jungle people.

It was 2:00 p.m. by the time the missionary men were ready to take the sharpened tools back, and they made the short trip directly across the river to where Iroquois and the chief were waiting. As they hiked the seventeen-minute trail to the Meadow together, the chief devoured a good portion of the sweetened rice that had been meant for the entire group. It seemed the Yuquí must be camped close by as they stayed until 5:00 p.m. before heading off into the jungle. It had been a profitable day of language acquisition and friendship building.

As the nomads were preparing to leave, the chief was able to communicate to Les that he'd really like him to bring some fish the next day. They seemed to have a preference for the soft flesh of fish.

On one visit, Bob took a small palm nut over to show the nomads but kept it concealed in his hand. Then slowly and with much pomp, he opened his hand and showed only one man what was in it, not allowing any of the others to see. Meanwhile, the missionaries all listened closely, hoping to hear one of the other nomads ask in their language, "What is it?" Their ploy didn't succeed nor did other methods they tried. It wasn't until many days later when the chief's wife pointed at Les' watch that one of the alert missionaries managed to capture the important phrase as she said, "*Ba ua?*"

The missionaries began testing that phrase, pointing at different objects, some of which they had already learned the word for, and the responses they got seemed to confirm their suspicion. Now they could get object-like words more quickly, but they still needed a phrase such as, "What are you doing?" something that would allow them to gather verbs. That would prove a greater challenge!

On the afternoon radio schedule, the mission supply man advised the team that a flight would be arriving in Puerto Yuca, bringing corn as well as other supplies for the missionaries. The round trip to and from the airstrip was eight to nine hours, so the next morning, Les and Bob made a quick trip across the river to see the Yuquí and drop off foodstuffs. In response to the chief's request for fish the day before, God had graciously allowed Les to catch a twenty-pound shovelnose catfish overnight, so they took that along as well as cooked sweetened rice and a kettle of hominy.

Les did his best to communicate with them that he was leaving to get more corn for them and then, after dropping Bob off at the houseboat, left for Puerto Yuca. While he was gone, Bob and Dick walked up the beach two different times where they could see the Yuquí at the Meadow and reassure them of their presence. The nomads seemed to have camped there for the night.

Little by little, the missionaries were getting acquainted with all the Yuquí and didn't think there could be many more, although another young man showed up the next day, forty-seven people to date. Clearly, they were losing their fear of the missionaries and beginning to see that their guns were effective in providing meat. Now they wanted the missionaries to bring their shotguns and go hunting with them. They imitated the sound a razor-billed curassow makes as it calls its mate and wanted the men to shoot some for them.

First, the missionaries wanted to get them used to the explosive noise of the gun in a more open environment, so they stayed near the Meadow. One of the warriors pointed out a blackbird for Les to shoot. Toughy, Roughneck, Iroquois, Witchy, and the chief watched while Les warned them repeatedly of the loud noise the shotgun would make and then fired, dropping the bird. Then they went into the jungle nearby with Bob taking the lead.

A macaw had the misfortune to be the only game they saw, and Bob was able to bring it down. The warriors were impressed with both the noise and the effectiveness of the guns. This was a good start in helping them lose their fear of the missionaries and their guns and enough for one day. They returned to the edge of the Meadow, leaned their guns against a stump, and spent the rest of the morning working on a farm for the chief.

The nomads knew that Les' trip the day before had been to pick up corn, so they gave him a basket and asked him to bring corn in the afternoon. Only two men showed up that afternoon, Freddy and the newest young man they had met. Even so, they had an excellent visit with the two as they tried to communicate and pick up more of the language. It was slow going, but they were making progress.

Living on a houseboat had numerous advantages and a few disadvantages. One of the perks was being able to have fishing lines in the water 24/7, and the missionaries habitually did. This morning, they were awakened by the aluminum boat banging vigorously against the large wooden boat. The heavy-gauge handline tied to the aluminum boat had succeeded in catching a large black catfish known locally as a *muturu*, and as it fought the line, the boat was being jerked forcefully around. The fish weighed well over one hundred pounds, and it took two men to get it into the aluminum boat. To do so, they pushed the end of a canoe paddle through the mouth and out the gill slit, and each man took one end of the paddle to lift the monster into the small boat. Since the nomads should arrive soon, the men left the fish in the boat to take over as a gift. This ought to impress the jungle dwellers!

Eighty-five pound "yellow" muturu catfish caught by visitor.

It was midmorning before a group of nine nomads made their appearance. The six warriors seemed suitably impressed as Les and Bob carried the imposing fish up the bank and laid it in front of them, indicating it was for them. The two women and one child also clustered around, eyeing the behemoth with evident pleasure. They would eat well today!

It wasn't long before the Yuquí began cutting the fish into smaller portions suitable for transporting to their camp. Then they wove palm carrying baskets, attached vines that would go around their foreheads to support the weight, placed the dissected fish into the baskets, and indicated they would be back later in the afternoon.

Around noon, just as the missionary team was sitting down to eat lunch in the houseboat, they heard calling from across the river. Another group of Yuquí had come to see them. Evidently, the fish had been a big hit, and others were hoping for similar bounty. Lunch could wait.

Bob, Les, and Dick gathered up a few gifts, including candy, and went over to greet the new arrivals. All except two were men. The chief had brought his wife along as had Roughneck. Fatty, as Roughneck's wife had come to be known among the missionaries, had been Wide Eyes' wife but, upon his death, became Roughneck's spouse. Many years later, the missionaries learned that she was to have been killed to appease Wide Eye's spirit when he died, but Roughneck insisted she not be sacrificed as he was interested in her. She was a contented spouse, and Roughneck was an excellent hunter and provider; consequently, she was well-fed, hence the name Fatty.

The missionary team made several trips back and forth across the river, taking hominy, cooked rice with sugar and milk, cookies, and on one trip put Yogi the dog on a leash and took her over so the nomads could get familiar with her. Yogi was left in the boat; even so, the nomads were apprehensive and made it plain they didn't want the terrifying animal brought up the bank. Bethany had also come across and was contentedly playing with the lone Yuquí boy child who had come out with the adults.

Eventually, Yogi was taken back across to the houseboat and, as the visiting continued, Les and Bob encouraged the Yuquí to come across the river in the boat and see Lois at the houseboat. The chief seemed to trust Les and showed some willingness to go across, but his wife objected vigorously, so he got back out of the small aluminum boat. Roughneck, Fatty, and Straight Hair got in.

Roughneck knelt on hands and knees to sniff the boat and then spat as if bothered by the offensive smell. Even so, he squatted for a few moments in the boat as if planning to go, but after thinking it over more, the three changed their minds and climbed out at the last minute. Around 3:00 p.m., they headed off into the forest after indicating they would be back the next day, so the missionary team returned to the houseboat.

That night, one of the handlines tied to the launch yielded a nice fifteen-pound shovelnose catfish. Bob and Les also went hunting early in the morning but only shot a hawk. It seemed there weren't many animals or birds the nomads didn't eat, and they were always pleased with the larger birds as they also yielded feathers for fletching their arrows.

The nomads had heard the gunshot when Les killed the hawk and, upon his return to the houseboat, were excitedly waiting across the river to see what he had brought. He held up the bird so they could see it and could hear them discussing it among themselves. Bob had yet to arrive back from hunting, so Dick and Les went on across the river to interact with the nomads while waiting for Bob.

The group that had come out was impressive—thirty-two people consisting of eleven men, eight women, and thirteen children. Evidently, yesterday's remarkable catfish had been a big drawing card. The fifteen-pound shovelnose catfish would be a nice follow-up to that and would show the nomads that large fish weren't that unusual. While waiting for Bob, Les and Dick pulled out small fishlines and stood on the shore fishing for small catfish and other little fish. Eventually, they were able to convince some of the young Yuquí men to try fishing. It was easy enough; Les had tied six feet of line and a hook to a slender five-foot-long sapling, and they just needed to dangle the line in the water and wait for a fish to bite. The young men were a little apprehensive about this new way of fishing but willing to try as they had seen how effective the missionaries had been in catching small fish. Their exhilaration knew no bounds when Wooly Hair pulled in his first small fish!

The chief and Roughneck both slapped the back of their heads showing just how pleased they were. Toughy also pulled out a small fish, and there was more slapping of heads as they showed how thrilled they were. Eventually, the missionaries headed back across the river after assuring the Yuquí that they would return shortly after the sun reached its zenith and would bring their wives and Bethany when they returned.

The afternoon contact brought new advances in the trust relationship between missionary and nomad. Lois, Mary, and Bethany went across the river and stayed there with Dick, Bob, and a large group of Yuquí, while Les convinced Witchy, Freddy, and one of the older women to accompany Les to the houseboat. Crossing a deep river in the small aluminum boat was initially a terrifying experience. The missionaries didn't learn until months later that the three individuals who went with Les were considered the more expendable in the tribal hierarchy as they were all slave class, not descendants or relatives of the chief and his wife.

While at the houseboat, Les treated his three guests royally, loading them up with cookies, candy, and other goodies. They, on the other hand, while his back was turned, were into mischief, throwing a pillow from Les' bed near the door of the launch out onto the front deck and stealing a can. Nothing too drastic, and it being the first time they had visited the boat, he made little of it.

When he brought his guests back over to where the rest of the tribe waited, he found that the whole group, excluding the passengers, had been crying. They had taken a great risk in sending their slaves across the river and thought they might never see them again. Even after the brave voyagers returned to the welcoming arms of their tribal companions, the crying continued, and it was several minutes before everyone calmed down. Oh, how terrifying is the unknown!

Even so, once the missionaries expressed to the Yuquí that they were going to take Lois, Mary, and Bethany back to the houseboat, two of the young men expressed a desire for the experience of a lifetime—a trip across the river to the marvelous houseboat. Once again, Les feted his guests with candy and cookies, and they waited as he sharpened axes and machetes on the grindstone before taking the young men back across to their worried families.

When they arrived on the other side, Witchy and White Joven expressed a desire to go to the houseboat. Evidently, candy and cookies were worth the risk to one's life. As the small boat began to pull away from the shore, White Joven's bravery evaporated, and he jumped quickly out of the boat. Les pulled back to shore and pantomimed, "How about just a short boat ride near shore, and then I'll bring you back?"

The two not so brave warriors assented to that, and Les gave them a very short spin in the boat before pulling back in and letting them off. One thing he definitely did not want was a passenger who changed their mind once they were farther out in the river as the Yuquí didn't know how to swim, and he didn't want to try and rescue a frantic drowning person.

After the short boat ride, he headed back to the launch to repair one more machete handle, and when he brought it back to its owner, they disappeared into the forest. It had been a very good day with much trust being built.

After the big day they and the nomads had experienced, the missionaries were pleased when the nomads didn't show up the following day. Everyone could use a little time off from the stress that each contact induced. Les went to work enlarging the missionary clearing where they planned to build houses and plant crops, but it wasn't long before he was back in the house as he had splashed poisonous sap from an *ochoó* tree into his eye and needed to wash it out.

The following day, only a few Yuquí showed up. Witchy was first, followed by the chief and his wife. Eventually, George and his brother, Freddy, showed up as well. Much later, the missionaries would learn that Witchy was George and Freddy's father, and all three of them were slave-class, George being the chief's slave. Witchy had no fear of the boat and was happy to go across the river and eat cookies while Les sharpened an axe. Then they went back across to where the chief wanted them to work on his farm clearing.

After a time, George indicated a desire to visit the houseboat, so Les took him across so he could eat some cookies, and then the two of them went on a very short hunt. By now, the chief was worried and calling anxiously from across the river, wanting George to come back. Evidently, he was concerned he might lose his slave to the missionaries.

Les took George across and left Dick and Bob there visiting with the chief and his wife while George told them all about the hunt he had gone on with Les. By midafternoon, the Yuquí began making preparations to head into the jungle, and the missionaries motored back to the houseboat. No sooner had they arrived than an eighteen-pound *surubí* (tiger-striped catfish) struck on one of the fishing lines. Les began yelling and whistling, and soon the chief and George showed up again in the clearing across from the houseboat and waited while Bob and Les took the fresh fish over to them. When the Yuquí had once again retreated into the forest, Les and Bob went home and then headed out their trails to hunt. Bob was excited when he shot a collared peccary, something that didn't happen all that often.

By now, the missionaries had a routine of soaking a four-gallon kettle of Cuban field corn each night and boiling it up first thing in the morning to share with the Yuquí. As they sat together, eating the hominy, the missionaries would boil up a similar sized kettle of rice with sugar, sometimes adding powdered milk as well. This gave time to interact, "talking" together, slowly learning the Yuquí language, and teaching a few Spanish words to the nomads.

Learning an unknown unwritten language while having no language in common is a daunting and slow proposition. Pantomime, with facial and hand gestures were still the main method of getting things across. Watching the Yuquí men tell a hunting story was a special treat as much of it could be understood, even without a knowledge of the language.

Les was busy stoking up the campfire and cooking corn in anticipation of the daily visitors when Bob noticed there was a fish on one of the big lines. Before Les could get down there to help Bob pull in the huge fish, it got away. Thirty minutes later, they heard whistling from across the river and went over to see who had come to visit. White Joven and his wife were there along with Favorite Joven, his wife and girl child, as well as two other children. Les and Bob went across with no gifts and, after receiving fruit and honey from the visitors, returned to the houseboat for corn, cookies, and the peccary Bob had shot. The visit was going well until the wind began gusting, which caused the nomads to run and cry as if greatly frightened.

Much later, the missionaries would learn that not only did the Yuquí fear wind and storms due to trees or large limbs crashing down endangering their lives, but they also believed the spirits of their dead were "along the sky (up in the sky)," causing the wind and storms as they retaliated against the living who may have mistreated them in life. It was necessary to chant in fear to show proper respect to the departed as they could still affect the daily lives of the living.

Les was overjoyed with the way the friendship was moving forward, writing:

> It's almost unbelievable the way the contact is going. This is the same group of Yuquí Indians as before, but things have changed so much. Whereas before they were always threatening us with their bows and arrows, choking us, and mistreating us, now they are not at all that way. We have carried pistols on each contact, a thing they would not let us do before, while insisting they not bring their bows and arrows out, but rather leave them back in the jungle. We have freely taken our wives and little Bethany Garland over to be with the nomads and they have not mistreated them. A few times overzealous men have tried to touch Lois but after reminding them that she is mine, now they don't try to touch her. Lois is wearing her hair in bangs, much like the younger women, and all the women love to sit and stroke her hair. We are confident God has preserved them so that they may hear the Gospel. Pray that we may quickly master the language." Now that they had the phrase for, "What is that?" they were constantly using it to gather the names of new objects and at times were getting up to 50 new words a day. Mary and Bob were busy processing the words, assisted by Dick.
>
> On one early hunting trip Les took a young warrior of about 17 along and was impressed by how he headed off into the forest not following a trail, just bending over a twig from time to time.

As the young man heard birds or monkeys in the distance, he would guide Les to them and wait while Les shot them, then pick up the game and lead Les on as they continued the hunt. Les happened to shoot one of the monkeys in the eye and the young man was very impressed. When they eventually rejoined the group on the far side of the river the young man told the Chief in great detail all about the hunt and Les' marksmanship and the Chief seemed well pleased. No doubt he was thinking to himself, "Maybe these missionaries will turn out to be useful after all!

To date, forty-seven individual nomads—men, women, and children—had shown themselves during these contacts. Whenever the missionary wives went across to visit the Yuquí, women jabbered with them nonstop as the men fished or went hunting nearby. The contacts had become much more relaxed, and it seemed that the Yuquí understood the boundaries the missionaries had set. To date, seven of them had braved the river crossing in the aluminum boat, and all had been amply rewarded.

The nomads had begun calling Yogi the dog *Yagua*, the same word they used for tigers or jaguars, and were still very cautious when she was around. Whenever the nomads failed to show up or if the missionaries had a few spare hours, they kept busy enlarging the clearing on their side of the river and gathering jungle poles and palms, preparing to build the first permanent house. It would be for Bob and Mary Garland as they were the only family with a preschool child and really needed a place of their own, especially when their other children came home for vacation from boarding school.

The house would be all jungle materials, except for the corrugated tin roof and some screen wire to bug-proof a portion of the house. Mosquitoes, cockroaches, snakes, and other pests were abundant, and the family needed some protection.

It had been five weeks since the first friendly, but tense contact in the Meadow on the banks of the Chimoré River, and at last the area for the chief's farm was ready for planting. First to go in were 252 plants of manioc. It would take six to nine months to begin producing, but between the rows of manioc, they planted field corn, which would only take ninety days and be up and harvested long before the manioc was ready.

The Yuquí were still not too happy to see edible corn go into the ground but appeared to accept the missionaries doing this, evidently deciding that they knew what they were doing. A few papaya plants were also transplanted to the small farm. If weather, animals, insects, and river levels cooperated, in three months, the Yuquí could begin to see the benefits of growing their own crops.

A Short Break

THE MISSIONARIES AWOKE TO A cold wet storm from the south, a *surazo*, but decided to go down and check the original banana patch they had planted. They were pleased to see that the nomads had discovered the plantation and had harvested seven stalks of fruit, and another seven were nearly ready to be cut. The men dug twenty young rhizomes to bring back and plant on their side of the river and, when they got home, planted those and continued enlarging their farm area. By nightfall, the heavy rains in the foothills had caused water levels in the river to rise to where it was within inches of coming over the bank. They would soon see if the site they had chosen for their base was high enough, although they were pretty sure it was one of the highest areas along the lower section of the Chimoré River.

It had now been fourteen days since their last visit with the Yuquí, so they weren't surprised to get a radio message that sixteen Yuquí had been seen over on the Chapare River near the Yura mission where they had stolen bananas. The missionaries would redeem the time while the Yuquí were away, clearing, planting, building houses and hunting, while waiting for their friends to return; after all, the Yuquí were nomads and couldn't be expected to stay around for months on end! In fact, later on, as the missionaries learned more of the language, they would find that the two principal verbs were *Come* and *Go,* very appropriate for people who spent their whole lives coming and going!

In some ways, the respite from daily contacts with the Yuquí was beneficial. It was nearing vacation time, and the men were able to focus on getting the Garland house completed. Without a house, Mary and the children might need to spend the vacation in the city without Bob as he was really needed on the Chimoré contact base.

While the missionaries wanted to be in daily contact with the Yuquí, they also needed to have their families with them. As Les wrote, "We can't have contact and build houses at the same time."

The whole team was pushing hard, gathering bamboo, palm boards and matting, and other materials for Bob and Mary's house as they hoped to have it and a small kitchen shed finished before the Yuquí returned or school vacation started.

Les was having his own struggles. Lois had flown out for graduation at the boarding school where their oldest two children, Anna and Alan, were graduating from high school. Les wrote in his journal:

> Had a time of crying this evening, as I thought of tonight being graduation and picturing Anna and Alan both graduating and me not being there. In my mind's eye I could see sweet little Anna, all frills and nerves, walking slowly down the aisle to the stage followed by black suited, studious, serious Alan, tall and handsome. Oh Lord, what a price we pay at times like this!

With only three men on the contact base, none of them could be spared as they would all be needed when the Yuquí returned. Anna and Alan would spend their summer break at the Chimoré base before heading to the homeland in the fall to see what came next in their lives.

The nomads were gone for three weeks before they eventually reappeared. It was midmorning, and Bill Presson, Bob Garland, and Les had just crossed the river to cut bamboo for the house walls when they heard the nomads yelling from the clearing across from the houseboat. The group of eleven Yuquí spent five hours with the missionaries and might have stayed longer had it not been for a heavy rainstorm with cold wind. They were in a mischievous mood, taking Bill's machete and giving the missionaries a very hard time before they finally returned it. Bob's ball cap was taken and never returned. Alan had arrived a few days earlier and was busy catching fish for the nomads until they took his jar of bait. He stopped fishing and let them know he wouldn't continue until the jar was returned. They seemed to be "feeling their oats" after their time away, and some of the tension of the early contacts had come back.

An hour after the main group left, George, one of the slaves, showed up by himself and accompanied the missionaries across the river to the houseboat to have an axe sharpened. The missionaries had cooked up corn and shared many other gifts of foodstuff, cookies, candy, cooked rice, and meat with the Yuquí and were optimistic the people would return the next day.

Sure enough, even though it was raining with a cold south wind blowing, late morning saw the arrival of thirty-three men, women, and children. The missionaries had set up corrugated tin roofing as a shelter in case they had visitors so they could all sit around several small campfires out of the rain. Roy, a school friend of Alan's, had flown in to visit and shot three guans and a hawk early in the morning. Alan caught several fish, and the Yuquí were pleased with the assortment of meat.

Sharpening axes and machetes, cooking hominy and sweetened rice, and visiting took up much of the time together. When they were ready to head back into the jungle, several of the nomads handed gift cans with wire handles to the missionaries and let them know that they would like them returned full of corn the next day.

Late in the afternoon, Bill took a tape recorder across the river, and Les held the microphone as they recorded people talking. After recording, Bill would stop and play back what had been recorded, and at first, the Yuquí seemed to enjoy this. They would make remarks to the machine, and the machine would repeat it back to them. After a time, Toughy began to say what appeared to be threatening things to the tape recorder, and then, as it said the same threatening things back to him, he started getting upset and saying meaner things to it, which upset him even more when it repeated those things back to him. That little box with two wheels going around seemed to be just about as tough as he was.

Soon the chief joined in, telling that old box what he thought of it, and what do you know? That defiant thing just turned around and told the chief off in the same words! That was too much! The chief let Les know that he needed to throw that thing in the river. Bill and Les thought it better to take the recorder back over to the launch and leave it there. Maybe this hadn't been such a good idea!

More cold wind and heavy rain from the south moved in the next morning, and it was late afternoon before any of the Yuquí made their appearance, and then only a small group of seven people. Roughneck and his wife and two children, and Witchy with his wife and a child. They were pleased when Les came over with three of the cans they had left overnight. He had almost filled the cans with hominy for them and that, along with a string of small catfish Alan had caught, made a big hit.

An hour later, six more people showed up, Favorite Joven with his wife and two children, White Joven, and another child. Les went back across the river and brought cans of corn for them. They were overjoyed with that and left five more one-gallon gift cans and two smaller cans to be filled with corn and picked up the next day. The next day dawned rainy and cold, and the nomads must have spent the day keeping warm by their fires as none of them made an appearance. But after that one-day intermission, the nomads showed up daily for the next thirty days.

More and more, the missionaries were hunting with the Yuquí who were beginning to see the value of their guns. White Joven showed up one afternoon in an unhappy mood and told a long story of how he had spent the day hunting but missed all the game and returned empty-handed. Les pointed to his shotgun and pantomimed that the two of them should go find some meat. Within a relatively short time, they were back, carrying two large red howler monkeys.

Roy had earlier shot a big fat *coati mundi* (South American cousin to the raccoon), and the nomads were soon busy roasting it over a smoke rack of green sticks. Coati mundi is one of the few fat items of game and especially prized. The nomads would never think of skinning a coati mundi, preferring to burn off the hair so all the fat under the skin cooks into the meat. Just watching it sizzle over the smoke rack is enough to make your mouth water!

The dictionary Bob and Mary were compiling of Yuquí words continued to grow, and some days, they were able to capture fifty or sixty new words, mostly object-like words. They still had no phrase to ask, "What are you doing?" and no idea of the grammatical construction of the language.

On one contact, Les took needle and thread along and had Bob sew up a rip in his shirt sleeve. Fatty, Roughneck's wife, was quick to get the idea and took over, sewing up a tear in the back of Les' shirt. Fatty was thrilled when they let her keep the needle and gave her several spools of thread to go with it.

One morning, a group of twenty-seven showed up, and fourteen of them stayed with Bob in the clearing next to the river while ten men and three women headed up the trail toward the Meadow with Les to hunt. It wasn't long before Les shot a fat guan, then a squirrel monkey, and two red and blue macaws. The macaws were prized since not only were they considered edible, but their colorful wing feathers would be used to fletch arrows.

Soon Les ran out of shotgun shells, so he left the shotgun leaning against a tree just behind the corn patch. He was still carrying a pistol, but it wasn't much use for hunting. The men continued hunting with bow and arrow and shot a few squirrel monkeys before returning to the manioc patch nearby. The manioc was only an inch in diameter and smaller, not ready to harvest, but they went ahead and dug it all. As some of them harvested the manioc, Les watched as one of the men took a snail shell, broke a piece off so the edge was square and sharp, then used it to scrape his palm-wood arrow point, sharpening it.

By now, the nomads had lost their fear of having the missionaries in their camp, and often, when returning from the hunt, would swing by their camp in the jungle to drop off game or pick up some fruit to eat before returning to the clearing on the river's edge. On one such occasion, Les was squatting on his haunches in their camp, the same way they sat around much of the time. He watched as they repaired their arrows, and Roughneck made a new arrow.

Roughneck was one of the best hunters and had some of the highest quality arrows in the group. He was truly a craftsman. He used two *agouti* (rodent) teeth embedded in the leg bone of a guan to sharpen the "plug (notch for bowstring)" and then, when fletching or feathering the arrow, wrapped human hair as thread through the feather and around the shaft to hold the feather on, using bee's wax as a kind of glue to hold the feather in place and cover the "thread." It didn't take many weeks before Roughneck discovered he could use the thread the missionaries gave to his wife, Fatty, instead of human hair to hold the feathers on his arrows.

With the developing friendship, more and more of the Yuquí were coming across the river in the aluminum boat to spend time in the missionary's camp or on the houseboat. Les set up a small shelter and fire onshore to cook hominy, and his daughters, Anna and Beverly, often sat there with Indian friends tending the fire and sharing the corn or rice they cooked. Freddy, George, and their sister were all slave-class and would sit at the fire with them to enjoy the food and friendship.

One day, Freddy came across by himself, so the missionaries invited him into the houseboat to eat lunch with them at the table. Sitting on a chair was a new experience for him, and instead of sitting on it, he placed both feet on the chair and squatted, just as he would normally squat on the ground in his camp or elsewhere. The menu was turkey soup, fried ripe plantain bananas, and hot tea. He didn't like the pastas in the soup and pulled them out with his fingers, dropping them into Bob's cup of tea. Then he kept reaching over, trying to take pieces of turkey from the missionary's soup bowls. It was a new experience for him, but little by little, he would adapt to how the missionaries ate.

Occasionally, there continued to be tense contacts where the missionaries would have to end the time together and leave when the nomads started to mistreat them physically or threaten them in other ways. The day after one such occurrence, when the Yuquí showed up across the river, Bill, who was watching with field glasses, could see that only two of the slaves were in the clearing on the bank while other men with bows and arrows were hiding back in the bamboo. Thinking of possible treachery, the men loaded the double-barrel shotgun with blanks, and Bob took it to the upper deck of the houseboat. Bill watched through the binoculars as Alan and Les went across with a twenty-four-pound ripsaw catfish and a pair of macaws.

White Joven holding ripsaw catfish

When they got close to shore, Les yelled for the chief to show himself and waited until he came to the clearing on the river's edge before landing with the boat. Les and Alan dropped off the fish and game and then invited the two slaves, Freddy and George, to join them on a trip to the houseboat. As the missionaries ate breakfast, they treated the two slaves with sugar water to drink and cookies to snack on, and then after breakfast, Les took them hunting on one of the trails behind the missionary camp. It was a profitable hunt, netting a quail and five squirrel monkeys.

By now, six Yuquí had come out in the clearing across the river, but the missionaries waited until early afternoon to go over, giving the nomads time to abandon any ideas of treachery. After lunch, Bill, Bob, Les, Freddy, and George went across the river and headed upriver, hunting. It seemed that by now, whatever had been troubling the people had stopped bothering them, and the mood was good.

The hunt netted two macaws, a hawk, and a squirrel monkey, and when they got back, the chief seemed to be in a pleasant mood. Freddy once again accompanied the missionaries across the river and sat at their table, drinking sweetened water. He was so happy, he began singing, chanting, and beating on the table to keep time. The words to the chant sounded something like, "*Oh, wat a ichey cadichie cadoo oo, cadichie cadoo oo*" repeated over and over, and Bill recorded it.

Les and Bill laughed and laughed as he sang, and the chief, who had accompanied them to the houseboat, seemed very pleased to see everyone so happy. Iroquois and his wife had come across and were also in a good mood. During the day, two small colorful feathers had been plastered into Les' hair with beeswax, one by Freddy and one by Iroquois's wife. The nomads seemed to have taken Les in as one of their own. Bob had also had a good day, adding forty-five words to the dictionary he was working on.

On one of the hunting trips, Les had seen two nice balsa trees, so he and Alan went to cut them. Alan wanted the balsa to build model airplanes for use with the small engines he had. Some of the nomads heard them chopping the trees down and thought Alan and Les were chopping down a bee tree and not sharing the honey with them, so they attempted unsuccessfully to wade across the river. When they couldn't cross the river, they got upset with the two men.

Later, when Les understood what had happened, he took large quantities of cookies across to share with all the people who were there. Les gave cookies first to the chief who tried to grab all of them for himself, and when Les wouldn't let him have the whole batch, he angrily threw the ones Les had given him into the aluminum boat and announced that they were leaving on a trip. They had been telling the missionaries for several days that they would be traveling but continued to show up each day, and sure enough, the next day, a small group was back, acting as if nothing had happened the day before.

The next morning, Favorite Joven, one of the chief's sons, showed up and managed to communicate that his father had gotten drunk the night before, crying and crying and beating his head against a tree because of the cookie incident the day before. Many times, the missionaries had seen evidence that the chief had a tender heart, and this confirmed it once again. Not only could the missionaries sense the mood of the nomads, but the nomads had a good sense of when the missionaries were struggling with attitudes.

Later that same day, Les was hunting with Scar Face who pointed out a turkey to Les. In his excitement, Scar Face kept pushing Les on the back as he tried to aim the gun until finally Les, in irritation, commented in Spanish, "Let me alone so I can aim." It was immediately obvious to Les that Scar Face had sensed his irritation and was hurt by it, but Les had no verbal way of apologizing for his impatience. Later, when they returned from hunting, Les told Lois and others in front of Scar Face what had happened and acted as though it was a joke, hoping Scar Face would understand that he was admitting his mistake and accept his apology.

Each day, the nomads came out earlier and earlier, making it apparent they were camped close by. Most days, one or another of the missionary men would go hunting with them and always came back with several items of game. Alan often sat with those who waited in the clearing on the riverbank and cooked sweetened rice for them or fished for small fish along the edge of the river.

The chief's wife had a streak of mischievousness in her, and when Alan would squat near her to talk, she could see he was unstable in the squatting position and would reach over and nudge him so he would topple over backward. She thought that was hilarious, while Alan, for his part, learned to squat with a tree or sapling to his back so he couldn't be pushed over.

School was out, so Les and Bob made a trip over to Puerto Yuca to pick up Mary Garland and the Garland children. They arrived back on the Chimoré midafternoon, and a group of Yuquí were anxiously waiting to meet these children they hadn't seen before. Never having been close to naked nomads, the Garland children were reluctant to get out of the boat and be touched and made over by these unusual people. This didn't set well with Roughneck, and he grabbed Lorraine Garland by the hair.

When Les protested his treatment of the girl, Roughneck grabbed a stalk of sugarcane the missionaries had brought from Puerto Yuca for them and acted like he was going to beat Les over the head with it. Les had a shotgun lying in the boat, and when he picked it up, the whole group of nomads scrambled madly up the bank. Les laid the gun back down, but they continued to jabber angrily, and the parting that day was definitely not on a friendly note, so much so that the missionaries had some doubts they would see them the next day.

Amazingly, Roughneck showed up the next morning, acting as if nothing had happened and, along with Scar Face and Iroquois, went upriver with Les and Dick to hunt. After motoring to a creek that dumped into the Chimoré River and then a short way up the creek, the party tied the boat and continued on foot. As they hiked along, the Yuquí kept saying to Les, "*Tiyuyu, tiyuyu*" and seemed very excited. Soon they came upon a large flock of toucans, which normally they would have loved for Les to shoot, but this time, they restrained him from shooting and used their bows and arrows instead. With all their shooting, they only scored one bird. Even so, they were determined that Les not shoot his noisy gun, even making him set the gun down lest he be tempted to shoot.

They had gone only 200 meters farther when it became clear to Les as they pointed out what they had come for. There in a tall tree, seventy-five feet above the ground, was a nest of two "granddaddy birds," five and a half feet tall white cranes with black head and black and red neck, known in Spanish as "bato." These birds are so heavy they can't take off from a standing start from the sandbars where they fish but must run for about twenty-five feet to get up enough speed to hop from the sand and fly. As the group arrived in sight of the nest, the nomads waited patiently until one of the birds flew away, and once it was gone, the nomads indicated to Les that he should shoot the one still sitting on the nest. They were beside themselves with excitement, waiting for him to fire. It was an easy shot, but unfortunately, the dead bird remained high in the tree, lying in the nest.

Soon its mate returned, and this bird came crashing to the ground when Les shot it. Scar Face began climbing a tree to get the first bird down, and as he was going up, a third *tiyuyu* flew into a nearby tree. The excitement of the hunters knew no bounds as Les shot this one. It came down wounded and tried to flee by running, but the hunters finished it off with two arrows.

After gathering the three giant birds, the two high-class warriors smeared blood from the birds all over each other's chests and backs. As they did this, they were very serious, and Les wondered, *What is this all about?* Clearly the ritual had some important meaning to them.

By noon, the hunters were on the move again but stopped when they found a motacú palm with ripe fruit. After a snack of palm fruit and palm heart, they continued on their way. Les was interested to see how they used the sharp edge of a piece of the torn palm leaf stalk to scrape the meat off the motacú fruit for eating. He was constantly amazed by the resourcefulness of these people who had learned how to survive with a minimum of outside utensils, making do with the resources the jungle provided.

Soon they came to a swamp about fifty feet wide, and Les waded in, carefully trying to keep gun, ammunition, pistol, and smoke grenade dry, holding them above his head as the water was up to his shirt pockets. Shortly after crossing, they found a bee tree and stopped to eat wild honey before continuing on, eventually picking up a main Yuquí trail and following it to one of their small camps.

Before arriving at the camp, Les had begun smelling wood-smoke and realized they were getting close to one of their camps. This was the first time any of the missionaries had been in an inhabited nomad camp, so Les was interested in seeing what it was like. There were many small fires, one on each side of each bark rope hammock. Bows and arrows leaned against trees here and there, and other items such as kettles, glass bottles, axes, and machetes lay around the site, maybe a dozen campfires and three hanging hammocks.

As they entered the camp, Scar Face began beating the back of his head and jabbering in a high-pitched voice as he saw one of the arrows he had left in camp had been too close to a fire and was now smoldering. The excess honey had been placed in a container made from the base of a palm leaf and carried back to the camp. Dropping the birds and honey in camp, the group continued on to the river and then across to the houseboat where Roughneck and his son ate lunch with Les and Dick before returning to their side of the river.

At one point during their trek to kill the *tiyuyu,* a gust of wind had swept through the jungle, and the nomads stopped to beat their arrows ferociously against their bows, yelling at the wind until it stopped. The missionaries didn't understand at the time what they were doing but much later would realize that they were telling the spirits of their ancestors up in the sky to stop causing the dangerous wind. It had been an exciting and exhausting day with another first, a friendly visit to an inhabited Yuquí camp.

By now, the missionaries had come to realize that some of the corn and sugar they were giving to the Yuquí was being used to make an alcoholic chicha-like drink. Among themselves, the missionaries had taken to calling it "Chimoré Hooch." Some of the containers the people were bringing to have filled with corn smelled strongly like chicha. While the missionaries didn't approve of alcoholic beverages, they didn't feel they should cut back on the amount of corn they were giving the people as it only averaged two one-gallon cans of corn daily for the entire group of forty-seven people they had identified. They wanted to furnish enough food that the Yuquí would stay around as they worked on learning the language, and it was important to keep them away from the colonist's farms where they would kill and be killed. Better a little drunkenness than the killings!

More and more, the Yuquí seemed to be accepting Les as one of their own. No doubt his prowess with the shotgun played a large part in that. It seemed they were treating him as one of them, even plucking out all his eyebrows and sticking small bright-colored feathers into the front of his hair with beeswax. For the last twenty days, he had been hunting with them on almost a daily basis and was physically drained. Some days, Bob Garland or Bill Presson would also hunt with the Yuquí, and over time, they began to alternate days on and days off so as to get an occasional rest at home, although rest meant catching up on chores, planting crops, working on their clearing or houses, maintaining the houseboat, and many other details demanded by pioneer life in the jungle.

Daily, some of the Yuquí would come across to the houseboat and missionary camp while others sat across the river, also with some of the missionaries, never a dull moment while building friendship and learning the language of the nomads. With the missionaries' children on school vacation, many of them were spending their days with the Yuquí as well and learning a smattering of the language.

The Yuquí had discovered that the missionaries liked to eat lunch on a regular schedule when the sun was at its zenith, and soon the nomads were vying for the privilege of having the noon meal with their new friends. A typical lunch might be something like fried or boiled monkey, fried rice, palm-heart (coleslaw) salad, and a sweetened soft drink. It was a special privilege to eat lunch with the missionaries, and to keep things under control, only a few nomads were invited at a time. The missionaries had opted to pray over each meal but always with their eyes open or their portion would disappear onto the plate or into the mouth of a Yuquí. Leftovers were always carried away by the dinner guests to be shared with less-fortunate relatives or friends, and cookies were sent along to be shared.

Trust had reached a point where unless a warrior seemed especially out of sorts, the missionaries allowed them to bring their bows and arrows across the river when they came to visit as they might decide to make a short hunt together on the island behind the missionary camp. The chief had finally worked up his courage to make the boat trip across the river and, with his seniority, had become a regular at the dinner table, trumping most of the others who deferred to his status. It was worth risking your life for sweetened drinks and cookies.

Pastas were the least desired of the dishes served by the missionaries and might be thrown on the floor, deposited on someone else's plate or in their drinking cup, or bring angry words, letting the missionaries know that this wasn't food. One noon, Les knew that pastas were being served, so he didn't invite any of the Yuquí for lunch; however, the chief, George, and Straight Hair all insisted on going across with him at lunchtime. Once they arrived on the houseboat, Les gave them a kettle of hominy and told them to sit on the front deck and eat it while the missionaries ate inside at the table but with the door open. Within a few moments, the three Yuquí were leaning over Alan and Bill, begging for the food on their plates, evidently feeling left out.

Theft was a common occurrence, but the missionaries didn't let it go unchallenged. Respecting the belongings of others and being able to have a trust relationship were important principles. So when items would disappear from the houseboat and they knew what group had been there or who the likely culprit was, that group or individual would be banned from coming across for a few days. Usually, the item was quickly returned so the privilege of coming across could be restored. Various tricks were used by the naked nomads to "lift" items and get them across the river in the missionary's boat. They were ingenious.

A naked man might shove the head of an axe up under his "voluminous" armpit with the handle cradled closely against his side while others of his people collaborated by clustering around him to keep the handle out of the missionaries' sight. Smaller items such as silverware, drinking cups, and knives might be hidden in a palm-leaf base container with rice, corn, or fruit. Most of the time, the missionaries noticed almost immediately when an item was missing but occasionally didn't realize it until the item began showing up in use days later on the far bank of the river. By then, the Yuquí seemed to feel the missionaries had forgotten about the item and they could display it freely. Not so!

Alan had a bayonet, a relic of WWII and treasure he had received from his father. He used the knife constantly to cut bait as he fished. While fishing from the houseboat, he laid the knife on a barrel behind him and left for a few minutes. In the meantime, a boatload of Yuquí went back across the river and, unbeknown to him, the bayonet went with them.

Within minutes, Alan noticed the knife was missing and reported it to his dad. Les went across the river where only a small handful of the nomads still remained as the rest had headed back to their camp. The chief and Roughneck were both still there, and Les invited them over, then took them to the barrel and explained about the missing knife. Their reaction made it clear they were aware of the missing knife, although the missionaries knew they hadn't taken it since they were on the other side of the river at the time. Les explained that the knife needed to be returned. The chief and Roughneck were anxious get back across the river and asked for cookies and food before leaving. Les explained that there would be no more cookies, hominy, rice, or any other food until the knife came back. They were grumbling as he took them across the river, and Roughneck insisted that Les leave the shotgun behind.

Within an hour, Favorite Joven and his wife, along with Freddy, George, and Potbelly came out and began calling across the river, holding up the knife to show it had come back. Les climbed in the boat with a small kettle of corn and went over to retrieve the knife, bringing it back to the houseboat along with the three slaves, Freddy, George, and Potbelly. Evidently, their masters had sent them to "test the waters" before others returned to see the missionaries.

The next day, when the nomads came to visit those who came told the story several times of how they got the bayonet away from Iroquois. They made sure the missionaries knew who the guilty party was.

A few days later, a good-sized group came over for lunch and a visit. Both the chief and Iroquois were among them. Later, after Les had taken them back across the river and the aluminum boat was still tied on the nomad side of the river, he heard a big commotion down the trail, loud enough that it could be heard on both sides of the river, and soon the chief showed up again. The chief sounded so furious that Les thought maybe he had spilled the container of food he was taking home for his wife.

Les decided to edge his way toward the boat in case he needed to make his escape, but Roughneck took hold of him and wouldn't let him leave. The chief stared off into space as he jabbered to the group assembled there, and they all looked rather serious. Then the group looked at Les to see how he would take it as Iroquois appeared in the clearing with a cup in his hand. He had stolen the cup in which they had given him Kool-Aid at lunch. He was in a rather foul mood but marched up to Les, handed him the cup, and stalked off. The chief had seen him with the cup and insisted he bring it back before they were all punished for his theft.

Clearly, progress was being made. Lois and Anna, in the meantime, had been washing the lunch dishes, and Anna had just noticed that one of the cups was missing and mentioned it to her mother. Little did she know that the theft had already been dealt with. As Les prepared to head back to the houseboat, a few of the nomads climbed in and accompanied him back to the houseboat where he and Lois cooked up a big pot of fish head soup to share with them. While on this occasion, with the theft of the bayonet fresh in his mind the chief had dealt quickly with the theft, he was not immune to stealing items himself from time to time and missed a few meals on the houseboat because of it.

Straight Hair was a young man of about seventeen years of age and was one of the favorites of all the missionary team. His long black hair was cut with bangs in the front, and while he usually went around completely naked, on this particular day, he had on a holey T-shirt Les had given him. Straight Hair had requested clothing the previous day due to the cold weather, and Les was happy to oblige.

Straight Hair. He was one of the first to put his faith in Christ. He also helped a few years later in making friends with a second band of Yuquí and was shot, but not killed, by them.

Anna, Les' nineteen-year old daughter, was sitting, visiting with Straight Hair on the launch as Les sat nearby, busily writing letters on the typewriter.

Straight Hair was clearly above average, quick to understand what the missionaries were trying to communicate, even though words were still in short supply. He regularly addressed Les as *Miaru*, and insisted that Les refer to him in the same way. It pleased Les to have such a good relationship with this intelligent young man, not understanding that when he said *Miaru*, to Straight Hair, he was saying "son-in-law," and when Straight Hair said it to him, it meant "father-in-law."

Neither Les nor Anna realized it yet, but she had a serious suitor. What Straight Hair didn't know was that Anna had just graduated from high school and, along with her brother Alan, would be leaving in another month to begin life in the United States. Straight Hair wouldn't marry for another five years, and then he would marry one of Toughy's daughters.

For thirty-five days straight, contacts with the nomads continued daily, leaving the missionary team exhausted but thrilled to be making so much progress. Each day, a few nomad hunters would show up and want Les, Bob, or Bill to bring their shotguns and provide them with meat. Finding lost arrows and trying to get them down from high up in a tree took considerable effort, and arrows had to be repaired daily and their points sharpened. Guns had made their lives so much easier as all they had to do was find the game, point to it, and retrieve it after the missionary fired.

Roughneck was ready to hunt and had brought his slave, Scar Face, along to carry the game. Roughneck had also brought his wife and young son along, and the group headed off down the trail with Roughneck in the lead, followed by Les, then Scar Face, with the wife and son coming along behind. Roughneck was carrying an unusually large bundle of arrows, and his wife, Fatty, had a large woven palm-leaf basket on her back supported from her forehead by vines. This seemed to Les like more than the normal hunting trip, but strange things happened daily, so he gave it no lengthy thought.

Around one o'clock, the party stopped for a rest, and Roughneck explained to Les that this was an overnight trip. Les had brought no mosquito net nor provisions for an overnight trip and had no way to communicate to his colleagues or wife that he wouldn't be home that night, so he initially said no, expressing that he needed to go home for the night. After more consideration, he agreed to accompany them, planning to sleep on the ground next to a small campfire.

The party continued on down the trail for ten minutes before Roughneck came to a halt once again. After jabbering unintelligibly to Les for a few moments, Roughneck made it clear to Les that he should make his own way home. As Les described it later:

> There we were, three hours out into the jungle following invisible Yuquí trails and they

expected me to be able to find my way back home. I explained to them that I couldn't find my way home, so after a few minutes of talking Roughneck agreed to send his slave Scar Face to show me the way. I was instructed to feed him, let him sleep with us on the houseboat, and give him food for the journey back to their camp.

After agreeing to those conditions, Les and Scar Face headed back to the houseboat as Roughneck and his family went on their way to join a larger group of nomads farther out in the jungle. After spending the night on a cot in the houseboat, Scar Face got an early start the next morning to rejoin his people somewhere out in the forest.

Les had been nauseated with considerable pain above and to the right of his navel for several days, and with the nomads gone and a flight due to arrive in Puerto Yuca with supplies, it was decided that Les would make a quick trip to Cochabamba to see a doctor. There would still be three missionary men on the contact base, and eighteen-year-old Alan was well-accepted by the nomads and helping in many ways, so Les could be spared for a few days.

When Les arrived in Cochabamba, he headed straight to the doctor's office where the doctor's wife, a lab technician, took a blood sample as the doctor talked with Les and poked around. After viewing the blood work and symptoms, it was determined that the appendix was inflamed, and within thirty minutes, Les and the doctor were at the hospital where the appendix was removed.

Once Les awoke from surgery, the doctor let him know that he had come in the nick of time as the appendix had been close to bursting. Les was concerned about the expenses he had incurred with the flight out as well as surgery since their account in the mission office was already overdrawn, but before he even went into surgery, a coworker let him know that everything was completely paid for. In addition, Anna and Alan would be leaving for the United States in just a few weeks, but before Les headed back to the jungle, he learned that two additional gifts had come in that would cover the airfare with enough margin that he could send his two oldest children off with money in their pockets. He wrote in his journal:

> So I just cried! It's such a blessing to see how God supplies. Had I waited out there in the jungle any longer I probably wouldn't have lived. The appendix was that bad. So, I'm glad that I didn't let the lack of money keep me from coming in.

God is faithful!

Later, as Les looked back on all that had just happened, he could see the Spirit of God directing in so many ways and wrote this counterfactual:

> In thinking back, I wonder what would've happened had I gone with Roughneck and his group on the overnight hunt that day. We would've been out, at least a full day's travel into the jungle or maybe two-or-three-day's travel. As I became sicker and sicker with the appendix and unable to hike back to the mission base, I would likely have died of a burst appendix. Perhaps through fear of a misunderstanding by the missionary team as to cause of my death the nomads may have chosen not to return to the missionary camp and after a few days the team would have become alarmed and reported by radio to the mission and the authorities that I was missing. No doubt the Bolivian Army would have been sent in to look for my body, thinking the nomads had killed me and, if they found the Yuquí would likely have killed without mercy. And the whole misunderstanding would have been brought on by a purely natural cause, not by any treachery by the nomads.

Les was so thankful that God had prompted Roughneck and him to rethink the overnight trip.

By now, the nomads had been gone for three weeks, and the missionaries were pretty sure they had gone north to hunt in the low swamps now that dry season had arrived. Meat was scarce at this time of year, and the team wasn't even getting enough game for their own consumption, although giant catfish were abundant and easy to catch at this time of year. The easiest way to get game was to motor upriver before dark and then paddle quietly down the river after dark, using a spotlight to shine along the river's edge and locate animals that had come down to drink.

Alligators could also be gotten by this method, and with a texture similar to lobster, alligators were always enjoyed whether boiled and dipped in butter or deep fried. On this particular night, as the men were paddling down the river, Les spotted an unusual set of eyes. Alligator eyes reflect orange in the light, whereas these eyes were farther up the bank and reflected more yellow. Les' first thought was that it might be a jaguar or maybe even a tapir. The animal was too far away to shoot with the shotgun, so Les used the .30-30 Winchester rifle.

It was clear that he hadn't killed the animal, only wounded it as they could hear it thrashing around up in the edge of the jungle. Les wasn't at all eager to face a wounded jaguar, so he waited until the thrashing had subsided somewhat and then edged up into the bamboo with gun ready. The beam of the light shone on a snarling ocelot, ears laid back, teeth bared, ready to spring. Les put another shot into it, this time in the neck, and they took it home to eat.

These "little tigers," or *tigrecillos* as the local Spanish speakers call them, really do look like small jaguars, a beautiful animal. The missionaries found that it was also edible, tasting much like venison. A few nights later, Bob shot a buck deer, and they were able to have venison steaks along with their usual diet of fried bananas and manioc. Tapir was the preferred meat, tasting much like beef. A tapir dressed out at about 400 pounds and was more meat than the team had capacity to store without spoilage, although when the Yuquí were around, there was no waste as they devoured the excess meat.

* * * * *

It was four months before the Yuquí returned, and the missionaries were pleased to see them once again. Soon they settled back into the familiar routine—cook corn, cook rice, go hunting, bring people over for lunch, etc., etc. One day, Bill was visiting with the Yuquí on the west bank of the river and called over to Les at the houseboat to bring food over as the chief was getting restless.

Les loaded up a few Yuquí who were going back across with him, and after they squatted down in the bottom of the boat, they reached over and clung to his legs as if their lives depended on it. At least they had progressed from the early days when they would squat *and* cover themselves with palm leaves, so their fear of crossing the river in a tiny boat was slowly evaporating.

As Les neared the far bank of the river, he saw Bill lying there with two eight-foot long Yuquí arrows sticking out of him. The chief was yelling, trying to get Les' attention, and then he ran over to Bill, put his foot on Bill's chest and, grabbing the arrow shanks with much force, pulled them out. Then he picked Bill up, brushed him off, and there the two of them stood, grinning from ear to ear, just having some friendly fun!

Later, Bill explained to Les that the chief was very careful to plant the two arrows between his arms and chest, using the arm pressure to hold them up into the air. After the many colonists Les had seen shot by nomad arrows during his years based out of Todos Santos, he had a difficult time seeing the humor, although as he thought about it, he knew it showed that they had come a very long way in their relationship with the Yuquí, but the many shootings and close encounters were still too fresh in his memory.

The friendly times together still had the potential to quickly turn lethal as Les wrote:

We never know from one minute to the next what will happen next in this work with naked Stone-Age people. For them to kill a human appears to be no worse than to kill an animal. But the longer we are with them, the better we are getting to "know" them. They are people just like all others. They can be very affectionate with one another, and with us. When I recently suffered an appendix attack the chief pressed on the pain with his fist and blew on it. When a hornet stung me on the face, they all expressed their concern for me. When Roughneck found a tree with wild honey, he gave me more than he took himself and even gave me some to take home to my children. Even though at times they are a fierce people, yet I find it easy to love them. They are "my" people. God has given them to us as friends, to teach them of Christ and present them back to God as His people.

Fire was essential to the Yuquí, and there were always several campfires burning in their camps. When they migrated, the elderly, disabled, or women always carried several smoldering sticks, keeping the glowing tips together, and from time to time, the entire group would come to a halt when the fire was getting weak and take time to build it up. Not only did fire give smoke that reduced the biting insect pests in their camps and provide warmth during cold weather, it was also crucial for cooking their most important food—meat.

Meat was always eaten well-cooked, either boiled in a kettle or can, baked in the coals, or smoked on a rack of green sticks. Often you would see one of the Yuquí pinching or breaking open a piece of smoked meat, checking the moisture content as they wanted it well-done, very dry, with no visible redness. Blood was never swallowed.

If their mouth bled for some reason, they would spit and spit until the bleeding stopped. As to fire, if a small group of Yuquí was traveling and their fire went out, they might either send a "runner" to another group of their band to bring back fire or shoot a colonist in order to steal his fire. Fire was critical for survival.

Soon they learned that their new friends could make fire at any time, either with matches or more often with a cigarette lighter, and they were thrilled when the missionaries showed them how to use a butane lighter and then gave them their own to carry along with a warning not to put it in the fire as some of them initially wanted to do. They also discovered that the lighters could run out of fire (lighter fluid) so would bring them back to have more "fire" added.

With this new friendship, they now had a constant source of fire and often showed up asking for fire. They also felt no need to carry fire with them when returning to see the missionaries after a trip. The missionaries were proving valuable in more ways than one.

A group of nomads showed up—the chief and his wife, Roughneck and family, Wooly Hair, and a few others. Roughneck wanted to inspect Les' feet, and once his shoes were off, carefully cleaned a cracked area in his foot. Milk Shake Girl showed up, bringing her new baby for all to see. In the meantime, the chief's wife had gotten some lettuce from Lois and was crumpling it in her hands, squeezing the moisture out of it and rubbing it on her husband's chest in a medicinal manner before requesting more lettuce. Fortunately, Lois had started a small garden and was able to provide lettuce that had not been flown in at great expense.

About this time, Favorite Joven and Wooly Hair came over, bringing a nice piece of roasted tapir which they gave to Les and Lois. What a treat! Moments later, Les turned around to see Wooly Hair and Chinaman swiftly climbing trees. They had seen Yogi the dog coming their way and still didn't trust this animal they called a jaguar. Yogi was defensive of her family, the Fosters, and the Yuquí had seen evidence of that, so they gave her due respect.

The following day was not so laid back, and tension rose steadily throughout the morning until the contact ended with a bang in the late afternoon. When the nomads arrived, they had been carrying their hammocks, pots, axes and machetes, and some had huge bundles of arrows. One brought a thick palm board and was carving a bow from it. They had manioc and bananas with them, as well as meat.

The group of thirty-six who had come were demanding, restless, and getting physically rough with the missionaries. First, the chief wanted his wife to stay overnight with the missionaries. She was a mischievous demanding individual and one of the habitual thieves, often making their lives difficult. They didn't think keeping such a tough woman overnight was a good idea. When the missionaries said no, the chief wanted his slave George to spend the night.

Again, the answer was no.

Next he proposed that Wooly Hair spend the night, and when the answer was once again no, Wooly Hair got upset and began rattling his arrows in anger. At that point, Iroquois stepped up and wanted to wrestle with Les. Wrestling with the Yuquí was never a good idea since if their wrestler was losing, others would step in to help, and the situation would quickly get out of hand. Les had already seen this happen several times during the La Jota and El Naranjal contacts and had a firm no wrestling rule. Others insisted that he wrestle with Toughy.

With the situation going downhill, Bill and Les finally got in the aluminum boat to go back to their side of the river. As they were leaving, a few of the nomads pointed down river and yelled, "*Abaa! Abaa!*" *Abaa* was what they called anyone who was not one of them and could mean Bolivian national or enemy. Were there Bolivian hunters nearby, camped just down river? Les sure hoped not as the Yuquí might encounter the hunters, and someone would likely get shot.

The Yuquí had not yet reached a point where they trusted the world outside of their missionary friends. As Les and Bill headed to the houseboat, the Yuquí dispersed into the jungle, although an hour or so later, two slave brothers, George and Freddy, came back and called across the river to the missionaries until almost dark. Evidently, they were camped nearby.

As so often happened, the group of twenty-four that showed up the following day were a pleasure to have around. Overnight, the attitudes had dissipated and the tension was gone. Only three men had come along with six women and fifteen children. Bringing so many children in itself was evidence of the trust the nomads had in their new friends.

Later, two more men showed up, and Les went hunting with most of the men during the morning while Bill took the afternoon hunting shift. Favorite Joven had an injured knee which the missionaries medicated and gave him sweetened water to drink along with some cookies. When Iroquois arrived, he was carrying a palm heart and wanted to trade it for sugar. Little by little, the missionaries had been introducing the concept of trading—a machete for an arrow, an axe for a bow, sugar for a palm heart, and so on; although in the beginning, sometimes the Yuquí would come back later and want their item returned without wanting to give back what they had received.

It took time and patience before they understood clearly that the trade was a permanent exchange. On at least one occasion, a Yuquí warrior had drawn his bow and pointed an arrow at a missionary when they refused to give back an arrow he had traded. It had been a near thing as another missionary intervened, holding the shooter's hand to keep him from releasing the arrow.

George spent the night on a cot in Bob's kitchen and enjoyed being the sole object of attention for a number of hours, eating with the Garland family and enjoying a night in a screened house without the omnipresent insects he was used to in his camp. As the chief's slave, George spent most nights on a palm mat on the ground next to his master's hammock, keeping the campfire smoking and hammock swinging so his master could sleep. He also went hungry when food was in short supply, cleaned and cooked game for his master, gathered firewood, brought water from a swamp, creek, or river as needed and, in general, was the chief's "man Friday."

The following day, Dick and Les accompanied a group of hunters and were surprised when their guides led them through the jungle to the first abandoned nomad camp the missionaries had initially discovered in the area and where they had hung gifts. Nearby was a swamp the missionaries had crossed before discovering that camp. The Yuquí wanted to hunt capybara in and around the swamp.

The capybara, the world's largest rodent, stands as much as two feet tall, is three to four feet long, and can weigh up to 150 pounds. It has a thick skin with a generous quantity of fat under the skin, which the nomads prized as most game in the jungle was lean. In the swamp were areas of open water as well as sections covered with a thick matted grass that could, if one was careful, be walked on, always with the risk of breaking through to the murky depths below, not the kind of place the squeamish would want to go. It didn't help once you learned that vipers such as the water version of the fer-de-lance loved the swamp.

Anacondas, caiman, man-eating piranha fish, and many other fearsome creatures also lived in the swamp. But for a people such as the Yuquí, who had to hunt to survive, the succulent treasures of the swamp made the terrors worth the risk. Today, the capybara seemed to be hiding in their dens along the swamp edge as none were showing themselves, but Les spotted a campanilla turkey, a type of guan, and at the same instant he shot, a breeze sprang up.

The nomad hunters began yelling, "Waa! Waa!" rattling their bows and arrows together, threatening the wind to make it stop. Evidently, they believed the breeze was sent by the spirits of their ancestors who lived along the sky, but threatening the wind seemed to do little good. Were the spirits keeping them from finding capybara? Did the spirits need to be appeased?

The hunt yielded a few birds but no meat of consequence, and later in the afternoon, as they headed home, the nomads took the missionaries to their main camp where they stopped to rest and visit. The Yuquí were quite fearful as a tiger had come close by their camp the previous night. Would the missionaries be willing to bring their guns and spend the night? This would be a new milestone in the growing relationship and a chance to observe a unique culture close up while picking up new words. Seeing the Yuquí interact with one another in their own natural setting would be a special privilege!

After agreeing to spend the night, Dick and Les indicated they would need to return to the houseboat first for their hammocks. They had WWII vintage jungle hammocks complete with waterproof roof and mosquito netting.

Once they returned to the nomad encampment, they were told to hang their hammocks near where the chief had his hammock slung. There were fifteen ambaibo bark rope hammocks hanging in the clearing, and they soon discovered that most hammocks held a whole family. The Yuquí hung their hammocks low, only three or four inches from the ground, so they didn't have far to fall if the rope broke.

The chief, his wife, and two of their grandchildren relaxed in one hammock. People sat around in hammocks or squatted on the ground as the Yuquí shared food with Les and Dick, roasted squirrel meat, turtle liver (a delicacy) and turtle leg, bananas, corn, rice, several different kinds of wild honey, some boiled tuberous roots, as well as various unknown jungle fruits. Very young green *marayaú* palm fruit was cooked and eaten whole, seeds and all.

As dusk came, Dick and Les acted out with a flashlight how they would kill the tiger. If the nomads heard the tiger, they were to awaken Les by quietly calling, "*Tibakede! Tibakede! Yagua! Yagua* (Les! Les! Tiger! Tiger!)!" Then Dick would shine the flashlight in the tiger's eyes, and Les would shoot it.

As they acted it out, Les went to the edge of the clearing, made the tiger call, and started slowly toward the camp. Dick quickly turned his flashlight on Les who pretended to be frozen with fear. Then Dick made a loud "boom," and Les fell to the ground as a dead tiger. They were all very impressed and wanted the men to act it out over and over again. The Yuquí made a game out of it for quite some time until everyone knew the plan. As it grew darker, Les could see by the firelight a nearby hammock with arms, legs, and heads sticking out all over. Everyone had gone to bed at the first sign of darkness, although there was much talking in low voices and once, during the night, a hammock rope broke, dumping its occupants to the ground, eliciting some muttered imprecations. The spirit world was once again actively making their lives miserable. The hammock rope was knotted back together, and the family climbed back in, contorting themselves into the most comfortable positions possible.

Les didn't get much sleep that night with the nervousness of being in a nomad camp overnight for the first time and with trying to observe all he could of their camp life. For some time, he had noticed a caste system among them, and it appeared that even in the hanging of their hammocks, they were hung somewhat according to their rank in the group. He also observed that the principal warriors, the chief's sons, had younger boys tending the fires on each side of their hammocks, and the hammocks were kept swinging much of the night which, along with the smoke, helped keep the mosquitoes at bay.

Around 2:15 a.m., Les awoke after dozing briefly. He could hear a creature of some kind calling in the jungle, and the nomads seemed frightened. Several of the men started yelling, "Waa! Waa!" And then after a while, all was quiet again. Again, Les dozed momentarily, only to awaken to a noise that sounded like a large animal with a tin can on one foot walking on a cement sidewalk. The nomads paid no attention to the sound which was thumping an uneven rhythm. Once it might be four quick thumps, a pause, and seven quick thumps, a pause, and two quick thumps. Then there would be a long pause and it would start over with maybe six quick thumps, a pause, two quick thumps, a pause, and nine quick thumps.

This went on for some time as his imagination ran wild. He pictured one of them thumping to the spirits who were making the "tin can" sound out in the jungle. Finally, as one of the fires flared up a little, he could see Favorite Joven sitting in his hammock. He would take one of his arrows, run it through the fire to warm it, then hold it up, sighting along it toward the starry sky, then "thump" as he bent it to straighten it. Les made the mistake of clearing his throat, which showed Favorite Joven he was awake, and he called over and invited Les to join him beside the fire as he continued getting ready for the morning hunt.

By then, it was 3:00 a.m. as Les sat, warming himself, and watched as arrows were prepared for the hunt. At 4:00 a.m., Dick joined them, squatting by the fire, and soon Les, Dick, Favorite Joven, and Freddy were on their way looking for game. Even in the jungle, the "early bird gets the worm!"

It was still too dark to see where you were placing your feet, and Les knew well that most pit vipers were night hunters. He hoped that by 4:00 a.m., they had decided to go back to their dens as there was no chance of him seeing them in the early darkness. The God who stopped the mouths of the lions for Daniel could certainly close the mouths of fer-de-lances and bushmasters. Now Les mentioned that to God, trusting that God would have a word with His creatures, letting them know to ignore the hunting party.

The hunt was not too successful, only one *guaracachi* turkey, a type of guan. They also saw a large razor-billed curassow turkey but weren't able to get a shot at it, and shortly after daylight, they were back in the nomad camp where Favorite Joven began preparing the guaracachi for his family's breakfast. As he did that, Les and Dick rolled up their hammocks, getting ready to accompany the Yuquí to the river and back home to the houseboat.

The nomads were still concerned about the tiger, so Bob and Bill prepared their bedrolls and jungle hammocks and followed the Yuquí off into the forest to spend the day looking for capybara with the plan of overnighting in the nomad camp. While Bob and Bill were able to shoot an assortment of fifteen birds for the Yuquí, they shot no capybara, although some of the nomad hunters with them were more successful and killed three of the rodents with bow and arrow.

The following day, after the animals had been roasted over the fire on a rack composed of green sticks, the chief sent a whole roasted capybara leg for the missionaries to enjoy. Bob and Bill spent the night in the nomad camp but arrived home hungry, not having eaten as well as Les and Dick. One factor may have been that Les and Dick had many more years of jungle life and had learned to eat foods that Bob and Bill had not yet learned to appreciate.

Roughneck seemed to have developed a special friendship with Les, although it would be many more months before the missionaries learned that the Yuquí considered Les to be the reincarnated son of the chief and his wife, a son who died of snakebite. In the Yuquí kinship, this would make Les Roughneck's older brother, and interestingly enough, from early on in the contacts, the Yuquí had insisted that Les call Roughneck *Yaqui*, meaning younger brother, although the missionaries had yet to figure out the meaning of the term.

Toughy, Wide Eyes, and Favorite Joven were also sons of the chief and his wife, so Les was directly tied to the "ruling" family. This probably went a long way toward explaining their greater respect for him than for many of his coworkers during the contacts five years earlier.

Les had pulled a muscle in his left leg and wasn't able to go hunting. Roughneck had shown up with his wife, Fatty, and slave, Scar Face, and when he saw that Les was in pain, he had him drop his trousers while he massaged the sore muscle and then took achiote and rubbed it all over Les, not just on the leg, and then all over himself. How better to protect yourself from illness brought on by the spirits of your ancestors than by covering yourself in orange coloring?

By the following day, Les' leg was feeling enough better that he and Bob were able to go hunting with Roughneck, his wife, Fatty, Straight Hair, and slave, Scarface. They went north through the forest until they came to the original plantain patch the missionaries had planted and then made a wide circle west and south as they made their way back to where the Yuquí were currently camped. Along the way, they shot several birds, and soon, Les was nearly out of shells. It was then that a mother tayra (black weasel-like animal) ran out of a hollow *pachuba* palm log lying on the ground.

Straight Hair quickly ran to the open end of the log and tromped down on it so any other animals in it couldn't escape; then, with the tip of a palm hardwood bow, they began prying the rotten palm wood apart. Once they had opened a small crack in the log, they began tormenting the two young tayras who were still inside, making them cry. Soon the mother was circling around wanting to get back to her young but only showing herself for brief moments. As she came into view, Les took a quick shot but missed. Eventually, the Yuquí contented themselves with killing the two baby tayras and taking them along since the mother had disappeared after Les' shot.

The caste system was constantly in view in a variety of ways. One day, White Joven's wife, Queenie, came across to visit the missionaries and was willing to trade a baby sling, the bark rope skirt that the women wore, for two empty hundred-pound cotton sugar sacks. When Fatty showed up and saw the desirable sacks, she took them from Queenie and, in return, gave her two cotton diapers Mary had given her.

Later in the day, Les saw Fatty again, and this time, she had both the sacks and the diapers. Fatty was married to Roughneck, the chief's son, whereas Queenie's husband, White Joven, ranked lower in the caste system. While no longer truly a slave, he was lower in the social order. "Pulling rank" was observed often. After a time, the missionaries came up with ways to help the downtrodden without getting them in too much trouble with the higher ranked individuals. A simple example that was seen often was with foodstuff. If a sugar cookie was given to a slave, they wouldn't eat it but would carry it around until the missionaries weren't watching and then give it to their master; otherwise, they might be beaten.

As the missionaries picked up on this, they found that if they handed the slave a cookie and insisted he or she eat it then and there, everyone could see that they had eaten it "against their will," and the master wouldn't punish them. On the other hand, if the object couldn't be eaten and the master wanted it, there wasn't much the missionaries could do about it.

The day began with Favorite Joven bringing a bow and two arrows and wanting to trade them for an axe. His slave, Big Tummy, waited patiently on the far bank of the river while Favorite Joven made the trade and then stayed for lunch with the missionaries. Shortly after lunch, Favorite Joven and Big Tummy left after telling the missionaries that they were going on an extended hunt and would be gone for several days to the south. South was not a direction the missionaries liked to see them go as most of the colonies were to the south and west, and there was still no friendship between colonist and nomad.

Within an hour, the chief, Toughy, Favorite Joven, Scar Face, and Big Tummy were back, calling urgently to the missionaries from the clearing across the river. "Roughneck has been shot in the leg by an *abaa*, an enemy national," was the report. It was late in the day, so Bob and Les grabbed their jungle hammocks and gathered up an assortment of medical supplies. "Bring fire and many shells to shoot the enemies," commanded the chief.

The nomads were camped two hours away, and when the men arrived, they found Roughneck surrounded by the entire group who were crying and wailing. It wasn't easy for Les to get near him as everyone wanted to be close to the injured warrior. There was a long shallow gash and several smaller cuts on the front of his left leg above the knee that didn't look much like a bullet wound. It turned out that had just been a story the nomads used, knowing the missionaries would be sure to respond.

The missionaries were constantly advising them of the danger of going anywhere near the Bolivian farms, strongly discouraging them by telling them how deadly guns were. When they were finally told the true story, Bob and Les learned that Roughneck had been perched several feet off the ground on the hefty horizontal branch of one tree as he chopped into another tree to open a bee's nest and extract the honey. He had fallen from the limb and was in considerable pain, although no bones appeared to be broken.

Les cleaned the cuts and applied Merthiolate liberally as the Yuquí loved the orange color. Les had a syringe along which he sanitized by boiling and then was going to give Roughneck a shot of Demerol, an analgesic, but the nomads surrounding Roughneck refused to let Les inject the painkiller. Bob had brought along a bottle of aspirin, so Plan B was implemented as Les took an aspirin and swallowed it, demonstrating to Roughneck what he should do.

The chief's wife asked for an aspirin, stuck it against her tongue to see how it tasted, spit and spit, trying to get the taste out of her mouth, and again, the people refused on Roughneck's behalf. Iroquois bravely tried an aspirin, and when he didn't have any bad reaction, Roughneck took one but, instead of swallowing, began to chew it, spitting it out in disgust. Once again, Les explained that he needed to swallow it whole, and when Roughneck acquiesced, Les handed him a stronger analgesic instead of an aspirin. It seemed like that was all they would be able to do.

After an hour passed, Les gave him a second pain pill, and soon, Roughneck was drowsy, sleeping through the night with very little groaning. While Les was busy treating Roughneck, Favorite Joven's wife was busy flirting with Bob, offering him food and making sexual advances. Later, when Roughneck was resting, his wife, Fatty, tried a similar approach with Les, but both men made it clear they had wives back home and weren't interested.

Long before dawn, Iroquois came to Les' hammock and awakened him, whispering, "*Yaso piri ya* (Let's go hunting)." By now, Les knew what this phrase meant, so he climbed out of the hammock and into his clammy clothing, shaking out his shoes carefully before putting them on. You never knew what creature might have chosen to bed down in your shoes—a scorpion, centipede, tarantula, or snake—so it was wise to either sleep with them in your netted jungle hammock or shake them out before putting them on.

Soon, Les and Iroquois approached a swamp where they would look for alligators. To see the open water, they had to wade through shallow water and head-high grass heavy with dew. It wasn't long until Les was soaked from the moisture on the grass. The fog lay in low layers over the wetlands, and a large silvery moon made the whole scene look like a prehistoric setting. One could almost imagine huge dinosaurs rising up out of the swamps.

Eventually, they spotted an alligator, but it had seen them and made its escape. Next, they heard the loud weird cry of a cattle rustler bird or *tapacaré* as it is known in Spanish. This large condor-like bird has three-inch-long horny spikes, much like a rooster spur on the outer joint of its wings. The bird, known to the Yuquí as a *chaguahu*, took off before the two men saw it, but Les shot it in midair.

Iroquois was convinced he had missed the bird, but eventually, they found it where it had fallen in the dense marsh grass. They were able to sneak up on the bird's mate, but it was a little out of range for the shotgun, so they weren't able to shoot it. Much of the time they were hunting, they could hear two different troops of red howler monkeys, one on each side of swamp. Their roaring made one think of a lion, and it could be frightening if you didn't know what animal was making such a fearsome sound.

Iroquois wanted to continue to the far side of the swamp and shoot howler monkeys, but Les convinced him to return to camp. Along the way, they were able to shoot two more birds, one of them a razor-billed curassow.

The caste system displayed itself again in an incident that happened the next day. Lois had caught a large gilded catfish, a gorgeous silver and gold predator that puts up an exciting fight. Lois loved fishing, and while she sometimes used a handline due to the size of the tropical fish, she also had a deep-sea rod and reel she enjoyed using. This fish was caught on the handline and would have been too large for her rod and reel.

Les was busy dressing out the fish when Freddy, Toughy, and a few others showed up and spent some time going back and forth visiting the missionaries and before returning to their side, the west side of the river. When the missionaries and their guests finished lunch, Les took the last few nomads across the river along with a piece of leftover fish and some potatoes with a plan to give it to one of the Yuquí who hadn't had much to eat. Toughy had been well-fed, but Freddy, being a slave, had received little.

When Les exited the boat on the west bank of the river, Toughy saw that he intended to give the food to Freddy, so he grabbed him and tried to take the fish and potatoes by force, wrestling with Les and attempting to throw him to the ground. Les finally called to Bob and said, "Pull your pistol out." When Bob obeyed, all the Yuquí turned on Bob and started scolding him. The plan had worked. Toughy had released Les, but now the nomads were upset with Bob, and he was concerned as he felt that the people would lose trust in him.

Twice in the past, Les had needed to lift a shotgun or pull a pistol when a situation was getting out of hand, and he expressed to Bob that he didn't think it would have any long-term consequence. Lifting a shotgun or pulling a pistol in a threatening manner was not something the missionaries wanted to do unnecessarily, but Les heartily agreed with a statement he had read in the November 1965 edition of the *Reader's Digest*: "One of the tests of leadership is the ability to recognize problems before it becomes an emergency." Wrestling with the Yuquí could quickly become a life-threatening emergency.

For fifteen days, contacts continued on a daily basis, and when the nomads eventually let it be known that they were planning an extended hunting trip, Les let them know that some of the missionaries would also be taking a trip and would be gone for many days. The houseboat needed major maintenance work, rotting planks needed to be replaced in the hull, and after the work was done, the launch could be loaded with supplies for the missionary team and foodstuff for the Yuquí. It was far less expensive to bring heavy bulky loads by water than by air, although it was time-consuming. This would be the last trip to Todos Santos with the houseboat before selling it, so they needed to take advantage of the trip. Now that a permanent camp had been established on the Chimoré River the missionaries didn't need a mobile base.

On this trip, the missionaries would also have a smaller wooden boat built in Todos Santos, one that could be used in the daily trips back and forth across the Chimoré River with the Yuquí and could also be used for supply runs to the airstrip at Puerto Yuca.

Four days after the nomads traveled and the launch departed, five Yuquí showed up across the river from Garland's house, saw the launch and aluminum boat were missing and, after yelling back and forth for twenty minutes, went on their way. The aluminum boat was hidden behind one of the missionary houses, available in case of emergency so they could get to the airstrip at Puerto Yuca. With only Dick Strickler and Bob Garland on the base, the team had decided not to take the risk of having contacts with the Yuquí until Les, Lois, Bill, and Mildred returned. It would be two months before contact with the nomads resumed.

Les and Lois spent much of that time in Todos Santos and some in Cochabamba, buying supplies. The launch would take several weeks to be repaired as it had to be floated out of the river when the water was high and then left sitting up on barrels on dry ground while boards in the hull were replaced and re-caulked. Then they would need the river to rise again so the boat could be refloated. Much would depend on the weather cooperating.

Many people wanted to hear how the work with the Yuquí was going, so Les and Lois interacted with individuals, churches, and in other venues as they showed pictures and movies and told stories of the challenges involved in building this friendship. Countless people wanted to visit the Chimoré base and meet the nomads firsthand, but the missionary team was trying to protect the Yuquí by keeping them isolated from colds, flu, and other illnesses against which they had little or no resistance and did their best to discourage visitors. Little by little, exposure would come, but the slower it came, the more chance of survival this small band of forty-nine people would have.

While in Todos Santos, Les and Lois packed up the last of their belongings from the rooms they had been renting there for almost ten years and said their goodbyes to their many friends. They weren't sure if they would ever be back to the town where they had learned Spanish and adjusted to a new way of life. They also arranged for the eventual sale of the houseboat to Don Hilarión, personal friend and chief elder of the local church. They would let him know when they were finished with the launch and then make arrangements for him to pick it up at an agreed upon location.

There were many tearful goodbyes, especially from their land-lady, Doña María, as the whole Foster family had grown close to her. Knowing how much she, as a widow, had counted on the rent, Les paid her for an extra month as a last gesture of love and friendship.

Álvaro and a friend also came to have a last meal with the Fosters and to say their goodbyes. A very special chapter was closing in the life of the Foster family, and a new life was well underway on the Chimoré River.

* * * * *

During the two-month break from contact with the Yuquí on the Chimoré, numerous rumors reached the ears of the missionaries concerning the nomads. Four domestic pigs had been shot near the Yura mission on the Chapare River and many bananas stolen. Later, the rumor was verified by the nomads themselves when they returned and reported how sick most of the group had gotten from the heavy amount of fat the domesticated pigs contained. As usual, when they had an abundance of meat, they had "pigged" out on the excessively fat meat and learned that too much fat wasn't a good thing.

Next, a rumor came in that Bolivian hunters had their steel tiger traps stolen by the Yuquí, but due to where the incident was reported to have happened and the fact that the nomads had no use for tiger traps, the missionaries considered it much more likely that another Bolivian hunter "appropriated" the traps. It was always convenient to blame the nomads.

Later, it was reported that the nomads were seen near the colony of La Jota two kilometers from the Chimoré River. This rumor was likely true as the next day, Orlando and Francisco Blanco, friends of the missionaries, came to report that they had seen fresh tracks of the Yuquí while hunting in that area, and the nomads had raided one of their farms, cleaning out the bananas and manioc. The brothers wanted the missionaries to pay for their stolen crops and threatened "war to the death" against the nomads. Add to that the fact that their brother, Cristóbal, had been wounded by the Yuquí a few years previously, and it was understandable that they were fed up with the nomads making their lives difficult.

Francisco groused, "If one of us loses our lives to the savages, the government thinks nothing about it, but if one of you Yankees lost his life, the government might do something about it."

Les did his best to assure Francisco that he cared deeply about every individual in the area and was doing his utmost to settle the Yuquí down and bring about respect and friendship between them and the local people. Months later, Francisco and Orlando were two of the first outsiders to become friends with the Yuquí, and a few years later, Francisco taught the Yuquí to use canoes and to fish with gill nets, providing them with a method to more easily get a good supply of protein.

By mid-December, the houseboat had come out of dry-dock and was loaded and ready for its last trip to the Chimoré River. Day three of the trip, the launch was traveling up the Ichilo River when they saw a sight that Les described as "something straight out of Huckleberry Finn."

A large raft of logs was coming down the Ichilo River as they were going up. There were thirteen men aboard the raft, some in swimming trunks, who jumped overboard from time to time to check the lashings holding the massive raft together. A little hut roofed with palm leaves had been built on the raft, and a fifty-gallon gasoline drum had been cut in half to use as a wood stove for cooking. Two dugout canoes were tied to the raft and drifting along behind while three men in another dugout were also accompanying the raft but occasionally paddling closer to shore to shoot game, providing food for those onboard the raft.

The raft was heading for a sawmill down river, and at the speed they were traveling, it would take at least three days to get there, assuming they didn't get caught on a snag or run aground on a sandbar. It would be a leisurely float down one of the tributaries of the mighty Amazon.

By the third week of December, the houseboat was once again moored across from the clearing on the Chimoré River where the Yuquí normally came to meet the missionaries, but it would still be three weeks before they reappeared. Coming back from Todos Santos, Les had loaded the houseboat with three varieties of rhizomes or bulbs for eating bananas he intended to plant. He had also brought pineapple plants and an assortment of other plants he hoped to grow both for their own consumption and to abundantly provide for the Yuquí.

He worked at getting all the plants in the ground while they were still viable and then, two days later, took Dick Strickler by boat to the airstrip at Puerto Yuca. Dick was heading to the homeland to visit family and ministry partners. The flight that would take Dick out would also bring in the Foster, Garland, and Presson children for their month-long vacation from boarding school.

While in Todos Santos, Les had also had a new wooden boat called a *chalupa* built for making the supply runs to Puerto Yuca and for using daily as they brought the Yuquí back and forth across the Chimoré River. The new boat constructed of boards was twenty-one feet long and six feet wide and could haul more cargo than the smaller aluminum boat they had been using.

Once the houseboat was sold, they would have the two small boats for crossing the river and for making supply runs.

* * * * *

The first week of January, after their Christmas vacation, all the school-aged missionary children on the base boarded a decrepit Bolivian Army plane, the only small aircraft available at the time, to begin their trip back to boarding school. As the plane flew above the clouds on the hour-long flight back to Santa Cruz, the engine started acting up, no longer able to keep the plane aloft.

The pilot dropped through the cloud cover, fully expecting to try a crash landing in the dense, tree-covered jungle, but Praise God! As the plane came out of the clouds, a small grass airstrip came into view. He landed with no idea of whose strip it might be, and all aboard were pleased when they learned that it was a base for the Dick Moore family of World Gospel Mission.

Dick was able to notify the team on the Chimoré that their children were safe and in good hands as the two missions operated on the same radio frequency. It took a few days to arrange another plane and get the children to Santa Cruz, but the gracious WGM missionaries took good care of them in the meantime. As Les wrote in a letter, "The children could all have been killed in a crash in the jungle had it not been for this airstrip right under them when they needed it. It just shows me again that when we put our whole trust in the Lord. He will never let us fall."

The same day in January that the missionary children left for boarding school after their month-long Christmas vacation, the nomads showed up, back from their extended hunting trip. The second morning, a large group of twenty-eight Yuquí showed up, and the day was spent ferrying small groups back and forth across the river in the new chalupa as missionaries and Yuquí spent time together on each side of the river.

Les spent a good portion of his day cutting children's hair. The Yuquí had seen Lois trim Les' hair with her scissors, and the nomads loved how easy it was to shorten hair with scissors. Their method of cutting hair was to take a segment of bamboo and split it lengthwise. Sometimes it required splitting several times before getting the proper resultant edge, which was razor sharp, although the sharp edge dulled quickly. Using the sharp edge of the bamboo, they would saw off handfuls of hair. The result was somewhat ragged but eventually grew out more evenly. Scissors soon became a desired object, but for now, Les' free barbershop was the hit of the day.

Several of the Yuquí women were pregnant—Fatty, Queenie, Toughy's wife, and one other. With his wife, Fatty, in the family way, Roughneck would no longer let the missionaries touch him as that was taboo. Also, when he climbed into the wooden boat to go across the river, he covered himself carefully with palm branches. Over the next weeks, the missionaries began learning more about taboos related to pregnancy.

Soon Bill, Bob, and Les were back in a routine of daily hunts with the nomads. As Bill was cleaning his shotgun one day, preparing for the hunt, he failed to remove live ammunition from the chamber, and the gun went off, accidentally blowing a hole through his kitchen roof. Some of nomad hunters were there watching him oil the gun and were thoroughly shaken up, as was Bill. Thankfully, no one was injured, and it was a lesson in gun safety for all.

Bob and Les accompanied a group of nomads to their camp back in the jungle on the west side of the river where Bob spent the day interacting with those in the camp as he worked to gather more language material for Mary to analyze. As a mother with small children, Mary wasn't able to get out with Yuquí as much as the other missionaries were, so Bob especially, and the rest of the team as well, gathered words and phrases as they were able and passed them along to Mary so she could try to bring some logical order to it all. They were also keeping their eyes open for a Yuquí woman or young lady who seemed to be above average and might be able to spend time with Mary on a regular basis, helping her understand the intricacies of the language.

Leaving Bob in the Yuquí camp, Les took off hunting with Favorite Joven, George, Straight Hair, and Chinaman. After shooting a large razor-billed curassow, a macaw, and a small parrot, the men headed back to the nomad camp. On the return trip, Straight Hair, who was in the lead, reached over to take two small eggs from a bird's nest that George had spotted on the way out and indicated he planned to pick up on his return. George, a slave, made a grab for Straight Hair, the chief's grandson, and threw him down. They started wrestling and choking each other in anger.

Favorite Joven joined the fray on behalf of Straight Hair, pulling George's legs over his head to where Straight Hair ended up on top. Then when George started getting the best of him, Favorite Joven once again joined in, choking George and digging his thumbs into George's eyes.

Chinaman also jumped on George. It was a very unfair fight and very dirty with much slugging, eye-gouging, hair-pulling, slapping, choking, etc. Poor George was quite beaten up and abused all over two small bird's eggs. Once again, the caste system had raised its ugly head. Favorite Joven, one of the chief's sons, and his nephew, Straight Hair, saw to it that the chief's slave, George, was kept in his place. In a fair one-on-one fight, George could easily have bested Straight Hair, but the ruling class kept the lower class in their place.

Straight Hair, nineteen-year-old grandson of the chief, was above average intelligence and a quick learner. Even though Anna had left for the United States, Straight Hair still spent much time on the houseboat with the Fosters and was adapting well to the new way of life. He was showing interest in learning more about guns and, while it was still too soon to trust the nomads with such a weapon, Les saw no problem teaching Straight Hair to use the BB gun Alan had left behind.

Soon, Straight Hair was out shooting at every little bird he could find. He also spent many hours on the houseboat looking through *National Geographic* magazines. Initially, it took a little time before most of the Yuquí could recognize pictures on the pages, but once again, Straight Hair was quicker than the rest at distinguishing the pictures, and this proved to be an excellent way for the missionaries to gather many object-like words quickly.

As Straight Hair thumbed through the magazines, he let Les know what the pictures were calling all non-Yuquí people, *abaa* (enemies), and all unknown birds *etimaaguä* (chickens), but anytime he recognized an animal or object, he gave the word in his language. Les pulled out a picture of Dick Strickler who was gone for the year. "*Esaimaji*," Straight Hair responded. Dick wore glasses, and the name they called him by eventually turned out to mean "to have covered/ wrapped eyes."

While it appeared that the norm in a Yuquí marriage was one spouse, there were at least two cases where it seemed for a time that an individual had two partners. In both cases, it eventually became clear that the individual was transitioning from one partner to another and didn't retain the first partner for long after moving to the second one, even when children were involved. Promiscuity was rampant, and much cunning or guile was used to achieve the desired end.

The Yuquí women and teenage girls continued to unabashedly pursue the missionary men, and the Yuquí men did what they could to get the missionary women alone. That was almost impossible to achieve. On one occasion, Lois was alone on the houseboat, washing clothes with their gas-powered Maytag, while Les was up at Bill's house. Meanwhile, slave Freddy was trying to get into the houseboat but found the doors locked. Then he tried a window, but they all had wooden bars across them.

About this time, Les left Bill's house on his way back to the launch, and along the way, White Joven intercepted him and tried various stalling tactics to keep Les from proceeding to the houseboat. Evidently, White Joven knew what Freddy was up to and colluded with him. This type of behavior kept the missionaries alert and on their toes.

Bob and Mary continued, anxious to find someone who would sit down with them for hours at a time on a regular basis and "cooperate" with them in the language work. Les, in the meantime, continued showing pictures and magazines to various ones of the nomads. The quickness with which different individuals grasped what they were seeing seemed to be a good indicator of who the sharper ones were, but not always. Sometimes it was just a lack of interest or the person had something else on their mind, such as how to get another cookie, how to get invited to lunch at the houseboat, or some other concern.

Straight Hair was getting better at shooting the BB gun, and he and Favorite Joven jumped for joy when he at last shot a small fish. The next thing Les knew, Straight Hair headed off into the jungle along a trail that went from the missionary camp down and parallel to the river. Favorite Joven, George, and Les went trailing along behind, wondering what Straight Hair had in mind, and eventually caught up with him.

"Where are you headed?" questioned Les.

"I'm going to shoot howler monkeys," came the reply.

Les had to explain that the BB gun was for small birds and tiny animals and little fish but wouldn't work for monkeys, pigs and larger game. Straight Hair was rather disappointed as he turned around and headed back to the clearing.

The daily hunts Bob, Les, and Bill were making with the nomads were bringing in abundant game. Normally, one or two of the missionaries would go hunting daily, each with a separate group of nomads. Not only did they shoot great quantities of game, but often, the Yuquí spotted bee trees which they sometimes stopped to harvest and, at other times, marked and left for another day. On one of the better days, the two hunting parties came home with seven razor-billed curassows, fourteen assorted monkeys—including howlers, capuchins, Azara's night monkeys, and squirrel monkeys—two curassows, and two bee trees they spotted and left for the following day.

Petty theft continued to be an issue with Lois' saltshaker disappearing after a group which included the chief's wife came over for lunch. The next morning, when the missionaries failed to bring the accustomed kettle of hominy and explained that the saltshaker had been taken, it was quick to make its reappearance, although no one admitted blame. The chief's wife wanted to come for lunch again, and when Les said no and explained that it was because the saltshaker had been taken on her watch, she promptly slapped him across the face and sulked off to stay on the west side of the river.

That didn't trouble her husband, the chief, who joined his grandson, Straight Hair, and the two went across for lunch with the missionaries. The chief was looking around in the back of the houseboat, in the motor room, and soon the missionaries could see him back there, entertaining himself as he peered into the Fosters' large mirror. He would smile, turn his head to one side and the other, open his mouth, stick out his tongue, play with his hair, and talk to himself, making faces at himself. It was quite hilarious to watch him seeing himself for the first time. Not only was the mirror a big hit to him, but as he told others about it; they also had to come and see themselves in this amazing device.

Bob's group of hunters eventually showed up, bringing monkeys as well as honey from a type of bee that didn't sting but rather pinched. They shared some of the honey with Les and, while he was eating it, managed to get a live bee in his mouth. The bee bit Les on the end of the tongue, and he cried out, "Ohó! Ohó! Ohó!" causing the group of nomads to howl with laughter. In many ways, they were unpredictable, sometimes laughing when someone hurt themselves, while at other times showing great sympathy.

Two days later, the chief's wife still seemed to be out of sorts over the saltshaker. When she sent a can over with a request for sugar, Les placed a quantity of fresh honey and honeycomb in the can and took it back to her personally, expecting her to be pleased with the generous quantity of honey. Instead, she fingered the honeycomb while murmuring her discontent and then pulled out a piece of the honeycomb and peevishly threw it at Les. It seemed her reincarnated son was not treating her as well as she wished or possibly the quality of honey was below standard, but it was fresh honey others had given him the previous day and should have been acceptable.

Early one morning, around 3:30 a.m., lightning and thunder began and was soon overhead, crashing loudly. The missionaries, awakened by the storm, began hearing chanting on the far side of the river. "*Aaauuuaa, aaauuuuaa, aaauuuuaa, op, uum, op, uum, op uum, oh, wat a ichey cadichie cadoo oo, cadichie cadoo oo, cadichie cadoo oo,*" repeated endlessly as the nomads appealed to the spirits of their dead to stop their drinking party up in the sky. Soon the rain began, and the sound of chanting was muted. How miserable it must be to live in the dense, tall forest with little or no protection from falling branches, crashing trees, lightning and the elements, not to mention dangerous jungle creatures.

The rain continued well into the morning, and it wasn't until noon that a small handful of nomads appeared across the river, ready for brunch. Bill and Les transported a large kettle of hominy over to the group and then brought three of the young men over for lunch on the houseboat, after which they took a kettle of sweetened rice across to the rest of the Yuquí before proceeding by small boat up to the Meadow. There they picked up Roughneck, Iroquois, and Toughy and continued by river until they rounded a large river bend where they moored the boat and headed inland on the missionary side, the east side of the river to hunt.

As they hiked along quite a way back in from the river, they began seeing broken twigs such as the nomads used to mark their trails. The group with Les began showing great concern when they saw these signs indicating another group of nomads. One of the Yuquí was carrying an axe, and when they found a bee tree, Roughneck went to work, chopping into it to get the honey, but not before explaining to Les, "There are hostile nomads around here. You need to watch for them, and if any of them show up, shoot them with your shotgun before they shoot us with an arrow."

"I won't shoot them," responded Les. "They are your brothers, and I will not shoot them."

"Well then, just shoot to miss and scare them away," Roughneck replied. "If you don't shoot them, they will shoot you right in the eye with their arrows."

"If they come around, I'll call to them and tell them we are their friends," Les replied. And then he asked Roughneck, "Why don't you go out and bring this group in so we can be their friends?"

"They would shoot and kill me," came the answer.

Les had wondered right along if the various groups of Yuquí were aware of each other and friendly, but this pretty well answered his question. Clearly, they were afraid even of other bands of their own people. His hope had been that once the first group of Yuquí were settled down, it would be relatively quick and easy to find and settle the other groups. Evidently, this was not to be the case.

It had now been ten months since the initial contact at the Meadow, although there had been a few long spells where the nomads were absent. Even so, the missionaries were making progress on the language, especially when it came to the names of animals and hunting terms. They had gathered few verbs and had little understanding of the grammar as such, not knowing how to conjugate the handful of verbs they had collected. There was still a long way to go.

Les had little natural language ability but was highly motivated and wanted to communicate well with the Yuquí, although in the years he was with the nomads, he never reached a point where he could clearly communicate biblical truths. His strength was more in the area of building rapport, making friendships, and the Yuquí had come to love, trust and value him and, because of that, had come to trust the entire missionary team. Each day was physically exhausting but full of meaning. It had taken almost nine years of persistence to reach this point, far longer than any of them could have imagined when they began the effort to befriend the Yuquí.

Capuchin monkeys and squirrel monkeys often roam together in the jungle, and hunting them is a lot of fun, almost like going to the shooting gallery in a carnival. These monkeys seem to be the most abundant in the forest and easy to find. Often as the Yuquí and the missionaries hunted together, the nomads would stop and whistle the capuchin call. It was a rare day that some of the agile animals didn't respond. On this particular day, Straight Hair was leading Les through the jungle, and soon, the two of them found themselves running wildly through the forest beneath a large group of monkeys who were fleeing, swinging from tree to tree. Straight Hair would point at this big fat monkey or that one and tell Les to shoot it, not wasting shells on the smaller animals. At times, the furry creatures would pause in their flight, looking down in curiosity at their pursuers, making the shot easier.

Occasionally, many monkeys would come single-file down the same branch before leaping from the end of the branch to the next tree. Les and Straight Hair could stand there and shoot monkey after monkey as it ran down the same branch, pausing briefly to get its balance and calculating the leap to the next tree. All the nomad hunters were calling, "*Ooosh, ooosh, ooosh*" as they followed the monkeys, trying to slow them down and keep them corralled.

As monkeys fell from the trees, wounded and dying, Les, Bill, and the nomads let them lie where they had fallen and continued racing along the forest floor beneath the terrified fleeing monkeys.

Soon Les had exhausted the eleven shotgun shells he had brought along for small game and stopped shooting as the Yuquí hunters continued firing with bow and arrow. Les followed Straight Hair back through the thick forest as he zigzagged his way unerringly back the way they had come picking up the fallen monkeys. There was no way Les could have retraced their steps, but Straight Hair, having grown up in this life, had no problem finding the ten monkeys the two of them had downed.

Straight Hair gave Les an ecstatic grin as the two of them sat and waited for Bill and the rest of the hunters to return and join them. What fun they had and what good eating the seventeen furry creatures the group had killed would be!

One of the missionaries' corn patches was now producing, so Les invited some of the Yuquí to help harvest fresh corn for eating. Roughneck's wife was pregnant, and when it came time to shuck the corn, Roughneck let Les know that he couldn't touch the corn husks to shuck them; Les would have to do it for him. As Les was husking the corn, he dropped a piece of the husk to the ground and it accidentally hit Roughneck's toe. Roughneck was quick to jump back from the "dangerous" corn husk.

On another day, when they brought in monkeys, Roughneck began complaining because, with a pregnant wife, he wasn't allowed to eat monkey tails. What a loss! He also wasn't allowed to tie knots. When the aging bark rope on his bow broke while he was preparing to shoot, he had to have Les knot the rope back together and restring the bow. He also wasn't allowed to eat razor-billed curassow, one of the tastiest jungle birds. Having a pregnant wife introduced many additional challenges into an already difficult life.

Straight Hair was inquisitive, always wanting to learn more about things outside of his experience. Even a simple thing like the canoe paddle interested him, and one day, when they stopped along the river and were waiting for some of their companions, he asked Les if the wooden paddle was made from a tree. Les assured him it was, and Straight Hair followed up with, "And is the wooden boat made from a tree? Did one of the *abaas* (enemies/Bolivian nationals) make it?"

After Les replied yes to both questions, he went on to explain, "It was made by the enemies over where you go to take bananas," and then added, "over where Wide Eyes was shot in the lower jaw by the man with the beard." And as Les wrote, "Wow! That started it!"

Toughy, Favorite Joven, and George, who were present, began crying, wailing, and chanting. They cried and cried with broken hearts as tears ran down their cheeks. Their noses ran and dripped off their lips, and they didn't even seem to notice. As they went on their way in the small wooden boat, the crying continued, and once they arrived where they planned to hunt and exited the boat, Les stood on the bank with his arms around Favorite Joven and Toughy, both of them brothers to the deceased Wide Eyes. Bill put his arms around others to comfort them.

Les was soon overcome by the grief and cried with them for a time. Freddy, who was watching Les closely, stood there with Straight Hair, looking sober, but not chanting. Iroquois was chanting but not crying. Eventually, the emotions began to calm down, and they split into two groups, some with Les and some with Bill as they headed out hunting.

Les' group went to the same area where they had hunted the day before to harvest honey they had spotted. Les started a fire to smoke the bees while Iroquois and Straight Hair cut into the tree. These were a small, black, biting type of bee, not a stinging bee, and were flying all around and crawling on the men. One flew into Les' right ear and went all the way in, concerning him greatly, but as he prayed, the insect turned around and came back out. Soon they had an abundance of honey as well as cells filled with a pollen-like substance and others with larvae, both of which the nomads also ate. Les found the larvae to be rich and creamy, very delicious. Some of the underdeveloped larvae tasted much like buttermilk. Very satisfying!

The group of hunters arrived back happy and content with the game and honey they had gathered, but as they went up the bank, Toughy began telling the assembled group about how his brother, Wide Eyes, had died at the hands of the *abaas* (the enemies). Within moments, wailing, chanting, and weeping broke out again, and soon the chief, Wide Eyes' father, was standing, crying as Bill and Les comforted him. After Toughy recounted the story as he had heard it from Les, they wanted to hear it from Les, who explained, "There are many, many, enemies up there (in the colonies) with many, many guns. Don't go up there and steal from their farms. Stay around here, and we will protect you and feed you."

This was the first time that, instead of responding, "We will shoot them in the eye," the Yuquí seemed to begin to understand that their bows and arrows against a world full of people with guns such as the missionaries could use so effectively was not stacked in their favor. They appeared to be giving a lot of thought to what Les was telling them. Over the next few days, others of the Yuquí heard the story, and the missionaries had numerous opportunities to discourage the nomads from going to the colonies to steal.

A few days later, the chief came over to the missionary houseboat for ongoing medical treatment and, while there, asked once again about his son, Wide Eyes, and if he had been shot through the chin. Les assured him that was the case, that it was done by a bearded man, and went on to explain how after killing him, the enemies tied his wrists with vines and hung him between two trees. The Yuquí of course already knew all of this, because they had seen him shot and later found him hanging there, so it was confirmation to them that Les knew what he was talking about.

Les was crying as he begged the chief and other listening nomads not to go back around the colonies again, telling them, "There are many more enemies there now, and they all have guns. Don't go there! Let's plant bananas for you here. Stay here with us, we'll protect you."

Once again, the chief began crying and wailing, and soon, Toughy and Milk Shake Girl also joined in, chanting, "*Gazedn de, edn de, edn de...*" with the last "e" drawn out, then a sob, a catching of the breath, and then they'd start the chant all over again. Eventually they asked to be taken back across to the west side of the river where the chanting and wailing continued for some time. In fact, it continued intermittently over the next three days.

Les' ear had gotten inflamed internally from the biting bee that had flown into it a few days previously, and he thought this would be a good opportunity for the Yuquí to see him get an injection, a good teaching experience to prepare them for the future when they might need a shot for some reason. Roughneck, Iroquois, Straight Hair, and others were there to watch as Les prepared the syringe for Lois.

Lois jabbed the needle in easily, but there seemed to be a blockage, and the penicillin wouldn't flow. Les had her pull the needle out, and he changed needles. As he was doing that, the first needle prick started bleeding profusely. She wiped the blood off and again stuck him. This time, she got about half the penicillin in, and again it froze.

By this time, the nomads were about, splitting their sides, laughing. She finally pulled the needle out and gave up. If the ear inflammation didn't clear up in a few days, they would try again. So much for that teaching experience!

Les had also begun to notice that he had numerous spots on his body and head that were infected, and Straight Hair had an eye that was almost swollen shut. As he was pointing out these things to the Yuquí, they explained that the small, black, biting bees caused these spots. He and Straight Hair had both been bitten numerous times a few days before by those bees.

Being a nomadic people who roamed naked exposed the Yuquí to physical hardship and the vagaries of the weather; consequently, they constantly groused to the missionaries about aches and pains. The chief showed up one day, complaining of a severe headache and soreness in the neck, chest, and back. He wanted them massaged by hand, which Les did, but then the electric vibrator came to Les' mind, and he thought of how much better that would work on the chief's neck and back, although he had some doubt the chief would let him try the strange device on him. Les started up the small generator for electric power and then took the chief and some of his people upstairs and had him lie face down on a cot.

The chief was feeling so poorly that he didn't resist at all as Les plugged in the vibrator and began massaging his neck and back. Soon he was enjoying it so much that he didn't want Les to stop and insisted he continue for a full half hour. The Chief seemed to feel much better afterward and returned for treatments over the next several days. He raved about the treatment so much that every day, other nomads showed up and wanted the vibrator treatment, sometimes begging for it twice in one day.

As Les wrote to the friend who had given them the vibrator, "I'd like to have a movie of this to send to you. If you can, picture a big naked man with skin like leather lying on a cot. He has long black hair like a woman. He tells me to do the vibrator here and then there and then somewhere else. When I don't press hard enough, he takes my wrist and pushes it down harder."

On the daily hunting expeditions, liana vines were often used as rope or string for tying a variety of items. Lianas were tied around the neck of the game, and then a loop was made that could be placed around the forehead of the person carrying it to support the weight of the animal for transport. The ends of their *bareguaas* (a container made from the broad flexible base of the palm leaf) had to be tied with lianas for carrying honey or other liquids. It was taboo for a man with an expectant wife to wrap or tie the lianas, so often, the missionaries had to do this for a nomad hunter whose wife was pregnant.

Also, the man couldn't string his bow, so the missionaries learned how to make the two half-hitches and tighten the bowstring for the Yuquí hunters as well as how to wind the string on the plug end or the point end of the arrows when the string came loose. A Yuquí hunter with a pregnant wife was greatly hampered in many ways and always needed someone to go hunting with him to perform actions he wasn't allowed to do as they would violate the many taboos.

Straight Hair continued to show interest in learning all he could about the outside world and asked if he could accompany the missionaries on one of the supply trips to Puerto Yuca. The world was a much bigger place than he had ever realized, and he was excited to know more about it. The trip had to be authorized by the chief and others, but they trusted Les and Bob and readily agreed.

As they boarded the small wooden boat, the chalupa, Toughy handed Straight Hair a shirt to wear, telling him that he would need a little something to cover his nakedness when he encountered the "enemies." The chief insisted that another Yuquí accompany Straight Hair on this adventure and suggested George, his slave, whom he considered an expendable person. Les and Bob agreed to take George, and soon, the two nomads were on their way down the Chimoré River in the wooden chalupa (boat) with the missionaries.

Straight Hair took a bow and arrows along at Les' suggestion, knowing that the people at Puerto Yuca would be impressed with the armed nomad. As they motored along the river, Straight Hair had a great time as he recognized many spots and pointed out to the missionaries where they had shot capybara, where they had gathered peach palm fruit, and where they had shot a pig. They stopped once to pick peach palm fruit, leaving it on the bank to retrieve on their return.

Soon they reached the mouth of the Chimoré River and made the right turn to the southeast as they followed the Ichilo River to Puerto Yuca where they would meet the supply flight. By this time, Straight Hair had taken off the shirt his uncle had given him. He would meet this new world in the garb he was most accustomed to—no clothing!

After two and a half hours, they came in sight of Puerto Yuca, and suddenly, all of Straight Hair and George's aplomb evaporated. They decided they wanted to be left off in the jungle on the far side of the river as their fear of the "enemies" overcame their desire to see this new world.

Les and Bob understood and dropped them across the river where they could hide in the forest while the two missionaries crossed to talk with Don Enrique's wife. Once they learned from her that the three Bolivian men who lived there were out hunting and only women and children were on-site, Les went over and explained to Straight Hair and George that there was no danger before bringing them across the river to the upper end of the airstrip as far as possible from the houses.

As Straight Hair exited the boat with his bow and arrows, all the little Bolivian children fled to the safety of their houses while screaming wildly, "The savages are here!" Straight Hair found it hilarious that he with his bow and arrows could invoke such terror. Soon, pilot Leroy Lindahl of World Gospel Mission landed with a plane load of supplies, and the Yuquí were fascinated to see the aircraft up close.

They looked in the windows and saw the nice shiny aluminum cooking pots the missionaries had ordered and the hundred-pound bags of sugar and hugged themselves with joy! They knew most of these items were destined for their people.

Leroy was almost as captivated as the Yuquí to at last meet these people he had heard so much about. A large patch of sugarcane had been planted to one side of the airstrip, and when George and Straight Hair saw that, they quickly lost their fear and asked for machetes so they could cut cane to take back to their people. As Leroy, Les, and Bob unloaded the plane, the two nomads cut sugarcane until Les let them know that there was a limit to how much the boat could carry, then they each dug a plant of manioc to take home, and the missionaries said their goodbyes to the women and children and headed home for the Chimoré.

Four hours later, Straight Hair and George were animatedly recounting their fascinating trip to the nomads who were waiting to welcome them home.

While the missionaries had introduced the concept of trading in a small way, they felt it was time to do more both in that area and in enlarging the farm clearing for the Yuquí. They would need farms if they were to feed themselves without stealing from the colonists, and eventually, they would need to learn the idea of working for pay. Four very nice aluminum kettles had arrived on the last flight, and Les let it be known that two of the four were available for men who were willing to work with Les on enlarging the plantain patch. Favorite Joven was ready then and there, asking, "Where's an axe? I'll get started now!"

It was too late to begin work that day, but the next morning, six men showed up, and after some discussion, it was decided that Favorite Joven and the chief would join Les. They started at a regrown site they had previously cleared and put twelve banana plants in there before moving to their old manioc plantation and planting twenty plants there. After that, the two men, along with Les, finished clearing weeds from the old corn patch and did some weeding around the papaya trees before heavy rain hit and they were forced to quit.

Les was pleased. Favorite Joven and the chief had worked hard and steadily, but when they went to choose their cooking pots, they said they couldn't take the big one because Toughy had already laid claim to it, nor would they take the one George had seen and claimed when he had gone to meet the flight. That left only a small one for the chief who had earned a large one.

Bob and Mary Garland solved the impasse by offering a new large kettle that had come for them on the flight, but the missionaries learned that at least for the immediate future, they would have to keep trade goods well-hidden so one of the nomads wouldn't lay claim to it and others be unwilling to accept it as payment. The caste system also added to the challenges, since when a slave worked to earn something, either his master or another high-class individual would often take it from him or her, even if it meant beating them to get it away.

A few days later, Les took George, Freddy, Favorite Joven, and Toughy downriver to the first banana patch they had planted near the Chimoré. They needed more banana bulbs for planting in the Yuquí farm next to the meadow. As they dug the twenty-five rhizomes weighing four to five pounds each, Iroquois' daughter was busy weaving a palm-leaf carrying basket in which to transport the bulbs. She wouldn't have to carry it far, just to the boat, and then, when they arrived at the Meadow, it would need to go up the bank. Even so, she would be carrying close to one hundred pounds on her back supported by several loops of liana vines from her forehead.

On the way downriver to get the banana bulbs, Bill shot an eagle and a duck and let the people know that he was keeping the latter for himself. After digging the banana bulbs, the entire party headed to a bee tree Favorite Joven had spotted on the way in, but as they neared the bee tree, Iroquois yelled that he had spotted howler monkeys, so the hunters diverted to shoot them. Five monkeys were shot, all with bow and arrow, and soon the group headed back toward the river.

Les had been going first on the way back to the boat, but as they neared the river, Roughneck stepped up and began leading the way. As they approached the riverbank, Roughneck said to Les, "Watch out for the tiger" and then approached the boat cautiously. Les thought Roughneck was just playing around, joking with him, so he paid little attention until they reached the boat. Roughneck stepped into the boat, pointed to where the duck had been lying dead, and said, "Look! The tiger has stolen the duck!"

The eagle was still lying there untouched, and now Les understood why Freddy had left their group earlier on. He had come back, taken the duck, and was now heading home through the forest. Les commented, "Where is Freddy and the duck?" At that, Roughneck jumped out of the boat and let it be known he was walking home, but not before Les let him know, "There won't be any more rice, corn, sugar, or hunting until the duck comes back."

Favorite Joven was still in the boat, but when he arrived back at the clearing on his side of the river, he bounded out of the boat and went running down the trail to get the duck. Soon the chief and Roughneck showed up with no duck and gave Les a real tongue lashing. Les sat in the boat and listened to their tirade and, after it was ended, let them know, "I am going home to eat. Once the duck is back, yell across the river, and I will come and get it."

It wasn't more than an hour until Toughy was calling across the river, holding up the duck, and when Les arrived across the river, Toughy said, "I punished Freddy for stealing the duck." More likely, Toughy had told the slave to steal the duck and was in cahoots from the beginning.

Now that the duck was back, Les invited George and Favorite Joven over to eat, and the chief, his wife, and others also climbed in the boat, going across to visit with various missionaries. Later in the afternoon, when it was time to take the Yuquí back across the river, everyone seemed to be in good spirits. The stolen duck storm had passed quickly!

The next day, Chinaman and George worked on clearing jungle, each of them earning an aluminum pot. Meanwhile, Les planted the twenty-five banana plants as Bob continued gathering words in the Yuquí language. The language work was moving at a snail's pace. With no language in common, no regular language helper, and the fact that the Yuquí would be around the missionaries for a few weeks and then disappear on their nomadic wanderings for months at a time, learning the language was a massive challenge. Early in the contacts, the Yuquí hadn't seemed to realize that the missionaries spoke a different language and, at times when the missionaries didn't understand what they were saying, would come close and yell into the missionaries' ear as if they were deaf. Their frustration at times was very evident as they tried hard to communicate with all these "deaf" missionaries.

White Joven was working with Les as they began to plant corn. Les handed him an oatmeal can full of Cuban field corn as seed and showed his helper how he should put three kernels of corn in each hole that Les punched in the soft soil with his planting stick. Les kept a close eye on things in the beginning, and sure enough, White Joven came to the first hole and poured it full of corn kernels. Les patiently explained again, only three kernels per hole, and soon White Joven was doing a good job.

It wasn't long until it began raining and was soon pouring, so work stopped, and Les took most of the Yuquí back to their side of the river while a small handful stayed with the missionaries. Several times in the coming months, Les or Bill had different Yuquí work with them planting corn, and often, when the corn sprouted, a dozen or more plants would come up in many of the holes. "Be sure your sin will find you out" was the analogy that came to Les' mind as he saw this.

The missionary team continued encouraging the Yuquí to enlarge their farm area and implemented a policy of feeding those who came to work on it. The chief especially liked this idea and also liked it when Les told him that they should make the clearing directly across the river so the missionaries could guard it from the *abaa* (enemies) when the Yuquí were gone on their lengthy migrations. Off and on, they worked on the clearing, and soon, it was large enough to plant a significant number of bananas and manioc. Only those who worked on the clearing were fed, so if a man stood around watching without working, he received no dinner.

At first, this caused some attitudes but soon worked wonders as men began working half a day to get a nice hearty meal and then spent the rest of the day hunting. Usually they had enough leftovers from the meal that they could take food home for their wives and families.

Don Ramón, sugar magnate and owner of Puerto Yuca, the airstrip the missionaries used when flying supplies and personnel in and out, was ready to close down the airstrip and abandon the base. He had quite a bit of thievery and was suspicious his caretaker was behind it. He offered to sell the base to the missionaries at a "special" price, but there was no way the missionaries could maintain an airstrip that was located two and a half hours away, and even at the special price, they couldn't begin to afford to buy the base.

As Les wrote, "I feel we must put in our own airstrip here at the Chimoré." There were mixed opinions among the missionary team as carving an airstrip by hand from raw jungle was a major undertaking, and some of the team felt it was an impossible task. Les measured the airstrip at Puerto Yuca and found it to be forty meters wide. The runway would need to be at least 450 meters long and possibly longer. Plus, jungle would need to be felled at both ends to give an approach to the airstrip, bringing the total length to 1,000 meters.

The Yuquí, with no idea of the amount of labor involved, were more enthusiastic about the project than the missionary team and, when Les mentioned it to them, grabbed their axes and machetes and said, "Let's get busy!"

Les consulted with pilot, Leroy Lindahl, to see how large the strip might need to be and then went into the jungle with Lois to do some preliminary measurements and see if they had adequate room for an airstrip alongside the houses. Favorite Joven insisted on accompanying them and helped cut a survey trail the length of the proposed airstrip.

If they were going to get rid of the houseboat, Les and Lois would need a house on shore, so Les hired three of the nomads to help begin clearing jungle for his house. Two of the men worked diligently while one mostly stood around and had to be reminded from time to time to cut brush. They worked well until lunchtime when it began to rain. After lunch, they were ferried back across the river, and the chief came over to visit on the houseboat and make a "trick or treat" circuit of the missionary houses, ending at the houseboat for a trip back across the river.

Les went into the back room and, when he came out, found the chief had opened the sugar barrel and was happily helping himself, looking up guiltily when Les came in. As they were crossing the river in the boat, the chief yelled something, and all the warriors grabbed their bows and arrows and met them at the bank. Roughneck lifted an arrow and prepared to nock it to the bowstring. Meanwhile, Toughy jumped into the boat when it touched shore and began talking to Les, asking if he would give them corn and rice the next day and if they could still come over to work and go hunting with him.

Les refused to commit to any of it, and eventually, they went off in a huff. An hour later, Freddy the slave showed up alone on the far bank of the river, calling across to the missionaries. Bob and Les went over and treated him to bananas and cookies, and he headed back to his people with a report that all was well. Bob and Les had also assured him that they would hunt with them the next day, and any who wanted to work would be allowed; however, sweets such as sugar, candy, and cookies would be withheld since a quantity of sugar had been stolen.

Killing a Tapir

Upriver, a short distance from the missionary camp, was a small island which the missionaries had taken to calling Monkey Island since the first time they landed there, a troop of monkeys was trapped on it with no way to get to the mainland. Over time, the monkeys had disappeared; whether killed by other animals or starved to death for lack of food, they didn't know.

On this particular day, they moored the chalupa a short distance below Monkey Island and headed inland, hunting. Soon they had four assorted guan and could hear a curassow calling and were sneaking up on it. George was leading the way with Les, following closely behind while Toughy came along last. Les heard a quiet whistle from Toughy and turned to look back. Toughy was motioning for Les to come to him, and when he got near, Toughy said, "*Aribi* (tapir)" and pointed over into some brush.

The tapir is the largest game animal in the Bolivian jungle, weighing up to 500 pounds and tasting very similar to beef. Endowed by the Creator with negative buoyancy, the tapir can walk underwater across small streams and is a very elusive animal with a good sense of smell but mediocre eyesight. As Toughy pointed, Les looked closely, but all he could see through the twigs and brush was a gray blob. But as he peered into the brush, the blob moved, confirming to Les that it was the tapir.

Les had switched shells in his 12-gauge shotgun and now had a zero-aught-buck shell in the weapon and, although he couldn't distinguish which body part of the beast he was seeing, fired into it. There was much crashing through the brush as the "gray mound" lunged off through the jungle. Les knew he had hit it but had no idea where and motioned vaguely to Toughy that he had shot it in its side. The two men plunged off into the undergrowth, following the creature with Toughy leading the way.

Soon they came on a puddle of blood, which confirmed that it was badly wounded, and then as Les caught up to Toughy, Toughy pointed ahead and said, "It's dying."

Les looked, and there lay the tapir on the ground, struggling but unable to rise. A crimson stream was gushing out of the chest where many of the lead shot had penetrated. For ten minutes, the behemoth thrashed about, dying, and when the movement stopped, the two men inspected it carefully. By their count, nine of the twelve zero-aught-buck lead shots from the shotgun shell had penetrated the head and chest of the animal. The tapir lay in dense brush, so Les and Toughy tried to drag it to a more open area to butcher it into manageable pieces to carry back to the boat.

Les estimated the dead weight to be close to 400 pounds, and when the men found they couldn't move it, they realized they would need to carve it up where it lay. The only knife available was Les' small pocketknife, which Toughy borrowed to perform the task. Even though the shot had been in a vital spot, the tapir had run sixty meters after being wounded.

Soon George arrived with a machete to help cut up the tapir, but the machete proved too unwieldy for the job so Toughy continued with only the pocketknife. Now they would have to carry this treasure of meat back to the boat, so George began weaving palm-leaf carrying baskets and gathering lianas to use as cords as Toughy dissected the animal.

Now that the Yuquí understood how passionate the missionaries were to have them stay away from the colonies and the dangers there, some of the Yuquí began using that as a lever with which to pressure the missionaries to do more for them and give them more foodstuff, using the threat of going raiding in the colonies if the missionaries failed to give them all they wanted. Missionary resources were limited as the various banana plantations were still too small and not producing adequately, and the Yuquí were eating all the manioc as fast as it could be grown. Large kettles of corn were boiled into hominy daily, and huge amounts of sweetened rice with milk were also being cooked for the people, but corn and rice had to be flown in, which required river trips to the airstrip.

From time to time, the missionaries would take the twenty-foot wooden chalupa over to Puerto Yuca and bring back a boatload of bananas, but they would have needed to do that twice a week in order to fully provide for the nomads. It would be very helpful to have an airstrip on the Chimoré base, but with no heavy machinery and only two missionary men (Bill and Les) to work on it, it would be a massive task.

Bob and Mary were focusing on the language, while Bill and Les took turns hunting daily with the Yuquí with the occasional day off. It seemed like the best way to keep the nomads around was to keep them fed and happy, but that was proving to be a challenge.

Occasionally, when the hunters were far out in the jungle, they would stop and make lunch of whatever was available. On this particular day, White Joven was carrying two red-footed tortoises, expecting to take them home for his family, but when the party stopped to rest and eat, he asked Les to start a fire and then placed the turtles upside down on the fire Les had built and watched them squirm for two or three minutes as they cooked in their own shells.

It took over thirty minutes for the ten or twelve-pound reptiles to fully cook, after which the hunting party enjoyed them along with bee larvae and honey for lunch, a very satisfying meal! Evidently, the two turtles had belonged to White Joven and Toughy as they each cracked one open and ate freely before passing meat around to the rest of the party.

Favorite Joven had begun spending many mornings with Bob and Mary, assisting them with the language. He was not an especially good hunter, and by working with Bob and Mary, they saw to it that he received plenty of food to feed his family as well as other trade goods in payment for his help. His wife, Rosa, occasionally sat with him as he worked with Bob and Mary, and they found she was quicker than her husband in understanding what Mary was looking for.

Les and Bill were doing their part to help in language acquisition by laying claim to some of the meat they shot and then giving it to Bob for Favorite Joven and his family; otherwise, he would need to take time off to hunt, hindering the progress Mary was making with the language. Rainy season was nearing its end, but game was still abundant in the area, so the Yuquí would probably stay around for a few more weeks.

Neither Bill nor Les were gifted in language learning, but both men were servants to all, caring men who loved the Yuquí and exerted themselves beyond measure on a daily basis as they tromped through the dense jungle, hunting, or worked extending the clearing, planting, or building houses. Bill was struggling emotionally as the Yuquí had begun making fun of his poor pronunciation of words in their language, and both Bob and Les tried to encourage and help him.

Les encouraged Bill to take the same attitude he had taken, "When they laugh *at* you, laugh *with* them." Attitude is everything! Of the many coworkers Les had over the years, Bill and Mildred were two of his favorites, and he sure didn't want them to get discouraged and leave the work. Les was highly motivated to learn the language, which was a real asset since he had little natural language learning ability.

The team had two outboard motors for the small boats, but with the constant use crossing the river multiple times a day, hunting trips with the nomads, and supply runs to Puerto Yuca, both motors were having major issues. Bill and Les were both mechanical-minded with an aptitude for figuring out and repairing motors, but without parts, they were unable to make the necessary repairs. Parts would have to be ordered from the United States, which would take at least three months. Gears were worn out, water pump impellers destroyed by sand and silt in the river water, and propellers ground down by running over sandbars. They were now reduced to paddling the boats back and forth across the river, a challenging undertaking. They desperately needed at least one motor operational for supply trips to the Puerto Yuca airstrip.

As they mentioned their need on the mission radio network, Jim Morgenroth graciously offered to sell them his nine and a half horsepower Johnson outboard. He would see that it got sent to them on the next supply flight.

With the constant hunting, game in the area was getting scarce, and the nomads were finding little wild fruit. White Joven once again began threatening to go steal plantains from the "enemy" farms, and later the same day, Toughy began making the same threat.

With no working outboard, the missionaries had lost the option of going to Puerto Yuca for bananas. If they could get a motor working, they would need to save it for the trip to pick up the new Johnson outboard. The next morning, they learned that White Joven, Toughy, and Iroquois had taken their families and gone to steal bananas from the colonies.

After taking the kettle of hominy and one of rice across the river to the nomads who were assembled and waiting for the daily provision, Les brought Straight Hair, Wooly Hair, and Chinaman back to the east side of the river and accompanied them down a trail that paralleled the river, planning to harvest honey from three bee trees they had seen on a previous hunting trip. They also did some hunting and shot an assortment of small animals and birds.

Along the way, the three men spotted tassels growing from the top of many of the bamboo stalks and stopped to harvest a good quantity of these for use as arrow shafts. Each man gathered a bundle of twenty or so tassels and carried them as well as the honey and game back to the missionary camp. It had been a profitable day, and Wooly Hair was in a talkative mood. He was an excellent hunter and a good storyteller and always fun to listen to as he told stories of the hunt.

Soon he was telling of the three tigers Toughy had killed and then followed up with a story of how he and the chief, his grandfather, had killed one together. Now that he was in storyteller mode, Wooly Hair began telling Les stories of the different nomad warriors who had shot Bolivian colonists, describing what kind of arrow tips had been used, whether the lance-type bamboo tip or the barbed tip, where geographically the shootings had taken place, and where each arrow had physically struck the targeted person.

Les knew of many of the shootings, had seen several of the victims, and had now heard about them from the perspective of the colonists as well as that of the Yuquí, so he found it very interesting. He sure hoped there wouldn't be a new story to hear when the three nomad families returned from their current expedition to steal bananas from the colonists.

* * * * *

It had now been a full year since the first contacts at the Meadow, and Bill wrote a letter to their ministry partners:

> Over the past year we have had 153 days of contacts with the nomads and many of those days have been together with them for eight or nine hours. At present they have been here for 80 days straight, making this the longest series of contacts we have had. Some of the group have been gone for a couple of weeks but the chief and others are still here and come out every day.

Les was taking a boatload of hunters up the river, and as they passed the Meadow, George began recounting that first contact. "I looked across the river, and there you were on the beach," he commented. "Then you got in the boat and came across to see us."

Les couldn't hold back the tears of joy as he thought of all the progress that had been made over the past year. Among other things, Mary was making advances in the language and had concluded that the Yuquí had no word for God, no knowledge of a Supreme Being. Bob and Mary had recently discovered the word for "large" when one of the nomads requested that the missionaries bring "large" bananas from Puerto Yuca, so Bob decided to use the word "large" together with the word "father" to communicate the idea of God. He was sure the Yuquí would soon correct him if such a concept existed in the language. The correction never came. The Yuquí had no word for God, no notion of a Supreme Being!

Bob told Favorite Joven and his wife, "Big Father lives up in the sky and loves you and sees everything you do. Big Father doesn't like it when you steal from the 'enemies' or when you shoot the 'enemies' or the 'enemies' shoot you." Bob went on to explain that Big Father had told *Tibaquete* (Les) to come and look for the Yuquí and to cut trails and leave gifts for them and told all the missionaries to learn their language so they could tell the Yuquí about Him.

Favorite Joven replied, "I will come back every day and help you learn our language so you can tell me more about Big Father."

Later in the day, Favorite Joven stopped by the houseboat to visit with Les and Lois. White Joven and Straight Hair were there, having lunch with the Fosters, and Favorite Joven began telling them what he had learned about Big Father. After the meal was finished, Favorite Joven motioned Les over to sit beside him on the bed that served as a sofa and said to Les, "*Tibaquete* (Les), tell Big Father to come down and sit here with me." He repeated the request numerous times until Les assured him that Big Father was coming someday.

Favorite Joven seemed impressed and quite serious, and later, across the river, began telling others about Big Father, although it wasn't clear just how much he really understood.

The next day, Bill and Les learned that the chief had sent his slave, George, to tell Toughy to come back from his banana stealing expedition. Evidently, his son, Favorite Joven, had explained to him that Big Father didn't approve of stealing from the colonists. After hearing of this, the missionary men headed off downriver with Favorite Joven, Straight Hair, Wooly Hair, Chinaman, and a few others to an island where an abundance of peach palm fruit grew.

After collecting about 300 pounds of the fruit, they went back upriver where they found a group of wailing nomads waiting for them on the riverbank. The wailing seemed to have something to do with Big Father, although the missionaries didn't understand just what. Several times throughout the day, different ones asked more questions about Big Father, but Bill and Les were limited in the Yuquí language and couldn't understand and answer their questions. They would have to leave that to Mary or Bob.

Swimming, Anyone?

LES HAD ORDERED A DOZEN brass cartridges that could be reloaded over and over again for his 12-gauge shotgun and was sitting at the table on the houseboat, busily reloading shells. Not only was he exhausted from a long day of pushing his way through dense jungle hunting with the Yuquí, but he was also distracted as he told Lois about his tiring day. Brothers Straight Hair and Wooly Hair, grandsons to the chief, were watching as Les pried the old used primers out of the brass shell casings, preparing to insert new primers. As he pried each old primer out, he would toss it through the barred window of the boat into the river to dispose of it. With the tiredness and the distractions, he mistakenly threw one of the brass cartridges into the river instead of the primer. He only had twelve of the expensive reusable brass shells and was not too happy to have thrown one into the river, so after eating lunch, he put on his swimming trunks and walked in the water along the edge of the boat, hoping to feel the cartridge with his feet and retrieve it.

He never did find the cartridge, but the nomads were getting such a kick out of seeing him in the water in bathing trunks that he decided to show them how to swim. He swam around the back of the launch and then up the other side in deeper water as they all watched, yelling and showing great interest in this amazing feat. Later, when they went back across the river, they told the chief with great animation how Les went "*Poo...poo...poo...poo*" around the boat.

The chief wanted to see this exploit, so a few days later, after caulking a leak in the wooden chalupa, Les invited the chief and Chinaman to join him for a test ride in the boat. Off they went upriver. Once they were out in the middle, Les shut off the motor, threw Yogi the dog (who loved to swim) overboard, and then both

Les and Bill jumped out of the chalupa into the river, swimming around and around as the boat floated down the river. The chief was impressed and thought that was the greatest thing.

After those two incidents, the missionary men began going often to the beach to bathe instead of showering at home, and soon, groups of Yuquí began accompanying them, although they stayed in the shallows as none of them knew how to swim. They would chase each other around on the beach, and soon, the missionaries would dive in and swim out into deeper water to see if anyone dared follow them. It was a long time before some of the younger Yuquí began learning to swim, and most of the older ones never did.

For a lengthy period of time, the main topic of conversation continued to be Big Father, and both the chief and Favorite Joven asked Les numerous times to have Him come down so they could meet and talk with Him. The whole group was impressed that the missionaries knew Big Father and could talk with Him.

As usual, the larger part of the Yuquí band had gone away for several weeks, but now a few families began returning from their travels. Toughy had been gone the longest and had yet to return, although other returnees reported that he was ill and would be back soon. The chief was expected back the following day, and when he arrived, the missionaries found his wife to have a new and improved attitude, much more cooperative and not the compulsive thief she had been. That was encouraging!

The bad news was they reported that they had killed a colonist, although this news was never confirmed, so it was possible they were using the information as leverage with the missionaries. The hunting schedule was soon back in full swing, and progress on a house for Les and Lois slowed accordingly. Les was anxious to get the house built so he could sell the houseboat and invest that money into building the airstrip they needed.

Snakes were an ever-present reality, and a book could be written just on the many close encounters of a deadly kind the missionaries had with slithering serpents, although some incidents were more memorable than others. On one hunting trip, Les was following Scar Face through the jungle when he went under a low overhanging arched branch. As Les bent to follow Scar Face under the branch, he didn't realize that Scar Face had bumped the branch and knocked a snake loose.

Les ducked and looked forward, ready to proceed under the branch, and found himself face-to-face at eye level with a deadly viper. The front half of the serpent was draped down from the limb, and Les' nose was only inches from the reptile. He jumped back, yelling. Scar Face turned around to see what the commotion was and began slapping the back of his head in fear and anger while muttering imprecations. He made it clear that had one of them been bitten in the face, they would now be dying.

The snake is not described in Les' journal but was likely one of the short green parrot vipers. They prefer to lie in low vegetation, and their bite is often fatal since it is delivered to the head or neck.

Another day, Les took a group of four hunters—Toughy, Roughneck, Scarface, and George—upriver to an island where they found a troop of capuchin monkeys, but Roughneck restrained Les from shooting, saying that instead, they would shoot the animals with bow and arrow. Two of the Yuquí shot but missed, so Les went ahead and shot three times, killing as many monkeys but bringing on an angry tirade from Roughneck. "You wait right here," said Roughneck to Les as the four Yuquí took off to chase the monkeys.

Not wanting Les to shoot the gun seemed to have something to do with the fact that both Toughy and Roughneck's wives were pregnant, although Les didn't understand why he shouldn't shoot since he had often hunted with men during their wives' pregnancies. Les decided to go the short distance back to where the boat was moored and get a drink of water, and soon, Scar Face came looking for him there. Les told Scar Face to go back and hunt with the group and that he would take a hunt by himself around the perimeter of the island.

Les began on the west side of the island and soon found fresh deer tracks as well as tiger, tapir, and capybara tracks. Two thirds of the way around the island, he came on very fresh tiger tracks and, as he stood there, heard something large coming through the brush. Since he could hear twigs being broken, he assumed it wasn't a tiger, so he whistled the low sound the Yuquí often used to call to one another and got two low whistles in return.

Toughy, Roughneck, and George came out to join him, telling him that they were going the follow the island around in the direction from which he had come. He, on the other hand, let them know that was going to continue circling the island in the direction he was going, so Toughy decided to join him. They hadn't gone far at all when they came to an area the tiger had tromped down, leaving abundant tracks. Les and Toughy eased their way a short distance into the jungle, eager to find the jaguar, and then stopped while Toughy imitated a wounded collared peccary in pain, hoping the jaguar would be attracted to the sound. Nothing.

The two men advanced farther into the shrubbery, following the tiger tracks, and soon came upon a huge black muturu catfish which, by Les' estimate, weighed 125 pounds. The tiger had caught the fish in the river, then dragged it up a five-foot-high bank and forty meters back into the woods. The innards had been eaten as well as half of the head. Some of the meat was mangled and torn while the rest of the fish was still fresh and could be salvaged and eaten.

Toughy called loudly for his fellow tribesmen, and when they arrived, they proceeded to trim off the still edible parts of the fish and carry it back to the boat, roughly half the fish. On their way home, they stopped briefly at the nomad camp to leave off the fish, and then three of the four Yuquí accompanied Les back to the houseboat for lunch. Scar Face, the slave, was left to build a smoke rack and begin roasting the fish.

Vampire bats were a constant problem in the jungle, and several consecutive nights, they found and bled the Foster's dog, Yogi. One morning, Les found some of the vampires hanging upside down, asleep in the hold of the houseboat, and shot them. Yogi thought that was great and immediately grabbed the dead creatures and ate them all before Les could collect them and toss them in the river. Anna, Les and Lois' daughter, had been bitten once when her hand got outside of her mosquito net during the night. There was always a risk that the vampires might carry rabies or some other illness, so it was best to take precautions and not get bit.

The bats didn't like light, so keeping a barn lantern fueled with kerosene burning was sometimes used as protection from the nocturnal flying mammals for domestic animals such as chickens, ducks, or dogs. Unfortunately, the Yuquí campfires didn't seem to furnish adequate light, and as the Yuquí stayed more and more in one location, not moving constantly as they had in the past, the plague of the vampires began to affect them.

Evidently, the bats have very sharp teeth as the person or animal being bitten doesn't awaken when the vampire bites and then laps up the blood, much like a dog laps water. Unfortunately, when they fly away, the wound continues to leak blood, and with the Yuquí, when the individual woke up, they would find a puddle of blood on the ground beneath their hammock. If a person or animal was bitten repeatedly, they soon became weak from loss of blood. Chickens that were bitten regularly would stop laying eggs.

Les made a trip to Puerto Yuca to bring back one of the first groups of outside visitors that had come to meet the Yuquí. Dick Wyma, the field leader, was accompanied by his brother, Mel, director of a mission training facility in Pennsylvania, as well as Hendry Redyke, a man who had recently sold his construction business and planned to join the mission. The three men were visiting various mission stations so Henry could see the mission work and decide what equipment to bring with him when he and his wife, Margaret, finished the mission training and moved to Bolivia. Helping build airstrips using a caterpillar tractor was one of his desires, and here at the Chimoré, he would be able to see what might be involved.

A happy group of naked Yuquí were waiting on the opposite bank of the river as Les pulled up to the houseboat with the three visitors, and after unloading the few supplies that had come on the flight, Les took the visitors across the river to introduce them to the nomads for the first time. The chief, his wife, and others gathered around as Les explained that these men had come to visit for two days. The nomads looked the men over, had them take their shirts off, and then asked, "Which one is Big Father?"

Les explained, "These are others like me, none of them is Big Father."

The expressions on the face of the Yuquí began changing from one of happiness to one of sadness, and soon, several of them began to cry. They had expected Les to bring Big Father back to meet them. Surely the airplane, which came from the sky, could bring Big Father to meet them, and here Les had just brought other men like himself. What a letdown! The crying continued for quite some time. As Les wrote:

> Where words are limited misconceptions are a danger. We know that the Yuquí feel that we speak with God by radio, that God flies around in an airplane, and that He could just drop down and visit them and then go back up to the sky in His airplane anytime He wants. They don't know how unready they are to meet God. Christ said, "I am the way, the truth, and the life: no man cometh unto the father, but by me." I'm not sure how much they understand now, or just how much they must understand before they can be born again. It's hard to know just what ideas they are really forming as they hear these things. Since we don't know much spiritual vocabulary in their language it's hard to explain these things to them. But we praise God that at least they now know what we are here for. And if tears are any indication, they are eager to hear more. Pray we will make fast progress in their language and that they will not get wrong ideas that will be hurtful to them. Pray also that we will be able to keep these people isolated until the Gospel has had its effect on them.

The hunt was not always successful, even with the advantages a shotgun brings, and that was proven once again the next time Les and his guides came across a tapir. Six men had come with Les, and Favorite Joven was leading the way with his bow out in front of him to shake cold, wet rainwater off the brush and minimize the wetness for those who followed. Even so, Les was getting soaked and colder by the minute.

They were down near the original plantain patch when they heard a tapir whistle, and at that point, everyone stopped and stood motionless and very quiet as Roughneck motioned Les to follow him, leaving the others to come along at a distance. Soon, Roughneck pointed through the brush, and Les could see the tapir clearly through the bushes as it turned to flee. He was able to take a frontal shot at the animal and was sure he had wounded it badly. The cup-sized puddles of blood along the way as they trailed the beast seemed to indicate that they should find it at any moment, lying on the ground, kicking as it died.

It was fifteen minutes before they came upon the tapir again, and this time, Les was able to shoot it as it stood broadside before it fled, continuing to leave a trail of blood. Even before shooting it the second time, they had begun seeing clots of blood and foam that looked much like pieces of lung. Roughneck didn't like these signs as to him, it indicated the tapir wasn't badly wounded or losing enough blood.

For a total of thirty minutes, the hunters followed their prey before nearing the river. Roughneck, still leading the way, was carrying Toughy's bow and a lance-tipped bleeder arrow and got an arrow into the hind quarters of the tapir before it jumped into the wide river and began swimming across. Once they came out on the river, Les recognized where they were and realized that it was quite a distance back to where they had tied their chalupa.

With no other way to continue, they would need to go back to the boat and use it to cross the river and follow the tapir. An hour later, they found where the tapir had exited the river and began following the blood trail it was leaving. The tapir was leading them in a big circle, and eventually, the men saw the beast, but before any of them could shoot, it was off again. They chased it through thick tangles of vine and brush, almost crawling through at times and bent over much of the time to where Les would silently thank God when he could take three or four steps, standing upright.

Much of the time, he was stooped over, lifting his feet over obstacles such as vines and fallen logs. They were on a large island in the river and continued following the tapir for two hours, long enough that Les estimated they could have gone around the entire island twice. Finally, they came out on the riverbank about 200 meters upriver from where the tapir had crossed the first time, only to find that it had gone back across the river. At least this time, the chalupa was close by, but all the men were totally exhausted and had little to show for it, so they gave up the hunt and motored home.

Bill would go back the next day with a group of nomads to continue the chase while Les would stay in camp for some rest, recuperation, and light chores as he rebuilt his strength. He was sure glad he hadn't been forced to survive off the land as the Yuquí had with only a bow and arrow and other rudimentary tools…and no shotgun. What a difficult life! The following day, Bill and a few hunters went back and followed the trail until they lost the tracks of the tapir, coming home with only a few birds and monkeys.

As Les and Bill hunted with the nomads, they were finding the hunt hindered at times by the numerous taboos the husbands of the pregnant women needed to observe, taboos that made the already difficult lives of the jungle dwellers even more challenging. During the first weeks of a woman's pregnancy, the missionaries were not allowed to touch the husband of the pregnant woman. The husband of the pregnant woman was very careful to avoid strong odors, which included things such as kerosene, fumes from the outboard motor, perfume, insect repellent, gun smoke, foods cooked with added flavorings, and even clean, freshly washed clothing.

With the clean clothing, they would usually throw these on the ground and, after a time, carefully pick them up with two fingers and handle them as little as possible until the "smell" was gone. They were very careful about what meats they ate and what parts of certain birds and animals they would eat. At one meal on the houseboat, Lois greatly offended a man whose wife was pregnant by serving him the tail piece of a wild turkey. She also learned not to serve the man monkey tail, something that was considered almost a delicacy at other times. One hunter whose wife was pregnant not only refused to shoot squirrel monkeys but prohibited anyone, missionaries included, from shooting them while he was along. With monkey being one of the most available and easy to shoot animals in the jungle, not being able to shoot or eat them greatly limited the food supply available to a family whose mother or wife was expectant.

More and more, the nomads were allowing the missionaries to doctor their illnesses, and having a massage with the electric vibrator was a treatment they enjoyed. One of the younger girls had been ill for some time, so the nomads began painting her blue black with the juice of a round fruit they called *dija*. Not only did they paint themselves when sick, but when a girl came of age, she would be painted; or when they wanted to protect themselves from spirits or from the outside world, they would paint themselves liberally with the juice of the *dija*.

In this case, the girl was sick enough that neither they nor the missionaries were confident she would survive, so they were bringing her over daily for vibrator treatments and painting her with *dija*. The chief accompanied the girl, and while the vibrator treatment was going on, Les asked what the little "package" was that the girl wore on a bark string around her neck. The package contained part of her umbilical cord, about one inch in diameter and two inches long. The cord itself had been dried, wrapped in fine string, and then covered in beeswax. Les didn't know the language well enough to discover the purpose for carrying this keepsake.

On another occasion Les heard that Toughy was in pain, so he went across the river and into the nomad camp where many of the Yuquí were gathered around Toughy who was crying and moaning. He had an area on his cheek that was either a very large boil or possibly a staph infection, and the Yuquí had been treating it using traditional methods. There was quite a bit of swelling, and Les squatted beside Toughy, putting pressure on his temples in accordance with instructions given to him by the nomads as his mother, the chief's wife, "operated" on him.

Her nursing assistant, the chief, handed her two thorns shaped like rosebush thorns but about an inch in length. Les could see where they had previously stuck him with the thorns, and the chief's wife was trying to get the thorns back into the same holes she had poked before, but there were many holes where it seemed she had tried and failed to accomplish her objective. She was crying hard, and her eyes were so full of tears that she turned to Les and asked him to stick Toughy with the thorns.

Les was unsure what the procedure was all about, so she turned to White Joven, who was also crying, and he stuck Toughy with a thorn then left it dangling until the chief's wife took hold of it again. She shoved the thorn in until he groaned, then waited a moment before shoving it in again until he stopped her by taking hold of her wrist.

After the thorn had gone in about three quarters of an inch, she pulled it out, squeezed, and pus ran out. She wiped it or rather scraped it off his cheek with a leaf and passed the leaf to someone to throw away. Then she squeezed again. After each time she squeezed and released, the indentations caused by her fingers remained for a time. When she had squeezed out the infected material some four or five times, she quit, and soon, Les and the six hunters he had come with left but not before telling Toughy they would try to get a capybara for him.

After several hours of hunting, the big excitement of the day came on the way back to the river when a ten-foot-long snake came slithering past the hunters. Les, who was near the front of the group, heard some of the nomads call out and turned to see the snake stop, raise its head, and look around. They were all yelling, "Shoot it! Shoot it!" So without even changing shells, Les blasted it with zero-aught-buck, blowing the top of its head off. The snake was six to seven inches in circumference.

It was unusual for the Yuquí to tell Les to shoot a snake as normally, they would tell him not to waste a shell on a creature they didn't consider edible, but in this case, fright overcame other considerations.

Now the Yuquí were camped near the Meadow, and the expectant mothers had begun having their babies. Days earlier, two of the women had delivered, and today, Fatty was having labor pains. Assuming jungle deliveries would have a high rate of mortality for both infant and mother, the missionaries were desirous of doing what they could to help with the birth process and hoped to introduce sanitary conditions and modern medicines, but first they would need to be allowed to get involved.

Once they learned that Fatty was near delivery, they asked to see the baby. When they arrived at the nomad camp, Milk Shake Girl took them two or three minutes beyond the camp to an area enclosed by palm branches where Fatty was in labor "behind leaves" as the nomads referred to it. Pa's wife and Iroquois' wife were attending her, and each had their new little babies with them along with others of their children. Fatty was sitting directly on the ground, holding onto a six-inch diameter tree, straining against it. Occasionally, she would lie down on the ground and push against the tree.

Les, Lois, and Beverly who had come to observe and help, if possible, were told to stay about fifteen feet away, although some of the nomad women did break off branches and twigs that were blocking the view, allowing the three to see better. The older children were holding and caring for the new babies while the two recent mothers rubbed Fatty's stomach, always in a downward motion. They both wanted cloth for their new babies, so Beverly, Les, and Lois' daughter, who was wearing two blouses for protection from insects, took one off and gave it to Pa's wife, Big Tooth. She quickly put it on and buttoned it up as Les, Lois, and Bev remained there observing.

Fatty strained and moaned for the next ten minutes until finally, Les said, "Let's go." It looked like labor was still in its early stages.

Before they left, one of the midwives brought a *bareguaa*, a container made from the base of a palm branch, with water for Fatty. They were doing what they could to take care of her. The Fosters turned to leave, but Milk Shake Girl begged them to stay a little longer, which they did, before eventually going back to the main nomad camp.

There they found Roughneck, Fatty's husband, lying in his hammock, chanting and crying as his slave, Scar Face, watched sadly. Toughy was also lying in his hammock and seemed to be feeling a little better. The chief and his wife were busy, once again, tending to the boil on his cheek, keeping it open and squeezing out the infected material. After observing their ministrations for a few minutes, Les, Lois, and Beverly headed back to where their chalupa was moored and crossed the river to the houseboat.

Once he had left the two women on the houseboat, Les picked up a group of hunters, and they headed up the river to spend the day hunting in the forest.

Several days later, after Fatty had prevailed over the unsanitary conditions and successfully delivered a new baby, Les and Bill stopped by the nomad camp near the Meadow. The majority of the Yuquí were ill with deep chest colds and runny noses. When the missionaries saw George, the chief's slave, they were especially concerned. The Yuquí had been telling them about George, and when they saw him, Les commented to Bill, "He looks about dead."

The nomads were busy giving George the "treatment." He was sitting almost on top of the fire as they poured hot water over him, followed by cold water. His deep chest cough resonated painfully. The chief and Iroquois were also in a bad way, and the majority of the group, including the women with new babies, were struggling with deep chest colds and a racking cough. Les' first thought was, *I wonder if one of the missionary children brought this "bug" in when they came for vacation from boarding school?* There was no way to know for sure, but this was another warning that it would be good to protect the Yuquí from outside visitors as much as possible.

This was the third cold season the missionaries had been in contact with the Yuquí, and they had never seen anything this bad in the previous two "surazo (cold south storm)" seasons. Les and Bill went around hammock to hammock, pressing on their chests and blowing gently on them, showing their love and concern in the same way they had seen the nomads do to one another time after time. They had made a continual effort to get the people to wear the warm clothing they gave them, but much of the clothing had been unraveled and turned into thread or rope and, during the warmer time of year, the clothes were abandoned as unnecessary and left to rot on the humid jungle floor.

The task of providing fifty people with new warm clothing every surazo season was challenging and would require more cooperation from the people themselves. None of the Yuquí were up to hunting, so after leaving kettles of cooked corn and rice, Bill and Les headed back to their clearing where Les worked on the house he was building, and Bill went out hunting, only to return empty-handed. Evidently, the animals were keeping warm in their dens.

With the lack of game in the area due to the cold weather, the Yuquí let it be known that they were all leaving, heading north, where they hoped to find meat. Two days after the Yuquí left, Beverly happened to look across the river as they were eating lunch in the houseboat and observed, "There's a Yuquí over there!"

It was Pa and Big Tooth, both of whom were low on the social scale, and doubtless not being well-fed. The two were carrying a large pot and gallon can, which they wanted filled with cooked rice. After filling their containers with rice, Bill also gave them a large kettle of hominy and waited as they made a *bareguaa* container from the base of a palm leaf to transport the cooked corn. They had come only expecting to get rice.

The two were shivering with the cold and rain, so Bill and Les also gave them some warm clothing. As the two nomads left, they commented that although the people were camped quite a distance away, even so, they would come back the next day for more corn and rice.

It was three days before another nomad showed up, once again at lunchtime, and this time it was Scar Face. He had come to get cooked corn and rice but said that the people were camped so far away that he would need to spend the night and leave the next morning. He explained that all the people were hungry and that most of the group continued ill with a deep cough.

Les sat him down at the table where Scar Face ate like a starving man. He was tired and sleepy, even though it was only the middle of the day, so Les set him up with a cot and an army blanket and tarp to cover himself with and keep warm. He slept all afternoon and woke up around 6:00 p.m. long enough to ask for a drink of water before going back to sleep until morning, although he groaned and coughed often throughout the night.

Daily, Les continued working on his house, hoping to get it finished so they could sell the houseboat. With the Yuquí gone, he could focus hard on the work at hand. In a letter, he described the house he was building.

> The roof is the only part I had to buy, other than nails, door hinges, and some screen wire. The floors are of split palm logs, the corner uprights of whole palm logs, and the walls will be of bamboo. The overhanging corrugated-tin eaves are wide enough that the tropical rains will not wet us, but the cracks in the bamboo walls will let what breeze there is through to us. The floor is about two feet off the ground, set on stumps, as the river may occasionally flood over the bank, and our house will stay dry. We also have an upstairs for our bedrooms. Lois helps me gather bamboo and other materials as the other men are busy working on their own houses. The house will cost about $200.00 to build.

Their goal was to be moved into the house and have the houseboat sold before Dick Strickler arrived back from his year-long trip to the United States where he was visiting family and friends. Once Dick returned, Les and Lois would travel to the homeland for a year, and Dick would live in their house.

The next morning, Les took Scar Face across the river and then headed down the Chimoré River to Puerto Yuca. A supply flight was due in, and Dave and Elizabeth Lotz, teachers at the boarding school, were coming out for a short vacation and to assist as needed. The Yuquí had said they would be gone for a few days, but almost every day, a few showed up looking for corn and rice. Even though it was rainy and cold, they still needed to eat.

Favorite Joven, White Joven, and Big Tummy—Favorite Joven's slave—showed up while it was raining so heavily, the missionaries couldn't hear them calling from across the river, but Les saw one of them standing over there, so Bill went over and brought the three of them back to get them in out of the rain and give them something to eat. While the three Yuquí were visiting, they reported that the deep cough seemed to be improving for most of the nomads, although Toughy was still suffering much from his boil and one of the others had a bad burn on his back.

The group was camped a great distance away and not getting much meat, so they were hoping that these three would go hunting with Bill and Les and bring back meat for the entire band. After having Bill kindle a fire for them, the three disappeared into the jungle for the night, telling Les and Bill that they would be back in the morning to go hunting. They were no-shows the next morning, and it would be four months before any of the group returned. It was the time of year when they traditionally migrated north to the swamps to hunt, although this year had been wetter than most, so they might take longer getting there.

The missionaries were still expecting some of the nomads to show up but made the most of each day working on the houses, clearing jungle, and hunting to keep themselves provided with meat. Even though rainy season was officially past, they were getting excessive amounts of rain, and the river stayed full until it rose to the highest level they had seen since moving to the Chimoré. The river finally crested with Garland's house standing in twelve inches of water.

Neither the Presson nor the Foster house had water under them. With the jungle around the camp heavily flooded, many snakes moved up onto the higher ground where the missionaries lived, and they had several close calls with fer-de-lances and bushmasters. Les was almost bitten by a snake that came out of the brush less than a foot from his hands, poised as if to strike, then it slithered off into the water when he turned looking for a stick with which to kill the serpent.

Bill had a close encounter with a five foot three inch long bushmaster with inch-long fangs. Then Elizabeth Lotz accidentally hit a five-foot long bushmaster while clearing brush near the Fosters' house. Bill was able to slow the large reptile down by hitting it with his machete before Les arrived with his pistol and shot it through the head. The snake had two fangs on one side and one on the other; each fang was one and a quarter inches long. It was amazing that no one was bitten in any of the incidents, and they were all convinced that God was watching over them.

Before departing with the main group of Yuquí, the chief had explained to Les that they would be going south, initially, and then would make a large circle over a period of days, eventually returning from downriver from the north. By now, they had been gone for two weeks. With no counting system available in his language, the chief had explained that they would be gone many, many days and used his ten fingers to indicate that it would be much more than that.

The missionaries would keep busy, but there was one small problem. Dave and Elizabeth were due back at the boarding school where they were dorm parents and teachers, but a radio report from Puerto Yuca indicated the airstrip had flooded badly, and the soft silty strip would be unusable for the foreseeable future. At least the missionary team was getting an adequate supply of game as many smaller animals and snakes had moved onto the high area of jungle around them due to the flooding.

One of their favorite meats was the *paca*, also known as the *lapa*, or *jochi pintado*, a delicious rodent typically weighing ten to twenty-five pounds, and with the flooding, they were shooting quite a few of these. As a rodent, it was attracted to the manioc they had planted, so many of these nocturnal creatures had begun coming to dig and eat the manioc tubers. During the flooding, Les checked their proposed airstrip site and found that it was some of the highest ground around and was pleased to see that.

Dave and Elizabeth had expected to spend ten to fourteen days visiting on the Chimoré River, but due to the flooding and soft airstrip at Puerto Yuca, the visit stretched to five weeks. They would still make it back before school started but had little time to prepare for dorm life and classes. Their help in building and clearing allowed Les and Lois to finish their house, and within a few days, they were able to move from the houseboat to their new house on land and begin the process of coordinating with Don Hilarión, where to meet him, and turn the launch over to him. Another chapter in their lives was complete.

Now that the Yuquí had found them, a mobile base was no longer needed, but they would need an airstrip to make their presence at the Chimoré base truly permanent. It had been sixteen months since contact began on the Chimoré River, and living on the houseboat had been a special part of their lives. During the time they owned the launch, they had put a total of 587 hours of use on Old Michi (Old Cat), the D2 Caterpillar engine that powered *El Chori*.

A month later, Les, Lois, and Beverly were on APSA jet flight number 66 heading for Miami, Florida. They would spend a year in the USA while Garlands, Pressons, and Dick Strickler continued the work with the Yuquí. The Fosters hadn't seen the Yuquí again before leaving for the homeland but, in one of their last conversations with the nomads, had explained that they would be going by airplane to visit their parents far away and would be gone a long time.

"Don't go," was Toughy's first response. "Your parents must be old and will want you to stay and hunt for them." Then he suggested that Les just have his parents come to visit.

Les told him that he would be buying a new shotgun so he could kill more meat to feed the Yuquí, and with that, Toughy was content, telling Les, "Go and get a gun, but be sure to come back."

Two months later, a missionary living on the Chapare River reported that a large group of Yuquí had been stealing bananas from Yuracaré farms in the area, but there had been no known shootings, and shortly after, the nomads showed up again at the Chimoré base after an absence of four months. Rainy season would soon begin, so they had come back to higher ground.

As the routine settled into the expected norm, Mary got back into working on the language and soon found that having two or three women at a time as language helpers worked better than having a husband and wife. The women were more used to sitting around talking, caring for babies, tending the fires, or making bark rope and string, whereas the men wanted to be more physically active, hunting or chopping down bee trees. Since the language helpers were well-fed, the women fought over the chance to work with Mary and she soon figured out which ones were the most useful in advancing progress in the language.

There were more women willing to help than she could use, so she could be selective about who she worked with. None of the women yet seemed to understand what Mary was trying to do, but at least they would sit and talk with her for hours, and she could record stories they told and later transcribe those and ask questions about things they had said.

Bob wrote to Les, who was in the States:

> Mary has been having profitable days with the women that stay here. In fact, most days it has been from 8:30 a.m. to 4:00 p.m. She's gotten quite a bit of language material but not much time for analysis. This is the first time she has really been able to hear the language much and has enjoyed it.

Bob was considering accompanying the nomads on one of their trips in the jungle so he could be immersed in the language, but that would have to wait until the base had a larger complement of missionary personnel.

During the first two years of stable contact with the Yuquí, the nomads spent 391 days with the missionaries while the rest of the time, they were gone on their migratory wanderings. Now more and more, not all the Yuquí were gone at the same time; rather, a few would stay near the missionaries while others went off on hunting trips. They were happy to have a safe place where they could always count on something to eat and protection from Bolivian colonists, hunters, and farmers.

By this time, the Yuquí had 300 banana plants of their own plus a few hundred more on the missionary side of the Chimoré, so they rarely lacked for bananas. The 150 pineapple plants Les had planted continued to multiply and began to produce abundantly. Along with papaya, manioc, corn, rice, and plentiful fish from the river, the Yuquí diet was fairly good. Having a few Yuquí around all the time also meant that Mary was making progress in analyzing the language.

The year in the homeland was soon over, and Les and Lois arrived back on the Chimoré, quickly fitting back into the day-today routine with the Yuquí. Les went over to pay a visit to the Yuquí camp and was sitting on the ground, observing the unusual scene while thinking of the difficult life the nomads led, a life governed by fear—fear of the unknown, fear of the colonists, fear of the spirits of their own dead, fear of the wind and rain, jungle storms, falling trees, and the list goes on.

The chief was lying in his hammock, and there, beside the hammock, lay a palm-leaf basket about three feet long, twelve inches wide, and eight inches high. The open end of the basket revealed an adult human skull sitting upright, looking out on the camp with sightless eye sockets. It was shiny and smooth from much handling and had been painted a bright orange-red using the seeds of the achiote (urucú) which the Yuquí use for protection from spirits and other evils.

The skull was missing the lower jawbone, which led Les to believe that this was the skull of the nomad they had referred to as Wide Eyes on the earliest contacts in 1959. Wide Eyes was the chief's oldest son who had been killed by a burst of machine-gun fire from a posse of armed farmers. The position of the skull gave Les the impression that it had been placed so Wide Eyes could look out over the campsite and continue to be a part of the group.

As Les' eyes traveled around the campsite, he could see numerous baskets like this one, but of differing sizes. Most of them were tied shut but appeared to also contain the bones of their dead. Was it to the spirits of these dead the nomads were calling out when they heard them chanting and yelling in the night? With limited language, Les wasn't able to ask questions, and he also knew that to talk about the dead would set the entire group to wailing and mourning, possibly for days. Better to leave the subject alone for now.

Eventually, they would be able to explain to the Yuquí that God was more powerful than other spirits. The next day, one of the young Yuquí men told Les that he, along with another young man, had the job of moving the baskets of bones when they traveled.

Dry season was nearing its end, and the large swamps had shrunk to a small size, confining alligators and fish in a minimal amount of water. The nomads loved this as they had worked out various ways to easily gather abundant food. They took Les along to help shoot alligators. Placing Les and a hunter with bow and arrow at one end of a swamp, the rest of the hunters went to the other end of the water hole and waded into the water, slapping the surface of the water with sticks and jabbing into the water with them, slowly working their way in the direction where Les and his companion waited.

The alligators who were hiding under the water moved away from the slapping sticks toward Les, and as they neared the end of the swamp, the alligators came to the surface to see what was going on, at which point, Les or his buddy shot them. The first day, they got eight alligators this way.

Other times, before even entering the swamp to drive the alligators to the other side, the hunters would stand and call the gators by making the sound a baby alligator makes when it is in trouble. Often, the mama gators would surface and come toward the sound, thus allowing the hunters to shoot them.

The nomads were also getting an abundance of fish from the swamps and water holes that were drying up. The Yuquí cut eighteen-inch long pieces of a poisonous vine that grew in the jungle, tied it together in bundles, and then walked through the swamp, striking the bundle of vines with a stick, causing them to disintegrate, all the while dipping the bundled vines in and out of the water so the poison mixed with the water. In about an hour, the fish would come to the surface or to the edge of the swamp, and the nomads could either grab them by hand or shoot them with an arrow. The poison didn't seem to have any adverse effect on the person who ate fish caught by this method. In the dry season, a great abundance of fish could be gathered like this, and the smoke racks were piled high as the Yuquí gorged on meat.

* * * * *

It was pitch black at 8:30 p.m., and with group devotions over and a hard day of hunting with several Yuquí behind him, Les decided to take a relaxing walk down to the riverbank with flashlight and his

30-aught-six rifle before retiring for the night. Coming to the edge of the bank where he could overlook the large sandbar, he first shone his light downriver. Then he swept the beam out over the water and finally upstream and into the brush along the edge of the sandbar. It took an instant for his mind to react to the eyes his light had just passed over, and he swung the beam back around to focus on them. Sure enough, there they were!

It was too far away to tell what kind of an animal was connected to those two glowing reflectors, and as he edged closer, he could see the eyes become nervous, preparing to flee. He knew it wasn't his dog, Yogi, since she was behind him, between him and the house. He inched forward, keeping his light in the eyes of the animal so it wouldn't see him and run. Finally, at about seventy-five yards, he stopped, zeroed in on the eyes, and fired. A ball of fire shot out into the darkness, and all was still.

He sprinted down the bank and into the thicket where his game lay. As he ran, he thought of the nice meal a paca (fifteen-pound edible rodent) would make once it had been roasted slowly over the fire. His mouth watered as the scene played over in his mind. He was totally unprepared for what lay there before him as his flashlight illuminated the headless gray body. Garland's house cat had never been that far from their house before and never upriver. Leaving the body where it lay, he went to notify Bob that he had accidentally shot his pet cat. Bob was not too agitated, responding, "That's all right, Les, we can always get another one."

Les and Bob decided to use this opportunity to gather valuable language material, so he left the cat where it had fallen. The next morning, Les had been studying language for about an hour while seated under his mosquito net when he heard a yell from across the river. "*Tibaquete* (Les), what did you shoot last night?"

Without answering the question, Les walked down to the river and went across to bring a group of Yuquí over and showed them what he had shot. Bob was waiting with pencil and notebook and followed along as Les led the group up the sandbar. The men were hoping to make the most of this incident by trying to get the word for "accident" or maybe even the more valuable phrase, "I'm sorry," which might be useful for expressing to God our sorrow for our sins and disobedience against Him.

As Les approached the cat, the nomads started beating the back of their heads with their hands and yelling, "You shot *Pachïïnu's* (Bob's) cat!"

Les calmed them down and then proceeded to tell them the story of how he had seen the cat in the flashlight beam and thought it was an edible rodent but, upon shooting, found it to be Bob's cat. With trembling voice and fake tears as one who is really sorry for what they have done, Les asked them to tell Bob what he had done. Turning to Bob, they said, "*Tibaquete* is crying. May we eat your cat?" A very practical response! Why waste good meat?

While the missionaries didn't elicit the response they had hoped for, the next day, the Yuquí reported that roasted cat was excellent eating and they would welcome more any time. The missionary team was constantly alert for situations where they could capture abstract words or phrases while the nomads were attuned to the day-to-day struggle to survive.

Now, after almost three years of friendship with the missionaries, a few of the Yuquí were showing interest in having a more permanent roof over their heads, rather than sleeping under a handful of palm branches in the pouring rain. Favorite Joven asked Les to help him build a simple thatch house, and Les was pleased to work with him on that. The chief came by to see how they were progressing and let Les know that the house would need to be supplied with several fifty-gallon metal barrels of sugar, rice, and pasta, just like the missionaries had in their houses. He seemed to think that these kind of things were part of "having a house."

As they worked on the house, Favorite Joven continued asking Les about Big Father over and over again, and Les did his best to explain how Big Father lives up in the sky, looks down and sees us, and has a desire that the Yuquí become His children too. Les could see Favorite Joven processing this information, and soon, he commented, "When we build the trail for the airplane, I want it to carry me up into the sky."

From this and other happenings, it had become pretty clear that the nomads were associating the airplane and its trips to the sky with access to the spirit world they believed inhabited the sky.

While missionary fluency in the language was still rather rudimentary, Mary Garland, the linguist, had reached a point where she was able to give a limited Gospel presentation to her language helper. The young lady who was now helping her was quick and intelligent and seemed to understand what Mary was explaining to her and expressed her desire to become a child of Big Father. Only time would tell whether she truly understood the Gospel message, but the missionaries began to see such a change in her life that they were optimistic that the Spirit of God was at work in her. She also began sharing this new knowledge with others in her group, some of whom showed interest, while others made fun of her.

On another occasion, Les had gone hunting with a group of the nomads to a swamp, hoping to shoot cattle-rustler birds, a large swamp bird with a six-foot wingspan and "spurs" on its wing joints. These huge birds were not only good eating, but the feathers were excellent for fletching arrows. After looking unsuccessfully for game, the party sat and rested before heading back home, and the hunters began asking Les questions about Big Father. It had just thundered, which seemed to bring the subject to their minds as they asked, "Is that Big Father?"

Les replied, "No."

They began making other comments which made it clear that they were equating the thunder, lightning, and wind with Big Father. Les attempted to explain that Big Father cared about them and did good things for them, not bad, even sending His Son to earth to die for them so they could be "clean." He explained how Big Father's Son came to life again after three days and lives with Big Father now and can make us "clean" so we can live with Him after we die. With no words yet for accept, believe, sorrow, repentance, or trust, the best Les could come up with was "clean," a very rudimentary message, but one he desperately wanted to communicate to these people he cared so much about.

Les went on to say, "I asked Big Father to protect you until I can learn more of your language and tell you about Him."

At this point, Roughneck broke away from the group and ran wildly through the jungle until he came to an opening in the high canopy of trees large enough to see a part of the sky. Shaking his bow and arrows defiantly at the heavens, he yelled, "Big Father! Protect me!"

Les caught up with him and explained that "we don't need to "threaten" Big Father when we ask Him to protect us, but we go to him humbly."

Roughneck seemed to understand and stopped threatening Big Father. No doubt since hearing of Big Father, he had been threatening Him in fear the same way the Yuquí rattled their bows and arrows at the wind and chanted and yelled at it. Les would need much more language before he could adequately explain the message he had come to share with the Yuquí.

With dry season coming on the river level once again dropped, leaving the sandbar in front of the missionary camp long and level. Les talked to Leroy Lindahl, the World Gospel Mission pilot, by radio and asked if he would be willing to try using the sandbar as an airstrip. Leroy agreed to try it, and soon, the first flight was successfully accomplished. The sand was a little soft, but before the next flight, a light rain firmed up the sand, and it was much better. In fact, it was good enough that Leroy took Les and one of the Yuquí, George (a slave), up for a five-minute flight. In his anxiety at this new experience, George gave Les a bear hug throughout the entire flight, and as they flew, Les pointed out different swamps where they had hunted together.

George's comments back to Les showed that he recognized the spots where they had shot a variety of birds and animals. While the flight was in the air, the group of nomads on the ground did fine, but the minute the plane landed, the entire group began wailing as if someone had died. Les began joking about how George hugged him throughout the flight and all the things they had seen, and soon the wailing died off as George regaled them with his account of the flight. For a Stone Age nomad, a first airplane ride was a novel and terrifying experience, but he had survived it!

A few days later, Lois was talking with George and asked him where he would go after death. Now that the missionaries were doing some rudimentary teaching on biblical truths, she fully expected him to reply either "Big Father's camp (heaven)" or "to the fire (hell)" and was somewhat surprised when he replied, "When I die, I'll go up in the firefly (airplane) and travel around in it."

The Yuquí were anxious to have their own "trail (airstrip)" for the "firefly (airplane)" and told Les they would help him clear jungle for it. They had no idea of the massive amount of work involved but would soon learn. Les had contracted with a Bolivian friend to bring a work crew in and build the airstrip, but when that plan fell through, he decided to proceed with only the Yuquí to help him. He would pay them according to the pay scale that a Bolivian farmer would be paid, but instead of trade goods as he had done so far, they would be earning so much that he decided to introduce Bolivian coins, all of them in the fifty-centavo denomination to make matters easier. He would also stock a small "trading post" with goods they could buy with their earnings.

Lois was in Santa Cruz and planned to bring a plane load of cooking pots, machetes, knives, axes, shirts, cloth, string, rope, sugar, noodles, rice, and other items to stock the trading post. Then they would have a labeled jar with each worker's name where they could store their coins under lock and key in the trading post. Each day, Les would pay the workers, and they could buy what they wanted with the money he was "banking" for them or save up for purchasing more expensive items.

The first day, the Yuquí worked with great enthusiasm, not knowing how to pace themselves and, by the end of a few hours, had accomplished a full day's work but had numerous blisters and raw hands from swinging machetes and axes so strenuously. Now they all headed for the trading post where Les counted out the coins earned into each worker's jar. Because of the caste system, Les had to be careful to start from the top and work his way down as he paid the workers, and as he began selling items, starting with the chief and his sons and working his way down to the slave class.

When all had been paid and he asked what the workers wanted to purchase, they *all* plunked down their money and yelled, "*Sugar!*"

Les quickly became aware that supplying the trading post was going to be a time-consuming task and necessitated many flights. For the first several days, *all* the wages went to buy sugar only!

With no word for money in the language, Les introduced the Spanish word, *dinero*, not realizing how that would come across to the nomads. The Yuquí language has a prefix, "di," which means "your," and a prefix, "chi," which means "my." These are put on nouns to show possession; for example, they would say "*dirä*" for "yours to eat (food)" or "*chirä*" for "mine to eat (food)." In their thinking, the Spanish word "dinero" must mean "your money," therefore "chinero" must mean "my money." That made logical sense to them, so that is how they began referring to money.

Now Les was glad they had the sandbar to use as a temporary landing strip, and the next flight arrived loaded with 650 pounds of sugar. The Yuquí were extremely happy to help carry this bounty to the trading post Les had established in his work shed. Bill Presson arrived back on one of the flights, and now he and Les worked almost daily on the airstrip when not hunting with the Yuquí. Even young children wanted to work, moving light debris into piles to be burned and carrying small bags of dirt to fill low spots. Everyone wanted a chance to earn coins to buy sugar, sweetened condensed milk, canned meat, canned sardines, and other exotic goodies.

It was amazing the amount of work the small band of forty-nine jungle dwellers could accomplish with the right motivation, and for people who had lived a feast or famine existence, foodstuff was a powerful incentive.

Les and Bill were busy, daily, felling trees with their chainsaws and sawing them into small pieces that could be rolled or carried off the runway while the Yuquí dug dirt and moved the debris. Many piles of logs and brush were burned, and Les had been able to purchase three cases of dynamite for blowing out stumps. He soon found that by cutting a stump down to ground level and then drilling straight down into the center taproot of the stump before placing dynamite in the augered hole, he was able to blow most of the trunk and roots out so that very little digging was required.

After he had blown out a few tree trunks like this, some of the men came to him and complained that the pregnant women could feel their babies jump when the loud explosions went off. Les explained that instead of blowing the stumps out, they could dig around each one little by little with a shovel and then tediously chop them out using an axe. It didn't take long until all the workers agreed that the unborn babies could no longer hear the explosions.

Dynamiting stump while building airstrip.

The advantage of the dynamite was clear. Other than a hole in the roof of Les' house from a large piece of flying tree root, there were no known injuries or damages from the dynamite.

The work on the airstrip pressed forward as they knew they only had about six months to complete it before rainy season set in, which would slow or halt the work. This would mean having to transport supplies from the airstrip at Puerto Villaroel, a full-day round trip. Unfortunately, before rainy season set in, beach landings came to an abrupt halt. The river had come up and then gone back down, but what no one knew was that debris had been washed onto the beach and then covered with sand, leaving a soft, hidden "trap" in the beach. During the nineteenth beach landing and with Mildred Presson and her two daughters on board, the plane hit this soft spot and nosed up, damaging the cowling, propeller, and wing tip. Leroy was able to straighten the propeller to where he could fly the airplane back to his base for repairs but refused to risk the aircraft on any more beach landings. They would need at least 300 meters of usable runway before they could begin flights with limited weight on the airstrip they were building, and that would take several months at the rate they were progressing.

The previous year, while on a trip by launch from Todos Santos to the Chimoré, the missionaries had been flagged down along the Ichilo River by a group of Bolivian hunters. One of the men was a German immigrant who occasionally came hunting along the Chimoré River, even though the missionaries had asked him not to do so until the Yuquí were more settled and less of a danger. His response was that he would kill the "savages" and scalp them if he saw them.

The hunters had flagged down the launch, thinking it might be merchants selling cigarettes and alcohol, but when they saw it was the missionaries, the German fellow was quite antagonistic. Even so, Les led the conversation around to the Lord Jesus and how each individual needs to put his faith in Him if he wants to go to heaven. The German made the "smart remark" that he knew he was going to heaven because he himself was the Christ. His statement brought the conversation to an abrupt halt.

Now more than a year later, Les heard the distant blast of dynamite exploding far to the south and wondered what that was all about; possibly, the Bolivians were dynamiting fish. On the next supply trip to Puerto Villaroel, Les learned that the German fellow had indeed been dynamiting fish along the Ichilo River. As was customary when stunning and capturing fish by this method, he was using a very short fuse which he would light from his cigarette. The dynamite needed to explode just under the surface of the water before it sank too far. One fuse didn't seem to be lit, so he was blowing on it to get it started when, unbeknown to him, it was already burning. The dynamite exploded in his face, blowing him into the next world. As Les wrote, "I'm sure he knows now he is not the Christ."

The missionaries had been praying that this man, who had threatened to kill the Yuquí if he saw them, wouldn't continue coming up the Chimoré River, and God answered their request in an unusual manner.

Facing Death

"I DON'T WANT TO DIE alone. When I die, kill George to go with me!"

The chief was referring to his slave, George. Now put yourself in George's place. You are about twenty-two years of age, a slave to the chief of the Yuquí tribe, and the lowest of the social order in the group in which you live. Your master is old, racked with pain, and seemingly comes close to death several times a year. He has announced to the whole group his desire for you to accompany him in death and has even gone so far as to choose the executioner, Iroquois, a man who will cruelly and efficiently carry out his wish. Once his steel hands grip around your neck, struggle as you may, it will be only minutes until you pass out. As your body relaxes, his next move will be to bend your head backward, breaking your neck, and you will be in the great unknown of eternity.

Will you be up in the sky with the spirits of your ancestors? Or somewhere else? Truly, your life expectancy is short, and escape is next to impossible.

When the missionaries learned that George was facing this uncertain future, they could better understand the reckless, accident, and suicide prone ways they had seen him act during their years with the Yuquí. They had little doubt that George would be killed when the chief died and weren't sure there was much they could do about it. They discussed trying to hide George in one of their houses when the chief was ill, but as the chief's slave, George would be expected to tend to his master during any sickness, and if the missionaries weren't present, the deed would no doubt be carried out.

To smuggle him out to another mission station on a flight would undoubtedly cause them to lose the trust of the entire group.

About all they could do was try and convince the Yuquí that there was no need to kill George when the chief died, but the tradition of sending someone along to serve the high-class individual in the next life was a powerful motivator if the rest of the group wanted to protect themselves from the spirit of the dead person. It was engrained in their thinking. "Someone must die!" But what they didn't yet understand was that Big Father's Son had already died for all of them!

Les and Lois began taking multiday hunting trips with groups of up to eighteen nomads at a time. This gave them exposure to the language and culture 24/7. While traveling with the Yuquí, they lived simply, taking a jungle hammock apiece and modest amounts of rice, noodles, salt, and sugar to supplement the meat and honey they could get in the jungle, along with two small aluminum cooking pots for cooking they could get by. Palm cabbage and whatever fruit the jungle might provide supplemented the wild meat and honey.

A typical trip might be five or six days long as they traveled into more distant areas to hunt with the nomads. With all the hunting they had done near their base camp, game had gotten scarce, but on these trips, they were able to supply the Yuquí with large quantities of meat. Once the smoke racks were heaped full of roasting meat and the kettles full of honey, they could sit around camp, interacting with the Yuquí, hearing and trying out the language and observing new cultural experiences in their natural setting.

Even with a few modern amenities such as the shotgun, jungle hammocks, and cooking kettles, life was difficult in the forest. On the first five-day trip, Lois lost six pounds, and Les wrote to a friend, "If you know of anyone who has a problem with being overweight, this method of losing weight works good."

During one of these trips, Les was awakened out of a sound sleep at 4:15 a.m., and his first groggy thought was that one of the nomads he was camped with had crawled under the foot of his hammock, raising it up and then dropping it down again as a joke; but the "joke" theory lasted only for a second. He felt a large blunt nose push the mosquito net against his right ankle followed by a loud snapping noise! Next it was at the calf of his legs, sniffing, then at his knee. Les thought of the revolver lying beside him in the hammock, but it was between him and the creature that was sniffing him, and he was afraid to move lest he startle the animal and cause it to pounce on him.

By now, it was sniffing at his beltline, and then, as it pushed hard against the netting, it was sniffing at his arm, then shoulder, and the last very loud sniff was right in his ear! He waited patiently, wondering what conclusion the animal had come to, afraid to move, but nothing further happened. The creature seemed to have moved on.

Les rolled over quickly, grabbed his .357 Magnum pistol and flashlight, and shone around the small clearing, but by then, the animal had moved on into the surrounding woods. Les lay back in his netted hammock and tried to relax. Within a few minutes, he began to hear the low humming sound of a prowling jaguar calling for its mate. As he later wrote in a letter, "Needless to say, I am very happy to be able to write you again at this time." Oh, and what was the loud snapping noise? Jaguars are known to make a "snapping" sound with their ears!

After eight months of strenuous labor, 250 meters of airstrip were usable, and the pilot said he could try a landing, bringing a small amount of cargo to give some balance to the airplane. He wanted at least 300 meters before bringing larger loads or taking passengers out, but by coming in now, he could inspect the work and give suggestions on how they could improve the runway.

Most of the surface was already covered in a variety of native grasses that came up within weeks once the ground was cleared. Seeding was unnecessary. It would take eight more months to complete the 450-meter runway, sixteen months total, with the vast majority of the work done by the Yuquí themselves along with Les and Bill. By now, the nomads understood the value of money or at least of fifty-centavo coins. Coins had been introduced instead of paper bills because of their indestructibility. The trading post did a thriving business, and supply flights became a regular occurrence.

It had been ten years since the very first contacts at La Jota when Les wrote to his daughter, Beverly, at the boarding school to tell her of the first profession of faith among the nomads.

> I'm pretty sure that Mary's language helper is saved! She has sure changed! I have seen many indications that she may very well be born again. We are having good times with her talking about the Lord, and she shows real spiritual insight into those things. I have been experiencing real freedom in the language and in witnessing. I've talked with her much and she seems to drink up everything I tell her and believe it. I've also been talking to Freddy and George and I think they are both close to believing.

While groups of the Yuquí continued to leave for weeks or months at a time, now there was almost always a handful of them who remained behind to interact with the missionaries. Some of them stayed because they were receiving medical treatment, and others because they had a steady source of food. With the main part of the airstrip work completed, there was still work available for any of the nomads who wanted to do maintenance work, clearing brush with a machete.

The jungle never stops encroaching, and the missionaries were happy to pay them to help keep the weeds down. Most of those who worked would come over to the missionary camp and cut grass or weeds for three to four hours, earning enough to buy food for a few days.

Les and Bill still hunted regularly with those who wanted to go with them while Bob and Mary continued analyzing the language. Mary had also begun working on some simple Bible stories to share with the Yuquí.

Medical work continued to expand as the Yuquí found that the missionaries had effective ways of treating many of their ailments, so each morning, the sick and injured would show up for treatment. Injections had become a regular occurrence as two of the men were being treated for tuberculosis, and occasional other infections required antibiotics.

The nomads had gone out to a swamp and poisoned fish, coming back with many aluminum cooking pots full of small fish and many larger fish strung on vines. They were pleased with their haul, and as they came through the missionary camp, the chief's wife dropped off three small carp-type fish for Les to eat. Once she was gone, Les took the fish and used them as bait for larger fish.

By then, it was early evening, and he soon hooked a hefty catfish but lost it. About five minutes later, he hooked another large one and fought with it for quite some time. Each time he would get the colossus near the boat, it would dive, turn crosswise to the current, and head downstream, aided by the force of the water. It took at least five minutes before the fish tired, and he was able to get it alongside the boat where he hooked it with a large metal gaff hook and pulled it into the boat. By then, his hands were bruised and cut up from the handline he had been using. He left the fish in the boat for the night, and the next morning, when the Yuquí showed up on the far bank of the river and began calling to come across to work or hunt, he headed over there, still with the fish in the boat.

The chief's wife was there as Les pulled ashore. Pointing proudly to the 137-pound giant black catfish, he said, "It's for you!"

She beamed all over! After some of the men helped him haul it up the bank, three of the men hoisted it so he could weigh it with his 300-pound milk scale, although the rope broke the first time they tried, so they had to double the rope.

Les had begun getting requests from missionary coworkers for curios from the Yuquí tribe, items they could use as displays when speaking in churches in the homeland. Bows and arrows were a common request. Les answered one missionary's request with the following:

> I picked up another curio of handiwork
> from the Yuquí. It is called a *teecua*. These mats
> are made from the inner leaves of certain palm

trees. Small ones like this are used to fan their fires. Larger ones are used to sit or sleep on by women who are having their time of the month. The women spend that time at the edge of the main camp with a shelter of palm leaves between them and the camp so that no man or boy may look upon them. Also, the large mats are made in abundance when a person dies and the body is wrapped in the mats and tied up in a bundle. Then the body is placed on a platform 4 to 5-feet high and a shelter of palm leaves much like a teepee or wigwam is built around the platform. Later after the flesh has rotted from the bones, the bones are "renewed" by being put into an "*iiru*," which is like a double mat, or flat basket. The bones are then carried around with the group as they move from place to place. Later the less important dead are left in a central burial place, again on platforms. The more important bones like those of "Wide Eyes," who was the chief's oldest son, killed by a commission in 1960 are still being carried around. His bones and skull are in camp with them right now in an "*iiru*." His skull has been painted with urucú and is normally set in such a way that he is able to look out over the camp with his eyeless sockets.

Les went on to explain:

These *iirus* are not only used for the dead, but also are used as containers for personal belongings, which might consist of small snail shells for sharpening arrows, an agouti or paca tooth/turkey bone tool for arrow making, some achiote (urucú) to be used as needed for smearing on any "sick" part of their bodies, a few wing feathers from turkeys, ducks, macaws, or vultures which will be used to fletch arrows, a chunk of very sticky beeswax that has been cooked down for arrow making, maybe a ball of bark string for arrow making, and possibly a stickery pod to use as a hairbrush, or maybe a clamshell to use as a spoon.

Giving Birth

THE MORNING STARTED OFF MUCH like any other day. An average-sized group of Yuquí appeared on the west bank of the river, and Les went across in the boat to pick up those who were wanting to work. Iroquois and his wife were there, and she was in tears. Her labor pains had begun, and Iroquois was planning to stay there with her but asked Les to talk to Big Father on her behalf.

Throughout the day, different Yuquí came to the riverbank and called across, asking the missionaries to pray. Late that evening, White Joven and his wife came out to the riverbank, lighting their way with burning embers, and yelled across to Les, letting him know that the woman had not yet given birth and was in great pain. Again, Les promised to talk to Big Father.

The following morning, the woman still had not given birth, so after talking by radio with a doctor in Cochabamba to get his input, Les and Lois went across the river and hiked the twelve minutes into the main nomad camp. The chief lay in his hammock and stopped them so he could chat for a few moments. Beside his hammock sat the basket with Wide Eyes' bones, the empty eye sockets of the orange-painted skull staring vacantly over the camp.

After a short visit with the chief, father of the expectant mother, Les and Lois were escorted two minutes farther into the jungle by a bunch of girl children to where Iroquois' wife was being attended to by a group of women. Other than Les, no men were allowed to be present. Les and Lois timed her contractions and gathered additional information to share with the doctor they would be talking with on a noon radio schedule they had arranged.

The doctor recommended an injection of the opioid, Demerol, which the missionaries had on hand, so after the radio contact, Les and Lois went back over to the birth site. They explained to the woman and her attendants that the injection would help the woman sleep for a time and then she should wake up and give birth to the baby, all the while hoping that this would be the case as there wasn't much else they could do. The option of flying the woman to the city for medical attention was not yet available as the nomads hadn't reached a point in their trust relationship with the missionaries to where they would agree to such an extreme action, not understanding how it could benefit them.

Night fell once again, and occasionally, a Yuquí would appear on the west bank of the river to yell across that the woman still had not given birth. The last report came at 1:00 a.m. and indicated that the woman was in great pain. It was 2:00 a.m. when the missionary team heard the distant chanting change in pitch, volume, and intensity. They weren't sure what that meant, but it didn't sound good.

At daybreak, the first Yuquí showed up on the riverbank and reported that the woman still had not given birth. After talking with the doctor by radio once again, Les and Lois headed back across the river, carrying the doctor-recommended antibiotics. As they neared the place where she had been in labor, they saw a large group of men, women, and children with her. They noticed right away that the chief's wife was weaving a large palm-leaf mat of the kind they used to wrap the dead. As they came closer, they saw the woman, lying on her back with her head in her daughter's lap, and the bottom half of her body covered with leaves. They couldn't help but notice how pale she looked.

Les reached down and touched her chest. She was cold! He looked up at Lois and said, "She's dead!" Then he noticed the woman's teenage slave girl lying beside her also with the bottom half of her body covered by leaves. Knowing how tired the poor young woman had been the day before from waiting on her mistress, he at first thought she was sleeping from pure exhaustion. But then as he looked closer, he could see a thin red trickle of blood oozing from the corner of her mouth. He stepped over and laid his hand on her chest. She too was dead! He was horrified!

Les and Lois quickly discussed the possible cause of her death. Might she have died of exhaustion? Or did her master become so angry at her after his wife died that he killed her? Once recently, he had beaten her over the head with a shovel because of some minor offense.

Les commented to Lois that if they had killed her to go with her mistress to the next world and attend her there, it was possible that they might also want to kill one or both of them for the same reason. The nomads began begging Les and Lois to ask Big Father to bring the woman back. "Call the airplane and have it bring her back," they insisted.

They were very fearful and added, "We don't want her to wander over to where the enemies are. They might keep her."

"Where has she gone?" they questioned of Les and Lois.

Les whispered to Lois, "I think we need to go home before things get out of hand." The two of them made their escape and went back across the river where they informed their coworkers of the deaths. The slave girl had recently had a baby of her own, and it wasn't long before it too died from lack of care.

Later, when Les was alone with Straight Hair and his wife on the missionary side of the river and asked what had happened to the slave girl, Straight Hair commented, "They killed her."

"Who?" questioned Les.

"The chief," came the reply, and then Straight Hair's wife volunteered, "The chief choked her to death and broke her neck."

"Why would he do that?" inquired Les.

"Well, because she was the woman's slave girl, of course!" answered the woman. The answer strongly implied that anyone should naturally know that this was something that *had* to be done. "Someone must die!"

Les longed for the day when he could clearly explain to the nomads that "Someone had died!" The Son of God had not only died for them but could protect them from the spirits of their dead and any other forces of evil. Little by little, the Yuquí were coming to understand this truth, but they still had a way to go.

The next morning, Les and Lois went back across the river to meet with the Yuquí. Les wore his sidearm in case of trouble and carried a smoke grenade. The nomads had never seen a smoke grenade used, and the missionaries often carried one to use as a diversion in case of attack. Bill Presson watched through field glasses from the east bank of the river and had a gun at hand prepared to fire into the air if necessary. It had been a long time since the missionaries had taken such extreme precautions, but after the situation the previous day, they weren't sure what to expect.

Surprisingly, it appeared that the nomads appreciated the visit and guided Les and Lois to where the bodies had been placed a short distance back in the jungle. The Yuquí didn't bury their dead but had made a teepee shaped shelter of palm branches standing upright with the base of the leaves pressed into the soft soil. Inside the

Burial shelter for Iroquois' wife.

shelter was a table-like structure of slender poles about four feet high, and on the platform were two enclosed baskets made of woven palm leaf mats. A small smoky fire was burning outside of the shelter, possibly to keep predators away from the decaying bodies. Queenie took Les and Lois around the shelter and found an entrance near the fire, indicating to Les and Lois that they should stoop over and take a look at the burial baskets inside. Favorite Joven, brother to the

Palm leaf basket containing Iroquois' wife's body.

dead woman, had stepped inside the shelter to make sure everything was shipshape.

After viewing the unusual scene, Les and Lois followed their guides back to the nomad camp and spent some time visiting with the group assembled there. There were many questions asked about the afterlife, and Les did the best he could with his limited knowledge of the language to answer those queries, all the time realizing that much of what he said was being reinterpreted through the world view of the Yuquí.

Iroquois, husband to the dead woman, once again begged, "Have the airplane bring my wife back." And for many days after the death, he repeated his request. If the missionaries could fly through the sky where the spirits of the dead lived, surely it wouldn't be too difficult to bring back someone they had all loved.

After the death of his wife, Iroquois came across a few times to work for the missionaries but was so distraught, he would begin crying and couldn't work. Finally, he and a small group of Yuquí left on an extended hunting trip. In the past, when a death occurred, they could move camp as a means of disassociating themselves from the place of grief. Now that they were settling down, the best they could do was make an extended trip while they worked through the emotions of their loss.

Speaking of the dead was a forbidden subject, so the missionaries had to be careful when trying to learn more about departed ancestors of the Yuquí, especially those who had died in the recent past. Even so, after this death, Dick was able to elicit a word, *eyirogüëë*, for the "spirit (empty breath)" of the deceased woman, a word that would be helpful in communicating spiritual truth. Through another recent situation, the missionary team had finally gotten a phrase meaning, "What are they doing?" which made a huge impact on learning the language. Now they had a way to get verbs! Each one of these events were significant milestones for putting the language into a written form.

Toughy had begun showing a real streak of meanness, beating Mary's language helper, the first believer, several times. The missionaries weren't sure, but it seemed that he didn't like her talking about

Big Father and His Son. Then, after beating the language helper one day, Toughy followed up by throwing his old wife, whom he had discarded for a more desirable woman, into the campfire. She had three really bad burns on her chest and face, which Lois was treating.

Les continued to have a good relationship with Toughy and was sharing more biblical truth with him as they hunted together. Les explained to Toughy, "Big Father said that all of us—the enemies, the Yuquí, and the missionaries—are bad and, because of that, will have to die. But Jesus, the Son of Big Father, heard his Father say that and said, 'No! I'll die in their place!' So Big Father let bad people kill His Son and then made Him alive again for us. He will take those of us who love Him to live with Him forever."

With the lack of many key words, Les was working hard to get his simple presentation across to Toughy and to the other nomads. How much of it they really understood, only God knew, but Les didn't want to see any more of them enter eternity without learning of the Savior, so he did the best he could to communicate the message he was so passionate about.

Favorite Joven's wife, after hearing one of Les' "presentations," commented, "I am going to 'hold onto' you and go with you to Big Father's camp."

Les responded, "Hold on to Big Father's Son instead."

All of this contributed to more conversations with the Yuquí about spiritual things and enabled the missionaries to learn terminology related to spiritual matters as well as some of the beliefs of the Yuquí concerning the afterlife, the spirits of their dead, and reincarnation.

After five years of diligent effort, by early 1970, progress in the language and on the spiritual front were notable. Some of the hard to obtain words, such as *believe, love, think, remember,* and *obey* had been acquired, and Mary had begun preparing Bible teaching materials that Bob could use with the nomads. Several had made professions of faith, but only two showed evidence of a changed life. One was the young lady who was helping Mary with the language, while the other was her brother, Straight Hair.

One day, Straight Hair was talking with Les and commented, "If Big Father is so powerful, then we don't need to fear the spirits of our dead, do we?" As fear of the spirits became a thing of the past in his life, he changed from a somber, morose individual to an outgoing, joyful person. The change was so obvious that many people who didn't know him but saw pictures of him commented on the difference they saw on his face between the early pictures and later ones.

The language helper was sharing her new faith in an outgoing manner and suffered a fair amount of physical abuse, not only from Toughy, but also from some of the women in the group for being so outspoken in her new beliefs. At the same time, she was going through the rites of passage for puberty and, for several days, had to stay behind a palm-leaf wall where no man could look upon her. During that time, her hair was plucked out in front as was the custom among Yuquí women, making her look like a long-haired woman who was balding in front. Her entire body was painted the color of royal blue ink, using the juice of a jungle fruit called *dija* by the Yuquí.

After these rituals were completed, she would be considered ready for marriage. She was interested in Scar Face and would eventually marry him.

1970 Onward—I (Alan) Enter the Yuquí Work

WITH WORK AMONG THE YUQUÍ at the Chimoré River moving along well, discussions began among mission leadership and personnel about the need to begin looking for and befriending bands of the Yuquí tribe who roamed in other areas of jungle. After completing my four years of specialized training with the mission, I arrived back in Bolivia in mid-1970 and, by January of 1971, was living at the Chimoré base, learning the language with the hope of joining or creating a team that would locate and make friends with other groups of Yuquí.

Now that the language was available to learn, it made sense to take advantage of that and be able to communicate effectively right from the start as we encountered new bands of nomads. Being single, I could live among the Yuquí, travel with them, and absorb language and culture, much like a small child does.

As yet, there was no grammar book, and the dictionary Mary Garland was collecting was in its infancy, so living with the Yuquí in their natural setting, hearing the language spoken 24/7, recording what I could, writing out what I recorded, and then trying to make sense of it seemed the best approach to learning the language. In the mission training, I had received basic linguistics, phonetics, language learning, and culture gathering techniques; now I would put that training to the test in mastering the language of the monolingual Yuquí.

I had seen the value in being able to write sounds phonetically, so I had repeated that phase of the training a second time and was proficient in recognizing sounds and putting them down on paper.

Now I would need to attach meaning to the words I wrote down. As I gathered language material, I would often take it over to Mary and see if she knew what it meant, and if not, give it to her as new material to research with her language helper. Mary was our linguist and the most advanced speaker of Yuquí on the missionary team. The Yuquí at the Chimoré welcomed me as family, and I quickly discovered that the chief and his wife claimed me as a grandson since I was son to Les, whom they continued to believe was their reincarnated son who had died of snakebite.

Early in 1972, Chief Big Chest died, and his widow (my grandmother), Tame Pig, was happy to have me living in their camp in the jungle, especially since I saw to it that she ate well. Each day, around noon, I would make my way over to her hammock and campfire where I would give her a quantity of plantain bananas and manioc. As she squatted by the fire, roasting our lunch in the coals, I would lie in her hammock and listen to her as I used my tape recorder to document stories she related of the past or sometimes of more recent events. Also, when I went hunting with the Yuquí, I would bring home select game for her, and along with her sons, keep her well provided for.

As she considered me to be her grandson, she expected me to go above and beyond in providing for her and occasionally got "out of sorts" when I wouldn't do her bidding. After lunch, I would return to my "room," a large mosquito net I had installed under a modest eight by ten-foot palm-thatch hut. I built a small table/desk and bed from jungle poles and would sit on the bed as I used my Smith-Corona typewriter with Spanish keyboard to type out the material I had just recorded. Once that was done, I would go through the material, identifying and writing in, by hand, words that I knew.

Day after day, I gathered new recordings and went back over previous material to identify and write in words I had learned since typing the original material, and slowly, I began to understand some of the stories. Often, a Yuquí would drop by my shelter to visit, and I would use the occasion to ask questions about stories I had recorded and see if I could understand their explanation of words and phrases that I didn't comprehend.

I also cut hundreds of three-inch by five-inch index cards into three pieces, and as I identified useful phrases, I wrote the Yuquí phrase on one side of a card and the English equivalent on the other side. I carried packs of these cards with me everywhere for the next fifteen years, constantly creating new ones, reviewing old ones, and mixing the stacks of cards regularly so I wouldn't get familiar with them by their position in a stack. I would read the card in one language and translate to the other, visualizing in my mind how I could use the phrase. Learning a complex unwritten language with no language in common, no grammar book, and a minimal dictionary from a people who in the beginning thought theirs was the only language on the planet was a daunting task, and few missionaries became truly conversational in the Yuquí language.

Yuquí Captured by Loggers

AFTER I HAD BEEN STUDYING the Yuquí language for about six weeks, we received word by radio from Santa Cruz that Bolivians who were logging mahogany in another area of jungle had captured eleven ethnic nomads from another group thought to be Yuquí. I was one of the missionaries sent over to see what we could do for these people. Before we arrived at the isolated location, which required a lengthy, several day trip by swamp tractor and logging trucks, seven of the healthier Indians had escaped from the loggers and gone back to roam in the forest.

Of the four who remained, one was a small child who was taken to the city to be raised in the home of one of the loggers. Three Indians remained when we arrived on the scene.

It was cold season, and with no resistance to the flu bug to which the loggers had exposed them, the two adults were very sick, possibly with pneumonia, and rapidly headed for death and eternity without God—no knowledge of God's love for them. The old man among them succumbed before we could do much for him.

That left a crippled woman and her daughter who was about seven years old. The girl, whom we chose to call Sweet Pea, was fairly healthy, but the lady lay on the ground under a palm-leaf shelter,

Crippled Yuquí woman and her daughter who were captured by Bolivian loggers north of Santa Rosa del Sara. Picture taken after we had nursed them back to health.

refusing any food or drink we offered her. She had given up the will to live. When we arrived and saw the desperate situation, we radioed the mission supply buyer in Santa Cruz, the nearest city, and had him dispatch injectable medications on a logging truck headed our way. In the meantime, we spent much of our time trying to get a sip of broth or a morsel of food down the woman, bringing firewood to keep her warm, and trying to teach her to cover her naked body with a blanket for warmth, but none of our efforts met with success. She would die if something radical didn't change soon.

Each day, I hunted in the jungle nearby, looking for food for us and for them, hoping I could find something she was willing to eat. A short distance from our camp was a small pond, and I went by there often to see if I could shoot fish. One day, as I eased slowly through the woods along the edge and peered down toward the pond, my heart leapt. An alligator! Not a big one, but an alligator nonetheless.

With a whispered prayer, I lined up my .22 rifle on the gator's neck, just behind the head, and squeezed the trigger. When the shot rang out, his white underbelly rolled slowly into view. I collected my prize and dragged it through the bushes back to camp where I built a smoke rack of straight green sticks; then I began carving the gator and putting pieces of it over the smoky fire to grill.

Soon, all that was left was the innards. I found a slender stick and began turning the small intestines inside out on the stick to clean them, after which I braided them, much as you braid your daughter's hair. When I was finished, the braided intestines went on the smoke rack. As they began to sizzle, my mouth began to water, and that's when it hit me—*this was a delicacy she would never be able to resist!*

My heart sank at the thought of having to give up my prize. We were eating simple meals ourselves. We were miles from the nearest village. Would you give up your favorite crispy fried chicken dinner for an itinerant tramp on the street? For only a moment, my inner battle raged…I knew what I had to do.

Soon the succulent morsel was crisp and golden brown, and I carried it over to the thatch dwelling where the lady lay dying. In my extremely limited Yuquí language, I said, "Here. Try the alligator intestines."

Her eyes lit up. She couldn't resist. She began eating!

That was the beginning of a six-week process of nursing her back to health.

Even after eating the alligator small intestines, she was still not enthusiastic about eating, although she was easier to tempt with delicacies like monkeys and coati mundis (South American relative of the raccoon).

A day or two later, I shot a coati mundi, which is one of the greasier of the jungle meats. Since most animals in the jungle are lean, the fatter ones are prized, one of the reasons the people enjoy the intestines. When I arrived back in camp with the raccoon, I didn't even bother to dress it out. Carrying it straight over to where she lay, I dropped it on the ground next to her along with my hunting knife, saying to her, "*Chaye tu esää,*" meaning, "Try/taste the raccoon."

From her lying position, she carefully cut a small two-inch incision across the lower belly of the coati mundi. Slipping two fingers inside of the animal, she pulled out most of the innards, which she then wrapped in leaves and slipped into the coals of the fire to roast. Then she laid the entire animal over the fire and began burning the hair, scraping the singed hair off with her fingernails. When the process was complete, she lay the animal against the coals to cook.

When I came back thirty minutes later, she had been napping but awoke as I entered the shelter. She looked over at the raccoon and saw that the side that was against the coals was beginning to burn. She spoke to Sweet Pea, "*Ebiisiri* (Move it)."

Dutifully, the girl rolled the raccoon over, so a new spot would be against the coals. I jotted this new word down in the notebook, which I always carried, planning to ask our linguist later by radio if she knew what it meant. It turned out to mean, "Move it!" We were beginning to gather evidence that they were indeed a fragment of one of the scattered bands of the Yuquí tribe.

Another day, I was sitting by their fire, toying with a capuchin monkey skull they had eaten the meat and brains from, when Sweet Pea said, "*Quiäï itö ebuu che je* (Give me the monkey skull/head)." Amazingly, even though I had only studied the Yuquí language for a few weeks before going on this early assignment, I caught the entire sentence. It was definitely the Yuquí language.

One morning, I shot three coati mundis and two squirrel monkeys, and when I took them in and showed them to the lady, she looked at the coati mundi and said "*shaye*" at the squirrel monkey and said "*isa ririï*." I gave her one of each, and within an hour, she had the hair burned off and the innards roasting in the coals. She was the happiest we had seen her and jabbered incessantly, clearly pleased.

Unfortunately, I understood very little of what she had to say, but I became more highly motivated to continue working hard to master the language.

Not many days later, we carried some lunch over at noon to the hut where they had been living. The woman and child were gone! They had regained sufficient strength to slip off into the jungle. We never saw them again, but many years later, when a ranch worker was shot by nomads in an area a little northeast of there, I was part of a team that was sent to investigate. At that time, we learned that this woman, who could be easily identified by an arm that had been broken and healed very deformed, had come out of the jungle alone to another cattle ranch about nine miles away and was living there. Evidently, her daughter had died in the jungle, and the lady never found the other members of her group. Possibly they were killed by loggers or died of the flu bug that had almost taken the life of the woman. Her sole chance of survival had been to come out to that ranch.

As far as we know, that group of Yuquí never had the opportunity to hear the Gospel message. Another larger group roaming in that same area also disappeared without a trace before they could hear of the Savior who had left His own home for them!

Soon I was once again immersed in language study at the Chimoré River base while I was also more than a little puzzled by new missionary arrivals who expressed an interest to get involved in the effort to befriend other groups of the Yuquí but showed *no interest* in learning the language. How did they expect to make friends and build a relationship with these jungle dwellers if they couldn't communicate with them? It baffled my mind.

Searching for Other Bands of the Yuquí

A NUMBER OF SURVEYS FOLLOWED as we tried to identify areas where the various groups of nomads, presumed to be Yuquí, roamed. Tom Moreno headed up several of those surveys while Chi Ching Lora (a young Bolivian Christian) and I helped out along with assorted others. Once that survey team disbanded, Chuck Johnson, who had spearheaded a contact effort to a different tribe in northern Bolivia before leaving that work in the hands of other missionaries, headed up a new survey team, and I joined him. Chuck and I began looking for a location where we could set up a base from which to reach out to a second group of Yuquí.

We headed first for the Yapacaní River as there were abundant reports of hostile nomads on both sides of that river. As we met hunters who had survived deadly encounters with those nomad warriors, we heard stories such as the following:

> The first arrow was accurately placed and would have gotten me right in the belly if I hadn't been carrying my machete crossways in front of me. As it was the arrow glanced off the machete and stuck in the ground beside me. The other four arrows missed. If I and my two companions had walked into the ambush from the front as the ambushers had expected us to, instead of surprising the ambushers by arriving from the opposite direction, the three of us would not have lived to tell you this story.

You wouldn't believe the force one of those eight-foot arrows has behind it. When the first arrow hit me in the upper arm it knocked me to the ground, saving my life, for the other three arrows went over me. One of them stuck in a tree and the other two in the ground.

Even so, this hunter almost died from tetanus contracted from the arrow. Fortunately, he was able to make it to a hospital and his life was saved.

These are the kind of stories the Bolivian hunters, loggers, and road builders regularly told us in the Yapacaní area. Both of these stories were true, and the fellow who told me the second story backed it up by showing me the scars where the arrow punctured him. He wasn't the first one to show us this type of proof and wouldn't be the last.

During several survey trips into this area, lying northwest of Santa Cruz along the Yapacaní River, we found definite signs of two or three groups of what we believed to be more Yuquí Indians. These Indians were not only unfriendly but went out of their way to express their hostility to those entering their territory. Not only did they commonly set ambushes for people, but they were also known to hide sharpened hardwood spikes along trails, camouflaging them just off the end of a log bridge or on the other side of a log that must be stepped over in the middle of the trail. Woe to the individual who stepped on these spikes.

Some of these things we learned from another mission organization who tried unsuccessfully for about three years to contact these Indians. After suffering, one man killed, and another seriously wounded, they gave up the effort.

Eventually, Chuck and I located an isolated area along the Arroyo Hediondo where we were confident we could begin a contact effort without much interference from outside influences. Now the holdup was a lack of personnel. We would need at least five men in order to safely proceed. I returned to the Chimoré base to continue language study as I was convinced that the better I spoke the language, the more chance we had of success in a contact effort. Having seen the challenges the first Yuquí contact team faced by not knowing the language, I pushed hard to learn as much Yuquí language and culture as possible, knowing that I would never know enough but determined to give it my best shot.

As we waited for more personnel to arrive in country, we continued to get reports of hunters and loggers being killed by the nomads. The latest report was of two killings on the Chore River, and government representatives contacted the mission to ask if we could send a team in there. It wasn't exactly the location Chuck and I had in mind but was very possibly the same group of Indians.

We planned to set up on the northern end of that section of jungle while these two most recent shootings were on the southern end of that same area between the Yapacaní and Ichilo Rivers. Evidently, this group roamed the entire area, unless there was more than one band of nomads.

Growing up in the western Amazon basin, I had always been terrified of getting lost by myself in the jungle but was now slowly losing my fear as I traveled with and learned from the group of Yuquí at the Chimoré survival techniques they had discovered over countless generations. As a single missionary, I had freedom to take off with a few families of Yuquí for days at a time as we traveled through the jungle hunting, fishing, and gathering honey and fruit. I made several trips with them with the goal of mastering the language while we waited for contact personnel.

Being in the Yuquí camps in the jungle gave me exposure 24/7 to the language and culture. Since they considered me to be the chief's grandson, I was accepted as "family" and was required to use kinship terms while referring to them, not names.

On my initial trip with a group of them, my "older brothers"— Favorite Joven, Toughy, and Roughneck—took me with them and their families as we headed out to an old isolated oxbow riverbed that had become a swamp. The first thing I learned was the proper way to hang a hammock. As I began tying numerous knots to hang my hammock, one of them came over and graciously showed me a simple technique of wrapping the rope once around the tree, then back, and under the rope with *no knots*. The beauty of their technique was that it was quick and efficient and could be easily loosened to move the hammock up or down the tree so it could be set at the exact height the user desired. I also quickly learned to place the hammock very low to the ground so that when the rope snapped, a common occurrence with their bark ropes, I didn't have far to fall.

My hammock had nylon ropes which could be trusted not to break, so I opted to string my hammock a little higher than theirs so I could get in and out more easily. It was a rare night that I didn't hear one of their hammock ropes break and a few muttered imprecations as the family sleeping in it tied the rope back together and settled once more into a restless sleep. With no mosquito nets on their hammocks, they spent the nights exposed to myriad mosquitoes. I was thankful for my Vietnam-era nylon jungle hammock with mosquito net and water-resistant roof!

While this band of Yuquí had now been settled and hunting close to the mission base for six years, we were still able to kill a significant amount of game on this first trip, and I learned much about survival, Yuquí culture, and language. We arrived at our campsite late the first afternoon, and by the time we finished setting up camp, it was getting dark when a small chicken-like guan landed in a nearby tree. Roughneck jumped to his feet and said, "Let's shoot the turkey," by which he really meant, "Bring your gun and *you* shoot the turkey." This would be the first test of my shooting skills! How I did would build or diminish my reputation among them as a hunter.

It was so dark by now that I couldn't even see the sights on my .22 rifle, and the best I could do was sight down the barrel of the gun, hoping I might hit the guan. Amazingly, I got it! During my later years in the jungle, there were many times I had "amazing" shots for which I can take no credit and where I'm convinced God guided the bullet because of its importance in building rapport, trust, or confidence with the people with whom we were building friendship.

Over the next several days, I learned to call alligators and wait motionless while the mother alligator drifted slowly like a log across the swamp to see why her babies were calling her, then shoot her when she floated nearby. Day three of the hunt, I netted five alligators along with much other assorted game. Roughneck caught seven baby alligators and shot three carp-like sábalo fish with his bow and arrow, while Wooly Hair shot a collared peccary (javelina pig) with bow and arrow. The group I was with was composed mostly of sons or grandsons of the chief and were the top hunters and trackers in the tribe, so I was learning from the best.

I had chosen to carry a .22 rifle instead of a shotgun, even though a shotgun was better able to bring down large game. The advantages of the .22 were that it made less noise so was less likely to scare the game away. Also, I could carry far more ammunition since it was lighter, although I had to "place" my shots in a vital spot in order to bring down the larger game. Even so, most of my years in the jungle, I carried the .22 and only brought out my 12-gauge shotgun when we were truly desperate for meat. The lighter weight of the .22 also meant I didn't wear myself out carrying a heavy gun for the many hours we trudged through the dense forest on a daily basis. Experience soon taught me where the vital spots were for most animals, and I became quite effective with the .22 rifle.

Day four of the hunting trip, we were awakened by the roar of a large pride of lions, or so the sounds indicated. As my guides/teachers headed toward the loud roaring on the far side of the swamp, I realized that my little .22 rifle might not be the best weapon and was glad to see that my "older brothers" all carried their eight-foot long bows and arrows.

When we neared the lions, it turned out that they were actually red howler monkeys sitting high up in one of the tallest jungle trees I had seen. The troop of monkeys sat at least a hundred feet up in the large branches, secure in the knowledge that nothing could trouble them there…except our weapons, which they had never faced before. Shooting howler monkeys with an eight-foot arrow is a challenge in several ways. First of all, the monkeys see the ponderous arrows ascending toward them and often have time to dodge the missile. Secondly, if the arrow impacts a branch, it hangs high in the tree, and one of the slaves will later have to climb the tree to retrieve the valuable arrow. Or even if the arrow impacts a monkey, it is very likely the arrow and monkey will get tangled in branches and stay high up in the tree, once again meaning someone has to climb the tree and retrieve the monkey.

To get two or three howler monkeys in a morning with bow and arrow is an astounding feat, but to do the same with a .22 rifle is not much of a challenge. The monkeys think they are secure so far from the ground and don't flee quickly. Consequently, the warriors turned to me, the man with the gun. Soon, I had brought down five or six monkeys, and the rest had decided that they'd better flee with the Yuquí hunters following them. Eventually, we ended up with eight monkeys, one of them a baby that had been riding on its mother's back and was unwounded. Toughy's wife claimed the baby and, if it survived, would raise it as a pet. It didn't last long as within four days, she rolled over on it in the night while sleeping, and the next day, it joined the rest of our meat on the smoke rack.

Shooting howler monkeys took quite a few shots as they were tough to bring down, and after I shot up two days' rations of shells in one, the Yuquí told me not to shoot anymore. Rather, we went back to camp where we could sit near the smoke racks they had built and enjoy the fruits of our labors.

After a short rest, Favorite Joven decided to carry three of the smaller monkeys back to the mission base on the Chimoré and give them to his father, the chief. I accompanied him so I could pick up more ammunition from my house there and also brought back some powdered milk that could be used to feed the baby howler monkey.

Day six of our hunt was a highlight as Roughneck shot two tapirs (a beef-like animal). One of them escaped, but the other one was 400 pounds of excellent meat, and soon, his smoke rack was piled high. You've heard the saying about pigs: "Everything can be eaten except their squeal." That was how the nomads felt about the tapir and most other jungle animals. About the only thing that wasn't eaten was the hair, which was burned off. All the innards were cleaned and roasted or boiled. In fact, with most animals, the hair was singed off and cooked with the skin on since the small amount of fat in lean jungle game is directly under the skin and gives flavor to the meat. Skinning the animal was a waste of the skin and the fat under the skin.

Now that the smoke racks were piled high with an assortment of delicious meats—tapir, collared peccary, howler monkey, squirrel monkey, armadillo, paca (a delicious, small rodent), alligator, carp, turkeys, squirrel, and more—their interest turned toward honey. Each day as we hunted, they spotted bee trees, trees with colonies of different varieties of honeybees. Usually, they would mark the locations by bending over a sapling to let their companions know that this or that bee tree had been spotted and now had an owner. On a rare occasion, we might stop to harvest the honey, but more often, they would plan to go back another day with the express purpose of harvesting honey.

With plenty of meat in camp, we began going daily to harvest honey and averaged three or four trees a day. Soon all our kettles were overflowing with honey and its by-products, bee larvae and royal jelly. The larvae were especially tasty and nutritious with a creamy flavor, except for one variety of bee whose larvae tasted more like tobacco.

Each afternoon, after returning to camp from the day's activities, I lay on my hammock, outside of the net, alternately eating choice pieces of meat and different types of honey and larvae, while thinking to myself, "This life wouldn't be so bad if it could be lived with a rifle rather than bow and arrow and if there weren't so many life-threatening dangers."

At other times, I was so miserable I could hardly wait to get back to the mission base and my comfortable (by comparison) house. The most annoying things were the chiggers and the ticks, many varieties of tiny, almost invisible ticks, hundreds of them. Dry season was the worst time for these tiny tormenters, and we were coming up on the middle of dry season. The itching was unbearable, and by the time we eventually returned to the mission base, I looked like I had chicken pox on the legs and stomach from all the bites.

On the last day of the hunt, I was out with Toughy, and when he smelled pigs in the area, we stopped so he could call them. To call a javelina or peccary, open your mouth wide and begin drawing a large amount of air into your lungs while constricting the back of your mouth down toward your throat. This will make a loud, hoarse squealing sound, which is what a peccary that is wounded or being attacked by a jaguar or puma makes. Other pigs in the area are drawn to the sound as they come to help the wounded pig defend itself.

Sure enough, soon I saw a collared peccary approach and I placed my shot just behind the front shoulder, hoping to strike heart or lungs. As the pig fled, Toughy was sure I had missed it, so he wanted to leave the area and shoot some guan turkeys he had seen. I assured him I had struck the pig in a vital spot, so Favorite Joven, who was hunting with us, went to check and found the peccary dying about sixty feet from where I had shot it. Favorite Joven had his slave Big Tummy carry the pig back to camp as we continued hunting, and by the time we returned to camp a few hours later, the pig was already grilled and ready to eat.

They handed me one of the hind legs, and I lay in my hammock with a knife, carving and eating the delicious fresh pork. Maybe I should have been born a Yuquí as there were certain things about this life that appealed to me. Living on a diet heavy with meat and honey was definitely one of those!

On this hunting trip, I laid claim to no meat but let whoever I was hunting with take it all, and whenever I was hungry, I would mention the fact, and someone would offer me my choice of meat. Most of it had been grilled, smoked on green saplings over a wood fire and was delicious. Each morning, before leaving to hunt for the day, Favorite Joven would roast two plantain bananas in the fire and give them to me for breakfast, and by 7:00 or 7:30 a.m., we were on our way to hunt and look for honey.

For the first time in my life, I was enjoying hunting and began losing my fear of getting lost in the jungle. Daily we took off, hunting in a variety of directions with no trail, and yet, unerringly, my guides got us back to camp before nightfall. The only animal I was consistently having trouble shooting was squirrel monkeys. These small creatures stayed low in the jungle trees and fled quickly, faster than I could run, and on that first trip, I only shot two of them. Eventually, I would learn the trick of shooting them. Find a branch down which many of them run as they prepare to leap to the next tree and use it as a shooting gallery, leading them slightly with the rifle as they slow before leaping from that branch to the next tree. In the future, I would perfect the technique to where I would have a pile of five to seven monkeys lying below one branch which they had used as a runway. No need to run through the jungle, finding individual monkeys.

It was during my second year with the Yuquí that the chief died. It was a strange situation as he had been ill for three days but didn't seem to be too sick, and the morning of the night he died, his temperature seemed to be down near the normal range. One of the few concerns that Jane Wiebe, who was handling the medical work, had was that one of his feet was slightly swollen, and we were surprised when that night, around midnight, he died. We guessed at the time based on where the Yuquí told us the moon had been at the time he died.

At five o'clock the next morning, White Joven shouted across the river to the missionary camp and asked to borrow a shovel so they could bury the chief. Ed Wiebe and I went over to see what we could do to help and also because we were concerned for the chief's slave, George. The chief had told Iroquois some time before that when he died, he wanted Iroquois to kill George to accompany him in death. We had been exhorting them right along not to kill others to accompany their dead but weren't sure what might happen since it was the chief who had died.

Fortunately, the proposed executioner, Iroquois, wasn't in camp but was out on a multiday hunt with Favorite Joven, the chief's second-oldest son. George's life may have been spared by Iroquois being absent. White Joven and Straight Hair (the chief's grandson) were sent as runners to call Iroquois and Favorite Joven back to camp as they had no idea the chief had sickened and died. Roughneck wanted to keep the body in a palm basket as had been their custom to this point in time, but Straight Hair wanted the body buried. They opted to bury the body, and Favorite Joven arrived too late to see his father's body one last time.

Of all the chief's sons, Roughneck seemed to be the most broken up by his father's death and asked Ed and I, "Would it be all right if I killed a national (a Bolivian)?"

We replied, "You shouldn't kill anyone."

He accepted that, although his final comment was, "Dad was still strong and husky when he died, not like so many people who are skinny and frail." It was a puzzle to all of us as to why he died while appearing to be in such good health, but we were elated that for the first time, another Yuquí, Bolivian, or missionary had not been sacrificed to appease the spirit of the dead. Clearly, progress had been made during the seven years this group had been learning from the missionaries.

Another encouragement to the missionary team was that near the end of his life, the chief had expressed a desire to know Big Father (God) and to live in His Camp (heaven) when he died and not go to the fire (hell). We look forward to seeing him there.

While living in my palm-thatch shelter in the middle of the area where the Yuquí were camped across the Chimoré River from the missionaries, I continued learning from the people daily. As different individuals came in from hunting or gathering, they would often stop by to chat or to share fruit, honey, or meat with me, and I usually had something to give them in return—sugar, bananas, cookies, or other items.

In the early morning and late afternoon, guan would often fly in to roost in trees near the camp, and the Yuquí would come running and ask me to shoot the birds for them. It also wasn't uncommon for monkeys to come through the area, so I shot plenty of those for the people, even without leaving the camp area. One day, Roughneck came by to visit along with several others, and I found it somewhat humorous as he gave me a mini sermon on remembering Big Father (God) and His ways and reminded me that I shouldn't have affairs with the Yuquí women as that wouldn't please Big Father. All the Yuquí who were present listened intently, and several grinned at me as one of their own gave me the sermon they had often heard from the missionaries.

Several times a week, I went hunting with people as it was a good way to learn more language and enjoy unique cultural experiences while providing them with meat. On one fishing trip with George, his wife, and a few others of the slave class, we were fishing in the dark, tannin-laden water of a lazy stream a good distance from the river when George spotted a large eel about four inches in diameter and five-feet long. The mouth of the fish was near the surface of the water while the body extended downward at a forty-five-degree angle. I shot it through the head with the .22 rifle, but the fish disappeared into the murky depths, and I thought we had lost it.

A few minutes later, we saw it come up again and begin writhing about in midstream until eventually it came close to shore where I was able to shoot it two more times, whereupon George jumped into the water and pulled it out. They were thrilled with the catch and later, after it was cooked, shared some of the very delicious white meat with me. The only bone seemed to be the backbone, and there were no small bones to contend with.

After catching a few more fish, we headed home along the trail leading to their camp. On the way, we came to a log with a vine on it, and I was going to step over, but something about the vine caught my attention; it didn't look quite right. Then I realized I was looking at a green snake about three feet long but with its body contorted in such a way that it looked like a twisted vine on the fallen tree. After shooting it, I went on my way back to camp. It seemed there was always something unique to see in the tropical forest.

I might have lived longer in the Yuquí camp, but God had other plans. Ed and Jane Wiebe had flown to the city for a break, and while they were gone, I was tending their dog and house sitting for them on the missionary side of the river. One night, in the middle of February, a torrential rainstorm arrived with seven-inches of rain and a terrible storm called an *ibituguasu*, one of the storms most feared by the Yuquí as it had tornado-like winds which often leveled vast stretches of jungle. A large tree fell lengthwise on my thatch shack in the jungle, destroying it. God had kept me from harm by moving me out before the storm, and amazingly, none of the Yuquí were injured, although many trees around their camp had also fallen. Once again, I could see God's hand of protection.

* * * * *

The storm had been in February, and by May, new missionary families began arriving in Bolivia, destined to join Chuck and me in setting up a base for a contact effort in the Arroyo Hediondo area. I flew to Cochabamba to welcome some of the new missionaries and help them get adjusted to Bolivia. Wallace Pouncy's guns had been confiscated by Bolivian customs, so he and I went to La Paz, the capital, to see if we could get the guns back as he would need those in the jungle.

By June, the contact team was ready to head out on our first survey with the hope of finding a suitable location for a base camp where we could build houses and eventually have our families join us as we began in serious the effort to befriend a second band of Yuquí. The men on the team consisted of Chuck Johnson, Wallace Pouncy, Bob Curtiss, Larry Depue, and me, Alan Foster.

The third of June saw us heading down the Yapacaní River in a scow-like wooden boat Chuck had purchased new a few weeks earlier. This far up the Yapacaní, the riverbed was 600 meters wide but was mostly sand with the water coming down several shallow channels, which were almost unnavigable. Most traffic on the river took place during rainy season when there was more water, whereas we were headed down the river at the beginning of dry season. Fortunately, unseasonable rain brought the water level up to where we only hung up for a few minutes, twice on underwater sandbars, before we were far enough downriver to have mostly clear sailing.

By three o'clock, we were moving along nicely and even had four ducks and a collared peccary we had been able to shoot for supper. The pig had been trapped on the riverbank with a twenty-foot high clay bank behind it so it couldn't flee to the woods above and had been easy shooting for Larry, who shot it in the head, giving us meat for a day or two.

The first night, we camped on a beach in the middle of the river with the boat in an eddy that caused the boat to move around a lot, so we staked it securely with three bamboo poles driven deep into the sand. Even so, Chuck woke us up at 4:20 a.m. with the terrible news that our boat was gone along with all of our belongings and supplies. Now what? As the boat had moved around in the backwater, it had pulled the chain with which the boat was tied as well as all three bamboo poles from the sand and drifted away downriver and was long gone, out of sight…but God was gracious!

At daybreak, Larry and Chuck took off, paddling their way downriver on air mattresses to look for the boat, and just out of sight, around 200 yards downriver, they found that the weight of the dragging chain along with the bamboo poles had snagged in a logjam. The boat was weaving gently back and forth in the current, waiting to be retrieved. You can't begin to imagine our rejoicing as we thanked God for preserving our boat and equipment, and after that, every night, we also tied a rope to the boat with the other end tied to one of our tents so the tent with us in it would be dragged across the sand if the boat broke free of the chain. That would be sure to alert us!

Larry and Chuck had left their air mattresses on shore when they brought the boat back, so Bob and Wallace walked along the shore to retrieve the flotation devices. On their way back to our campsite, the two new missionaries had their first encounter with another reality of life in the Amazon basin as they narrowly missed being bitten by a three-foot-long fer-de-lance viper on the riverbank. After killing the snake, they rejoined us at the campsite, and after breakfast, now that our supplies had come back, we headed on down the Yapacaní.

A Bolivian/Argentine company called the Comisión Mixta had been clearing jungle, planning to build a railroad from Santa Cruz to Trinidad. This venture would have routed the railroad through the heart of nomad territory and was certain to have led to their demise as it would open the area for colonization and logging, but eventually, the project had been discontinued, leaving behind a long, straight, elevated dirt roadway and various complexes that had been used as maintenance centers and housing for workers. We stopped at one of the abandoned sites and found a true treasure beyond measure—abandoned aerial photo mosaics of most of the area in which we planned to work.

The three by five feet cardboard sheets with overlaid photos would allow us to plan where to locate gift trails, where to build our base, and where to position an airstrip in relation to our camp. With a magnifying glass, individual trees could be easily distinguished, allowing you to see where the belts of high jungle were located. While I was reluctant to remove these treasures, they were clearly abandoned and beginning to deteriorate in the jungle humidity. They were truly a gift from God!

Two weeks later, we arrived back at the Yuquí camp on the Chimoré River after having decided on a site for a base on the bank of the Arroyo Hediondo. The site was perfect in that it was an abandoned logging camp with established fruit trees, avocados, grapefruit, oranges, limes, and sugarcane. It was called Triumph One by hunters who were aware of its existence, no doubt the name that it had gone by when it was a logging camp. Rather than haul all our gear back out with us, we had hidden three fifty-gallon metal barrels of supplies in the jungle not far from our base to be.

Unfortunately, while we were preparing to move into the area, Bolivian hunters discovered our cache and helped themselves to a good quantity of items. We were surprised at this since, generally speaking, we had found the people along the lowland rivers to be trustworthy and very hospitable. We were sure the items hadn't been taken by the nomads as few if any of the missing items would have been of interest to them, whereas they would have been useful to settlers along the Rio Grande River into which the Arroyo Hediondo dumped. Not only did our confidence and trust in the settler's wane, but this also left us short on supplies we had been counting on.

By the middle of August, our team was back in the Arroyo Hediondo along with a team of short-term volunteers which included some young men who had come from the United States to help for a few months. We would be clearing an airstrip, building houses, cutting gift trails into the jungle, and making a road that would connect us to the road the Comisión Mixta had cleared only a few hundred yards from our base. We had brought a lightweight swamp tractor with us that could be used for dragging logs off the airstrip site, hauling dirt to fill low spots on the airstrip, and many other purposes.

With no other people in the area, we planned to use the long straight road the Comisión Mixta had made as a gift trail, placing gifts for many miles from our camp and using the swamp tractor to travel the road and monitor the gifts, thereby sparing ourselves much walking on the muddy road.

One week after our arrival at the Hediondo Cam, and Chuck drove the swamp buggy down to the end of the sugar-cane field and, on the lefthand side, the jungle side, found a spot where the nomads had been taking sugar cane regularly. The cut end of one of the cane stalks

Alan swimming the yellow swamp buggy across a swollen stream.

had been chopped off so recently that it was still wet. Chuck hung a machete there as a gift, and we were all encouraged as we realized we had found a prime campsite from which to reach out to the nomads. Now if only we could have a quick friendly contact with them and see a friendship begun!

It was not to be. Over the next four years, the nomads were seen by the missionary team on numerous occasions, and one of the missionary children, the high school-age son of Dave and Shirley Payne, was narrowly missed by an Indian arrow. Countless gifts were taken both near to and far from the camp, but there were no friendly contacts. The nomads were elusive, hostile, and wary of outsiders.

By the end of 1974, I returned to the United States for a year of home assignment while a team of missionaries continued to man the Arroyo Hediondo base, reaching out unsuccessfully to the nomads.

Finding a Life Partner

WHILE IN THE UNITED STATES, I visited the mission language school near Camdenton, Missouri, where my sister, Beverly, was finishing up her training before heading to Venezuela as a missionary. There were thirteen single girls in her dorm, and I asked her who I should date. She recommended Vickie.

Six months later, Vickie and I were married in Spokane, Washington, where her family lived. Vickie had finished the mission training and was planning to go to the Philippines until our paths crossed and she was redirected to Bolivia. Although before we "tied the knot" I showed her and her family my slides of the naked nomadic Yuquí and did my best to help her understand the reality of what she would be facing by marrying someone who was almost a Yuquí at heart, the true magnitude of her new life didn't hit home until a year and a half later when she found herself isolated in the western Amazon on our Arroyo Hediondo base.

We had initially gone to the Chimoré River base to help out but were hardly settled there before the nomads, after a lengthy absence, began taking gifts from the trails near the Arroyo Hediondo base. With no speaker of the Yuquí language on-site, the missionaries there were desperate for us to join them, which we did. Within a month of arriving in Bolivia, Vickie had her first glimpse of the naked nomads as they came out at the Hediondo base for the first time. Let me tell you a little more about that first contact.

It was almost noon, and I was sitting at my desk in the back room of the house we had "inherited" from Paul Johnson, memorizing conversation number 24 in the recently completed Yuquí grammar book, when Wallace Pouncy walked into the house and calmly said, "There are two Indians out under the gift rack."

My assumption was that the rest of the folks in camp had already been notified, so I got up from my desk, walked out the front door, and headed for the gift rack. As I got to where I could see it, I saw not only the two that he had seen, but back down the trail, I could see several more. Two were painted for protection with *dija* (the purple juice of a jungle fruit). I walked over to the gift rack to embrace one of the slaves and murmur phrases of friendship to him before doing likewise with the other one. Next, I called to the nomads who were farther down the trail, encouraging them to come out and talk to us. They didn't want to come any nearer than they already were, and after much talking and trying to convince them to come to the rack, they finally said, "You come to us."

By then, some of the other missionary men had shown up, so I asked them what they thought, and they said, "Go ahead." Taking bananas to use as a gift, I walked down to meet with the nomads. One fellow painted with *dija* seemed to be the leader of the group, but he wasn't doing much talking. I talked to some others and then to a painted one (who appeared to be related to Iroquois of the Chimoré group). The chief looked like he could be kin to the chief of the Chimoré group and his family. There was also a man who appeared to be a brother to the leader of the group. He was younger, not having the gray hair in his beard that the leader had.

I asked the leader if that was his brother, and he confirmed that he was. Other than those three, there was one six-foot tall slave-looking individual, fairly young, about thirty years old. He didn't say or do much and might have been related to Witchy of the Chimoré group. There was also an older man about forty years of age who appeared to be a slave. Later, he came and took bananas right next to our house. He also appeared related to Witchy, and the missionary wives were able to get some pictures of him once they figured out how to use the camera.

There were also two younger men—his sons, I believe—one of whom appeared to be slave to the leader of group, and the other was apparently slave to Iroquois's relative. I deduced these two slave-master relationships because later, around 2:30 p.m., we gave honey to the two leaders, and they designated these two slaves respectively to wrap the honey up for carrying home. At that time, the leader turned to his slave and said something like, "Wrap it for me to be the thing I eat when I get flat tummied (hungry)."

There were also two nice-looking young fellows who appeared to be high-class, and I got the impression they might be the sons of sisters of the leader of the group or a similar relationship.

Our banana plantation wasn't large enough and was producing poorly, so we were giving small bunches of bananas to the people, trying to save as many as possible to use to lure them back the next day. They kept wanting more, a great quantity, so they wouldn't have to return, and none of them were happy with the modest number of bananas we were giving them.

Finally, the chief got a little disgusted with how slowly we were giving fruit to them, and when I explained to him that the rest were too green, they disappeared and went to see for themselves. We heard them cutting bananas freely, taking even those that were far too green, and there wasn't much we could do to stop them. Eventually, the leader came back to the gift trail and, after a moment, got up and headed back down the gift trail toward the jungle.

As he neared the end of it, a woman darted across the trail to join him. I only had a brief look, but she appeared to be wearing a bark-rope baby sling running diagonally across her body. That was the only view I had of her, and it wasn't enough to ever recognize her again.

As they drifted off to cut bananas, we thought the contact was ending, but Wallace was able to interact with some of them for a time on the northwest end of the airstrip near the sugarcane and, in the process, took off his shirt and gave it to them as a gift. A few of them continued sitting on our gift trail while the others were checking out the bananas down at the end but far enough into the forest that it seemed unwise for any of us to venture down there to interact with them. As unhappy as they were with the scarcity of bananas, we were being extra cautious.

One of the slave men, the one with two sons, crossed the airstrip and began cutting bananas behind our house, and when the leader and a few others came back to our gift rack near the edge of the clearing, some of us went out as I began conversing with them again. Talking with the leader, whose wife I suspected I had seen, I said, "Have your wife come out and she can meet *Eteguayo* (my childless wife) so they can become friends."

He didn't seem interested in following up on that idea. Trying to keep the conversation going was a big challenge, but knowing that hunting was always a good topic, I went there. "We'll go along the river in the night and shoot meat for you. Come back tomorrow, and we will have meat for you," I encouraged the leader.

"Shoot a *yiquiareguasu* (caiman, a South American crocodilian) for me," was his reply. He seemed to approve of us hunting to provide them with meat.

Next, I began telling him what a great hunter Wallace was and how he "really brings in the game," hoping to stimulate their enthusiasm to return the next day.

Soon they were once again getting restless but had begun promising to come back the next day. Now I questioned the leader, "Would you like some honey?"

He showed interest, so Wallace returned to his house with a broad leaf on which he dribbled as much honey as possible before bringing it back to the leader. Dipping a finger into the honey and tasting it while making approving sounds to show how good it was, Wallace handed the leaf to the leader. "Try it," I suggested.

He replied, "You try it," which I did so he could see that I considered it safe to eat. Then he had his slave wrap it up for transport home.

When Wallace had brought the honey out, he started to give it to the man who appeared to be second in command, and I intervened, telling him to give it to the leader. The second in command acquiesced readily as if the other man was his superior. Even so, we didn't want to leave the second in rank with no honey, so Wallace brought out a second leaf with honey and gave it to him. Much like leader Number One had done, Number Two handed it to his slave and had him wrap it up and prepare it to take with them.

We conversed for a few more minutes as Number One kept assuring me that they would return tomorrow. I asked Number Two, and he also assured me of their plan to return along with a statement that seemed to imply that I was being childish by asking the question repeatedly. Not only did they promise to return, but they also promised to bring their women with them to meet our wives. Whether they meant this or were only telling us this since we had earlier suggested it to them was impossible to tell.

Soon the group under the gift rack stood and made their way into the jungle but not before I hugged the leaders and gave them a friendly goodbye. "Keep yourself warm by your fire." As I headed back across the airstrip to my house, I found Paul Short and a tall slave coming from behind the house with bananas and manioc. "Your others have already left, and your sons were asking where you were," I informed him. He seemed to acknowledge the fact that they were his sons as he headed on across the airstrip and disappeared into the forest beyond.

During all these happenings, the missionary wives stayed in or near Pouncy's house, observing from the riverside of the airstrip, letting us know when nomads were around and where they were. It was a real blessing to have them keep an eye on things, watching over the side of camp next to the river where the houses were located. Vickie was able to take about twenty-five pictures the second time they came out but had gotten no pictures initially as the women couldn't figure out how to work the complicated settings on the SLR camera.

We fully expected to see the nomads again if not the next day, then in a few days' time, but it was not to be. Within a few days, we heard the throaty roar of caterpillar tractors and road graders, and shortly afterward, a crew of loggers made a grand entrance into our clearing in the jungle. We learned that our base was now located in the Ibabo Logging Concession. They were rather surprised to find anyone living in this isolated location, and we were even more surprised at their sudden appearance. We also learned that the area for at least fifty kilometers south of us had been divided into logging concessions as the loggers began taking advantage of the road the Comisión Mixta had made and poured into the area, intent on stripping the valuable mahogany. The nomads would need to flee the area or be killed by the invaders.

Our time at the Hediondo would soon be over. The loggers were very active for the next several months of dry season, and then, when wet season began, they pulled out of the area. We were hoping that the nomads might return to the area during the rainy season so left many gifts along the vacant roads and drove the swamp buggy or hiked extensively as far as forty kilometers south, looking for any indications that the nomads had returned to the area. Nothing!

Come dry season, the logging would pick up in earnest once again. After all the years of effort we had expended in this location, it now looked like we would be forced to relocate. The logging would go on for many years, and the nomads would avoid the loggers by staying far to the south.

The Domain of the Yuquí

PICTURE AN EXPANSE OF JUNGLE about the size of the state of Connecticut dotted with innumerable swamps, many small streams and modest rivers covered with thick foliage, and you will have an idea of the area in which we needed to find the migratory routes of the Yuquí and set up a base from which to reach out to them. The area we would be searching was not included in the photo mosaic maps that had once been so useful.

Suspecting that aerial photos of the new area might be available, Vickie and I made a trip to the capital city of La Paz to visit the Instituto Geográfico Militar (Military Geographic Institute) and see if we could purchase aerial photos from them. Once they understood who we were and what we needed the photos for, they were happy to oblige. They also sold us paper charts of the area that we could carry with us as we went into the forest. Knowing how valuable this information was, I studied them to where I carried a detailed map of the area in my head, and over the coming years, it would prove to be worth every minute I spent memorizing them.

God had been working on our behalf and on behalf of the Yuquí we were determined to preserve from annihilation as He now sent a missionary helicopter to Bolivia.

Bölkow Bo 105 Helimission helicopter which helped us with surveys in the Víbora River area and transported personnel and equipment as we established our base.

When the Helimission pilot learned of what we were doing, he offered to fly for the cost of the fuel it took to operate the Bölkow Bo105, a helicopter with the distinction of being the first light twin-engine helicopter and one that could perform aerobatic maneuvers such as inverted loops.

The cost of fuel was equivalent to what we normally paid per hour to fly in the small mission Cessna, a real bargain, and what a machine the Bo105 turned out to be! God brought it along at a time of great need as the area we wanted to investigate was in the middle of nowhere with no easy access. In a few days' time, we would be able to explore territory that on foot would take many weeks or even months.

We gathered two teams of three men each with a Christian Yuquí from the Chimoré on each team, a Yuquí speaking missionary to interact with our Yuquí guide, and a third missionary to complete each team. We wanted to look over the area along the upper Chore River as it was notorious for the number of hunters and loggers that had been shot there over the years by the unfriendly nomads. Clearly, they frequented the area.

Arriving at the Chore by helicopter, we found a high beach where the helicopter could land and spend the night, and the next morning, the helicopter lifted off with one of the teams and flew parallel to the river but about four kilometers to the east of it, looking for a small clearing or swamp where he could hover and drop the team off. From there, they would hike westward until they encountered the river and wait there until the helicopter flew along the river in the late afternoon, picked the team up, and brought them back to our temporary camp.

After dropping both teams in different areas, the pilot returned to the beach and waited until he could pick us up. By hiking across the high belts of jungle, we should be able to locate some of the trails the nomads used in their migratory travels. The second day, we "struck gold!" The other team had been on the west side of the Chore River where they found several Yuquí camps along with at least one well-traveled trail.

Now the challenge would be figuring out the easiest way to move in close to that area without having to rely solely on the helicopter. The nearest we could get by land was the tiny village of Puerto Grether, fourteen kilometers due south of where the Yuquí camps had been spotted. Or we might be able to come in by way of the Víbora River. If we based along the Víbora River, we would have access by river in the rainy season and, in the dry season, could use an abandoned logging track to get to the upper Víbora River with our swamp tractor and then boat a short distance downriver to the base camp site we chose. This would put us four kilometers from the nomad trail and camps our team had spotted.

By November, we were hard at work clearing jungle and building houses, but it wasn't an easy task. It seemed that Satan had unleashed all his forces to block the arrival of the Gospel message to the band of jungle dwellers. As we began clearing jungle, we were attacked by swarms of stinging bees on a daily basis, and Phil Burns contracted malaria and had to be evacuated by way of an arduous river and swamp tractor trip. Our swamp tractor broke down numerous times, and some of our short-term volunteer helpers abandoned us, finding the task too daunting, and then the final straw, as he was felling a leaning tree on the river bank to clear an approach for the helipad we were making, Wallace lost his balance and, as he went to catch himself, leaned his hand on the spinning chainsaw blade, suffering a severe cut in the wrist area. We were already reduced to three men, and now two of us would be needed to transport Wallace to the city for medical attention.

Interestingly, all the hardships we were going through convinced the core group of contact team members that Satan was fighting so hard, because God was at work to bring these jungle nomads to Himself. We were encouraged to press forward, although the opposition didn't stop. When a small group of us returned to continue clearing and house-building, we also began cutting a gift trail the four kilometers from our base to where the nomad trail and abandoned camps had been seen. As we cut trail, I stirred up a hornet's nest, literally, and suffered twelve or fifteen stings to the face.

The next day, my face was so swollen I could hardly see, but Paul Short and I headed out to continue cutting the gift trail. Around midmorning, we stopped chopping for a few moments to take a short break, and as we stood there, we heard a strange noise. Looking to my right, I saw a short creamy-green and mottled viper looking me in the eye. His tail was wrapped around a sapling, and the noise we had just heard was him as he repeatedly struck at us. We were just out of reach, but had he bitten either of us, it would have been in the head or neck and most likely fatal. I had never seen one of these before but believe it to have been a parrot snake whose bites are often fatal due to where they strike.

The day didn't end there as shortly after that, I almost stepped on an anaconda tail sticking out from its den under a log. Satan seemed to know where to attack me as I am terrified of snakes ... strange; why would God send someone like me to the jungle? So that I could learn to trust Him? Often, as I walked through low, dense vegetation where I couldn't see what lay at my feet, I would be talking to God, reminding Him that He had shut the mouths of the lions for Daniel and pleading that he do the same for me with the snakes. He heard and answered my prayers!

Footprints in the Sand

FOOTPRINTS IN THE SAND! WE weren't even 200 yards from camp when we began seeing them. The Indians had walked right down our trail, making no effort to hide their presence. To me it was a good indication that they knew who we were and weren't worried about us harming them. It appeared they had come through about ten days previously, taking most of the gifts we had hung along the trail and then moving on. We had now been back in the area for five days, so we only missed them by five days. Doubtless they were still in the area, we replaced the gifts and, after discussing the situation, decided that two men should make a trip out to buy bananas from the Bolivian farms twenty-two kilometers away.

Early the next morning, Paul Short and Phil Burns set off up the river, leaving Larry Depue and me behind. Only thirty-five minutes upriver from camp, Paul and Phil found an Indian bridge no more than two days old. This seemed to indicate that the nomads were heading south and, on their return, would doubtless pass close to our camp. With abundant bananas on hand, the prospects would be good for luring the Indians to our camp. If they were the same nomads who had come to us at the Arroyo Hediondo, they might have already identified us from the gifts we were hanging out and might come to us quickly. It was not to be.

Rainy season ended, and with dry season underway, the expanse in which the Yuquí could roam expanded greatly; although if they went north, they would be in the area which was now dangerous with heavy logging activity. We hoped they would stay away from the loggers and closer to us. The helicopter was no longer available as the pilot had left Bolivia, and Helimission was trying to find another

ALAN FOSTER

pilot to operate it. This left us rather isolated in the middle of nowhere without our families and with no easy way to get supplies.

Now that construction of the first houses was moving along well, we began going out farther from our camp, getting to know the area, finding the best places to hang gifts for the nomads. On one of these trips, we came across a mound of decaying palm leaves which was a real puzzle. What could it be? It was almost as if a palm thatch house had fallen in, leaving its roof piled up there. Knowing that the Yuquí don't normally build houses, I knew there had to be some special significance to this.

I questioned our Christian Yuquí guides and received a brief explanation, which I failed to understand, so I continued pondering the puzzle as we went on following the old Indian trails through many abandoned camps. There were camps in abundance and of all vintages. Some were only a few months old while others were a year or more old. It was encouraging to know that the nomads had spent a portion of the rainy season camped only four kilometers from us and to realize that they would no doubt return eventually.

After following the trail for half an hour, we decided to turn back and investigate in another direction as well. When we once again passed the mound of leaves, light dawned on me. Could this have been a shelter for the dead? It had been. We later found a second shelter in much better condition. Inspection revealed that the bones had already been moved (the bones are carried with the tribe as they migrate).

Two shelters. Two more souls into eternity without Christ! Or maybe more if they had killed others to accompany the dead.

As we followed the nomad trail to the southeast, we saw three old camps and discovered a major Indian trail skirting around to the east of a half-moon swamp. Moving on from those three camps, we found an assortment of palm-leaf baskets as well as four additional camps, one of them larger than the others and quite new, so we left a fish-shaped pocketknife hanging in it as a gift.

Next, we came to a burial shelter with the platform still inside where a high-class individual's body had rested. The shelter was about two years old, if that. We stopped long enough to boil up a monkey for lunch before moving on and later shot two coati mundis for

▶ 364 ◀

supper before setting up camp for the night. The next day, we headed west and found the newest camp we had seen so far as well as another burial shelter, well-preserved and new enough that we initially thought it might still contain a body.

Straight Hair thought it had probably been for a high-class child, and Phil Burns

Yuqui burial shelter and platform found between Víbora and Chore Rivers. (Drawn by Phil Burns. 1979)

Yuquí burial shelter found near the Chore River in 1979.

took the time to sketch a drawing of it as well as take pictures of it. Then we came upon another camp with a separate corral-like enclosure where Straight Hair determined that a woman had given birth. Leaving a small aluminum kettle, blue enamel drinking cup, and some yellow thread as gifts, we headed home. We had seen enough to know that the nomads frequented the area. Now we just needed them to find our gifts and follow the trails to our camp so we could become their friends. How long might that take?

Eventually, Helimission found another pilot, Joe Belson, who was happy to meet our transportation needs. It was a beautiful sight to watch the orange and white Bo105 helicopter on final approach. The roar of the twin turbines as it settled gently onto the grassy helipad on the riverbank was a constant reminder of the miraculous ways God had worked on our behalf during the past year.

The helicopter itself was the first miracle. With it in service, our families had been able to join us on the contact base. Household goods were flown in, food supplies and other necessities were easily transported; even a kerosene operated refrigerator and gas-powered washing machine were transported in a net beneath the helicopter. Also, a load of bananas was flown in each flight day to be kept on hand for the Indians if they showed up. The helicopter continued to be a valuable aid for survey work too, although we weren't using it much now for that.

We could also see God's hand in a road which had recently been completed to the town of Puerto Grether, ten kilometers due south of us. We needed this alternative means of transportation in case the helicopter was not available on some occasion. The road was only a mud track during the rainy season, but with our swamp buggy, we could travel it if necessary. Fortunately, the lightweight buggy and its aluminum trailer could swim the water-filled gullies along the way. Travel by swamp buggy was preferable to hiking out or to traveling by river. The river was narrow, swift, and log-filled, making it dangerous for travel, especially when small children were along.

The nomad camps and burial shelters indicated that the nomads had spent a fair portion of rainy season only a few kilometers from us on a belt of high jungle, and now they began taking gifts, so we anticipated that it wouldn't be long until they followed the gift trails leading to our clearing. Our bananas were beginning to produce, and the manioc was ready to harvest anytime they showed up. We were ready; now when would we see them for the first time?

* * * * *

For three days, the pain in Vickie's tooth grew worse and the swelling in her face increased. We consulted with doctors by radio and received conflicting advice as to what course of treatment to follow, although we were advised that it would be best to seek medical help without delay. As we considered the twelve-hour trip by swamp tractor to the highway, the additional three hours from there to medical attention in Santa Cruz, and her condition as an expectant mother, we could only commit the situation to God.

For one full day, we tried to get in touch with a helicopter to fly her out. Failing in that, we determined to leave early the next morning by swamp tractor along the logging track. By this time, the pain was nearly unbearable, even using the full allowable dose of painkillers. Calling in some of our coworkers, we committed the situation to God in earnest, praying over Vickie and anointing her with oil. Within thirty minutes, the pain lessened, and she was able to sleep soundly for the first night since the pain had begun; in her exhaustion, we even overslept our two alarms.

A coworker woke us in the morning, and by 4:30 a.m., we were on our way by swamp tractor. Vickie lay in the trailer as the tractor pulled her along the deeply rutted mud track that served as our "road." For the entire trip, God kept the pain at bay, only allowing it to return gradually during the final hours of highway travel before arriving in the city of Santa Cruz twenty hours later.

Rain had begun shortly after we left home, and soon, we were thoroughly soaked and cold from the south wind. Vickie was sloshing around in the water that puddled in the trailer but was content in the knowledge that she was on her way to medical help. In two places, local people had blocked the road and weren't allowing travel in order to keep it from being torn up, but after we explained that the giant tires of our swamp tractor wouldn't damage their valuable dirt road, God worked in their hearts, allowing us to proceed.

We reached the highway at 5:30 p.m., too late to get public transportation into the city of Santa Cruz that day, but God had already made plans for us. As we left the mud track and drove onto the gravel road, Larry Depue, traveling with us, spotted the owner of a sawmill, a friend of his, climbing into his pickup truck. Senor Cuellar very kindly offered us a ride about seventy kilometers up the gravel roadway to his other sawmill. As we rode, we were able to present the Gospel clearly to this man who claimed never to have been exposed to it before and showed interest. God also touched his heart regarding Vickie's illness and as we neared his second sawmill, he graciously offered to take us on into Santa Cruz that very night since he had business in town the following day. Truly God had prepared the way for us.

During the two weeks spent in Santa Cruz attending to Vickie's abscess, God made available to us a newer, heavier duty, diesel-powered swamp tractor, which the Depues and us, the Fosters, purchased jointly. Helimission was no longer available to serve us, so the two swamp tractors would now be our principal means of travel, and we were very grateful to God for His provision of this powerful machine.

September 1980—Effort to Befriend Víbora River Yuquí in the Jungle

BY NOW, WE HAD BEEN established at the Víbora River base for two years, and since beginning to put out gifts for the nomads, they had taken them every two to three months. The first few times they had come within a few hundred yards of our camp, but now, instead of coming so close, they were staying farther away, mostly taking the gifts near the end of the trail about three kilometers from our base.

In the early days, they had come into our camp once when we were all absent and stolen machetes and a few other items. Were they fearful that if they came to us, we would retaliate for that? After discussions among the contact team and with mission leadership, we began to feel that we should go looking for them in the jungle. It would be dangerous as we would be in dense forest if we encountered them where they could easily fire arrows at us without us seeing them. We thought a crew of three American missionaries and four Yuquí believers from the Chimoré would work well on such an endeavor.

As I was praying and looking to God through His Word as to whether I should be involved in such a venture, He showed me Acts 21:11–13, KJV, where the prophet Agabus warns the Apostle Paul against going to Jerusalem because there, the Jews would do him harm. Paul's reply was, "I am ready not to be bound only, but also to die at Jerusalem for the name of the Lord Jesus."

God's message to me was clear, and I was prepared to die in the jungle for the name of the Lord Jesus. I was ready to go looking for the Yuquí, regardless of the personal cost.

Interestingly, I soon received a letter from my father, Les, referencing this same passage, which God had led him to, and he took it as a message from God that we shouldn't go because something bad would happen, and yet God had used this passage in my own heart to tell me not to worry about what might happen, that He is in ultimate control. While appreciating my dad's input, I elected to follow the message God had given me through His Word.

There are those who say of isolated people such as the Yuquí, "Leave them alone, they're happy like they are." I had learned during my years with the nomads that there was little or no truth to that statement. Like the majority of people, the Yuquí prefer having food to going hungry, prefer staying dry under a nice roof during a rainstorm, prefer not being shot at and killed by those who were invading their territory, prefer a chainsaw over an ax when cutting down a tree for honey, prefer not to be killed when someone else dies—and the list goes on.

As we prepared to look for their hostile relatives in the vastness of the forest with few trails to follow until we encountered nomad trails, I suggested to our Yuquí coworkers that we travel with little food, living mostly off the land as they had done before settling down near the missionaries on the Chimoré River. "Let's live off the forest as you did," I commented. "If we carry a lot of food, our packs will be too heavy."

They were unanimous and quick to refuse this suggestion, stating, "That life was too difficult."

A day or two later, as we piled the foodstuff in front of them and divided those items into seven equal piles so that everyone would carry the same weight, none of them wanted to carry the foodstuff, complaining, "That's too much to carry."

"Okay, we'll leave most of the food behind," I replied.

"No, no, you guys can carry it," they whined, so each American missionary ended up with a pack that was significantly heavier than those of our guides. I guess you could say they wanted to have their cake and eat it too. I would have preferred a lighter pack, even if it meant going hungry from time to time as cutting your way through dense jungle while wearing a heavy pack is exhausting. Even though we carried food, the amount was modest, and we would still tolerate hunger.

We departed the Víbora River base by following our gift trail to the Chore River where we had seen so many abandoned nomad camps and then took a heading of 120 degrees, southeast toward the Bolivian colonies that had sprung up near an abandoned oil drilling platform called Cascabel (Rattlesnake). Almost immediately, we began finding indications that the nomads had passed through within the past few weeks—trees had been cut for honey, palm branches had been cut and discarded—and as we continued, we found more and more nomad camps, some of them years old, others newer, of all different ages. Near the end of the day, we ran into white-lipped peccaries (a type of javelina pig), and although we wounded some, we got none. Now we began to appreciate the food we were carrying. Even with guns, living off the land was not an easy endeavor.

The next day, we began hearing axes chopping in the distance, and our guides indicated we should all be very quiet as they were sure it was the nomads chopping down honey trees. We headed toward the sound and soon came to a large clearing; a new farm was being felled by Bolivian colonists. They had seen no indications of hostile Indians in their area but were able to give us directions to the Cascabel oil drilling site. We were looking for a man named Orlando Antelo, a hunter/woodsman who reportedly knew the area well and had seen many signs of the Yuquí as he wandered through the forest. He was knowledgeable and a great source of valuable information, telling us of the various waterways that flowed through the area and where the nomads roamed in relation to those as well as giving us directions to farms where the Yuquí had recently stolen bananas.

Orlando graciously hosted us for the night in his modest, dirt-floored, thatch-roofed home with no walls, which we really appreciated since a cold, wet storm had moved in from the south. We set up our mosquito nets on the floor and enjoyed what would be our last night under proper shelter.

The next day, we went to look at two of the farms the nomads had been raiding and, at both, found trails they had made as they hauled their loot away. At the second farm, which had the fresher trail, we decided to follow it if we could. Wooly Hair, one of our four guides, was possibly the best tracker of all the Yuquí from the

Chimoré with his younger brother, Straight Hair, being similar in ability. Wooly Hair led off with Straight Hair following, and the two paused often to consult together.

We were now on the fourth day of our expedition and not doing too well at living off the jungle, and even though we were carrying food, the amount we had brought was modest, so when Wooly Hair spotted a bee tree, we stopped to get the honey. It was wasted time. The honey, made by a small yellow bee, had the consistency of snot and was not much better. The weather continued cold and drizzly, so occasionally we would stop, light a fire, and warm ourselves. I soon learned a new Yuquí phrase from our guides: "*Tata amama ta yegua* (I'll huddle around the fire and keep warm)."

Now Straight Hair was leading the way, and I was very impressed with his abilities in the jungle. I would give him a compass heading, and even though the day was gray and cloudy with little indication of where the sun might be, he kept going in the correct direction as he weaved and wound his way through obstacles in the vine-choked jungle. Occasionally, I would give him a minor heading correction from the compass, although his directional intuition was amazing and he only varied a few degrees.

Eventually, we came to the Espuma River, another river notorious for hostile Indian activity, and Wooly Hair found another honey tree, this time with *quigögua* honey, a variety which we all enjoyed. Two small guan turkeys were also shot and could be used to flavor the rice we would have for supper.

After our rest stop and a light lunch at the Espuma River, our guides began suggesting that maybe the jungle would be better, more passable, on the west side of the river, commenting, "*Ibi ete tu cue subai* (Do you suppose it could be good jungle on the other side)?"

So after eating, we headed west, crossing the river and coming right into a large abandoned Indian camp. Smaller camps were also scattered around nearby. Even before crossing the river, we found a tree where the nomads had gathered honey. Now we went north for two hours before our guides said, "*Susu ya* (Let's set up camp)."

Fear had begun to build in them as they realized that the camps we had seen were new enough that a hostile nomad out hunting might spot us at any time. The nomads seemed to be active in this area of jungle. The first time Straight Hair suggested stopping, I questioned it because it was so early, and he replied, "I was *going* to set up camp, but there is a lot of sun left." Fear was controlling his behavior, but then, I could understand as I was somewhat nervous myself.

We continued on, although it was clear that our guides had begun to realize the magnitude of risk in what we were doing. They knew the mindset of their hostile relatives as it had only been fifteen years since they themselves had been the ones shooting the *abaa* (the enemy outsiders).

The next day, we continued our course to the north and east until we made our way back to the Espuma River and again found a large abandoned nomad camp. Abundant alligator bones littered the clearing, and many palm hearts had been cut. Two of our guides, Favorite Joven and Big Tummy, were both feeling quite ill, not from fear but more likely from our inadequate diet and poor sleeping conditions. Over the next four days, our diet improved slightly as Big Tummy caught a catfish large enough that we could all eat our fill. Two large red-footed terrapins and a small one also supplemented our diet along with a small guan, and then, Straight Hair shot a collared peccary (javelina pig), which allowed us all to eat until we were content.

Even so, our guides were discontented with the insufficient food and fear of their kinfolk and would have abandoned the undertaking and gone home had there been an easy way out. They had more than enough of this dangerous venture!

We were no longer finding fresh Indian signs along the Espuma River, so we headed west toward the Chore River, stopping once along the way to set up the radio and let our Víbora River base know where we were and what we were seeing. The jungle was dense and full of vines, which required strenuous cutting with a machete, so we were taking turns, chopping our way through; even so, by 4:30 p.m., we were all dog-tired and stopped to camp for the night. The day had been rainy, and although we stopped often during the heaviest downpours to huddle under a tarp until the rain lightened, we were all soaked to the skin from the sodden vegetation we had been forcing our way through. A warm fire would dry us off and warm us before we crawled into our mosquito nets for the night.

After only three hours of travel the next day, we reached the banks of the Chore River. It had taken nine hours from the Espuma to the Chore. Now we wanted to cross the river, but it was swollen from rain, and our guides didn't know how to swim. We worked our way upstream along the bank for an hour, hoping to find a shallow place where we could ford the river since we were desirous of looking over the terrain on the other side. Larry, a brawny individual, was able to accompany our guides across the river one by one so that they weren't swept off their feet by the current, and soon we were all safely on the west side.

We were surprised by what we now found. Only a few yards into the jungle from the river bank, a capybara (world's largest rodent) lay dead although missing its head and skin. The nomads had killed the animal but left the carcass and flesh behind. It was so unusual, and we had no idea what the significance of this might be. Initially, Straight Hair suggested that they had only taken the head and skin because their camp was far away and they hadn't wanted to carry the meat. The head is a preferred delicacy, and the skin has a nice layer of fat under it, so it is also greatly desired.

We hadn't traveled much farther before we found a large Indian camp near the river with four main fires. It was surrounded by long walls of palm branches, giving it protection and concealment from people who might pass nearby. In the camp was a capybara skull, howler monkey jawbone, blue macaw feathers, turtle skeleton, and assorted other camp debris.

Shortly after leaving that camp, we found three additional camps, and now, due to the proximity of these camps to the capybara carcass, Straight Hair and Wooly Hair revised their theory about the capybara carcass. "Very likely a high-class individual died and the people aren't eating capybara meat since it was that person's favorite meat in life," opined Straight Hair.

Wooly Hair nodded his approval of that idea; while the older brother might be the better woodsman and tracker, he deferred to his younger brother's overall intelligence. We all knew the implications of a high-class death; the nomads would need a victim. "Someone must die" to accompany the individual in death. Would this increase the likelihood of us being targets of their arrows? We worked our way south and then southwest along the river but couldn't determine for sure which way the Indians had gone, north or south. Wooly Hair said north; Straight Hair said south.

A few days previously, a thorn-covered palm sapling had sprung back as I was walking the trail and embedded a thorn deep into my left knee. The thorn had proven impossible to extract, and now the knee was infected and swollen, very painful, making walking difficult. We stopped in one of the abandoned camps so I could rest and soak my knee in saltwater, hoping it would fester to where the thorn would come out. As I rested, some of our guides went a little ways south and soon found another Indian camp but still couldn't determine which direction the nomads had traveled.

Once they returned, they left Big Tummy to tend to me while the other five men went to search the area north of us, planning to return and spend the night with us. By this time, my knee had stiffened to the point that it was doubtful I would be able to walk at all the next day. There was no firewood in this abandoned camp, a sign which our guides said indicated the nomads had only traveled a short distance to make their next camp and took the firewood with them. How frustrating. Here we were, so close to our objective, and I could no longer walk. Would we be forced to abandon the effort and call for a helicopter to extract us?

The next morning brought no improvement in the knee, although in the night, much infection had drained from it along with the thorn. Even so, it remained hot, inflamed, tender, stiff, and walking brought agony. Straight Hair could see the pain I was in and offered to carry my pack, but I refused and walked last in line so my companions wouldn't see the tears I was trying not to shed. Soon, Favorite Joven, walking ahead of me, insisted on carrying my pack. With a knee that was stiff and unbending, I was holding up progress, and eventually, we came to a halt.

Wallace, Larry, Straight Hair, and Wooly Hair left the others of us there as they went once again to look at nomad camps to the north and the south, eventually concluding that the nomads had traveled north. Now if only I wasn't hindering us from doing the same.

Our guides were becoming uncooperative, and it was evident they no longer had any desire to encounter their kinfolk under these conditions. It was just too dangerous! We were hunting for killers, treacherous people who would shoot without thinking twice about it, and they had proven it on many occasions. As we foreigners discussed our options, we realized that if we stayed where we were until I could walk, our guides would insist on returning home due to low morale, fear, and inadequate food.

On the other hand, if we called for a helicopter, we could have Bob Garland, who spoke the Yuquí language, flown in, bringing food supplies, raising the morale of the "troops," and I could be flown out for medical aid.

The decision was made to hire a military helicopter out of Cochabamba, the only helicopter available and costing $450 an hour. I had a bad night. I had to squeeze the knee at midnight to get enough relief from pressure and pain to be able to sleep, and then it drained all night.

The next day, the helicopter stopped at the Chimoré River base to pick up Bob and then headed our direction. The first time the helicopter came out our way, they didn't come far enough east but mistook a long swamp for the Chore River and returned to the Chimoré without having found us. Now they were low on fuel and had to fly to the town of Villa Tunari at the base of the mountains where they accessed fuel reserves stored there before returning to the Chimoré to talk to us by mission radio and heading our direction once again. They had no radio with our frequency in the aircraft, so they couldn't communicate with us once they were airborne.

It was 3:07 p.m. when the helicopter finally flew over the tiny beach on the Chore River where I was hoping to be picked up and Bob and supplies dropped off. The helicopter, a large Huey, was forced to hover with one skid over the small sandy beach, and the other skid out over the river. Even though we had repeatedly told our colleagues by radio to let the military pilots know that this would be a "hot stop" so they should come as lightly loaded as possible, the word had never reached them, so the helicopter arrived overloaded with two military pilots, our mission pilot Chuck Henson, a flight engineer, Bob Garland, and supplies.

When they flew over and saw the narrow river and tiny beach with overhanging trees, they circled a few times, looking the situation over, and we started to think they were going to abort the mission, but they didn't. As the helicopter hovered between beach and water, Bob threw supplies out onto the beach and hopped out while I hobbled painfully to the craft and crawled aboard.

Soon we were in the air, and Chuck gave me a warm welcome as we headed west toward the towering range of the eastern Andes Mountains that we would need to cross to get to Cochabamba. As Villa Tunari, the small town at the base of the foothills, came in sight, Chuck, who was listening to the chatter among the flight crew, turned to me and said, "They just figured out that they don't have enough fuel to return to Cochabamba." Now that they had used the fuel reserves stored in Villa Tunari, they opted to fly as far as possible before setting down along the highway high in the mountains.

Clouds from the Amazon basin had drifted westward and were pressed tightly up against the mountains, but with the shortage of fuel, the pilots didn't dare climb above the clouds to go "over the top" but rather opted to follow the winding mountainous two-lane highway leading from Villa Tunari to Cochabamba. Even that approach was questionable as at some elevation, we would reach the cloud ceiling and need to punch up through it, not knowing what might lurk in the mist above. As missionary pilots often said, "There could be rocks in those clouds." Also, high-tension power lines came down from the hydroelectric dam at Corani, higher up the mountains, and we would need to avoid hitting those cables, so we didn't dare penetrate the clouds.

Eventually, as we neared the cloud ceiling, we flew around a lengthy road tunnel, avoided the high-tension lines at the western end of the tunnel, and landed at the highway maintenance facility at a place called Paracti. The employee in charge of the National Road Service (Senac) facility was pleased to be of service to the Bolivian military and treated us graciously, serving us an excellent supper and kindly putting us up for the night in individual rooms with comfortable beds. While we were eating supper, the pilots informed us that the Air Force would be sending fuel down the next day from their reserves at Corani, the hydroelectric plant a few miles farther up the road, and we would be able to fly on in to Cochabamba if the cloud cover in this rain forest area dissipated.

Paracti was far enough up in the Andean foothills that I lay in bed, shivering violently while burning up with fever. My knee was hot and so sensitive to touch that I couldn't bear to have the sheet touching it, much less a blanket. The knee continued to swell and was draining continually but didn't seem to be improving at all, leading me to wonder if I had a staph infection. I knew it would be a sleepless night, but at least I was much nearer to medical care than I had been earlier in the day.

The night was still young when at 9:40 p.m., I heard familiar voices in the hallway, and soon, two missionary coworkers, Bernie Murrin and Cam Hurst, showed up in my tiny room. Bolivia was under a curfew, but Bernie and Cam had gone to the Air Force base in Cochabamba and gotten a special travel pass from the general in charge along with two barrels of jet fuel, then borrowed a pickup truck from Jim Wilhelmson to bring fuel to the pilots and to transport Chuck and me back to Cochabamba. Three hours later, we arrived at the mission guesthouse where Cam was a big help in getting me bathed, soaking the knee, and getting me settled for the night. Praise God for caring coworkers!

It was early afternoon the next day by the time a doctor arrived at the mission guesthouse to evaluate my knee, and after prescribing Gentamicin injections and limited walking, he was on his way out the door. Even better news arrived by radio at 4:32 p.m. The team in the jungle had made contact with the nomads near the Chore River and were interacting with them at that very moment. No one had been shot, although one arrow had been fired but fell short as the nomads first fled from the trespassers.

My emotional response was a *big* smile and joy. I didn't feel in the least bypassed but rather marveled at how God allowed my illness forcing us to use the Huey so Bob, with his greater experience and ability in the language and contact work, could be there at this critical time. Anything less severe than my abscess would hardly have prompted those measures. I was confident that God knew what He was doing.

After a two-hour contact with seven men, three women, and three children, the missionary team pulled back to set up camp for the night after receiving a promise that the nomads would come back the following day to spend more time with them.

Contact Gone Bad

THE NEWS WAS NOT SO good the next morning. At 7:13 a.m. we learned that in the night, by the light of the moon, the nomads had surrounded our men and fired arrows randomly into their mosquito nets, shooting Wallace, Wooly Hair, and Straight Hair—all of them in the leg. Wallace had seen the warriors moments before they started shooting and was reaching for his gun to fire it into the air and frighten them away when an arrow impacted him in the thigh. Wooly Hair's wound was not too serious, but Straight Hair was losing a lot of blood. Unfortunately, the military helicopter was not available to evacuate the team, so we had missionaries in both Cochabamba and Santa Cruz searching desperately for a helicopter, any helicopter to get the men out.

By 11:45 a.m., a helicopter was in the area but had trouble locating the team, which was hard to understand since our mission-owned Piper Aztec, with pilot Chuck Henson was circling the area and in radio communications with the helicopter guiding him to the site. By 1:15 p.m., my sister, Anna, who had been going back and forth between the radio room and the room I was lying in came to report that Wallace and Wooly Hair had arrived at our Chimoré River base and that Wallace was in a lot of pain. Both Wallace and Straight Hair had been hit with lance-tipped arrows meant to bleed the injured person to death. Wooly Hair had been hit with a barbed arrow, which was not quite as deadly.

Initially, the helicopter pilot showed great reluctance to go back in and bring the rest of the team out but eventually relented, so by evening, the three injured missionaries had been airlifted to Elizabeth Seton Hospital in Cochabamba, and all were recovering well.

The shooting incident had shaken me badly, even more than I cared to admit. As a single person, death had held little fear; but as a married man, I hated to think of leaving my family, such a young family, to grow up without their daddy. Now I began to doubt that the nomads would ever come out to us on their own, especially after this. It didn't seem that we had anything strong enough to lure them into our camp at the Víbora River.

As the men improved and were released from the hospital, each of them joined me at the mission guesthouse to recuperate, and I was able to ask both Straight Hair and Wooly Hair about the contact they had with the hostile nomads. I taped their stories for later, more detailed analysis. Straight Hair was convinced they were the same Yuquí who had come to us years before at the Arroyo Hediondo, commenting, "One of the leaders died, and now the other one has that one's widow as his wife."

Wooly Hair agreed, adding, "When the jungle people saw Wallace, they said, 'He is the one who hung things far away and fed me.' He went on to say, 'It was the one who was really dark, the one who looks like Iroquois who said this about Wallace.'" Then he described the others, "Three of the men were very light-colored, like White Joven, one looked like Scarface, one was like Witchy and had two or more sons." Not only did it sound like the same group we had interacted with at Arroyo Hediondo, but it also seemed that these were their closest relatives, Chief Strong Arm's group, from whom they had split in the late 1940s or early 1950s.

Later, Bob Garland gave additional details. The day they made contact in the jungle, they had been following the nomad trail from abandoned camp to abandoned camp until eventually, at the fourth camp, they found the ashes still warm. "This one is from this morning," Straight Hair announced. All the members of the team knew what they would find at the next camp.

They had been hiking for well over six hours since early morning. The terrain was very broken, up and down steep ravines, but most of the team weren't sensing their exhaustion as the excitement of being this close to the nomads gave them the added impetus they needed.

It was then that it happened. They heard the voices of children and the sound of splashing water break through the jungle's silence. Several Indian children were playing and fishing in a small creek. The team froze in their tracks. Straight Hair and Favorite Joven, who were walking side by side in the lead, stood motionless for several minutes until the rest of the team encouraged them to go forward. If they didn't proceed while they had the advantage, they might be spotted first.

The two Yuquí looked at each other and then advanced, offering a gift. But when the Indian children saw them, they ran off, screaming hysterically. The team ran toward the Indian camp, and as they neared it, they could see several adults and children already fleeing. Suddenly, one of the fleeing warriors turned toward the group and shot an arrow that landed just short of the team. A few minutes later, they spotted another man coming up the trail from behind, possibly just returning from the day's hunt. When he realized they didn't belong in that setting, he got ready to draw back his bow. Favorite Joven and Big Tummy rushed up to him yelling, "No! No! Don't shoot! We aren't going to harm you!"

The man lowered his bow and arrow.

For fifteen or twenty minutes, the team conversed with this man, encouraging him to go and bring the others to meet them. He left and, after thirty minutes, returned with others of his group, including six more men. The four Yuquí from the Chimoré explained who they were and assured the nomads they wouldn't harm them but would protect them. The fact that Bob could speak their language seemed to make no impression at all on them. But then again, why should it? These jungle people only knew their own language and had no idea that anyone in the world spoke differently. Undoubtedly, they believed these missionaries to be the spirits of their dead relatives reincarnated. Their worldview offered few other explanations.

Likely they had seen or heard the helicopter the previous day as it extracted me, but if they did, they may have linked it to the fact that now all these dead relatives were appearing in a reincarnated state. They know that the sky is where the dead live, so it all fits together. That's where the missionaries had to have come from. The experience was doubtless traumatic to the whole group.

The missionaries gave them a variety of gifts, including hard candy and bananas, and Straight Hair pulled out a file to begin sharpening their dull axes. For the next several hours, the four Yuquí from the Chimoré talked with the hostile nomads and encouraged them to visit the missionary settlement at the Víbora River.

As the sun began to set, the missionaries explained to the nomads that they were going to go and set up camp for the night but would come back to see them in the morning. They seemed agreeable to this, so the missionaries began setting up camp and hanging their mosquito nets. The entire team was exhausted enough that they needed rest more than food, so didn't bother to eat. They were encouraged with how well the contact had gone and were looking forward to seeing the Indians again the next day.

While often the missionaries would sleep in jungle hammocks, on this occasion, all the missionaries were sleeping on the ground under mosquito nets. The netting was a heavy, white gauze net that couldn't be seen into from the outside; however, from inside the net, you could see out. By 10:30 p.m., most of the team was asleep.

At 12:30 a.m., Bob was awakened from a deep sleep by screams, and then a series of rifle shots rang out. He hollered, "What's the matter?" realizing even as he asked the question that he knew what was happening—they were under attack!

Larry yelled out, "Wally's been hit!"

Two of the Yuquí guides, Favorite Joven and his brother Wooly Hair who had been sleeping together under one net had also been shot.

Wallace had been unable to fall asleep. The moon was almost full that night, and as he lay there, he suddenly caught sight of men standing about ten feet away with bows and arrows drawn. He knew what was coming and tried to yell out, but before he could find his voice, an arrow ripped into his thigh. He pulled it out, almost as fast as it penetrated and then, with lightning speed, reached outside of the net and grabbed his .22 rifle from the bag in which he had it hidden. He quickly fired four or five times into the air.

As screams came from the two Yuquí guides who had been struck, the attackers fled into the night. They hadn't seen the .22 rifle earlier and didn't know that the team had a gun. It appeared their plan had been to massacre the missionary team.

Flashlights went on as the men took stock of the injuries. Wallace and Wooly Hair had been shot in the thigh, and Straight Hair in the lower leg. Straight Hair bled profusely and gave the most concern. Larry began ripping up sheets to bandage the wounds, moving about calmly and handling the emergency efficiently. Then the team settled down to pray and wait for day to dawn. Periodically, throughout the night, Wallace fired the rifle into the air to keep the attackers from returning.

As the men surveyed the scene later, they could see how God had protected them. The attackers hadn't been able to discern through the heavy nets where heads or feet were. It was only God who prevented anyone from getting wounded in a vital spot, and although Bob had a see-through net, they hadn't shot at him. Absolutely amazing! Of the four arrows shot, three hit their marks, and one missed. That one stuck in the ground about twelve inches from Larry's head!

At around 6:30 in the morning, the men began attempting to make radio contact with anyone tuned into the mission frequency and, at 6:45 a.m., finally got through. After explaining their plight, they asked for a helicopter to be sent in to evacuate the team. Other missionaries swung into action, praying, and trying to find a helicopter. There was no helicopter available in Cochabamba because the president was expected in the city that morning, and the helicopter would be needed to take him around to various places.

Finally, Ed Wiebe located a privately owned helicopter in Santa Cruz that would fly for $500 an hour.

Chuck Henson, our mission pilot, knew exactly where the team was since he had accompanied Bob Garland on the army helicopter just two days previously. He flew over with the Piper Aztec and kept circling the area to indicate the location to the helicopter while the men on the ground started a smoke fire to help him spot their location. While the vegetation was dense, praise God, the men were near a swamp with enough space to land the helicopter.

The helicopter arrived around noon and didn't even land but just hovered low as Wallace and Wooly Hair got aboard. Larry was preparing to move Straight Hair over and get him aboard, but the pilot didn't want to take more than two men on that first flight, so the others had to wait. Altogether, it took three flights and almost six hours to complete the evacuation.

After the first flight, the weather started closing in and threatened rain, but God held it open long enough to get everyone out. Chuck Henson then flew the three wounded men from Chimoré to Cochabamba, and by late afternoon, they were in the hospital, receiving medical attention.

For the next two years, the contact base on the Víbora River lay abandoned as the missionary team disbanded and helped out in other ministries around Bolivia. The hiatus would give the missionaries an opportunity to recover from the trauma of the shootings and time for the hostile nomads to cool off. We moved back to the Chimoré River where Vickie began handling the medical work, and I partnered with Bob as we took turns teaching the Yuquí from God's Word. I could continue improving my knowledge of the Yuquí language as I interacted with the people daily, assisted them in planting crops and fruit trees, and helped them with animal husbandry, especially poultry.

Our time at the Chimoré base saw numerous snakebites among the Yuquí, which Vickie had to deal with, although not singlehandedly as others of us stepped in to assist her as necessary. Many of the bites were minor, although from the screams and tears of the Yuquí when someone was bitten, you would have thought that each bite was fatal...and one was.

Death by Snakebite

THE FRESH DIRT WAS CLAMMY and clung to my tennis shoes as I stood on the mound, gazing with moist eyes into the hole. Only two-and-a-half hours before, she had been a normal, healthy, expectant mother. Now they were preparing to lay her on the fresh green banana leaves in the bottom of this yawning cavity. Her mother's wailing and her husband's broke in on my thoughts, and I wondered how it felt to lose his wife so suddenly. I wondered too if he was thinking of how she had trusted in Christ as her Savior several years previously and of how she must be rejoicing now or if he had other thoughts related to their cultural beliefs concerning the spirits of the dead.

She had been harvesting rice in the hot sun, was already overly tired and wanting to rest, but her husband forbade her. There was much work to be done, and every hand was needed. She continued harvesting, and it was then that the pit viper struck. At least one other person had walked close by that very spot without noticing the snake. It was just a small snake waiting for her. When it hit, she cried out, ran a few feet, and sat down, saying, "I'm going to die! I'm going to die!" Then she passed out, never to come to again.

Now we were burying her. There was no coffin for her. No change of clothing. Just as they had brought her from the rice field, they would place her in the ground.

They had brought her the last part of the distance from the rice field to the clinic in a wheelbarrow. They were wailing as they came down the airstrip. When I asked why they were all crying so much, no one answered. I had no idea that she was unconscious and not breathing or I might have begun cardiac massage and mouth-to-mouth right then and there.

Now they were handing a variety of items to the men standing in the grave—cups, cloth, a knife; these things would be buried with her. Her dog and chickens were already dead and buried; her mother-in-law had taken care of that detail half an hour earlier.

The certainty of her death had not really gripped me yet. It was too sudden. Her young son, Juan, stood alone to one side. I don't think the reality of it had come home to him yet either. Everyone's sympathy was for the husband; Juan was ignored.

Early the next morning, her husband, Jaime, came to my door and handed me his shotgun, asking me to keep it for him for a time. He explained, "I don't want to be tempted to shoot myself." Then he and close family members took a few of their belongings and headed out into the jungle to get away. They traveled in the forest for a few weeks, assuaging their grief in the comforting jungle that they loved. Others remained behind, continuing the rice harvest.

1983 Contact on the Chore

By early 1983, a contact team, which included several new families, was once again installed at the Rio Víbora base, and an airstrip had been built to make access to the site less challenging. Gift trails were once again active, but as before, the nomads were reluctant to approach too closely, mostly taking the more distant gifts and staying far from the clearing. The quantity of bananas now growing at the farm should have been a big attraction for the jungle dwellers, but they avoided the missionary camp and were again stealing bananas from settlers near the abandoned Cascabel oil exploration site.

Vickie and I continued living at the Chimoré base where I had just completed building a new school building of lumber. We were helping with the medical work, Bible teaching, and community development.

We had requested a supply flight, so I was on the radio, communicating with our pilot as the Piper Twin Aztec, call sign CP-1370, made its way to our base when there was a "breaker" on our frequency. "Hello, this is Lester Finkbinder of World Gospel Mission calling. Am I talking to Alan Foster?"

"Greetings, Lester. Nice to hear from you," I answered. Lester and Clara had helped us during our travels a few years previously and were familiar with the work we were doing among the Yuquí.

Lester continued, "Orlando Antelo was by the house the other day to let us know that the colonists near Cascabel are having trouble with the Indians. They had a farmer killed up there, shot full of arrows. Now they are threatening to get the military in and annihilate the Indians, if possible." Lester let us know that the military had already gone in once, but rain hindered their search for the Indians. The government-owned oil company, YPFB, which was also doing exploration in that area, had begun official paperwork to authorize a battalion of soldiers to go in and deal with the hostile nomads once and for all.

I let Larry Depue and Jack Jones know what was going on, and they made a road trip to the Cascabel area to get a better understanding of what was happening there. Their report raised even greater concern among the missionary community for the safety of the nomads. Those of us working at the Chimoré base and the Víbora base all began asking God what His plan for us might be.

Bob Garland and I also began discussing the situation with the Yuquí Christians at the Chimoré as we knew that if we once again went into the jungle, looking for their kinfolk, we would need their help. Not only were the nomads their blood relatives, but they could communicate with them better than any of us could. At the same time, two of the Chimoré Christians had been shot the last time they encountered their kinfolk in the woods, so they knew the risks involved. The Yuquí wives all made it clear they didn't want their husbands facing such certain death! They had had enough of their volatile cousins. Among the expatriate missionaries, there were also those who initially were strongly opposed to such an effort, but eventually, all became convinced that without such a measure, the jungle nomads would all soon be killed.

Straight Hair, Favorite Joven, Wooly Hair, Jaime, and Lorenzo—all believers from the Chimoré—agreed to take part in the effort, and soon, they and their families were flown to the Víbora River base where the team was being assembled. Jack Jones and I joined them there. Larry Depue and Steve Parker, already living at the Víbora, would complete the team that would go to look for the nomads.

Soon after arriving at the Víbora base, both Straight Hair and Lorenzo pointed out that someone on the base had a dog that barked all the time and that this would be a hindrance to the nomads approaching the base. This observation wasn't accepted well by the missionary team, few of whom had any experience with the Yuquí and little idea of what might or might not hinder the jungle dwellers from approaching the base. Weeks later, when we made contact in the jungle with the nomads, one of their first questions as we invited them to our base was, "Is the barking dog still there?" Clearly it was a hindrance to them approaching our base and would need to be dealt with before they came to us.

As the day drew near for our team to head into the forest, some of our Yuquí guides began getting "cold feet," expressing a desire to return home to the Chimoré, but as we met and prayed together, reminding them that their hostile relatives would all be killed by soldiers or settlers if we didn't find them first and convince them to settle down, they all recommitted to accompanying us. My fear was as great as their own, and without the confidence that God was sending us, I wouldn't have gone.

Within a few days, our team of nine had flown to Buena Vista and then traveled by road to Cascabel. Once again, as we had done three years previously, we spent the night with Orlando Antelo and, the next day, accompanied him to several farms where the Yuquí had recently stolen bananas. At Aramayo's farm, the westernmost of the farms we visited, we took off following a ten-day-old nomad trail northwestward into the forest. A few hundred yards from the farm, we came to a site where the colonist farmers had camouflaged themselves inside a circle of palm branches and lain in ambush to shoot the nomads as they came to steal bananas.

Moving on, we came to a large abandoned farm roughly ten acres in size. As we worked our way through the dense regrowth that had overtaken the farm, we had trouble following the nomad trail, but when we came out the other side, we found abandoned palm-leaf backpacks, some of them small ones for children to carry. Not only were the backpacks still fresh and green, but we found sweet potatoes wrapped in leaves and still in good condition as well as sugarcane stalks and banana stalks from which the bananas had been removed. As the trail became harder to find, we left Jack, Larry, and Jaime to watch the packs while the rest of us went ahead, trying to locate the trail.

Eventually, we came to a creek where the Indians had crossed on a fallen log, so we returned to let the pack watchers know what we had found and bring them up to the creek where we ate a lunch of oatmeal trail mix at 12:30 p.m. After lunch, we crossed the creek and continued working our way to the northwest. We had some difficulty following the trail, and now Jaime began proving himself as a tracker along with Straight Hair and Wooly Hair. We began picking up the occasional footprint, although the trail was getting poorer and harder to follow.

Eventually, it seemed to prove out that we were following two men and two women. One man, at least, had big feet. Later in the afternoon, around 2:30 p.m., we found fresher evidence, a three-day-old backpack among other items. Soon we came into an older camp where a woman had been behind leaves for her time of the month. In this camp, they had eaten collared peccary, white-lipped peccary, and other game. As we continued, we found a newer camp, but still not an up-to-date one. This was a larger camp with smaller campsites around the main one. There they had left the jawbone of an alligator which made us think we might not be far from a waterway.

By now, it was late enough that we wanted to camp and would need water, so some of our team went scouting nearby for water without finding any. This seemed unusual as the Yuquí normally camped near water. We picked up our packs and headed west, not following a trail, until we hit a swampy area where there was a large puddle of water we could draw from; not too great, but water.

A tiny piece of higher ground rose a foot or so out of the marsh around it, and we were able to set up camp there for the night. We had picked up two tortoises, red-footed terrapins, earlier in the day, one of them in the last few minutes from the nomad camp to our campsite, so God had provided meat for us. The turtles had abundant eggs inside, which added to the good eating when we boiled rice with soup mix for supper.

In the morning, we returned to the last nomad camp we had seen the previous day and, from there, sent out two scouting parties to see which direction the people had gone. Within minutes, we had found and were following their trail. Our guides were carrying bows and arrows to more readily identify with their hostile relatives, so when we saw quail, they shot two of them with arrows rather than make noise with our guns. A short distance further, we came on a much fresher nomad trail crossing the trail we had been following. Dropping our packs, some of us remained there as the rest of us scouted farther ahead, soon coming on a secluded, tannin-laden waterway that didn't flow.

It was apparent the nomads had camped nearby and spent much time in the area as countless palm hearts had been cut, many alligators had been shot, and ashes that had dropped from the fire they carried as they traveled onward were still fluffy and fresh. We continued forward, following the waterway, and sure enough, about forty yards to the east, we found a camp the nomads had recently abandoned. They had spent a considerable amount of time in this camp, leaving heavier duty shelters than usual, many more animal bones, fruit peelings, banana skins, and other assorted trash. As I looked around the camp, I counted fourteen fires, and none of them appeared to have been rained on. The ashes were still light and fluffy, not compacted at all. It was now 10:45 a.m.

Hoisting our packs, we headed north, following what appeared to be a trail cut by Bolivian hunters or loggers until we came to a spongy, swampy area of jungle called an *izozo* (by the Yuquí). The surface of the water had a floating carpet of growth while small trees and shrubs protruded where soil had built up. In some ways, it looked like a maze of ruts and ditches, and we slogged our way through the muddy ditches comprising the swamp for the better part of an hour, until noon, before coming cautiously out onto high ground on the far side and then stopping at a spot where it was obvious the nomads had taken a break. We were thirsty, hungry, and tired and, with no clean drinking water available, opted to take a lengthy dry break before continuing our journey.

We were still following an exploratory trail made by Bolivian nationals and assumed the nomads would continue along that trail, but almost immediately, after getting through the swamp, they left the trail and headed west. We were successful in following their trail, partly because they had stopped often to build up the fire they carried, and much ash had fallen from the smoldering sticks they carried. Soon the ashes led us to another camp, and shortly beyond that, we found a dead tapir (large beef-like animal) killed by a jaguar.

Just a short distance farther, we came to a small waterway which wasn't flowing but would flow in the rainy season. We followed along it for a time before stopping to eat lunch and enjoy some of the cool, refreshing, tannin-laden water. One of the fellows took a kettle down and brought water for the group, and as we were getting out the oatmeal trail mix, preparing to mix water with it for lunch, a giant anteater (also known as an antbear and weighing seventy to ninety pounds) came into view. I had tried giant anteater meat in the past and found it inedible with a flavor similar to the smell of a fox. Even so, Jaime shot it and then dragged it, still writhing, through the waterway, stirring up the water and making it unfit to drink.

After separating the two hind legs from the anteater, he brought them along for supper, although we foreigners didn't eat any of it. The nomad camps we found during the afternoon were overnighters, camps where they had only spent one night, and it appeared they were traveling fast with a particular destination in mind. One camp had a smoldering log, but as it was a large log, our guides estimated it had been smoldering for two or three days, so we weren't too far behind the nomads. We walked warily and quietly at all times, not wanting to get caught off guard.

Supper that night consisted of rice to which we added three aqua-colored quail eggs and two quail we had shot earlier in the day, making a nutritious meal. While the meal was being prepared, Straight Hair, Jack, Wooly Hair, and two others, me included, went a short way down the trail we would follow the next day and found the paper label from a tuna can the nomads had taken from a small house we had built at the Chore River. Along with the fact that we had been traveling west and north for two days, we were pretty sure that we weren't far from the Chore.

Returning to camp, we went on the radio and reported to our coworkers at the Víbora River base our location and what our plans were and then, as we ate supper, discussed how we could best approach the hostile jungle dwellers the next day. We would have very little control over the situation but deliberated about various scenarios and what our responses should be to them. Our primary plan, if it worked out, would be to come on the nomad camp near sundown as they were setting up for the night, run into their camp, grabbing bows and arrows so they wouldn't be able to shoot us, and grab any men present so we could talk to them. From that point on, we hoped to maintain contact while taking axes, machetes, and bows and arrows away from them for the night, if possible, while encouraging them to accompany us to the Víbora base for bananas. A tall order, which didn't sound too practical, but at least we had some idea of what other team members were thinking and would be better able to respond as a team to whatever situation we faced.

When we went on the radio, we learned that our colleagues at Rio Víbora had checked the gift trail leading to the Chore River and that the nomads had followed that trail and taken gifts one or two days previously. This gave even more confirmation that we weren't far behind them and that we might find them quickly the next day. Either we would need to find them first thing in the morning before they left their current camp, or once we knew we were approaching their next campsite, wait until late afternoon to approach. What we didn't want was to run into them while they were on the move as they would be strung out along the trail and could quickly disappear.

Now that we seemed to be so close behind the jungle dwellers, we decided to begin setting a night guard, taking two to three-hour shifts. I would stay alert until 9:00 p.m., followed by Steve, Larry, then Jack at 1:00 a.m., and me from 3:00 a.m. until dawn. We would listen throughout the night for movement, twigs cracking, etc. We let our Yuquí guides know what we were doing but exempted them from guard duty as we wanted them fresh and alert during daylight hours. They were in full agreement as we all expected to encounter the jungle people the next day.

We were on our way by 7:07 a.m. the next morning and, by 8:30 a.m., were standing in the camp the nomads had abandoned only a short time before. Their eleven fires were still smoldering, and fresh footprints led the way out of camp. Straight Hair noticed a tuna can in the camp and commented, "One of the men will be back for that. He will want it for heating beeswax for his arrows and must have forgotten it. We might run into him along the trail."

That began a discussion among us. "Should we stop, hide, and try to surround and talk to the man on his return?" We continued following the trail while watching for a spot to stop and setup an ambush. Larry and I saw a number of promising locations, but each time we pointed one out, Straight Hair vetoed it.

Now the terrain began changing, and I commented, "This jungle is very much like the forest along the Chore River." At 10:00 a.m. we came to an open area of forest where Straight Hair stopped. "This would be a good place to watch their back trail," he suggested. "We can wait here and ambush them in this clearing if they come back for the tuna can."

I wasn't happy at all with the places my companions were setting their backpacks, pointing out, "If you leave your packs out in the open, the warrior will see them as he comes into this open area. We need to hide our packs." On the northeast edge of the clearing was a fallen tree almost four feet in diameter, a perfect blind behind which to hide our packs, so I suggested, "Why don't we move our packs over behind that fallen tree?"

As the first man arrived at the fallen tree and looked over to find a good spot to set his pack, he found that the nomads had the same idea. *Their palm-leaf packs were lined up behind the log!*

Either the nomads had left their packs there as they hunted in the area or, more likely, they had cached them there as they went to check the gift trail leading from the Chore River to our Víbora River base. Later, events seemed to show the latter as the more likely explanation.

Now we were in possession of most of their belongings, other than their bows, arrows, and possibly a few machetes and axes.

We looked around for somewhere else to position our packs out of sight and then dispersed around the area to hide while keeping an eye on the log behind which their palm-leaf backpacks were located. Maybe we could talk to them when they returned for their belongings. We spent the day in silent hiding, paired off, and watched each other's backs and the surrounding jungle, waiting until 5:30 p.m. They still hadn't come. Somehow, they knew we were there. Either their women had been hidden nearby and after seeing us went to warn their men, or more likely, they picked up our back trail or heard or saw us as we waited by their packs.

Now we decided to move sixty or eighty yards from their packs and set up camp for the night, giving them opportunity to retrieve their belongings. We had no water but found that by digging a hole in the bottom of a nearby gully, water would eventually seep in and was drinkable if you didn't mind the sewer-like flavor. Some of us opted to drink while others preferred to suffer thirst.

Once again, we chose to set guards for the night, but now we were much more serious about it, setting two-man teams to keep alert throughout the night—Larry and Favorite Joven from 9:00–11:00 p.m., Wooly Hair and me from 11:00 p.m.–1:00 a.m., Steve and Jaime from 1:00–3:-00 a.m., and Jack and Larry from 3:00 a.m. until dawn. After much discussion about guard duty, most of us expressed a preference that the guards remain outside of their mosquito nets, watching and listening well with no risk of them falling asleep. The weather was threatening, and if it rained, with all the pattering on the leaf cover, there was no way we would hear an approaching threat. We were also unsure how to proceed now that the nomads knew we were on their trail. While there was a small chance the nomads had planned to spend the night away from their belongings, it was unlikely.

Straight Hair wanted to spend the next day watching their packs, although most of us thought it improbable that they would return for them while we were nearby. There was also a chance they would come by moonlight and pick up their possessions as we had moved far enough away to allow them to do that.

After a mostly sleepless night, we were up and ready for action by 3:45 a.m., so I suggested that we sit hidden near the packs again. Six of us went over and sat by the packs until 7:00 a.m., and when the nomads failed to appear, we decided to hang gifts around their packs—an ax head, two paring knives, a machete, a shirt, as well as a small bag of eight hard candies in each pack so the Indians could see that we had found their packs but hadn't taken anything or hurt the packs in any way.

At Larry's suggestion, we went over with our file and sharpened the five axes and two machetes that accompanied their packs.

The machetes were in terrible shape, with no handles, just loose rivets hanging through the holes where the handles should have been attached. After sharpening their tools and leaving the gifts for them, we decided to move our camp farther from their belongings, giving them safe and easy access while we lingered for a day or two, waiting for them to recover their belongings and flee.

As we headed west, away from their cache, we only traveled about 200 meters before coming to the Chore River. Now we had a good source of water and the area was open enough that if they shot at us, it would be from a distance, not too close up. Our western side was protected by the river. We decided to spend all of today, Sunday, resting and waiting as well as most or all of Monday. Then we would go back over to see if they had picked up their belongings.

Now that our guides were sure the nomads knew we were trailing them and after the way the similar situation had ended three years previously, our guides didn't want to go any farther. I was hopeful that the waiting time would cause a change of heart, but Straight Hair told us, "My wife said that if the jungle people know you are following them, don't go any farther, just come home."

Wooly Hair and Favorite Joven were quick to chime in, letting us know that their wives had given them similar orders. With Straight Hair and Wooly Hair both having been shot by the nomad warriors once before, I wasn't about to force them to continue on, although I did what I could to encourage them with the importance of what we were doing. Without our intervention, their kinfolk would soon all be annihilated.

Knowing that the nomads were in the vicinity, our whole team was aware that we were prohibited from firing our guns so as not to frighten the hostiles. Any shooting had to be with bow and arrow. It didn't take long for the rule to be broken. As Jack was serving lunch, I heard him say, "He's gonna shoot a tapir!" I turned around and saw a tapir as Jaime fired. I didn't have a chance stop him, but we didn't want any shooting, and he knew that but chose to shoot. The temptation was just too great for someone who had been raised in a feast or famine society. The tapir ran off as I remonstrated with Jaime, reminding him that we didn't want any shooting, and he knew that.

Jack had told him, "No! No! No!" at the time, but he didn't listen to Jack and shot anyway.

Our guides went over to look and found that it was a full-grown male tapir. It had run thirty yards or so and fallen down dead. It was shot near but not in the heart with a Remington Yellow Jacket Hornet .22 shell. Now our situation had improved greatly as we were next to the river with abundant fresh water and had all the fresh beef-like tapir we could eat.

The guides built a smoke rack of green saplings and soon had the meat grilling and smoking over the fire. After several hot sweaty days on the trail, we were all happy to be able to bathe and wash clothing. At 4:15 p.m., the rain set in and continued off and on throughout the night along with a cool south wind. Jack and Larry didn't fare too well as it turned out that they had both camped in a low spot on the jungle floor, and by morning, they were almost afloat in a small lake!

We spent the day camped by the Chore River while drying our soggy belongings on sticks over smoky fires. Smoky clothing smelled much better than sweaty or mildewed clothing. Steve and Larry went with Favorite Joven to see if they could figure out where we were on the Chore River, relative to our Víbora River base, while Straight Hair, Wooly Hair, Jack, and I went up to check the gifts we had left at the packs. We had hung a machete at our first campsite. It was gone. The gifts and nomad packs were gone. We had also left a lance-tipped arrow of Wooly Hair's as a gift. It had also been taken.

When we saw that the packs were gone, we also saw evidence that they had found the hard candy and began eating it immediately as wrappers were scattered around on the ground. Later, Larry told us that the nomads had tried both hard candy and sugar on the failed contact three years previously. Evidently, the candy was a real treat to them. The hostiles had headed north, leaving a well beaten down trail we should be able to follow. The occasional clear cellophane candy wrapper also indicated where they had traveled.

After looking the area over and determining that we were two kilometers north of where our Víbora River gift trail came out on the Chore River, we went on the radio and reported to both the Víbora and Chimoré bases, letting them know where we were and what our plans were. The fellows on the Víbora informed us that the day we had spent ambushing the nomad's belongings gifts had been taken on the trail between the Víbora and the Chore Rivers. As we had been waiting near their packs, they had been busy taking gifts from our trail two kilometers away! Our coworkers at the Víbora replaced the gifts and would inform us by radio if anymore were taken.

We planned to spend the rest of the day, Monday, where we were, allowing the nomads time to calm down before following them. Our guides were once again showing reluctance to follow their hostile relatives, fearing, among other things, an ambush along the trail. I told Straight Hair, "I'll walk first with you second so you can tell me where to go if I can't follow the trail."

We were excited about what God was doing with the nomads receiving gifts not only along our gift trail, but also the many we had left in their packs. Surely, they would understand that we wanted their friendship. Even so, we planned to stand guard duty throughout the night as was now our custom. We didn't want any shootings to destroy what might well be our last opportunity to spare these people from destruction by outside forces.

The next morning, we were on our way by 8:00 a.m. and soon passed the log where we had discovered the nomad's packs. I was going first, and within half an hour, we found where the nomads had camped the night it rained so heavily. They had stayed nearby, no doubt, to retrieve their packs when possible. The rain shelters they had built were covered thickly with an abundance of palm leaves, much heavier than usual, but they hadn't fenced in their camp with palm leaves as they often did. In many places along their trail, candy wrappers indicated where they had passed, and at one place, they had stopped to make a new ax handle, possibly for the ax-head we had left for them by their packs. We followed their well beaten down trail through dense jungle thick with brush and vines until 11:00 a.m., seeing many places where they had cut palm heart and a spot where they dug an armadillo out of the ground. They had also chopped honey out about fifteen feet up on one tree without felling the tree balancing, doubtless, on a very small horizontal sapling next to it while doing the chopping. An amazing feat!

We also saw, even before finding their first camp in the morning, places where some of them had remained, watching their back trail, setting ambushes for those of us who might come along after them. Repeatedly throughout our travels, several times a day, we stopped, committed ourselves the job we were doing and our guides to God in prayer. We also prayed regularly over decisions, trusting Him to give guidance as needed. Around 11:20 a.m., we crossed a stream on a fallen sapling and once again found where they had waited in ambush.

This stream was flowing swiftly, and the "bridge" they had built, the sapling spanning the stream, had to be repositioned by Straight Hair and Favorite Joven since it had drifted out of position. Straight Hair fell in the creek while doing that.

It seemed that we might be nearing another of their camps as we kept seeing where they had stopped to build up the fire they carried. Soon we came to where they had felled another tree for honey and where they had set up a camp with eleven fires. All indications were that this was last night's camp, so the next camp should be active with people! It was 11:50 a.m., and after a short break, we set up the radio to inform Paul Short at the Víbora and Bob Garland at the Chimoré of what we had found and what we planned to do next. Those plans were to stay in this camp until about two o'clock, and then move on, hoping to find the nomads later in the day as they were setting up their next camp. They were keeping a close watch on their back trail as indicated by the several ambush sites we had seen, so we suspected they would see us before we saw them.

It had taken us three hours to travel from their previous camp to this one, so we anticipated two to three hours to their next camp. If we left at 2:00 p.m., we should come on them as they were setting up their next camp, and they might be making enough noise that we could show up without them spotting us first. As we left the abandoned camp, Larry and I began taking turns leading the way with Straight Hair walking second to help us. During my turns to lead,

I intentionally slowed the pace, not wanting to arrive at the nomad camp too early.

The trail was well beaten down and good enough that I could follow it with little help from Straight Hair, and soon we came out into a beautiful area of jungle, much like an open woodland. We passed through older nomad camps of various vintages as we continued along their trail. Now the trail turned, and we began to wonder if we had somehow gotten onto an older trail, one they weren't presently using. We slowed the pace further as we looked carefully until we found signs indicating that the trail was recently used.

At 3:37 p.m., we heard the sound of axes chopping. Two guys chopping trees. We knew then that they were nearby. I said, "Why don't we hide our packs here and have our guides take off their clothing?" When I translated my thoughts into the dialect, the guides suggested we go a little farther before they disrobed for better acceptance by their kinfolk.

As we approached a massive finned tree, Straight Hair remarked, "Here's a good place to leave our packs, guns, and clothing."

Larry, Jack, and Steve were all wearing revolvers, and since we doubted the nomads would recognize those as weapons, they continued to carry those. Our guides removed their clothing and picked up their bows and arrows as we advanced with Larry leading. At Straight Hair's suggestion, we had also removed the baseball caps that we typically wore in the jungle.

At 4:10 p.m., we were boldly walking down the trail when all of a sudden, I saw a black head and brown skin bobbing up the trail toward us. I ducked, hit the deck fast, but she had already seen Larry and hollered, "*Abaa* (enemy)!" and ran.

The whole camp broke into pandemonium as they all started fleeing. Larry hollered, "Come on! What are you guys waiting for?"

I took off running after him. We ran into their camp where there were many kettles sitting on fires. They had just begun cooking. They hadn't even set up camp. They had only had time to build up their fires and begin boiling palm cabbage for their evening meal . They hadn't been there much time at all.

As we ran into their camp, I saw women running for the jungle, some carrying children. I think one of us saw a man running too. I didn't think I should grab women or children, so I didn't. Larry didn't either. We ran through their camp and a little way farther in the direction in which they had fled. The nomads were all hooting to each other in the woods and hollering. We could hear different one saying things like, "Where's Papa?"

Others were hollering, "*Abaa! Abaa!* (Enemy! Enemy)"

There was much hooting back and forth and some whistling. It also sounded like some were calling, "Papa! Papa! (Father! Father!)" but they may have been saying, "*Abaa!*" We could tell they were frightened.

As we had come into their camp, we were all yelling phrases in their language. I could hear Jack and Steve trying out Yuquí phrases along with Larry, mostly calling, "*Dicuateja yo che aiquio* (I'm the one who regards/cares about you)." We went on over to a big tree on the far side of their camp where there was a raised mound of dirt, kind of a clearing, and stood there, calling out phrases to them.

Finally, Straight Hair told us (the foreign missionaries) all to be quiet, so we sat down and let the guides call as he requested. George became courageous at this point, contrary to his prior character on the trip (In a testimony weeks later, he told us that God took away his fear at that point). He, Straight Hair, and one of the other guides went down into the woods toward where the nomads had fled and began calling out to them, attempting to initiate a conversation. We four men with clothing (such was the distinction the nomads later made) went back to the now abandoned camp, sat down, joined hands, and prayed. We poured out our hearts to God, asking him to give a friendly contact and to protect our guides whom we could hear but not see.

We heard our guides calling to the jungle dwellers, and they began to get responses. They asked the other Yuquí, "*Taso nde saa* (Let me come to you)." We couldn't hear all of what was going on, but we could hear a portion of it. After a while, maybe fifteen minutes (time was hard to judge), they came slowly back accompanied by a group of nomads, a fair-sized group of men and even some women and girls. As Straight Hair brought them up, he pointed to us and said, "See! They are not *abaas* (enemies)*!* They are our others! They are just like us! They aren't nationals!"

One dark-skinned girl, whom we later referred to as Giggles, looked at us and laughingly said, "They wrap their feet." She thought that was humorous, us wearing shoes.

We also were smiling too broadly for their liking, and they commented on that. We kept our hands in sight and sat there quietly, letting our guides interact with their kinfolk. Pretty soon, quite a crowd had gathered. One was a tall, dangerous-looking light-skinned guy holding a very hefty bow and bleeder-tipped arrow with a look that seemed to indicate he would have liked to try it out on one of us. To me, he looked like one we would need to work on making friends with.

They talked with our fellows for a while, and Straight Hair asked us in the Yuquí dialect for the file so that he could sharpen their axes and machetes as he had promised them he would do. Favorite Joven and another of our guys went to get our packs and the file. The nomads, meanwhile, began bringing their axes and machetes to us to be sharpened. Giggles looked over at Steve and I who were whispering to each other and said to the whole group, "They are talking to each other!"

Straight Hair had told us to keep quiet as some of them didn't appreciate our talking among ourselves. I stood up after a while, but *Tä*, the matriarch of the group, said, "Sit down!"

I sat.

Then she looked at Steve who was half lying down, leaning on one elbow, and said, "Why is he lying down?"

So he sat up.

Our guides leaned their bows and arrows up against the trees, leaving me somewhat concerned as they sat and interacted with the armed nomads. Many of the warriors, at least eight men among them, were standing, holding their powerful bows and lance-tipped arrows as well as other arrows in their hands, while our guides sat there, unarmed. While three of us had revolvers, this group had no idea what those were, so we couldn't count on them to respect the revolvers as guns. It could have been a bad situation since in their thinking, they had the upper hand...except that they considered those of us who wore clothing to be, in some ways, an unknown quantity.

Our guides kept up a running conversation with the nomads as they sharpened their axes and machetes. The other four of us, the clothed ones, sat there listening, and occasionally I would translate some of the conversation for my buddies, although I was having to listen closely to follow the multiple conversations going on around us. We eventually began making a few comments to our guides, sometimes in the dialect, and at other times offered input or guidance in the limited Spanish that I knew Straight Hair understood.

When Straight Hair had offered to sharpen their axes and machetes, he told the nomad leaders that some of us would have to go and retrieve our packs to get the "thing for sharpening (file)." When our two guys, Favorite Joven and someone else went for the file, they came back with the wrong backpack, one that didn't contain the file. Once again, they returned to where our belongings were hidden and this time came back with Jack's pack which contained the file. The file was possibly the most important thing we carried on our trip and seemed to be the most appreciated.

Earlier, we had sharpened machetes and axes when we found their packs behind the log and now, the thing they seemed to desire most was to have their tools sharpened.

With the confusion in locating the file, several of us now had our packs, although not all of us. Straight Hair was busy sharpening their tools while conversing with them, telling them of the abundance of bananas we had at our base and how we would love to give those to them if they would come to visit. Those of us who had our packs began opening those and offering additional gifts to the nomads. We were carrying some of the roasted meat from the tapir Jaime had killed and shared that with them.

As I opened my pack, several of them crowded around, anxious to see what treasures it held. Soon I had given away a knife and a lightweight nylon hammock I carried. The matriarch of the group now joined the crowd around me and was quick to accept my shirts and other cloth items. Meanwhile, the dangerous-looking, tall white man, the one I wanted to butter up, came over, so I offered him my beautiful filleting knife with razor edge, one of my treasured possessions. He accepted that, and Straight Hair warned him not to cut himself with it. He gave the sheath right back as he had no idea of its use, so I explained to him what it was for and that it would keep the knife sharp. He took it then, but I imagine he threw it away the first chance he had.

By this time, we only had two machetes left. Favorite Joven had just given one of those two away and was preparing to give the last one—mine—away when I stopped him, explaining to the nomads that we had to have one for setting up camp. I took my machete back, although they kept asking for it and wanted it badly, especially the tall guy that I was wanting to befriend.

Now we let them know that we had an abundance of machetes at our Víbora River camp and promised that if they came there, we would give them axes and machetes and repair the broken handles on their machetes.

Two of our guides had gone to bring the last of our packs along with our two rifles. Larry and I were concerned as to what the reaction of the nomads might be to the guns, but they didn't even seem to show awareness of what the guns were. When the guns arrived, Larry moved over quickly, laying one gun down and leaning the other one against a tree where it was clearly visible. They didn't seem to recognize what it was and showed no curiosity.

On the contrary, they showed much curiosity about the revolvers and the mini recorder I had been using to record the contact from the time my backpack had been brought in.

Soon the nomads began expressing that they were very hungry, and we could see evidence of that. They had no meat racks, and we saw little evidence of meat in their camp. Meat was the most important food in their way of life, yet all they were preparing for supper was palm heart they had cut along their travels. In many of their most recent camps we had come through, it appeared that all they had been eating was the occasional turtle, some armadillo, and palm heart, but not much else in the way of meat. They said, "We are really hungry. *The people* (spirits of the dead) are hiding the meat from us continually."

The contact seemed to be going relatively well. No major problems, although we remained alert, and they made it clear they didn't really appreciate us, the people with clothing, around. They still considered us to be "*abaas*," even though Larry and I had taken our shirts off. They were impressed with Larry's physique and called him "*Equitä*," meaning "Big Chest." Finally, about 6:10 p.m., I suggested we back off and go find a place to camp for the night before it was too dark.

The number of nomads with us had been slowly decreasing as they drifted off to camp somewhere nearby but out of sight. We suggested to some of the few who were left that they should let us camp with them, to sleep the same place they did, but they ignored our repeated suggestions. Consequently, excusing ourselves, we said, "Keep yourselves warm" and picked up our packs to leave.

There were still more axes and machetes to sharpen, and our hope was that they'd return in the morning for that reason if for nothing more, so we left some unsharpened. They insisted, "Do it now!"

We replied, "Tomorrow!" No doubt they didn't want to have to come back to us but had to accept our refusal.

We picked up our belongings and headed back down the trail the way we had come. Unbeknown to us, whichever one of us had last been sharpening axes and machetes dropped the file on the ground and walked off, leaving the file behind. Fortunately, the nomads didn't notice our blunder. Now we would do our best to avoid being shot in the night and could only hope that they would be willing to meet with us again the next day.

Down our back trail, about 150 yards, was a large tree with an open area under it, kind of a clearing, and the fringe of bushes around that clearing seemed like a good place to spend the night in hiding. After setting up the radio to let our coworkers at Víbora and Chimoré know that our contact with the nomads had been successful, we prepared for the night. Our goal was to make it difficult for the nomads to find us if they came looking in the night, so we paired off, although Jack had Wooly Hair and Lorenzo with him since there were nine of us.

Larry had Straight Hair to keep him company, Steve had Jaime, and Favorite Joven was with me. Each pair looked for a spot where they could blend in with the bushes or foliage, using no mosquito nets, tarps, or blankets—nothing that would help make us discernible to prying eyes. We lay on the cold, damp ground, quietly swatting mosquitoes as we listened to the night noises and gently poked our companion in the ribs if they dozed off and began snoring. Jack had suggested that instead of setting a guard, we all try to stay awake, so that was our plan.

With no thought for our peace of mind or comfort, the large tree we had chosen to lay under dropped small inedible fruits all night long, adding to the sounds of the jungle and forcing us to listen closely for the stealthy sounds of approaching warriors. If one or more of us were to get shot, it was unlikely that the nomads would have another opportunity to settle down peacefully.

Early in the evening, Larry and I conversed softly with Straight Hair, discussing our plan for the next day, and decided that at 4:00 a.m., we would make our way back to where we had spent the afternoon with the nomads with the hope that they would return to us there. By going early, we thought we had a better chance of avoiding an ambush if they chose to set one. The night dragged on, and I checked my watch repeatedly, anxious to see what the morning might bring.

Eventually, 4:00 a.m. came, but the moon was so bright, we agreed it would be better to wait until five o'clock, once the moon had gone down. Darkness was our ally. At 5:00 a.m. we jumped up, grabbed our backpacks, and headed up the trail by flashlight to within thirty yards of where we had met with them the day before. We had survived our sleepless night!

At daybreak, 5:30 a.m., we walked the few yards on up to the camp they had abandoned the night before and where we had first met them. Immediately, we heard them whistling to us. Our guides began whistling back, but the nomads refused to come to us. One by one, our guides made their way toward the whistling jungle dwellers, calling as they went to let them know they were coming. Soon, those of us wearing clothing were sitting alone in the abandoned nomad camp, wondering what was going on farther into the jungle and with little we could do to help our guides. Time passed, and our level of concern began to reach its peak. Should some of us head down that way?

Before we had reached a decision, some of our guides returned and reported that the contact was going well. The jungle dwellers, especially the womenfolk, had really taken a shine to Favorite Joven, and he was basking in the attention. Now Straight Hair came back and reported that they were meeting quite a distance back in the jungle, and the nomads didn't want the ones with clothes down there. Even so, we impressed on him that the nomads needed to begin accepting us sooner rather than later, so it was decided that I would accompany him down there.

As we started off, he quickly disappeared, leaving me to make my way alone. While the jungle people didn't like very much having me around, I stayed with the group for a lengthy period of time and could see that the contact was going extremely well. The two groups were very happy with each other, laughing, smiling, and joking together.

I had a micro-recorder in my hip pocket and turned it on shortly after joining the party. They were quick to notice the unfamiliar device and commented on the fact that I had it with me again. I pulled it out of my pocket to show it to them, and as one of them reached for it, I said, "Let me show it to you."

He grabbed it from me as he demanded, "Let me see it" and then proceeded to try and tear the case from it.

"I'll show you," I replied as I gently took it from him and showed him how to remove the case. He was satisfied and allowed me to put it back in my hip pocket as I tried to keep my hip with recorder aimed toward the general conversation.

Larry had also suggested I wear his revolver when I went down to join the group, and the gun was a concern to them, although they didn't know what it was. Fortunately, it was strapped in and not easy to get out, but they didn't like the revolver or tape recorder as they were unknowns. *Tä*, the matriarch, asked if I had children, and I let her know that I had a boy, a girl, and another boy. As I stood conversing with them, I smoothed the bangs of one of the men with my hand, and he liked the attention. I had done the same thing the day before as well and knew the gesture was meaningful to them.

I got out my pocket comb and demonstrated what it was for before giving it to someone who showed interest in it. After I had been there for thirty or forty minutes, the matriarch turned to me and said, "*Eso, Equitä* (Go, Big Chest)."

So I left. I went back up to where Larry, Jack, and Steve were waiting and reported to them that the contact continued going well. A few minutes later, Lorenzo came up with a report that right after I left, they had brought ten children out, including at least one baby. Also, another heavyset lady, similar to the other two but younger, showed up. That made a total of twenty-nine people we had counted, although there were doubtless others whom we had not seen, so the group seemed to number close to forty.

During the contact, they twice brought up the subject of the barking dog at our base. It seemed the dog was a hindrance to friendship with them and would need to be flown out.

Our guides continued encouraging them to come to us at the Víbora River, because we could feed them and shoot meat for them, and they were excited about that. They said, "We are not getting meat. We're hungry." They kept repeating this theme. You could see in their camps also that they were not getting adequate meat. It seemed that in God's perfect timing, He sent us at a time when they might sense a need for us in a way they hadn't felt before, and I began to feel optimism that they might eventually show up at our camp. Progress was being made!

During the contact, while I was down there with them, the matriarch came up to Favorite Joven and began stroking his stomach and crying over him at the same time. She seemed to be equating him with one of their people who had died and now came back reincarnated and accepted him very well. The young ladies had by this time lost their fear and were beginning to crowd around our guides, and it looked as if they were seeing them as potential husbands.

By 9:00 a.m., the group finally told our guides to leave and go back to the Víbora, promising that they'd come to see us there. Because of the hunger they were currently experiencing, we were confident they were sincere in their promise. Now all our guides came back to where "the ones with clothing" were waiting and let us know that the nomads had asked our team to leave. We wanted to establish credibility with them by honoring their request, so we picked up our belongings and headed down the trail toward home, excited about the successful trip.

We hightailed it for home, realizing we had a good chance of making it all the way to the Víbora base that same night, which we did. For me, the hike was long and difficult as I had been sick for two days with a sore throat and high fever. The night on the ground in the damp, and shivering uncontrollably while feverish hadn't helped at all. Favorite Joven and I had spent much of the night trying to cuddle together to keep at least a little bit warm. At least when we lay close together, my uncontrollable shaking stopped.

We were in a hurry to get home and moved along nicely until we realized that Favorite Joven and Jaime were no longer with us. Earlier, they had mentioned to Larry that they had dropped a hat and wanted to go back for it. He told them not to go, but they chose to go anyway. For almost thirty minutes, we sat and waited with ever-increasing concern for them as they searched for the hat. Had they encountered the nomads and been shot? Eventually they returned and we hurried on our way.

Shortly after passing the Indian camp where we had eaten lunch the day before, we stopped to cook a lunch of rice with a double ration of soup mix for flavoring. No need to conserve rations as we hoped to be home before nightfall.

As we neared the Chore River, we turned south to intersect one of our gift trails, which we then followed to the river. After wading across the river, we followed the trail the last four kilometers to the Víbora River base where we arrived happy but exhausted around 5:00 p.m. A hot shower provided by Wallace Pouncy relaxed my tired and stiff muscles before I collapsed into bed for a refreshing night's sleep.

Waiting for the Nomads

While our hope was that the nomads would soon appear at our Víbora River base, based on their past record, we knew it was more likely they would not come. Even so, our Yuquí guides, their families, and I spent the next two weeks waiting for their appearance before being flown home to the Chimoré River by Joe Kemper of SAM Air (South American Mission). Four flights in a Cessna 206 were necessary to complete that mission. Now we would settle back into our normal routines at the Chimoré while waiting for the missionaries at the Víbora base to call for our help if and when the jungle dwellers showed up at their clearing. They would need our help as none of them spoke more than a few phrases of the language.

Two more weeks went by. It had now been one month since our successful encounter with the nomads, and we were all anxious to follow up on that friendly encounter. Since they hadn't appeared, a strategy meeting was held at the Rio Víbora. Mission leadership flew in, and I accompanied them to the Víbora where we met with the team there. The decision was made to give the nomads four more weeks, and if they hadn't shown up by the third week of November, we would once again go looking for them.

As the third week of November approached, the rains began a month earlier than usual, and soon the rivers were uncrossable, except by boat. The nomads would be unable to approach the Víbora River base as the Chore River would be impassable. It would also be too challenging for us to go looking for them as our Yuquí guides didn't know how to swim. Now we would need to wait for the rains to slow and water in the rivers to go down.

Another month went by, and the waters receded slightly so our team assembled at the Víbora, ready to look for the nomads. Before we even left camp, heavy rains began again, and the mission was aborted. The Yuquí guides and I flew back to the Chimoré to wait for the weather to improve.

The day after we left, Wallace, Paul, Steve, and Grant headed out the trail leading from the Víbora River to the Chore River for a routine check of the gifts along the trail. It was unlikely that the nomads had been in the area since the Chore River was swollen with rainwater, and as the men approached the Chore River, they were talking in normal or slightly louder than normal voices. Above the sound of their voices, first Grant, and then the others, heard talking. They looked across to where our gift trail continued on the far bank of the Chore, and there stood a group of nomads.

The swollen river and forty-yard distance precluded crossing, except by boat or swimming. Even so, the two groups of people called back and forth as our men began throwing bananas and other gifts across the river and pantomimed, since none of them spoke the language, that they would return the next day. After a forty-five-minute contact with a group of fifteen nomads, the missionaries headed enthusiastically homeward, anxious to share their excitement with the rest of us.

Only the day before, Straight Hair, Favorite Joven, Wooly Hair, and I had flown back to the Chimoré from the Víbora, anticipating that the nomads wouldn't come to us and that we couldn't go looking for them because of the high water. While we had been there at the Víbora, preparing to go into the jungle looking for them, God's plan was to bring them to us.

As soon as Grant and the others arrived back from their encounter with the nomads, they turned on the radio and were able to talk to pilot Steve Valentine of SAM Air as he was flying to our mission boarding school. After dropping his passengers at the school, Steve flew directly to our Chimoré base.

At the Chimoré, Bob Garland and I were walking down the trail from his house, discussing the situation at the Víbora, not knowing that the missionaries had seen the nomads a few hours earlier. I had just expressed to Bob that I thought I should be at the Víbora since they needed someone who could talk to the nomads if they showed up there. Right about then, we heard the sound of the approaching airplane, and Steve landed. We walked over to the airstrip to meet Steve as he taxied in and shut the engine down.

After explaining to us about the encounter with the nomads at the Chore River, he said, "If we can get off the ground within thirty minutes, I can take two loads today;" which would mean one load with the men and a second load with Yuquí wives and families. We rushed around as Bob did a masterful job helping organize the first flight before preparing the second flight. Within minutes. we were on our way back to the Víbora River, only one day after we had flown home.

The next morning, we arose at the early hour of 4:00 a.m. to make the four-kilometer trek to the Chore River. Straight Hair, Favorite Joven, and Toughy had accompanied me from the Chimoré. Now we filled our packs with bananas and manioc. The manioc had been flown in with us from the Chimoré while the bananas were from the Víbora base. By 7:00 a.m., we arrived at the Chore, and I laid down in the little shack we had there to take a nap. Soon, others followed suit.

Grant was watching the clearing on the far side of the river closely, and shortly after 9:00 a.m. we heard him say, "Here they come."

Sure enough, here came the nomads, slowly emerging from the jungle onto the bank of the Chore River. What a sight! How many years had we waited for this to become a reality, them coming to us of their own volition! The warriors stood there, gripping their bows and arrows as people of assorted ages clustered around them. There were more than twenty of them, although I don't think any of us counted their number on that first contact.

Soon we had built a palm-log raft and, after paddling it across the river, tied a rope from a tree on the far side of the river to a tree on our side. Now the raft could be moved back and forth across the Chore, hand over hand, along the rope. We had tried paddling the raft across the river, but with the swift current, the unwieldy raft ended up too far downstream. Hand over hand along the rope was the better method.

We began taking foodstuff across to them, and they were quite pleased with all the gifts. For two and a half hours, we interacted with them before explaining that we were going to head home and do some hunting and fishing so we could bring meat back to them the next day. They were overjoyed with the abundance of bananas and manioc and expressed their pleasure at the thought of the meat we might bring the next day.

The next morning, we were once again on our way at 4:00 a.m. and any hope for a brief nap at the Chore River was dispelled immediately upon arrival as I heard someone say in Yuquí, "Here they come."

I'm pretty sure it was Rosa, Favorite Joven's wife, as she had accompanied us along with Toughy's wife, Justina. It had been necessary to use a canoe to get the women across the first gully near our Víbora base as the water was quite deep, but it was well worth the extra effort as they became an immediate asset when the nomads appeared. Rosa wasn't at all shy and was soon chatting playfully and flirtatiously across the river with her newly met kinfolk.

I had brought along a movie camera, hoping to film some of these early contacts and, since I hadn't had opportunity to set up the tripod before the nomads appeared, had to wait until their attention was diverted, watching our men raft across the river before setting up the camera. Even so, some of them noticed me setting up the strange device and seemed to be somewhat concerned.

I left the tripod where it sat, and later, after they lost interest in it, moved it to a better location right on the river bank where we could shoot pictures of the raft, the nomads on the bank, our men passing out gifts, and the whole contact scene. Soon I had taken fifteen minutes of footage, and my five rolls of film were used up.

The contact was going well, and with the picture-taking done, I rafted across to join the group on the far side of the river who were continuing to interact with the nomads. We kept at least two of our men and the two Yuquí wives on the Víbora side of the river at all times as a rearguard, and so the nomads would think twice before starting anything on their side of the river. The two men kept busy, preparing bags of bananas and manioc which they continued to send over by means of some of our fellows who were shuttling back and forth across the river on the raft. Straight Hair made numerous shuttles back and forth while Curt made quite a few as did Paul Short. Grant came over and made himself useful, sharpening axes and machetes for them for which they were very appreciative.

We had learned from experience with the first group of Yuquí we befriended that cooking kettles of rice or corn was an excellent way to keep the nomads around while we interacted and built a friendship with them. Sitting around waiting for the food to cook while talking together gave them something to look forward to. Now I filled an aluminum cooking kettle with rice, sugar, and water and took it across, explaining that we were going to cook food to share with them.

I sat by the fire, chatting with a few of the nomads, and about that time, the raft arrived from the other side of the river, diverting our attention momentarily from the kettle. The nomads and I all stood to see what was arriving on the raft, and when I turned to sit back down, the kettle was gone. Stolen! Loudly, in the dialect, I raised the cry, saying, "They took the kettle as they shouldn't have." Then in Yuquí, I told Grant, while signaling with my hands since he didn't understand the language, "Stop sharpening." First, though I proclaimed loudly in dialect, so I could be heard on both sides of the river, "Don't bring anything else from the other side of the river." Then, directing my attention to the nomads, I said, "Bring my kettle back or we won't give you any more food."

Favorite Joven and Toughy were quick to come to my aid, telling the nomads, "The kettle has to come back or else."

They all realized that we meant it, and the nomads began whistling toward the forest, beyond the riverbank where we stood. In no time at all, the kettle was brought back still with the rice and water in it and was placed back over the fire to continue cooking. Favorite Joven took over and began tending the kettle, watching it closely. God had brought us through an incident that could have turned deadly, and the situation had been tense for a few minutes.

One or two of them had grabbed up their bows and arrows, rustling them around and muttering. After the kettle came back, the old lady, matriarch of the group, turned to me and said, "Leave!"

This was not the right time to bow to her anger, so I replied, "I've got to stay and finish cooking the rice so we can teach you to eat it, then I'll go."

Failing with me, she tried to force one of my companions to leave, but we all stayed, again letting her know that we needed to cook the rice and teach the people how to eat it. Now my years of hard work learning the Yuquí language were paying dividends. Without the language, this incident could easily have been the end of our friendship with this band of nomads. Also, the Yuquí from the Chimoré who were working with us, people who understood what we were trying to accomplish, were able to step into the situation and back me up, explaining with clarity to the nomads the need for them to return the kettle. Thank God for a positive ending to a precarious situation!

And that wasn't the only tense standoff of the morning. Later, Curt came over on the raft with a large bag of hard candy, intending to share it with all the nomads. By now, for use among ourselves in identifying the nomads, we had begun putting names on them. As Curt arrived with the bag of candy, Macho, a tall, muscular, white fellow who looked unpredictable and dangerous (hence the name Macho) went down to the raft as Curt arrived, grabbed the bag of candy, and attempted to take it from Curt by force.

In God's providence, I happened to go down at the same time and came to Curt's aid, telling him to hang on tight and not let Macho take the candy by force. In dialect, I called out to Toughy to join us, saying, "Take the hard candy and give it out to *all* the people."

Curt relinquished the bag to Toughy who was able to convince Macho to let go of it. As Toughy distributed the candy, Macho ended up with a fistful of the sweet delights and was soon sitting on a log, grinning from ear to ear as he popped candy contentedly into his mouth. His enjoyment was obvious. Much like a spoiled child, it didn't take much to make him happy, but beware if he became angry.

Three hours passed, and the interaction between our team and the nomads was going well, a good time to let them know we were heading home to hunt and fish for them. Curt went across the river to see how our companions felt about that. Much better to leave while they were enjoying our company as they would be more likely to return tomorrow. Soon the missionary team was all back on our side of the river, saying our farewells to the nomads and assuring them that we would be back early the next day. "Keep warm by your fire," we shouted across the river, and they gave the same reply.

Rosa and Justina had both been a big asset, and while neither of them had crossed the river to meet face-to-face with the nomads, both had spent much time talking and joking with their kinfolk, building rapport. As we hiked the four kilometers back to our camp we had much to talk about and were all exhilarated that the stressful time had gone so well.

We slept late the next morning, not getting up until 4:15 a.m., breakfasted, and then headed for the Chore River. Although we had hunted and fished after arriving home the previous day, we hadn't been successful in getting meat. We had been keeping two live red-footed tortoises for just such an emergency. Added to that, Favorite Joven took part of an armadillo and a piece of fish he had been preserving on his smoke rack. The fish would be for Tapir, a nomad woman who had recently given birth and whose food could not be shared by others due to cultural considerations.

Both Rosa and her husband, Favorite Joven, had worked hard on two previous contacts to build a friendship with Tapir and wanted to give her some special treatment. Tapir's husband was a warrior we were calling Smiley among ourselves, so by giving Tapir special attention, we were also ingratiating ourselves with Smiley. He almost always had a big smile on his face, and we wanted to keep it that way.

As we hiked to the Chore River, Straight Hair and I led the way, hoping to shoot additional game along the way. While we scared up monkeys, we were unable to shoot any of the agile creatures.

It was almost eight o'clock before we arrived at the river, and the nomads were there waiting for us, seemingly in a good mood. We had left our rope for the raft strung across the river and had told them previously not to take the rope as we would need it daily to cross. Something didn't look right about the rope, and my first thought was that maybe they had cut off a portion of it. We were desirous they learn to respect our property as eventually, especially when they began coming into our base camp, we would lose control and maybe our lives if there wasn't a mutual respect.

We briefly discussed the rope, and Straight Hair volunteered to cross the river first to see what had changed with the rope. His report was encouraging. The nomads had retied the rope on the far side but hadn't taken any of it. Straight Hair untied the rope and stretched it taut as it had stretched from much use the day before and then retied it tightly before rafting back to our side of the river. Now the gift-giving could begin.

The nomads had been observing with interest all of our actions, and now their excitement began to build as they watched our men begin to bag gifts to be taken across. One of the tortoises was among the first items taken across by Straight Hair.

Steve Parker and Joe Ed Pouncy had brought hook and line along and began fishing, something the nomads had never seen done before in this manner. They were amazed and thrilled as they watched the two men pull small catfish from the muddy water and send them across to them on the raft.

Straight Hair's wife, Loida, had accompanied us to the Chore, bringing their son, Moses, as well as her sister, Susan. Thirty minutes into the contact, Loida turned to me and said, "They're upset over there. They're tightening their bowstrings (a bad sign), and they want Wallace to leave. They said he's trying to take their pet monkeys and wanting to kill their monkeys and eat them."

Some of the nomads had pet monkeys sitting on their shoulders or heads or moving around from nomad to nomad. Wallace had just been showing what we would consider to be "normal" attention to the pets, but the nomads were interpreting it otherwise. Once Wallace understood their concern, he stopped paying attention to their monkeys, but they continued insisting he leave, and the overall mood was more tense than it had been. While we wanted to show respect to the nomads, we also didn't want them to dictate all of our actions, so we told Wallace to stay there for the moment and later, after time passed, he came back to our side of the river of his own volition, not in response to their earlier demands. They were still resistant to having those of us who were non-Yuquí around, but we were trying to get them to accept all of us.

As Wallace returned to our side of the river, I went across to their side, taking an empty kettle as well as rice and a bag of sugar. Once I joined the group, I filled the kettle with river water, and they watched as I added rice and a generous amount of sugar. By now, they knew what sugar was as we had given them some on more than one previous contact, and they began clamoring for the leftover sugar. They held out broad leaves and palm leaf base containers as I emptied the bag, giving the sugar to them before carrying the kettle up to the fire and saying, "Let's get it on."

As I sat down by the fire to watch the rice cook, *Tä*, the chief's mother and matriarch of the group, said, "Leave!"

I replied, "No, I have to sit here and wait for the rice to boil."

"Well," she said, "you go down and catch some fish. Go get some fish! You go down and fish too!"

Again I said, "No! I have to stay here and let the rice cook."

Once again, they were only desirous of having their kinfolk around, whereas we were trying to force them to accept us, "the ones who wear clothing," although this description was no longer accurate as our guides and their wives were now all fully dressed. Even so, the distinction between Yuquí and non-Yuquí was obvious.

The matriarch continued, insistent, trying to push me down to the river. Now Paul arrived on the scene, and she continued, unrelenting, wanting both of us to go fishing. I replied, "We didn't bring the things with which to catch fish (hooks)," although both she and I knew this wasn't about fishing but rather about removing us from the scene. Paul promised her he would bring his fishing line tomorrow, and both of us, over her protest, sat down by the fire.

The atmosphere seemed tense, so I sat with my back to the river, facing the woods as I felt some need to be watching for danger from that direction. For one thing, Macho had disappeared, and as he seemed to be an unpredictable individual, I had been trying in vain to locate where he had gone.

Paul was sitting beside me, trying out some of the few Yuquí phrases he knew when Straight Hair came up and said to Paul in Spanish, "Don't talk, remain quiet!" Then he said, "It would be better if you went back across the river."

I encouraged Paul to leave, and he went back across the river. Now I realized that there was an Indian behind the palm tree directly in front of me, and it was Macho. I had been asking the nomads where he was, and he had been there all the time behind a pachuba palm with a wide root system that hid him from my view. He had his bow as well as a bleeder-tipped arrow and a barbed arrow with him. Now that I knew where he was, I let him know, "You are the one I have been looking for. I wanted to bring sugar over for you, but I didn't see you here, so I didn't bring it."

That upset the small group of nomads sitting nearby, and they informed me, "He can't eat sugar. He has a boil (sweets such as sugar, honey, candy, etc., can't be eaten when you have a boil)."

The previous day, he had tried to take the whole bag of candy, and now today, he couldn't have sweets. Straight Hair took control, directing his voice to all the people around us and particularly to Macho behind the palm, since he also sensed we were in a dangerous situation, saying "We are going to leave. You are threatening to shoot us. You have that man hidden back there with the bow and arrows. We don't want to be shot. We are going to just leave and go," he said. Then he said, "Send him away!"

Nobody moved, so Straight Hair said, "Okay, that's it. We are going to leave. We don't want to get shot." Again, he said, "Send him away!"

Macho stood to his feet. He had a childlike temperament but was a big, husky, white-skinned fellow with broad face and broad shoulders...and a big black bow. He appeared volatile, like he could just explode in a moment and kill you and yet childish at the same time. Now he acted as if his feelings were a little bit hurt. He took his bow and arrow and started to leave. I had mentioned about wanting to give him sugar, but he couldn't have that, so I asked loudly, "What could we do for/give to him?"

Someone, I think it was Straight Hair, answered, "Bananas."

Macho left, and a short time later, I heard what sounded like a couple of arrows clack over to my left, so I looked over there. The nomads could tell that I was investigating the noise. They said, "What are you looking at?"

I said, "I heard a noise over there."

They started reassuring me.

When the next load of bananas came over, Straight Hair made a point to bring the food up to the fire where I was sitting. Then he asked, "Where is he?"

So they called Macho, and he came out. Straight Hair gave him the bulk of the bananas from that bag. When Macho had gone away, Sunday, one of the young, nicer looking girls, fourteen to sixteen years of age, commented proudly but with a touch of sadness, possibly so I would feel sorry for him, "That's *Yagua* (either a grown brother or the husband of a sister)."

After that, each time Macho came to get bananas from Straight Hair, Macho would hand them to Sunday to take care of for him. Eventually, Macho's mood improved to where he stayed with us and sat down by the fire. I was standing there, and he called me over and said, "Come sit here." I went over and sat down with him. From then on, he was in a very good mood.

We talked and talked and had a very excellent time together. The atmosphere of the whole contact changed. Straight Hair had asserted his authority, and the group responded to his leadership.

Soon, Macho and I were talking about hunting and a wide assortment of other subjects, and in the process, he asked about the dog at our camp. "Do you still have a dog?"

I assured him that we didn't, that it was dead, and then I realized I shouldn't have said that, because it wasn't really dead but had been flown out. But I stayed with that story rather than try and explain the intricacies of our flights. Changing the subject, I commented, "You are probably a real good hunter."

At that, he got all excited, and I could tell that hunting was his "thing." It was quite clear that he was an excellent hunter. After talking about hunting for a time with his excitement building, he said, "*Piri ya* (Let's go hunting)."

I said, "I'll go hunting with you. We'll go hunting together one of these days." Then I tried to explain about our guns. I told him that I would have to show him our guns first and help him lose his fear of those and the noise they make, and then we would go hunting together.

With the mood of the contact now going well, it was time to begin ending it for the day. We rafted the rest of the goodies across and gave most of the sugar away; also, half a bag of candy, since earlier on in the contact, they had asked for sugar and candy, and we had promised to give those out around noon. They were quite cooperative.

Sadly, some of those we had seen on previous contacts had not shown up today, and they later told us that the matriarch, *Tä*, was taking most of the things we were giving away and hoarding them for herself, so some of the people got upset and traveled farther away, saying, "When she dies, we'll come back."

Also, Tapir, who was "behind leaves (time of month)" along with some other young ladies who were hidden off to one side of where we gathered around the fire had been complaining that we, especially Paul, but all of us to a certain extent, breathed heavily, and sometimes (especially Paul) would stick his mouth in the water and make funny sounds. The people said that Tapir was afraid of the noises we made and had left on account of that. They asked Straight Hair and Favorite Joven to tell us to stop making funny sounds with our mouths in the river water, because Tapir was afraid of them.

Slim, one of the taller, white-complected men, had spent much of the morning flirting remotely from across the river with Rosa, Favorite Joven's wife. They traded teasing coquettish comments back and forth, enjoying the banter. Shortly before we crossed back to our side of the river to leave, I told him, "Make sure you hoot (yell loudly) when you come to our camp to get gifts so we can bring out more gifts for you."

He responded, "Like this?" He hooted. It was a beautiful hoot. In fact, he liked it so much himself, that he stood up and went down to the edge of the river and hooted across to the ladies to show off to them. It was a resounding hoot that would carry far through the jungle.

They responded, joking and laughing with him, and thought it was quite a lovely hoot too, so he carried on doing that for a good while.

Later, after we returned to our camp on the Víbora, we had a strategy meeting regarding our handling of the contact. One thing we decided was that we would take a two-day break from visiting with the nomads. We would tell that that we were going to sleep three nights first and then return to visit with them. We wanted to see what their response would be and see if they would follow through in coming back to us if they said they would. It would give them and us a chance to hunt and fish before returning to see each other. Each encounter with the nomads was laden with tension and a high level of stress as each group learned to trust the other. A break would give all of us a chance to relax mentally and be refreshed.

Straight Hair and Toughy went out hunting and came back with two capuchin (whistler) monkeys and a tree anteater (the smaller variety of anteater). Grant and I went fishing, and each of us caught a nice fish. His tiger-striped catfish weighed in at twenty-eight pounds, and mine was eight pounds lighter. Fish, monkeys, and an anteater—the nomads should be pleased with this amount of meat.

The next morning, we got up at 4:30 a.m., loaded our packs, and headed for the Chore. As gifts, we were carrying the tiger-striped catfish Grant had caught and the catfish I had caught. We hadn't cleaned the innards from mine since it was full of roe, fish eggs, and we knew they would value it more for the roe. We planned to hold the lovely fish up and show it to them from across the river before taking it over. They should be suitably impressed.

On our way out, Straight Hair found another red-footed tortoise to add to the two capuchin monkeys and tree anteater. Added to the bananas, manioc, sugar, and a few other odds and ends, we should be able to show the nomads that it was worthwhile for them to have friendship with us.

When we arrived at the Chore, the nomads were waiting, and the rope was intact, so we followed through with our normal delay of talking to them from our side of the river, telling them of all the goodies we had brought. This also gave us a chance to read their mood of the day, which could vary widely. On this day, Straight Hair was quick to let us know that they seemed edgy, afraid, and unhappy, so he warned us to keep alert. Strangely, once we crossed the river and began talking with them, they were more friendly than usual, jovial and happy.

When I first got over there the matriarch, *Tä*, called me over and wanted me to come and sit with her and visit, which I did. She let me know that Tapir, who had just had a new baby, was hungry and needed certain things. After promising *Tä* that we would take care of Tapir and get things for her, I sat and visited for a while longer with *Tä* and then assisted Favorite Joven as he got started on cooking rice. Speaking in the dialect so the nomads were sure to hear, I said, "Cook it quickly and then have more rice brought over. The people are hungry, so we need to cook a lot for them."

As Favorite Joven squatted by the fire and adjusted the wood as necessary to keep it blazing so the rice boiled vigorously, the nomads squatted around him, chatting and visiting. He and his wife, Rosa, had quickly become two of the favorites of the people with whom we were building friendship and were a tremendous asset to our team.

As the rice cooked, Grant kept busy, shuttling back and forth on the raft, bringing bags of bananas, manioc, and meat while Wallace was busy on the nomad side of the river, fishing. Eventually, Grant joined the group by the fire, trying to interact with the nomads. Initially, they wanted nothing to do with him, and almost as soon as he sat down, *Tä* said, "*Eso* (Go away)*!*"

Grant accepted her dismissal, returning to the raft, and the next time he came across with bananas and manioc, he carried some of the food over and gave it to her personally. With this overture, she allowed him to sit with the group for a period of time. Acceptance of "those who wore clothing" by the nomads was coming, but it would take time, although it seemed that my grasp of the language and the fact that the nomads could see that I often gave instructions to others quickened their acceptance of me. They were accustomed to the master-slave relationship and would expect us to have a similar culture. It would take time for them to understand that we worked on the principle of mutual respect.

While I was sitting with *Tä,* she started asking about my mother and my wife. She questioned, "Why didn't your wife cut your bangs?" My hair was a little long in front by their standards, and I didn't have proper Yuquí bangs. "Where is a knife?" she wanted to know.

So I handed her my belt knife. She found it too dull and couldn't cut my hair with it. A little later, she was still unhappy with my haircut and once again insisted on trying to cut it. She called another older woman over to assist, and I handed them my pocketknife, which was sharp enough to shave with. They tried it and managed to saw some hair off, leaving me with a set of Yuquí bangs before handing my knife back and commenting, "It's too dull." It seemed that little by little, I was being accepted as a member of the tribe and needed to look the part.

Later during this contact, I was standing on the riverbank with some of the younger nomads, looking to the west with the open sky beyond. We were talking about bananas and manioc, the perfect opportunity to tell them about our faraway farm at the Chimoré River and how the airplane, the thing that flies through the sky, brought food for us from there. I worked into the conversation how that beyond our faraway farm, lots of white-lipped peccary roamed. One of the young ladies asked, "Have you gone up in the sky in an airplane?"

I assured her I had, and she responded, "How do you stay in it and not fall out."

I explained as best I could. They seemed quite interested in the airplane, so Straight Hair explained more about the airplane and told them that beyond our camp on the Víbora River, they would hear an airplane landing and taking off. "Don't be afraid if you hear it when you are coming to our camp. It brings people, bananas, manioc, sugarcane, and other things that we ask it for and will bring things for you if we ask it to."

They were thrilled with the idea of someone or something bringing requested items for them.

The contact was going exceptionally well. It had taken about an hour to get the first kettle of rice cooked and distributed, and then Favorite Joven started on the second kettle. By then, we were finishing up bringing over the gifts we had brought, and they all seemed quite content with the amount of meat and other foodstuff we had provided for them. As the second kettle of rice finished cooking and we were giving it out, we let them know that we would soon be heading back to our camp. We had been with them for two and a half hours.

Before crossing the river to leave, we also explained to them that we would not be coming back the next day but that we would

sleep three nights first and then return to them. We really empha-
sized three nights and worked on it over and over with them, that
we would sleep three, and then come back, and that they should
hunt and fish in the meantime while we did the same near our
camp. We also told them, "If the river begins to drop, come to us at
our camp, and we will give you many more bananas, manioc, and
meat."

They liked that idea and assured us that they would come if the
water dropped enough.

After rafting back to our side of the river, we continued talking
to them across the river on the far side, and I picked up my gun,
preparing to leave. Now one of the nomads said something to our
guides, and Straight Hair turned to me. "They want you to shoot
your gun!" I couldn't believe my ears and had doubts I had heard
correctly, so I looked at Straight Hair for confirmation. Not only
Straight Hair, but other Yuquí said, "That's what they want."

So I hollered over and asked them myself, and they said they
wanted me to shoot it. I said, "You really mean that?"

They said, "Yes."

So I said, "I'll shoot it now up into the air. Don't you all be
afraid. Here I go." And I shot it up into the air.

They all jumped, kind of scared like. I thought that was that,
but then they said, "Shoot it again."

So I said, "Don't be afraid."

They told me which way to aim it, and after repeating to them
not to be afraid, I shot it again for them. We shot three times right
there on the riverbank, and they enjoyed the last two shots very much.
Then as we left and were a short distance out into the jungle, Straight
Hair said, "Now shoot it again." So we shot a total of four shots that
they could hear. We had earlier assured them that when they heard
our shots, we were shooting meat for them, that we weren't going
to shoot at them but were shooting meat for them to eat and they
shouldn't be afraid of our guns since they were for shooting meat.
They were quick to let us know that they wanted us to shoot lots of
meat for them with the guns. We were all thrilled to see that fear was

being replaced by friendship and trust. Clearly, progress was being made in our relationship with the nomads.

* * * * *

After our three-night break in meeting with them, we headed out to the Chore to see if they would come to us. Not only had they arrived at the river before our 8:00 a.m. arrival, but they had begun constructing a bridge of saplings across the river. We had also planned to build a bridge, so we brought a chainsaw with us. After finding a suitable tree on the bank of the river, we felled it into the river and, along with their saplings and some of our rope, soon had a crude bridge for crossing the Chore River.

While many of us and them had been working from both sides of the river to construct the bridge, Favorite Joven had been busy on our side of the river, cooking a kettle rice for them. The warriors crossed first, bringing along their bows and arrows and stood around, nervous to be on our side of the river, a little tense, but not too bad. Then we all went over to the small building we had built near the riverbank and began handing out the gifts we had brought along.

While we were in the building, Giggles, one of the young women who had crossed, tried to steal one of our machetes, picking it up surreptitiously and dropping it out a hole in the wall to pick up later. We were able to retrieve the machete, although nothing left unguarded was ever safe, so we had to continually keep an eye on our belongings. One theft could escalate into a permanent break of our budding friendship, and none of us wanted that, so we were ever vigilant.

Once the rice was ready, we sat around the fire, eating and chatting, until one of them said, "We want to go to your camp."

We hadn't expected that but were surprised and pleased, responding "Let's go!"

"We need to bring our belongings over first," Matador, the chief, commented. Some of their people were sent back across the rustic bridge to bring their belongings over.

By 10:00 a.m. they were ready and said, "Let's go."

We gathered up our empty packs, and they picked up their bows and arrows as we headed away from the river along our trail home. What a surprise this would be for our wives and children when we showed up with the armed naked warriors!

Right after leaving the Chore on our way to the Víbora River, we heard squirrel monkeys just off the trail in the trees to our right. Everyone stood waiting on the trail as Toughy and I went off to see if I could shoot some monkeys. My gun was not well sighted in and I had been missing almost everything I shot at recently, but on this day, God directed the bullets, and after only four shots with the .22 rifle, I had downed five monkeys. One of them was a mother with a baby on its back. Toughy gathered up the animals, and we rejoined the group on the trail. God had given us an opportunity to impress them with our ability to easily and quickly provide abundant meat for them, and they had seen the effectiveness of our guns.

Toughy gave out the monkeys to our new friends, making sure that the leading individuals such as Matador, the chief, got the largest, fattest, and most desirable animals.

They followed us all the way to our camp and as we got near, seemed to get tense, but not too bad, stopping at the edge of our clearing.

"We'll bring bananas for you," we offered as some of us went on into the clearing while others remained with them.

After we loaded them down with all the bananas they could carry, they left, but not before informing us, "We won't wait for you to cook rice for us now but will come back tomorrow bringing *yiti* (wife/child) to eat the thing you cook (rice)."

After they disappeared into the forest, we men remained near the edge of our clearing for a while, keeping an eye on the banana patch so they wouldn't return and steal fruit. We wanted them to have all the bananas they could use but needed to teach them to respect other's belongings, and that included our bananas and manioc. They had told us they would be moving to our side of the Chore River to camp and would come to us at our camp. Progress!

We would no longer need to make our early morning expeditions the four kilometers to the Chore River. Although during this first visit the nomads had stayed in the edge of the jungle at the fringe of our camp, some of the missionary wives were able to see them, and Sharon Short captured a few color photos. Now that the nomads had departed for their camp in the forest, most of us men would need to head out, hunting and fishing with the hope of getting an abundance of fish and game to share with the nomads when they came to see us the next day.

Rain was pouring down when the new day dawned, and the weather was quite chilly. It would be surprising if the nomads showed up in this weather, although if they were camped nearby and short on food, they might decide to leave their shelters and warm fires. I spent much of the day sitting in Pouncy's house, keeping an eye on our gift rack while looking at *National Geographic* magazines. My family, wife Vickie and three children, were still living at the Chimoré base but would join me at the Víbora as soon as we could work out housing arrangements. We were more needed here at the Víbora now than at the Chimoré. Without our Yuquí coworkers from the Chimoré and me, the missionary team at the Víbora would be unable to communicate with the nomads.

The gift rack was on the edge of our clearing, and we kept bananas or manioc hanging there all the time, so it was there we expected the nomads to appear. The rack was a hundred yards from the house, and the cinnamon-skinned warriors could easily blend into the shadows of the jungle beyond, so we kept a sharp eye out and often used binoculars to see better.

It was 3:50 p.m. when I thought I saw movement behind the gift rack, so I called Wallace over to look. He confirmed that there were two men moving toward the gift rack. We went out the door to notify Straight Hair that our visitors had arrived and at that precise moment, the nomads hooted to let us know they had come. Straight Hair hooted back to them, letting them know we were on our way as we headed to the rack with a kettle full of water. We had already added salt to the water since they were unfamiliar with it and might be concerned if we added it in their presence. The rice and sugar we carried along to add as they watched. Near the gift rack, we started a fire as some of our guys began bringing bananas and assorted other items out for them.

They began by explaining that they had stayed by their fires, keeping warm while it rained, and went on to let us know that they were camped out where they had made a gift rack on our trail, near the tree that contained the *eresari* (a type of kinkajou).

The contact went well. It was a little strange at first, but not bad as they were all standing by the gift rack and our men were too. I tried unsuccessfully to get everyone to move closer to the fire and sit around it, and after a few minutes, one or two moved slowly toward the fire, and eventually, the rest followed suit. That eased the tension somewhat as they sat around the familiar environment of the fire, chatting.

Straight Hair was able to talk with them some, as did Toughy who was cooking the rice. Two of the young men, Tom and Dick, sat there with us as we cooked and chatted with them. Eventually, near the middle of the contact, Steve suggested he bring his family out and introduce them to the nomads.

Barbara Pouncy had come out earlier, and the Indians had not shown much interest. Now Steve brought his family out, bringing along some fish to make the visit more appealing. The nomads kept wanting to look at little Susie Parker, and she was terrified of them. Her older sister, Raquel, also had a hard time as the nomads began touching her, pawing all over. The nomads were, of course, curious, wanting to touch and see. For us, it was not easy to accept their manner of satisfying their curiosity.

We only cooked one kettle of rice during their short visit but had a kettle of field corn (hominy) already cooked and gave them the cooked corn. Straight Hair ladled it out to one of men, and we let them know that we would cook more for them the next day. Straight Hair also told them that he and some of our guys would be going in the morning down the river to shoot large red howler monkeys and told the nomads not to be afraid if they saw our boat.

Straight Hair had killed and smoked a capybara and brought it out to them, and they were thrilled to get the meat. We told them that we had caught many fish, but all of them went bad since they were so late in coming due to the rain. Now the nomads let us know us that one reason they had moved in closer to us was because they thought they had heard nationals out on the Chore. Whatever the reason for their move, we were thrilled with their growing trust.

Two young ladies, non-married ones (Sunday and Jane), sidled up to Favorite Joven when he showed up, just back from a fishing trip, and cuddled up a little too close to him. One of them also began paying attention to me and started asking for things, cloth especially, and began telling me about the matriarch, *Tä*, and how poorly she was treating the rest of them. As the chief's mother and "queen" of the band, it seemed that *Tä* "lorded" it over the rest of them and was not well-liked.

Overall, the group that had come to us seemed content and told us much about what they had been doing the last few days. Soon Macho began telling a hunting story, and we all listened with enjoyment as he told about shooting *iö* (brown monkeys with gray tails), mimicking the sounds the monkeys made as they fled, the sounds of arrows being fired, and the thumps as arrows impacted the creatures, along with their cries of pain. It would have taken a movie camera to adequately capture the storytelling.

As he mentioned the arrows impacting the primates and their agonized cries, most of his listeners hugged themselves, grinning and making sounds which showed their delight as they visualized the scene he was painting.

The next morning, Grant was having a turn sitting in the chair in Pouncy's house, watching the gift rack, when the nomads showed up at 9:45 a.m. I happened to be in the house with him when he spotted them, and as we exited the house to notify the rest of our team, Wallace showed up from somewhere. The three of us gathered up two kettles, one of rice and one of corn, and headed out to the edge of the clearing to meet our guests.

It looked as if they had brought most of their families, children and wives, including several people we hadn't seen before, most of those being children as well as a young lady about twelve years of age. We dubbed her Spooky among ourselves. The time went fairly well, even though it rained and drizzled off and on. We were overjoyed to see the trust they had shown by bringing small children to our camp, and our Yuquí coworkers were quick to reciprocate by bringing their families out to sit with their jungle relatives for most of the morning.

We put corn and rice over the fire to cook as we boiled up three kettles of rice and one of corn. Our guides brought out all the meat they had and gave it to their relatives. Some of it was still uncooked, so once the corn was cooked, they had Favorite Joven boil up some of the meat in the kettle for them. There were so many conversations going on among the two groups of Yuquí that I had trouble understanding much of what was going on, but it was obvious they were enjoying one another's company.

The slight variations in speech that had taken place during the thirty or more years the groups had been apart made their dialect a little bit challenging to understand at times for those of us from the Chimoré, and they seemed at times to have some difficulty understanding us, but overall, communications were not too hard for the Yuquí, although more so for me as I was less fluent. The differences were minor, considering the years they had been apart.

One noticeable difference in pronunciation was whereas we said *tso* for meat, they used a fronted "t" and then "o"—"*to*"—leaving the "s" out.

It wasn't long until we had given away all the bananas in our two groves, including some stalks that weren't fully developed, yet they continued to ask for more bananas. We gave them manioc, but we were running short of that as well. We would either need to send men by river to buy bananas from Bolivian farms located a day away or have bananas flown in, although with all the rain, that might not be an option.

More of the missionary families came out to be introduced. Paul Short brought Sharon and their two children out. Barbara Pouncy came out again. The Mayer family came, and their young son, Chippy, was a big hit. Macho found Chippy especially interesting and enjoyed teasing him, blowing in his face and playfully tossing a monkey at him. At one point during the morning, one of the pet monkeys belonging to the nomads bit Pedro, young son of one of our Yuquí guides, on the ear. The nomads were quick to scold the monkey and shoo it away.

I returned to my house around 1:30 p.m. and had a bite to eat before going back to rejoin the group at the gift rack. The missionary team had taken turns going in to eat, and throughout the course of the day, all of us had been able to go out and interact with the nomads. We could tell that they had still not fully accepted those of us who wore clothing, so we were determined to spend as much time with them as possible until they accepted our presence. The plan seemed to be working, though at times, it was apparent they didn't appreciate us being with them.

They stayed until 2:30 p.m. and then, as they were leaving, Matador, the chief, informed us, "I'm going far away on an overnight trip to get my pack. I would like some sugar to take with me."

We were quick to oblige his request, not only because he was the leader of the group but also appeared to be eldest son to the matriarch, *Tä*. If those two people were on our side, they could influence the entire band in our favor.

After the nomads departed for the day, I had a talk with Straight Hair and suggested we push to go hunting with them the next day. He had a wise and slightly less risky answer, suggesting that we instead take them out to a bee tree he had spotted not far from our camp and harvest honey together. Honey or meat, either one was of great interest to the jungle people, and honey would be a good place to start. If that went well, in a few days, we could hunt together.

Now we needed to do some fishing and hunting in order to have meat to offer the people the next day, so Straight Hair, Wallace, and I headed upriver in the boat to see what we could find. Later, as we headed home empty-handed, we saw a tapir (like a small head of beef) swimming across the river. Straight Hair fired at it twice, and I got off one shot before my gun jammed. The tapir climbed up the bank out of the water and kept going into the jungle where we were unable to find it.

The 400 pounds of meat a tapir provides would have been a real treat and would have fed all of us, plus the band of nomads, but it was not to be. Maybe another day.

Two days of rain followed, and on the first of those, the nomads failed to appear. No doubt they were huddled around their fires, keeping warm and dry. We had a flight scheduled for the second day to bring bananas and manioc from the Chimoré base, but the flight was canceled, both due to weather and the fact that water was now running across a low spot in the middle of the airstrip. If we hoped to keep the nomads coming to visit us, we desperately needed bananas, so we decided to send Curt and Paul by river to Puerto Grether and buy bananas from the colonists there. It would be a two-day round trip, but with all the rain, at least there would be no lack of water in the rivers.

On the second day, the nomads showed up at 9:00 a.m., a little later than usual. The contact was more relaxed with less tension than normal. We went to the edge of the clearing next to the gift rack and built a fire. The nomads leaned their bows and arrows up against nearby trees and sat down. Macho and Matador, the chief, seemed to have lost their fear of us and lounged comfortably on the ground, waiting patiently as the corn and rice kettles were brought out and the cooking began. Between kettles of rice, they used the rice kettle to boil up some fish we had caught for them.

Steve stood nearby on the bank of the river, fishing, as I sat, talking with the nomads. After a while, some of the nomads drifted off to shoot fish with bows and arrows in a nearby swamp, and I asked those who remained if they would like to try fishing with a hook and line. With the river near the top of the bank, we were unsuccessful in catching fish.

The two groups of Yuquí, which included a number of women, spent much of the day discussing their common ancestors and were convinced that they were close relatives. To me, it was obvious just by looking at them as the family resemblances were notable. They were all thrilled to know that they weren't alone in the world and hugged themselves with joy as they pieced together the relationships.

When the nomads had first arrived, we warned them several times that our boat would be coming down the river and pass us in a few minutes on its way to pick up bananas for them, so when it finally came by, all of them, except Blanca, went out to the river bank to watch it go by. We thought it would be exciting for them to see the boat arrive the next day loaded with bananas as it should impress them with our ability to provide for them and hoped they would return for that event.

Our relationship with the nomads was continuing to improve to the point that it seemed like we should be able to begin hunting with them in the woods. We weren't letting down our guard and continued to wear our revolvers, although they still had no idea that those were weapons. We hadn't yet encouraged them to come into our camp as we thought it better to keep some unknowns until they learned to respect us and our belongings. Better to keep building rapport at the edge of the clearing and begin hunting with them as they learned how we expected them to behave around us.

Before they left for the night, one of the men turned to Joe Ed Pouncy, one of the missionary children. "Shoot or catch something and bring it out for us tomorrow."

Then they told Grant the same thing. They also wanted Grant to bring Chippy out again. Of all the missionary children, Chippy had been the biggest hit and hadn't been at all shy with the nomads.

By the next day, the water on the airstrip had receded to where a flight was possible, so we would be getting bananas and manioc both by river and by air. With the nomads asking for these items on a daily basis, we could never have enough, so we stockpiled them as fast as we could. Months later, they told us that they had been testing us to see if we could really supply all that we promised and had been piling the bananas out in the jungle where many of them rotted. Soon they were convinced that we had the capability to keep them fed, although it might have cost us a few extra flights.

When the nomads showed up, only two young women had accompanied the men to our camp, and they explained that the water in the gully a short distance behind our camp was so deep that none of the other women or children had chosen to cross. However, when they learned that Favorite Joven and his wife, Rosa, would be leaving on the airplane to fly back to their camp at the Chimoré, they sent one of the slave boys and a slave girl hurrying back out to their camp to call the older ladies, *Tä*, the matriarch, and the other grandma.

These two women had become especially close to Favorite Joven and Rosa and would want to tell them goodbye.

Unfortunately, by the time the two grandmothers arrived, Favorite Joven and Rosa, with their family, had gone to the airstrip to meet their outbound flight. The older ladies showed up just about the time the flight was to land, but as the airstrip was on the far side of the river, they had no opportunity to tell their friends goodbye. We informed the nomads that the flight was headed to our other camp and would be bringing back bananas and manioc for them, so they settled down to wait.

The contact continued very relaxed and easygoing all morning long. We cooked up three kettles of rice early on, and then, when more nomads arrived, cooked two more kettles of rice as well as one of corn. As we sat by the fire, eating and visiting, the flight took off, heading for the Chimoré. The pilot, Steve Valentine, turned left off the end of the runway and flew low, right over us, engine roaring.

A few of the nomads were terrified, leaping to their feet and running for the deep woods, although others kept their cool and continued lying or sitting where they were at. We had explained that the airplane would be noisy as it left but hadn't expected it to fly right over us.

The matriarch, *Tä*, elderly, sickly, and frail, leaped to her feet and was going to take off, fleeing, but Loida grabbed her by her bark skirt and held on for dear life. The old lady was grumbling and wanting to run, but Loida just held on so she never got away. Loida let go once right as Steve cut the power, and once again, *Tä* started to take off, but Loida took hold of her again. A few of the children ran and a couple of men too, but Macho and Matador just stayed put. Macho was lying on the ground. He just lay there coolly and took it.

The flight returned thirty minutes later, and after it had landed, we told them that bananas, sugarcane, and manioc would be brought across the river pretty quickly. As the group was anticipating that we heard the sound of a boat motor, I commented, "Hey, I think I hear the boat coming."

We listened, and then we said, "No, it's an airplane."

They had all jumped up to head for the riverbank, but now we all sat back down. Now we heard the outboard motor again as it hit debris in the river and kicked up, giving a slightly different sound, so we knew it was the outboard. We all got up and dashed to the bank and stood there. In five minutes or so, the boat, loaded with bananas from Puerto Grether, went roaring by, so we told the nomads, "We'll go bring bananas to you."

Now we had both a boatload of bananas and an airplane load, so we would be in good shape for a few days. Steve Valentine, the pilot, came over to get acquainted and accompanied our team as we brought bananas and other gifts out to the edge of our clearing for the nomads, explaining to them that Steve was the one who flew the "firefly (airplane)." Now all the missionaries began carrying bananas out to the edge of the clearing where Straight Hair was busy distributing them, making sure the leaders of the group got what they wanted and that no one was left out. After giving out half a boatload of bananas, we let them know that we would give them manioc the next day.

"The airplane is going to our other camp to bring more food for you and to bring Iroquois and his family to meet you," we explained to the nomads as pilot Steve and a few other missionaries headed back to the airstrip. We were rotating families of Yuquí from the Chimoré in and out so that none of them became too worn out as they helped us build a relationship with their jungle cousins. We also wanted the nomads to see that the group at the Chimoré was larger than their group and hoped to encourage the two groups to settle down together, increasing greatly their chance of survival as a cultural entity and enlarging the gene pool.

The Chimoré band of Yuquí had numbered forty-nine individuals when they first settled at the Chimoré, and it appeared that the group we were now befriending numbered close to thirty-six people.

The next morning, I sat down to enjoy an inviting breakfast of two hot pancakes and then added two generous spoonsful of sugar to my coffee before picking it up to have my first sip. Another rainy morning, so I should be able to enjoy my breakfast before the nomads showed up, it was only 7:35 a.m., and I would be surprised if they showed up before 9:00 a.m. I set the cup down, and before I could take another sip or even have my first bite of pancakes, Wallace called, "The nomads are here." So much for breakfast.

I headed over to notify our Yuquí colleagues that their kinfolk had arrived and then picked up the kettle and rice as I headed out to start a fire near the gift rack at the edge of the clearing. A large group of nomads were standing, waiting for us at the rack, and it was evident from all the freshly woven palm-leaf backpacks what they had in mind. They were going to hold us to our promise of the day before to give them manioc.

The airplane had also brought a limited amount of sugarcane, so we carried all the manioc and sugarcane out and distributed it. We didn't offer more bananas as they had hauled away an abundance of those the previous day. After receiving the foodstuff, they were happy to sit around the fire and talk as the rice cooked. The rice cooked quickly, within thirty minutes, but the corn, even though it had been soaked overnight, took much longer to soften, so we could spend time visiting while watching it boil. We started a second fire and soon had both rice and corn cooking. Wearing no clothing, the nomads seemed to have very tough skin and were much less sensitive to hot and cold than we were. It never ceased to amaze me, though, as the corn cooked, from time to time, one of the warriors would reach his hand into the boiling water and lift out a few kernels of corn, chewing them thoughtfully to see if they were soft enough to eat. He seemed oblivious to the heat of the boiling water.

I had seen the same thing as we made friends with the first group of Yuquí; they seemed much more inured to the boiling water than I was. There was no way I was going to dip my hand into boiling water to pick out some kernels of corn.

Occasionally throughout the day, one or another of the nomads would ask for sugar, bananas, or something else, and we let them know that we would give them sugar before they left and that they could have more bananas tomorrow. They were content with our answer as they had seen that we followed through on our promises. Right about then, Paul Short came out. "Two ducks have landed in the water behind Curt's house," he reported. We had been watching for opportunities to use a gun in their presence, wanting to demonstrate how effective the weapon was in shooting meat.

Straight Hair explained to the nomads, "There are two ducks behind the house. I'm going to shoot them for you. Don't be afraid of the noise."

While they had seen and heard me fire the .22 rifle previously, this would be their first time hearing the blast of a shotgun so nearby. Within a few minutes, we heard four loud explosions, and then Straight Hair rejoined us, carrying two ducks, which he handed to the nomads. It seemed like God so often provided in His perfect timing. We had been looking for the right occasion to demonstrate the effectiveness of the shotgun, and God sent two of His ducks to be sacrificed for that purpose!

Now that they had seen the shotgun in action, Straight Hair thought we should follow up on that, so he told the nomads, "We're going to go in the boat and shoot ducks and turkeys for you. We're going to take the big gun, so don't be afraid of the noise when we shoot."

"Take the little gun (.22 rifle)," the nomads responded.

Straight Hair insisted that they needed the big gun to be effective or they wouldn't go, and after some discussion back and forth, the nomads agreed to the big gun.

Wallace and Straight Hair headed out around 10:00 a.m., and I anticipated they would be gone about two hours. Sure enough, shortly before noon, we heard the outboard motor as they came back. God had guided them to a troop of howler monkeys, some of the larger monkeys in the jungle, and to a guan. Not only did they bring sufficient meat to share with their jungle kinfolk, but they also had enough for their own families. We were thrilled to see how God first brought the ducks so that the nomad could hear the shots nearby and see the ducks produced so quickly and easily, then the guys go hunting for two hours and bring back an abundance of monkeys. God was working step by step to take the fear out of the hearts of the people and to show them that we could provide for them. It was a stress-free day together.

Matador and Macho lounged around, seemingly without a care in the world. Around 10:30 a.m., I came in and got Iroquois' arrows and brought them out for the nomads to see. I used the opportunity to bring my gun out too and have it available in case any animals came around. Some of them asked about it, so I showed it to them, removing some bullets and explaining how they worked. When Straight Hair arrived back from hunting, he brought the shotgun out and showed them the shells from it as well. They seemed suitably impressed.

Early in the afternoon, they picked up their heavily laden palm-leaf packs and hiked off to rejoin their families in the forest.

The new day awakened gray and threatening rain; even so, the nomads arrived at our clearing shortly before 8:00 a.m. Curt went out to start a fire and get the rice cooking while others of us carried out the manioc we had promised them the day before. Although they had already hauled away an abundance of bananas over the past few days, they always wanted more. It seemed they never had enough.

I was pleased when Macho asked if he could take a stalk of bananas he had seen in our plantation, but he was not so pleased when I replied, "It's not well-developed. Let it mature first." He insisted that the two of us go and look at it more closely, which we did, but he was unhappy when I once again told him it wasn't ready to cut.

We had been explaining to them that axes, machetes, and cooking kettles were quite valuable and that if they wanted those, they would need to trade for them. The concept of trading was foreign to them, so Straight Hair explained it to them several times. Now Macho said, "I'd like an ax."

We had designated Wallace as the one to handle trade goods, so I replied, "I'll talk to Wallace about that."

I let Wallace know what was going on, and he headed into our camp to bring out some ax heads. While Wallace was gone, I once again explained to Macho that he would need to give us two of his arrows for the ax. I could tell that he didn't like that idea, but even so, he said, "Bring the ax."

When Wallace arrived with the ax heads, he took Straight Hair with him to make sure things were communicated well. Straight Hair told the assembled group, "Two arrows for an ax." *Equitä*, an old one-eyed man, went and got two arrows right away and traded for an ax. Someone else—I think it may have been the chief, Matador—was also quick to trade two arrows for an ax-head.

Macho, on the other hand, only wanted to trade one arrow, and when we wouldn't do that, he pouted. Wallace came back into camp to get some hatchets and let me know what was going on, so I went with him when he took the hatchets out. We were going to trade them for one arrow apiece. One of the people traded for one. It wasn't clear whether he traded his own arrow or possibly someone else's arrow, but I could tell that the nomads were getting kind of edgy, and things weren't going well.

Dick, the chief's younger brother, was one of the last ones to trade an arrow for a hatchet and now, as they prepared to leave, he said, "Give me my arrow."

I answered, "Give me the hatchet back, and you can have the arrow."

He wasn't happy with that answer and kept getting more and more insistent. Finally, Macho took Dick's part and headed over my way to try and take the arrow by force, so I said, "I'm going to hold onto it tightly, and you'll break it if you take it." In the meantime, I called to Straight Hair to reinforce me and to Matador, their chief, to call Macho off, which he did. Even so, Macho attempted to pry my fingers from the arrow, although he wasn't brutal about it. He was just letting me know that they really wanted the arrow.

As they continued getting more upset, our womenfolk jumped up and headed toward our camp, and some of the nomads also started disappearing down the trail into the jungle, leaving the scene. Matador kept his cool the whole time. Smiley just sat there and ignored the whole incident. Slim didn't seem too sure what to do or which side to take.

As more of them started pulling back, we did too. I went over and took the kettle off the fire. Giggles came up and held out a leaf, wanting corn, but I refused her request, turned, and handed the kettle to Wallace, and we began to leave. Wallace was walking last. He turned around to look, and there was Macho with a drawn bow, lining up an arrow on one of us. Wallace said, "No! No! No!" to him.

Macho lowered the arrow and disappeared into the jungle. Contact had ended on a bad note, although we didn't feel *too* badly as we felt that ground had been gained. They needed to know that we would stand our ground and that they couldn't walk over us with impunity. We were sure they would be back; maybe not tomorrow, but likely in the near future. We felt it was necessary for us to hold our ground and let them know that they couldn't have and do every-thing they wanted. The only two who seemed disgruntled and upset were Dick and Macho, but we would need to be extra cautious in future contacts until it was clear they had gotten over their anger.

Illness and a Setback

THREE WEEKS WENT BY, AND the nomads hadn't returned. While waiting for them, my family—Vickie and our three children—had flown over to join me at the Víbora River base while Paul and Sharon Short replaced us at the Chimoré base, swapping houses with each other. During the three weeks of moving, I had been quite sick with fevers, extreme sweating, and constant bad headaches. Others on the team had also been ill, but now we were all well enough for contact to resume.

Our team had diminished in size as Steve and Vangie Parker had left for Cochabamba to study Spanish, and all our Yuquí coworkers had returned home to the Chimoré. We were reduced to four families, Curt and Dawn Young, Wallace and Barbara Pouncy, Grant and Alana Mayer, and Vickie and me. We would be shorthanded if and when the nomads returned and would need to quickly fly in other missionaries to help us.

Two weeks went by, and we received word by radio that the nomads had killed a Bolivian woodsman a few kilometers north of us, and although they didn't know it, the nomads had once again raised the risk of the Bolivian military going in to find and eradicate them.

Three more weeks passed, and in the meantime, Vickie and I flew to Santa Cruz. I had begun losing vision in my left eye and, after consulting by radio with an eye doctor, had traveled to the city where toxoplasmosis in the left eye was diagnosed. It was destroying the vision, and I would need several weeks of monitoring and medication. We would have to be in the city for an extended period of time. In our absence, Lorenzo Cruz and his wife, Antonia, Yuquí Christians from the Chimoré, had gone to the Víbora River as reinforcements for the contact team. Lorenzo knew a little Spanish, so he could interact with the missionary team through that language as necessary.

Now almost ten weeks after the nomads had left in anger, and with only a skeleton team of missionaries on hand, the nomads once again showed up at the Víbora River base. As Grant Mayer, Curt Young, and Lorenzo headed out to the edge of the clearing to meet with the visible nomads. Grant spotted others of them hidden in the trees with bows drawn, waiting to shoot the missionaries. Grant yelled to Lorenzo, who was leading the way, and the two of them turned to flee. While two arrows passed close to Grant, he wasn't struck, but a barbed arrow impacted Lorenzo in the middle of the back, dangerously close to the spine, although it didn't seem to have penetrated too deeply. Curt, who was rear guard and carrying a rifle, fired three times into the air to scare off the attackers.

After learning by radio and phone call that the nomads had reappeared and before the shooting occurred, I had called Steve Valentine, South American Mission pilot, to see about getting a flight to the Víbora River since the team was shorthanded. Now we would need an emergency flight to bring out Lorenzo and his family. Later that afternoon, we landed at the Víbora River base, and Lorenzo was flown to Santa Cruz for medical attention.

After only two or three days, Lorenzo was released by the doctor and flew back home to the Chimoré to recuperate. However, instead of healing, he became feverish and got sicker by the day. A flight was called, and we flew him to Cochabamba for medical attention. One of the first things the doctor did was to order an X-ray of the injury. The X-ray showed nothing unusual, yet none of the antibiotics they administered seemed to be having a beneficial effect.

Vickie and I had joined Lorenzo in Cochabamba as my eye condition still needed attention, so I was overseeing Lorenzo's care and interacting with the doctor on his behalf as Lorenzo's Spanish was limited. Eventually, the doctor told me, "If we don't do something, he's going to die. How about if we do exploratory surgery?"

I approved. The surgeon cut into Lorenzo's back and found a piece of the palm arrow point as big around as a pencil and one and a half inches long still lodged in his back. It hadn't shown on any of the X-rays. After the large, foreign object was removed, Lorenzo healed quickly and, within two weeks, was able to return home to the Chimoré, healthy and in good spirits. Amazingly, he harbored no anger or desire to avenge himself on those who shot him but rather expressed a continued desire to see his kinfolk befriended and help them hear of the love of Christ.

After returning to the Víbora River, I began raising pigs, thinking they would be a drawing card for the nomads and a quick and abundant source of meat for them and for us. The four piglets, two males and two females, we had flown in from the mission boarding school were growing nicely, and I had fenced a portion of the jungle next to the camp so the pigs could roam and forage in the enclosure. Felix Ovales and his wife, Victoria, Christians from the village of Puerto Grether, decided to join us in the effort to befriend the Yuquí, and once they arrived on the base, Felix was anxious to help in any way he could.

He offered to do maintenance work on the pig enclosure fence, and he and I walked down there so I could show him what needed to be done. It was almost 4:00 p.m. and as we turned, facing back toward camp, we saw Curt Young frantically signaling us from up near one of the houses. He had just discovered that three stalks of cooking bananas had been taken from the gift rack, although none of us had seen the nomads come. The three of us along with a visitor at the base made our way cautiously toward the gift rack, watching carefully for any indication of an ambush, and as we got within forty yards, I began calling out in Yuquí in case the nomads were still nearby. It had been four and a half months since Lorenzo was shot, and as far as we knew, this was the first time the nomads had come near our camp since the shooting.

My calling brought no response. Evidently, the nomads had come earlier, and we had failed to see them. After hanging additional bananas from the gift rack, we returned to the houses to discuss our next step.

After dark that night, Curt and I carried a jug with rice, hard candy, and thread thirty minutes out the gift trail and hung it on a rack the nomads often visited when they came looking for gifts. Along the trail, we could see bare footprints which seemed to indicate that there had been at least three people and, when we arrived at the thirty-minute gift rack, we could see where they had made palm-leaf backpacks to carry the bananas they had taken. If they needed backpacks to carry the bananas, they were likely camped a fair distance away. Even so, when they arrived in their camp with bananas, others of their people might decide to come and see what they could get. Most likely, we would see them soon.

For the next six days, we kept someone watching the gift rack at the edge of our clearing during daylight hours, but none of our gifts were taken. We also hiked the four kilometers to the Chore River and hung candy and cloth at the river so they could see those if they came to the far side of the river. Felix and I continued working on the fence for my growing piglets in our spare time.

Now it was Sunday, and the team had assembled at our house to worship God together. As we all settled into our seats, I moved over to sit by Vickie and asked her, "Can you see the gifts at the rack?" We wanted someone watching the gift rack even during the meeting.

She replied, "Almost."

That wasn't good enough for me.

Seeing her hesitation, I stood and looked toward the gift rack. The gifts were gone! The last time any of the team could remember looking had been one hour previously. Even so, we walked out and called to the nomads. No response. At 3:15 p.m., three of us headed out to replace the gifts at the Chore River. All the gifts between our camp and the river had been taken.

Monday morning, Jack was busy watching the gift rack while I worked on the pig pen. At 11:00 a.m., thirteen nomads appeared near the rack, but most of them stayed in the edge of the jungle while they sent Giggles, Potbelly, and Friday out first to see what kind of welcome they might receive. These three were slaves and looked on as expendable members of the group.

I went out first, carrying bananas, while others of my coworkers followed along, also carrying bananas. I called to the nomads, most of whom continued to peer cautiously from farther back in the woods, and soon, the chief, Matador, showed himself. I assured them that we weren't mad at them and wouldn't shoot them and then approached a little closer to the edge of the woods where I set the bananas down, backed up a short distance, and said, "Come and get them."

They were still showing reluctance to come out of the woods, so I removed my shirt and laid it and my gun down, showing them that we had no intent to harm them. Now Giggles and Potbelly came boldly up to me, and Friday soon followed. Soon, ten more people came cautiously out to join us, and we spent the next hour talking with them as we brought out additional bananas and stalks of manioc. We gave out twelve stalks of bananas and ten plants of manioc, and they seemed to be happy with that. "I'll tell the airplane to bring 'your others' to see you," I commented before they departed.

That afternoon Wooly Hair, Straight Hair, Lorenzo, and Toughy were flown over to help us.

For the next nine days, we had no visitors, and I used the time to install an alarm system that would set off a warning buzzer if gifts were taken from the rack on the edge of our clearing; that way, we would know the instant gifts were taken. Too often, the nomads had taken gifts and left without us having an opportunity to interact with them. First, I added a spring-loaded hinged board to the bottom of the gift rack. As long as there was weight on the board, it would hang down, but once the bananas or other weight was removed, the spring would pull the board up, causing two metallic contacts to come together, completing a circuit. I buried lamp cord from the rack to my house, a distance of one hundred yards and, in the house, installed a battery-operated buzzer that would activate when the two metal contacts at the gift rack came together. Now we would hear the buzzer, even as the gifts were being taken, and could quickly go out and call to the nomads, letting them know they had been spotted.

On day nine, early in the afternoon, I was sitting in my study with the radio turned on when suddenly, I heard a loud buzzing noise coming through the radio speaker. I was puzzled as to what was making the sound, and as I stood to investigate, I realized it was the buzzer in our house sounding. I ran down the stairs to see Vickie dashing out of the house to look for me. She had heard intermittent buzzing as the nomads jiggled the board on the gift rack up and down while removing the bananas.

After looking out the window and seeing the nomads at the gift rack, she hurried from the house to look for me. Now she returned to the house to switch the buzzer off while I called Lorenzo and headed toward the rack, hooting as I went to let the nomads know we had spotted them. Matador made his way out of the jungle first and, by that time, Straight Hair had joined me and instructed Matador, Slim, and Smiley to leave their bows and arrows behind as they came out to see us.

Jane, Matador's daughter, had accompanied the three men, so it was just the four of them who were paying us a visit. Now they informed us that Macho had a child stolen on the Chore River and was the one who shot the Bolivian woodsman a few weeks previously.

God had sent the nomads back to us just in the nick of time as a flight was already in the air, coming to take our Chimoré Yuquí coworkers home. Now, instead of taking them home, the flight would go to the Chimoré and bring their wives and families to join them at the Víbora River. The contact was brief but friendly, ending with the nomads promising to return the following day. Once they disappeared into the woods, Felix and I headed out hunting, as did Straight Hair and Lorenzo, hoping to find meat and fish to share with the nomads the next day.

By 3:50 p.m. the following day, we had given up on the nomads appearing as it was so late in the day. I headed for the radio room, planning to turn it on for the 4:00 p.m. radio schedule. There was quite a bit of noise in our camp with motors running and children playing noisily as we were all confident it was too late for visitors. At that moment, the buzzer sounded. I ran back into the house to shut the buzzer off and looked out the window. A fair-sized group of nomads was clustered near the gift rack, although none of them had called out to us. Once again, we were pleased that the buzzer had alerted us to their presence.

As I approached the gift rack, one of the young men asked, "How did you know we were here?"

I felt a little dishonest as I replied, "I heard you." There was little chance I would have heard them, even had I been nearby as they approached our clearing. With their bare feet, they walked silently in the forest, but they weren't aware of my secret weapon—*the buzzer*. They spent only a few minutes with us before promising to return the following day, and we were confident that they meant it.

For the next five weeks, we had almost daily contacts with the nomads, each one filled with its customary mix of friendly, relaxed, enjoyable time together and moments of stress and tension. Without the Yuquí from the Chimoré, the task would have been impossible as they could "read" the moods of their jungle cousins, and this made it possible for us to make adjustments as necessary to address situations before they got out of hand.

There was no way our plantation could provide sufficient bananas and manioc for the thirty-six jungle dwellers and our missionary team, so supply flights occurred regularly, which also allowed us to rotate Yuquí from the Chimoré base in and out so none of them became too exhausted by the demands of their jungle kinfolk. Hunting and fishing were also a routine part of each day as we worked hard to provide an abundance of protein for people who looked on meat as the only true food; all other foodstuff took second place to meat. If there was no meat, they felt they hadn't eaten.

On the first contact, we refused to sit with them at the edge of the jungle, instead insisting on sitting a short distance into our clearing. We were still close enough to the jungle to be shot but were sending a message that we didn't trust them. They needed to make an effort to regain our trust. That first contact lasted over six hours, and they were happy with the capybara (world's largest rodent) we gave to Matador, the six-foot long electric eel we presented to Macho, and the two alligators Curt had shot for them.

Within a few days, several of the nomads began reporting sore throats and other symptoms. Unfortunately, some of the Yuquí from the Chimoré hadn't been well when they were flown over, but we hadn't been informed of that. Our policy had always been to avoid contact with the jungle people when we were sick as we didn't want to expose them to illnesses to which they might not have resistance.

Exposure would come with time, but we didn't want to hasten the process unnecessarily.

As their trust in us built, we continued to see people who hadn't come out to us previously. One day, Matador and his wife, Vera, showed up with their youngest son, Little Turtle, who was still too young to walk but would have difficulty when he reached that age as both of his feet rotated inwards at the ankle; he was clubfooted. Many years later, we were able to fly him to Cochabamba, where Bolivian doctors graciously and freely corrected that condition, allowing him to lead a normal life. As small as each band of Yuquí was, the effects of close intermarriage was noticeable in both groups with one of the Yuquí at the Chimoré having two thumbs on one hand.

Now that we were coming into dry season, we needed to work at clearing the Víbora River of logjams so we could hunt farther afield. We would be using the chainsaws while doing that, so we warned the nomads, "If you hear the chainsaw, don't be frightened, it's just us clearing logs from the river so we can hunt farther away for you."

They liked that idea, replying, "Good!"

We continued, "Would you like to hear the chainsaw from a short distance here? We'll start it, and you'll know what to listen for."

They said, "Sure." They were excited about a demonstration of the saw as we explained to them how effective it was.

I brought the saw to where a tall stump stood in our clearing and sawed off the upper part the stump. They were impressed, saying, "Come closer and cut one off." I went nearer to the group and sawed off another stump. They were quick to see the possibilities with this wonderful machine, and one of the nomad women spoke up, "How about coming out and cutting honey trees for us?"

We were thrilled with their response, and it was clear they could see that we were useful friends to have.

Earlier the same morning, I had also introduced another new concept to them by taking a notebook and pencil out to where the group was sitting. Since various ones often asked for sugar, candy, knives, thread, and other assorted items, I thought I would show them how the paper and pencil could "talk" to me. As the nomads made their various requests, I would say, "I'll let the leaf talk to me" as I wrote their request in the notebook. I explained to them that the "leaf" could "talk" to me so that I could remember everything in detail and order.

One by one, I turned to different individuals and asked what I should get for them, carefully repeating the item in the dialect as I jotted it down in my notebook, making a big deal out of the process. "I'm going to go and get the items you asked for," I informed them as I headed for our storage room. Before long, I was back and went down my list as I read off each request before fulfilling it. "You asked for sugar, you asked for lard, you asked for bananas."

They didn't seem nearly impressed as I was, but it was part of the learning curve as they faced the outside world.

After the chainsaw demonstration, Macho turned to me and said, "Is that what you mow the farm with?"

We had told them that I did the grass cutting and clearing, keeping our plantation maintained. Now I answered, "No, it's a different machine."

He wanted to see that too, so I brought the brush cutter out, started it up, and cut some brush and grass for them to see. A couple of the children ran in fear of the machinery while the rest of the group sat and watched.

Our day went well and was also profitable from a spiritual standpoint. In the morning, before the nomads showed up, I had given our Yuquí from the Chimoré a pep talk about being more aggressive in their witness and in sharing the most important purpose in our being here. Straight Hair practically preached some sermons as the nomads listened intently.

Macho especially focused on what Straight Hair was saying as he introduced a word for God, a concept the nomads were unfamiliar with, and then told them much about God and His desires for those of us He had created.

The nomads also did some storytelling, relating an incident that happened several months previously when they shot a Bolivian logger who had been rolling logs near the mouth of the Chore River. It turned out that Macho had shot this fellow, and he related the story in some detail. We took this as an opportunity, Straight Hair especially and other Yuquí from Chimoré, to encourage them not to shoot nationals. Straight Hair and our other helpers related to them how the loggers had lain in ambush for them for days after that and how the nationals have dogs to chase them, cornering them so they can shoot them with guns, set tiger traps for them, and things like that. We were working hard to get them to stop their killing and doing our best to share biblical concepts with them. It would be a long, slow process but was a priority to us.

Now the nomads informed us, "We are going on a two-day *juä* (overnight trip) and then will return."

We appreciated them giving us advance notice of their absence and replied, "That's fine, that's good." It showed we were growing in our relationship with them. "Stay far away from the *abaas* (nationals/enemies) while you are gone, and don't take bananas from their farms. If you need bananas, come to us," we reminded them.

While we didn't expect visitors the next morning, we weren't too surprised when Vickie called out around eight o'clock that the jungle people were standing at the gift rack, whistling for us. Wooly Hair and Grant had also heard them. It was a small group, only four people—Macho, Old One-Eye, Slim, and Harry, a teenager. As we chatted with them, they informed us that the group hadn't traveled because *Equitä* (Matador, the chief) and others were sick and didn't want to travel. We stood around visiting and, surprisingly enough, they didn't ask for anything. It appeared they had only come for a brief visit and were acting like they would depart soon.

Finally, I commented in dialect, "We can't let them go away empty-handed after they came to see us. How about if I bring some sugar out for them?"

Straight Hair thought that was a great idea, commenting, "Fine!"

Curt and I went to get sugar, about three cups apiece and five candies each and distributed it among them. They were pleased, and now Slim mentioned the ripe eating bananas hanging at my house, asking if they could have some of those. I headed back to the house, gathered up a good quantity of bananas, and when I arrived back, he expanded his request, "*Detibotibo mama tasää* (Can I have/try some of your leftovers?).” I headed to the house to see what Vickie might have and was in luck. I came back with a piece of pumpkin pie which I cut into smaller pieces and gave to the four visitors.

They smacked their lips and slapped the back of their heads approvingly with their palms. Curt had also gone home for leftovers and returned with cake-type brownies and some muffins. Macho didn't like the brownies at all, but Old Man One-Eye ate them and really approved of them. Later on, when Macho wasn't around, Old Man One-Eye commented, “What's wrong with Äätäyiba (Anteater's Arm or Macho)? Those things were sure good. They were really great. I really like those!”

Dawn Young's brownies were a big hit. What had started as a short visit kept growing longer, and as they seemed in no hurry to leave, Wooly Hair suggested, “Why don't we cook them some rice?”

I questioned, “Do you have that much time? Would you like us to cook some rice?”

They liked that idea, responding, “Yah.”

As the rice slowly boiled, Straight Hair told Curt, “Bring the chainsaw out and fell that dead tree to get some firewood.”

Curt brought out the saw, giving another demonstration of the chainsaw at work, and soon we had an abundance of wood along with a blazing fire. As we sat around the fire, a flock of parrots landed in a tree a short distance back in the woods. With only a small group of men present, I had previously asked Straight Hair, “Wouldn't this be a good time, with only four men here and no women, to demonstrate the shotgun to them up close?”

Straight Hair sent Lorenzo to get the shotgun, and when he returned, Slim, Harry, Straight Hair, and Lorenzo went out to shoot the parrots. Macho stayed right with me near the fire, showing more trust than I had expected from him, but after they headed into the woods with the gun, he retrieved his bow and one arrow from the jungle nearby and leaned them up against a tree where they were handy before once again sitting down with us.

Old Man One-Eye continued sitting with us the entire time and seemed completely unconcerned. After the fourth shotgun blast, Lorenzo came back to get the rifle to try and knock down a parrot that had hung up in a tree. When he headed back out with the rifle, it was too much for Macho; he couldn't resist any longer but had to see what all the shooting had accomplished, so he picked up his bow and arrow and ran into the forest, following Lorenzo. I began praying fervently, committing my colleagues to God. Who knew what thoughts might come into Macho's mind as he saw them there? I knew they each had a gun, but in the dense jungle, Macho could easily come up on them without their knowledge. With his reputation and lack of value for human life, anything could happen.

My fears proved to be unfounded as soon they all reappeared but with no birds. At least the shotgun had been fired a few times and they had seen and heard it fired up close and had handled the loud noise all right. Sadly, we hadn't been able to demonstrate the gun's effectiveness, but we had gone into the jungle with them on a brief hunting trip and survived to tell about it.

The contact continued going well, and a short while later, Straight Hair told them, "Well, we were going to go hunting." The four nomads began collecting the food items we had given them, and one of them politely asked, "Can we take this?" referring to the cardboard box we had used to bring the bananas out to them.

Sometimes they surprised me with their politeness, since it was unusual, and we were quick to assure them, "Sure, you can take the box. Come back to see us tomorrow."

"We'll come back to see you," they responded, and I was pretty sure we would see them again the next day. Our day together had gone well, and I was encouraged that Macho had been so trusting.

The next day proved to be long and draining. Initially, eight nomads showed up. Among them was a young woman we began referring to among ourselves as Jane. She looked much like Sunday but with a broader face. Jane seemed to be daughter to Matador, the chief, and was always close by his side. She was the only woman accompanying the seven men who had come to visit us. Among them were Macho, Smiley, Slim, Matador, Tom, Dick, and Harry.

Later on, another young woman, Blanca (White), whom we called that due to her very light skin-tone, also showed up, as did Friday, Old One-Eye, and Potbelly. These later arrivals were mostly slave-class individuals. We had already cooked two big kettles of rice, eight cups each time, and a large kettle of corn before the latecomers arrived. We were doing our best to delay their departure, even though they let us know they wanted to leave right away so they could travel. We had two shuttle flights coming, bringing bananas and moving personnel around, and on one of those flights, Bob Garland was coming so he could meet and interact with the nomads.

As noon approached, Matador was getting more and more anxious to leave, but we let him know that *Pachïïnu* (Bob) was coming on the airplane in just a few minutes and was bringing a knife and a piece of cloth for him and wanted to meet him. We also reminded him that the airplane would be bringing lots of bananas for them.

When Bob and Steve Valentine, the pilot, finally approached where we were sitting with the nomads, Macho jumped to his feet and put on a serious air. I could see that the unfamiliar situation puzzled and confused him briefly. Lorenzo, one of our helpers from Chimoré, read Macho's confusion well and began reassuring him, spending time talking with him as the two of them sat back down and conversed together.

By 1:30 p.m., the nomads headed off into the jungle, and the plane departed, taking Bob back to the Chimoré. Those of us who remained behind headed out to hunt and fish. The nomads had indicated that they would be back the next day, although with them, you never knew; in either event, we wanted to have plenty of meat to share with them if they returned.

I took my six-year-old son, Sam, along as Straight Hair and I headed down the river in the boat to hunt and fish. We saw plenty of game, although we had to work hard to get it. After first missing a coati mundi (South American raccoon) and numerous catfish, Straight Hair was finally able to shoot a capybara, but the animal disappeared into a cave on the riverbank. Since we expected to be hunting late, we were carrying a flashlight, and after shining it into the cave to assure that the beast was hiding in there, Straight Hair shot it again and then dug a hole which allowed him to get the rodent out of the cave. At least now we weren't empty-handed. Six-year-old

Sam was really enjoying all the excitement as it wasn't often he got to accompany his dad on such a great adventure!

Next, we saw a log lined with turtles, sunning themselves, and a little farther on, an alligator was stretched out on a log, but all of them dove into the river before we got close enough to shoot. Straight Hair was paddling the boat now, and I was doing the shooting, so when we saw another alligator on the left side of the river, up a bank, just lying there sound asleep, I upped with the rifle from across the river and hit it, first shot. It kind of twitched and remained lying there. We shot it again to make sure it was dead and wouldn't go into the river before paddling over to retrieve it. A capybara and an alligator—not as much game as we had hoped for, but a great father-son time with Sam. I was so glad I had taken him along as he thought it was a super time.

Now the Yuquí, both those from Chimoré and the nomads, were all sick with deep chest coughs and runny noses. We were pretty sure the illness had been brought in by those who had come from the Chimoré and thought we would take the opportunity to try and introduce medicine to the nomads, explaining that the medicines we were offering could help them feel better. We had introduced the concept of God to them in recent days, and it seemed they had begun to equate Him with the "spirits along the sky" they already believed in; they expressed that God was the one making them sick.

We let them know that on the contrary; God wanted to make them well and went on to tell them that we talked to God, asking Him to make them feel better. While Bob had been visiting from the Chimoré, we had mentioned medicine ("the thing that makes one well"), and Bob took an aspirin in their presence so they could see how it was done. After watching Bob swallow the aspirin, Slim decided he would try one, and although we explained to him, "Don't chew it, just swallow it," he crunched down on it and commented, "That's bitter" and spit it out. We would try again another day.

I had no sooner finished talking on the radio the next morning before Vickie let me know that the nomads had arrived. It was only 7:30 a.m. They not only seemed to be moving up their time of arrival, but almost half the band had come to see us, including one of the older women. Each day, they had been telling us that they were leaving on a trip and, once again, today they indicated they didn't plan to stay long, so I commented, "Let's not cause the sun to go up completely so I can go fishing."

The previous day, we had seen many large catfish dozing in shallow water near sandy beaches, so Lorenzo and I were planning to see if we could harpoon a few of those.

Grant had prepared two kettles with rice and one with corn to cook but had mistakenly added sugar to the kettle of corn. When he began serving the cooked grain to the nomads, we quickly realized that the corn had been cooked with sugar, and as we apologized, their response was, "Do that next time, put sugar in it." Everything with sugar.

Now they began asking for lard. Several of them had brought along cans in which we had previously given them lard and wanted refills. Jungle meat was so lean that the added fat was a much enjoyed addition to their diet.

While we had not yet invited any of the nomads farther into our camp than the edge of the clearing where we generally spent time together, Blanca, one of the slave women, took it upon herself to go into our camp and explore. Our concern was that if the group came in before they had learned to respect us and our belongings, they might begin helping themselves freely to everything and anything, and we could soon lose control. Not only did they outnumber us, but they were willing to use force, whereas we didn't want to be in a situation of having to control them by force.

When Blanca showed up near our houses, Vickie saw her coming and went out to interact with her. Blanca was content with the ripe bananas Vickie gave to her, but once Blanca rejoined the group at the edge of the clearing and told of her adventures, Old One-Eye and a few others of the nomads expressed a desire to come in and see our camp. We ignored the suggestion for the moment, but I was pretty sure they wouldn't be put off so easily the next time they returned. We would need to be sure not to leave axes, machetes, kettles, buckets, and other items they might desire lying around in the open or we would be forced to make an issue of it as items were stolen. We needed to "police" our camp before they came in, most likely the next day.

After passing out sugar and hard candy and giving them the capybara and alligator we had shot the previous day, Lorenzo and I said, "We're going to go shoot fish," and off we went.

The day was young, only 10:30 a.m. when Lorenzo and I headed downriver fishing. The fish seemed wary, and we were missing many of the fish as we threw the spear at them, but eventually, we harpooned a five-foot long electric eel. The Víbora River was notorious for the abundance of electric eels, and we saw scores of them over the years and shot or harpooned quite a few. We didn't find them to be good eating, but both groups of Yuquí considered them quite a

Alan with tiger-striped catfish, abundant and excellent eating. Catfish on right is red-tailed Amazon catfish weighing about 30 pounds.

treat. Eventually, we were able to harpoon several tiger-striped catfish and an "army-camouflage" catfish, most of them weighing seven to eight pounds. Not an abundance of fish, but enough to impress the nomads. With their fishing techniques, they would be fortunate to get two or three such fish in a day.

It seemed that the fish near our base were getting more wary, and harpooning them was getting ever more difficult. It was time to switch to using my crossbow so I could shoot them from a greater distance.

Late in the afternoon, after we returned from fishing, we began making preparations in case the nomads insisted on coming into our camp the next day. We wanted them to eventually have that liberty but didn't want things to get out of hand when it happened. We didn't want them to know where most of the foodstuffs and gifts were stored as they would likely force their way into the storage building and take everything, so we brought a moderate amount of goods to the Pouncy home where we could keep control as necessary. Their house was in the center of camp, and Barbara would always be there along with others of us as the situation warranted.

I also had a chat with our Yuquí coworkers, telling them not to encourage the nomads to come in and explore our camp but, if the nomads were insistent, to accompany them as they came in and never leave them unattended. Our helpers had gone through a similar process nineteen years earlier as they were being befriended at the Chimoré, so most of them understood exactly what I was talking about, although then, they had been the ones trying to steal anything they possibly could so knew well how their kinfolk thought.

By now, the nomads had begun learning some of our names in Spanish, a language they would someday need to acquire. They had begun calling Grant "Guido," although more often, they mispronounced it as "Guiroro," which had a better "ring" to it in their dialect. After talking with my Yuquí coworkers ahead of time, we had decided to see if we could learn the names of some of the nomads. This would liven up our time with them, and we might learn more about them. I began by pointing to Grant and asking the nomads, "What do the people call him (Meaning: What is his name)?"

Several were quick to respond, "Guiroro."

That was close enough for me. It seemed they were getting the idea. After pointing to a few others of my coworkers and getting similar responses, I pointed to one of the nomads and asked Slim, "What do the people call him?"

He was quick to reply, "That's younger brother."

I pointed to another. "That's younger brother," he again replied.

I knew that the chief, Matador, was older than Slim and not his brother, so I pointed to Matador, "What do the people call him?"

"That's *Equitä* (Big Chest)," came the answer once again not a name as much as a term of respect.

Now I pointed to his mother. "That's *Tä* (Mother)," came the answer.

Next, I pointed to Old One-Eye and asked Slim what his name was. "That's *Ai* (Father? Grandpa?)," came the reply. All I could get was relationships. No names.

Straight Hair was doing his best to help me and tried explaining to them in various ways what we were looking for, but we just couldn't get any names. Finally, with Tapir, they did call her *Iäquiägua*. Then I pointed to Blanca, whom I had heard Old One-Eye call *Tiasura*, and they said, "That's *Biguachi* (Mud Duck)."

They had already told us that another young lady was *Biguachi*, and we really didn't need two people with that name. We continued working on names for a time, but nothing was forthcoming. Kinship was the name of the game; relationships seemed to be all important. Names would have to wait; they might be important in our culture but not so much so in theirs. Even when we eventually learned some of their names, we generally found them to be derogatory, based on some negative physical attribute, so we preferred not to use them.

There was some grumbling from the nomads during the morning as they complained we didn't fill the rice kettles full enough, although the irritability seemed to begin when Tom, the chief's brother, didn't receive as large a portion of rice from the kettle as he wanted. Soon his attitude began to infect others, including Straight Hair who also began complaining about the kettles not being filled full enough. Straight Hair knew enough Spanish that I was able to question him about what was happening, and he explained that not only was Tom complaining about not getting enough rice but was also talking about taking us out to cut honey trees for them and then ambushing us while we were out there.

We suspected that Tom's younger brother, Dick, who had traded for a hatchet and then wanted his arrow back several months previously had been the driving force behind shooting Lorenzo in the back, and there was no doubt Tom was just as volatile. Now, even though he was talking about ambushing us, Tom spent much of the day smiling and interacting pleasantly with us. The next time a kettle of rice was ready to be doled out, Straight Hair made sure Tom received a generous portion. We had already been favoring Matador as the leader and Macho, since we perceived him as one of the greater dangers among them; clearly, we would need to also show extra favor to Tom and Dick, the chief's brothers.

The next day, I noticed that whoever brought the rice out doubled the amount we normally cooked so we only cooked one large kettle instead of two smaller ones. Corn was cooking in another kettle. Even so, Straight Hair detected an undercurrent of discontent and continued concerned that a shooting might occur. Having already been shot by the nomads in 1980, he had no interest in repeating the experience.

I spent my afternoon interacting with the nomads in order to keep an eye on how the contact was going while Curt took Straight Hair and Woolly Hair upriver to go hunting. Being away from the contact scene was always stress-relieving. Late in the afternoon, after the nomads had left for the day, Straight Hair and I went for an evening hunt, killing one small alligator. As we paddled along the river, talking quietly, Straight Hair let me know that he wasn't yet convinced we had won the nomads over but felt they could still turn on us at any time. He could read his kinfolk better than anyone else on our team, and I had no doubt we needed to remain constantly vigilant, while at the same time, we needed to show trust if we expected to generate trust. Again, today, the nomads had told us that they would be leaving on a short trip, just a night or two away.

We gave out the last of the lard, and as they were preparing to leave for the day, Slim handed me three cans of lard and asked me to keep them for him until they returned from their trip. Dick also handed me a can of lard in a red tomato paste can and asked me to keep it for him. To me, this was an indication that they were serious about leaving for a few days and didn't want to have to carry the extra lard.

While we expected the nomads to be gone for a few days, they only missed one day before a group of nine came to visit once again. They started the day by telling us, "Don't bring women and children out, we're sick (They wanted peace and quiet)." They weren't interested in rice or corn, so we didn't cook any, although we brought out the plentiful fish Sam and I had caught the night before. We had netted a twelve-pound pacú sunfish, a twenty-five-pound tiger-striped catfish, as well as eight large piranha. The nomads were very happy to receive the nearly fifty-pounds of fish.

During many of the contacts with the nomads, I had noticed that when one of them began telling a hunting story, he would stare off into space, not making eye contact with the audience as he related his story, and I had wondered if that would be a good way to share more of God's Word with them. I decided to give it a try, so during this contact, without any preamble or notifying anyone that I would be telling a story, when there was a brief lull in the conversation, I looked off into space and began telling about Big Father and how He created the world, how He made angels, and later created man.

I noticed right away that several of them jerked to attention, listening closely to me as I spoke, so I continued on letting them know that angels were God's servants, doing what He asked, and then introduced the aspect that God is eternal, He doesn't die, He has always been. As I paused, Straight Hair and his wife Loida both began adding to what I had been saying. I was happy to let them continue explaining as they were speaking much more fluently and clearly than I could.

After they stopped talking and other conversation once again picked up, several minutes passed before Slim suddenly looked up and, with a look on his face that showed he was thinking about what we had said, commented, "So, so, this guy God is the one who created everything, huh?" or something like that. It was the most pondered upon feedback of any that we had received since beginning to introduce Big Father, the God of the Bible.

Later in the morning, something about traveling came up, and the nomads let us know that they would be gone for two nights before coming back. Then they asked for us to bring Favorite Joven and Toughy back to see them. I said, "Well, when Lorenzo here travels in fifteen days"—as I held up and counted off fifteen fingers to give them an idea of how many days since they didn't have a counting system—"maybe we could bring one of them, Favorite Joven or Toughy, over from the Chimoré."

Now that the subject of travel had arisen, Straight Hair let them know that eventually, he would be going home since he needed to work on his farm. When he informed them of that, Matador, the chief, was very concerned and told Straight Hair, "Well, if you all (the Yuquí) go, they—these people here (the missionaries)—might kill us."

Straight Hair explained to him how this was the missionaries' farm and that the missionaries were the ones who planted bananas and manioc for them and were their friends and that nothing would happen to them, even in the absence of the Yuquí from Chimoré.

As Straight Hair explained this, Matador looked at me and, speaking to Straight Hair about me or possibly about the whole missionary team, said, "*Oo guriquio tuti na che rese* (He has his hands on me fully; in Yuquí, this is a strong way to express that someone has their loving hands on you, caring for you)."

I was thrilled, excited beyond measure. Matador seemed to understand that we, the missionary team, loved them, wanted to take care of them and protect them from those who might do them harm. Now if only the rest of the nomads would come to that same understanding.

With their deep chest coughs continuing, we thought we would once again try to introduce medication. Cough syrup might be a good starting point as it was flavorful. Curt Young brought out some grape-flavored cough syrup with a great taste. It was purple-colored and looked delicious. After Matador tasted a small amount, he wanted to drink the whole bottle. We gave him two teaspoons full and gave the same amount to a few others, telling them, "This is all you take at one time. You take more later."

Shortly after noon, Matador reminded us that he was ready for more, so we made the rounds again. If one tiny drop got spilled, they were very bothered by that, scooping it off the ground or leaves and licking it off their fingers. Later, as they prepared to leave, the chief wanted to take the bottle along for his sick children, but we didn't let him take it. It did seem to slow the coughing down a bit, even though we were only using a child dose. We wondered if maybe the whole group would show up the next day, wanting cough syrup and, of course, we didn't have anywhere near the quantity we would need in that case.

During the next three and a half weeks, the nomads came to see us almost daily, missing only four days. Between the hours spent with the nomads, time spent hunting and fishing to get meat to share with them when they came, time with our families and keeping up our own homes, we were being drained of energy. Roger Nebergall flew in to help out as did Dan Naldrett, and we were rotating Yuquí coworkers in and out from the Chimoré, but those of us who lived full-time at the Víbora River were fatigued from the never-ending stress and lack of sleep.

God was providing an abundance of game and fish that not only could be shared with the nomads, but our helpers, the Yuquí from the Chimoré, were also predominately meat eaters, voracious in their meat hunger. I had three gill nets, each about thirty meters long, and most nights, I found backwaters, calm areas in the river where we could stretch the nets, although we had to bring in the nets before daylight as the piranha came awake once there was light and would devour any captive fish. We learned that the hard way early on as one morning, we didn't go to bring in a net until 7:00 a.m. and found that instead of a fifteen-pound tiger-striped catfish, all we pulled in was its bony skeleton, which had been stripped of meat by the piranha. After that, we left at 4:30 in the morning to have the nets in before daylight.

Wooly Hair shot a jaguar, a not too frequent occurrence, although we often saw their tracks. They were elusive with their spotted skin blending seamlessly into the mottled sunlight and shadows of the forest. Another day, he came in with a giant South American otter, a rare creature with a wide flat tail like that of a beaver. To the Yuquí, these were considered edible meat, and after burning the hair off, they were cut up and piled on the smoke rack with the rest of their delicacies.

We never knew what time the nomads would appear or if they would show up at all, so camp chores had to be fitted in as possible around their appearances. The next morning, they didn't show up early, so two of us were out mowing the lawn near the missionary houses when they arrived shortly before 10:00 a.m. The group was small, only seven individuals—Blanca, Old One-Eye's wife or sister (we weren't sure yet which she was), Old One-Eye, Macho, Smiley, Harry, and one other.

Straight Hair and I had shot three alligators and had netted a nice selection of fish to give to the visitors. One of the alligators was full-grown, over six feet long, and quite heavy. Wooly Hair was busy cutting up the tiger as many of us watched. She was a full-grown female, very beautiful, and we were all exclaiming over her the size of her teeth and her claws.

The time seemed to pass slowly as we sat around the fire, waiting for the corn and rice to cook, and after a while, Macho asked to see my bow and arrow. On several occasions, when I brought fish out to them, I had commented that I had shot them with my bow and arrows. Now Macho wanted to admire this device that seemed so effective. He would be surprised. Rather than being an eight-foot long piece of palm wood as his was, mine was a metal crossbow with arrows only about two feet long. I took the unusual bow out and let him look it over. He had never seen anything so strange and wanted to see how it worked. "Shoot it," he commanded.

I cocked the bow, loaded it with an arrow, and fired it up into the sky. The arrow quickly disappeared against the white clouds, and then, after a moment, reappeared as it fell to earth. Next, I brought out my forty-five-pound test fiberglass bow with three-foot-long arrows I had made. These arrows looked much like his arrows but whereas his were eight feet long, mine were a mere three feet in length.

He wasn't too impressed and went to retrieve his bow and showed us how a real hunter could shoot. He shot several arrows up into the air for us, and it was an impressive sight. Beautiful! I would have loved to have gotten a movie of him shooting. Watching him pull the thick, massive bow back to his ear and hold it there while aiming gave some idea as to the shoulder and arm strength of this powerful warrior, and the force that would be behind each arrow he fired. I would not have liked to be his target.

Later, near the end of the morning, Pablo, Woolly Hair's son, came out, and Macho wanted to show him how he could shoot arrows up into the sky. As he began pulling back, the bark-rope bowstring broke. After tying it back together, he pulled back a second time, and again the rope snapped. "I'm going to get a new bowstring for you," I let him know as I went back to my house and found a length of nylon rope to give him as a new bowstring. It worked, all right; at least it didn't break, but nylon didn't prove to be good as a bowstring as it stretched and constantly had to be tightened or restrung. Whether he would be happy with that, only time would tell, although I sure hoped he didn't use it to shoot any nationals or one of us. Maybe I should have left him with a bowstring that might break if he was shooting at the wrong thing.

Old One-Eye's wife/sister asked for a kettle, and I gave her a small one since Smiley had come and was also asking for one. Had I given her the larger one and him the small one, he would've gotten upset as he was in a feisty mood, demanding everything from everybody and wanting more than his share. He wanted to take everything and cut everybody else out.

Blanca was being treated like dirt under their feet. They had put her to work making palm-leaf baskets to haul their foodstuff away, had her doing all the cooking for them, and were denigrating her in various ways. Her position as a slave had never been more evident. Up until now, I hadn't been too worried about Smiley, but with the superior attitude he was showing today and the way he was treating all of us, I realized I had been underestimating him. He clearly had more wily intelligence than I had given him credit for and was a man to be reckoned with. We would need to do more to keep him content while not catering to his demands. Slim, on the other hand, always appeared to be a little bit more "out of it." Now I worried that maybe I was underestimating him as well.

The deep coughing and sickness continued to linger, and the next day, when nine of them showed up, including the old lady we had begun calling Grandma, they let us know that Old One-Eye had tried to come with them but was so sick, he gave up and returned to their camp. From the way they described it, the matriarch, *Tä*, was the sickest of all of them. Clearly, we needed to protect them by not letting them have exposure to any of us when we were sick as the nomads might not have resistance to illnesses to which we might expose them. As they told us about people who were sick in their camp, Grandma wailed; their weapons against illness were limited and left them with a sense of hopelessness.

We sat around the fire as the rice and corn cooked, and after a time, Tom asked if he could see my bow and arrows. Evidently, Macho had mentioned them to him, so I obliged him by bringing them out and showing both of them to him. As we chatted, we learned that Macho's name was Äätäyiba (Anteater's Arm) and that Sunday was his "woman." I had also brought a Bible and a notebook of teaching materials out with the hope of introducing some additional biblical truth. With their focus on food and daily survival, the more mysterious concepts of spiritual truth were not something that generally held their attention for long; but to us, it was extremely important, and we would continue, day by day, trying to add to their understanding of what we considered the most important reason for us being with them.

Ricky Depue, who had flown in to assist us for a few days, brought out *National Geographic* magazines and began showing pictures from those to the nomads, although it took some time before a few of them began recognizing the pictures for what they were. Grant added to the entertainment by playing a game with Macho. "Choose the hand the candy is in." Macho would have preferred to have the candy without having to play the guessing game and, while he acted a little peeved, he didn't get overly angry.

We were innovating as we went along, trying to keep each day interesting and a little out of balance as we didn't want too much of a routine so we would always have room for changing things up as necessary. Some of our attempts worked well, others not so much.

Due to all the rainy weather, we had built an unwalled shed roofed with corrugated tin on the edge of our clearing and had our cooking fires under that so we could sit or squat out of the rain as we visited with the people. With all the rain, the ground under the shed was getting somewhat muddy, and they suggested we widen the roof and make a raised floor in the shed. Some of them even suggested they might come in and sleep there if we had a nice shed like that.

Grandma pointed over to our plantation and suggested we build a private house for her among the bananas. That they would even suggest spending the night with us showed they were progressing in their trust of us and as our long-term goal was to encourage them to move to the Chimoré and join the Yuquí who were settled there, consolidating the two bands into one, we were happy to make changes that might help further that goal.

That evening, Straight Hair and I went hunting and fishing downriver while Curt and Roger went upriver. Straight Hair and I got two capybaras, although one sunk in the river and, for a time, we despaired of finding it. We also shot two alligators, and once we had the reptiles aboard, we decided to switch to fishing. I had brought the crossbow and fishing arrows along, so I stood in the bow of the canoe as Straight Hair paddled quietly down the river. He had never seen the crossbow in use before and was impressed as I shot the first two carp I aimed at. After that, I shot another one and missed several.

As we turned the canoe around to motor back up the river with our 2 HP Yamaha outboard, rain began pouring down, and soon, we were quite wet. We could smell a troop of white-lipped peccaries, who travel in large herds, but didn't see them, and with the rain, we didn't feel much like traipsing through the jungle, getting wetter as we looked for them.

The next morning, Roger and I left well before dawn to retrieve the nets I had left out the previous night. While we hadn't caught much, the four large piranhas would be a welcome addition to the game we had shot the day before. The Yuquí from the Chimoré had their smoke racks piled high as they preserved the meat we gathered, and it was a good thing they did, since with all the rain the nomads didn't show up, and the meat would have spoiled had they not been smoking it. Between the rain and their deep coughs, the nomads were likely staying close to their fires under tiny shelters of palm branches, a miserable life.

When the nomads next came to visit the chief, Matador was with the small group. They arrived with numerous axes and machetes which they wanted sharpened and also asked for new handles on machetes which had long ago lost theirs. They let us know that they had moved farther away and that the group was still quite sick. In fact, Matador and Blanca, both of whom had come to see us, were sick enough they were willing to try a liquid antibiotic, although neither of them liked it enough to try a second dose. They were still planning to travel, but with the sickness the group was experiencing they didn't have the strength to move far.

They had brought so many axes and machetes and were in such a hurry that we brought our manually operated grindstone out, mounted it on a stump, and did the "rough" sharpening with it before finishing the operation off with a file. They had never seen a grindstone before, and after watching us for a while, Slim wanted an opportunity to turn the handle and help with the process. He was an enthusiastic helper and seemed to enjoy the novel experience.

Now they let us know, "We brought baskets and would like to fill them with manioc."

The number of baskets they had brought would clean out all the manioc in our patch, plus would be a lot of work to dig, so I asked, "Who's coming to help?"

Friday got up to come on orders from his master. Blanca followed Straight Hair and me as Grandma, Tapir, Vera (the chief's wife), and Slim also joined the crowd headed to the manioc patch located just behind my house. None of them, except Blanca, had been this far into our camp before but were willing to face the unknown if it meant filling their baskets with manioc.

As we were digging the manioc, they saw Victoria, Felix's wife, whom they had never seen before. They got very excited when they laid eyes on her, and Vera said to Tapir, "Quick, go tell your older sibling that *yiti* (young lady or girl) is here."

With their belief in reincarnation, it seemed that they thought Victoria was Old Lady One-Eye's daughter returned from the dead. Victoria, who was heavyset with black hair and caramel-colored skin, looked like she would fit right in among the older women in the group. It was no wonder they looked on her as one of their own. The next day, almost the entire band, including the sickest among them, made the trek to our camp to meet Victoria and welcome her as family.

Around 2:30 p.m., the nomads left for the day, so Roger and I boated up the river to hunt and fish. I had discovered a pond-like area with little current, which fed into the river, the perfect place to string my nets. I could join two nets end-to-end as the pond was more than eighty meters across and the water was murky, so we could string the nets in the daytime without the risk of the piranha seeing and devouring what we caught.

As I began stringing the first net, we had only gone twenty yards when the net started jerking and swishing around as fish swam into it. I continued setting the two nets and, after they were both fully extended, followed them back across the pond, removing the fish we had already trapped. We had never captured fish this quickly. The nets already contained four twelve-pound pacú (large sunfish) and a good-sized piranha, maybe a pound and a half. What might we have by morning?

We spent a few minutes fishing with handlines, waiting for it to get dark so we could paddle down the river, "spotting" game with a flashlight. Animals came to the river at night to drink, and we could then shoot them on the riverbank. As we fished, we saw two giant South American otters playing but didn't shoot either of them, although I was somewhat worried they might eat fish that got caught in my nets. I was suspicious that these rarely seen otters were or would soon be an endangered species, and they were one of the few animals I refused to shoot.

Once it was dark enough, I began paddling the boat down the river as Roger shone his light along first one bank and then the other, looking for the reflection of eyes in the light-beam. We came to a bend in the river right before a long straight stretch, and there stood a beautiful puma on the right bank, standing as still as a statue out in the open. It was a majestic sight and was standing broadside with its head turned toward us. Roger said, "Look at that!"

I whispered, "Shoot it!"

He shot with his twenty-gauge shotgun, and the puma went into the river real fast like it was wounded, thrashed around a bit before coming out of the water a short distance upriver, and then bounded into the woods. It was moving rapidly enough that, while it may have been wounded, there was no way we would be able to catch it, and I wasn't about to go into the jungle looking for a wounded cougar in the dark. By now, it was late enough that we fired up the outboard and motored on home. We would need to be up early to bring in the nets.

In the morning, Straight Hair and I went up and collected both nets. What an abundance! We had never had a catch like this—five pacús, the largest of them fourteen pounds; three tiger-striped catfish, the largest of which was thirty-three pounds, and the others twenty-nine pounds and seventeen pounds. Added to the four pacú we had netted the night before while setting the nets, we had netted almost 200 pounds of fish, and all of them excellent eating.

By noon, the nomads hadn't appeared, but the Yuquí from Chimoré weren't letting any of the fish spoil. Their smoke racks were piled high and they would eat well if their kinfolk failed to appear. At 1:30 p.m., I was over at Milk Shake Girl's fire when she said, "I think I hear Indians whistling."

I went to check, and sure enough, the nomads had arrived. Macho hadn't come, but a good-sized group including Old Man One-Eye, Spooky, Smiley's oldest boy, Sunday, Tapir, Vera, and Matador were there. For some reason, they wanted to see Straight Hair whom they perceived as the chief among the Yuquí from Chimoré. Straight Hair and Woolly Hair had gone hunting, and we weren't sure how long they would be gone. The nomads let us know, "We'll wait for Straight Hair, but don't cook anything. We'll get that tomorrow."

Even so, we took out five pacú and various pieces of catfish and placed those items on the rack to smoke over the fire we had built. We were doing our best to keep things interesting as they killed time, waiting for Straight Hair. Even so, it was a slow, boring contact and, at times, they were demanding and pushy. We really needed a key Yuquí leader such as Straight Hair on each contact, one who understood them and could keep things moving, someone they respected and looked up to.

Eventually, Straight Hair and Wooly Hair returned, and by the time the nomads left, they were content, carrying away an abundance of smoked fish. I never did figure out why they were so insistent on waiting for Straight Hair.

The following day was the beginning of a major change. Now that a few of them had been into our camp and lived to tell about all the things they had seen there, most of them were ready for this new adventure. We sat for a time at the edge of our clearing, cooking and eating rice and corn together, and then Macho asked Grant, "Can I have a chicken?"

Grant's chicken pen was located right behind his house well into our clearing. Grant replied to Macho, "Come on, let's go get it. Let's go to my chicken pen."

Macho wasn't sure he wanted to face the risks of venturing into our camp, so he remained seated, as did Grant. After a few minutes, Macho stood reluctantly to his feet. If going in to the missionary camp was required in order to get a chicken, he would face the hazards that might be involved.

As they headed for the chicken pen, the majority of the nomads jumped up and followed them, leaving me with Slim and one or two others. When they reached the chicken enclosure, Potbelly jumped over the fence, snagging it, and almost tearing it down. Before others, including Macho, could follow suit, Grant called to them and showed them the gate, which he opened to let them in.

Grant picked out a young chicken and gave it to Macho. Even though it was one of the smaller chickens, Macho was thrilled to get it, and soon the group rejoined us on the edge of the clearing. While the group had been gone, Slim inquired whether my chickens laid eggs and if he could have some. I asked him to wait until the group with Grant returned, and the minute they came back, he leaped to his feet, ready to go, telling me, "Let's go!"

As he jumped up, the whole group jumped up and were going to come with us, until I said, "No, no, not everybody! Just a few of you."

So about six came, and we went to my chicken pen. Vera came along with Grandma, Smiley, Slim and Friday. We looked in my chicken pen, but there were no eggs, so Slim asked about a chicken. After I gave him a plump old black hen, Smiley asked if he could have one of the nice young ones, so I gave him a skinny brown laying hen I had brought from the Chimoré. He was happy with the smaller chicken and didn't insist on a big fat one.

When we rejoined the group sitting at the edge of the clearing, they inspected the chickens carefully and commented, "We're going to keep them and raise them."

I knew that was an unrealistic expectation and that the three birds would be in the soup pot within a day or two. When they eventually settled down, we could help them learn to raise chickens, although we would cross that bridge when we came to it.

During the contact, they kept insisting that Felix, Victoria's husband, come out to where we were sitting, visiting. Macho hadn't met him and wanted to get acquainted with him. Macho was wanting to leave, and I could tell he was disappointed at not having met Felix, so I sent someone in to ask Felix if he would come out and spend some time with them. Eventually, he showed up along with Victoria.

When Macho had gone to get the chicken from Grant's pen, the nomads had also spotted Freddy, a Bolivian national who had come to help us for a few days, and they expressed a desire to meet him. The nomads were beginning to get the picture that there were many more of us than they had at first thought, and I was convinced that was a good thing as they were less likely to think they could overwhelm us by force. It was interesting too that they had no problem at all accepting our Bolivian coworkers. Rather, they identified better with them than they did with the whiter-skinned expatriate missionaries.

Our Yuquí helpers and the Bolivian nationals received the quickest acceptance and seemed to be immediately identified as reincarnated kinfolk. They had Felix take off his boots so they could look at his feet and expressed sympathy when they saw he was missing the little toe on one foot (a barrel had fallen off a truck, cutting off the toe). While they were on the subject of toes, they decided they needed to see my feet again, although it appeared the main reason was that they liked my socks. Socks unravel easily for thread, and they were always asking for socks. I had begun wearing my holey socks so I could give them away.

We had reached a point in our friendship with the nomads where we were ready to take the risk of hunting together with them in the jungle, if they were open to that, so while Macho and Slim were still there, I said, "I'm not going hunting or fishing tonight. I'm going to rest and relax, and tomorrow, I'll go hunting with you." I had discussed this with Woolly Hair ahead of time and knew that he was in agreement. Now he joined in and discussed the subject of hunting together with them.

Slim pondered on the idea some and, after a while, said to Woolly Hair, talking about me, "Maybe he'll shoot me while we are out there together."

Woolly Hair reassured him that he didn't need to be worried about that, and it appeared that Slim accepted his reassurances, although Macho, when he left for the day, seemed to be still pondering the idea of hunting together as if the idea might be a little too deep and dangerous.

After a time, Macho and the group that had come with him left, but others, including Slim, stayed and visited longer. Slim let me know he would like a machete, and I told him the airplane could bring one for him but that it was sure to want some item in return, since we always give the airplane something for bringing things. I said, "I think one of your arrows would be satisfactory."

He said, "Okay, tell him I'll feather him an arrow for a machete."

I promised to ask the airplane to bring a machete for him. We had begun working on the idea of trading again, but more slowly this time since the last time, it had resulted in Lorenzo getting shot. I was using my notebook constantly as I wrote down numerous requests from the nomads and let them know we would get the requested items for them.

Our camp and houses now held little fear for most of them, and the next morning, when they showed up Matador, Slim and Smiley were more than halfway into our clearing and approaching the houses before Curt saw them coming. Macho and a few others had stopped at the edge of the jungle to wait for us, but when we didn't go out to them quickly enough, they too came on in and chatted with us.

That left only a few of their womenfolk out near the gift rack, and I commented, "I'm going out to see the people," and then went out.

The women let me know that *Tä*, the chief's mother, was on her way in but was very sick. Even so, she wanted to see Victoria and meet her husband. I suggested to slave Friday that he go and help *Tä* along the trail, so he and Sunday went out to assist her. When she arrived, she looked so ill that I brought out a bark rope hammock made by Fatty, a Yuquí woman at the Chimoré, so *Tä* would have a comfortable place to repose.

Victoria brought out a cup of hot sweet tea for her to drink, and we were able to convince her to try a liquid antibiotic, although we had to mix it half-and-half with honey and a little water before she would swallow it. Even so, it was bitter, and she wasn't too keen on it.

Smiley had taken a shine to my wife, Vickie, and kept asking where she was, wanting to go to my house and see her. Finally, after I'd been in and out of camp several times getting clothing and other items the nomads asked for, I let him know, "Let's go see my wife."

Slim followed us to camp where Smiley greeted Vickie, stood smiling at her for a few moments, and then asked if she had any bananas he could have. After chatting with her briefly, he was content and followed Slim and me down to my chicken pen as Slim wanted to once again check for eggs. I was happy to see that there were two eggs, and he was thrilled when I told him he could take them.

Now I took the two of them on a tour of our camp. Everything was so new, and they were intrigued as I showed them my gill nets for fishing and explained how I used those. They had already seen and sampled the results enough times to know the nets were effective. As we passed the outhouses located behind each missionary house, I explained what those buildings were for, and they thought it was hilarious that people had a building for that. Soon we rejoined the main group of nomads at the edge of our clearing where Smiley and Slim recounted the exciting guided tour they had just experienced, and then the whole group expressed a desire to go in and see the sights.

Matador the chief and the bulk of the nomads, excluding *Tä*, the sick matriarch, and the few who stayed to attend her, followed me into our camp and took the grand tour. Last but not least, I took them down to see the houses where the Yuquí from Chimoré were living. I had warned our helpers ahead of time so they had moved much of the meat from their smoke racks and hidden it in their houses so they wouldn't have to give all of it to the nomads. The tour was a great success, and I was pleased they had respected our belongings, and as far as we could tell, nothing was stolen.

Matador hadn't seen a shotgun fired, and when Straight Hair offered to show him how it worked, I reminded him that Matador's mother was out at the edge of the clearing, lying sick in a hammock. He changed his mind about shooting, although we did take Matador and the group to the edge of the river where they could see our assortment of boats as we demonstrated how the motorized boats worked.

With all the new experiences and activities of the day, we dropped the idea of going hunting with them. We could do that another day. I was pleased with the respect they were showing for us and our property. Even when Matador asked Grant for a chicken and Grant said no, Matador accepted the refusal gracefully with no evidence of annoyance.

Now that they were comfortable coming into our camp, the next day, some of them decided to take the next step, crossing the river in our boat to see not only the "firefly trail (airstrip)" but also the bananas we had growing near the airstrip. While the men were across the river, Tapir began wailing, possibly worrying that she might never see her husband Smiley again, but some of the Yuquí wives from the Chimoré began calming her fears and reassuring her.

Once again, I was grateful for our Yuquí coworkers and appreciative that we had people helping us who spoke the language and could communicate effectively with the nomads. How different from the first several years of friendship with the Yuquí at the Chimoré and the challenges we faced there with no knowledge of the language.

All the nomads who had come to see us were in our camp, interacting with the missionary team, showing no signs of distrust or fear when, late in the afternoon, Lorenzo and Straight Hair told them, "We are leaving to go hunting."

"Where will you be going?" questioned the nomads. "Upriver," came the reply.

The jungle people said, "We'll come and see you off."

Our guys answered, "We've got to get our stuff together first."

Before our two guys could get ready to go, the nomads decided to leave. Straight Hair had picked up some hints that the nomads might have decided to go upriver and set an ambush, so he and Lorenzo decided to wait until later in the afternoon to take off hunting. Four of our missionaries had been shot by the nomads over the past four years, so we continued to be alert and on guard while acting as if we trusted them.

Another day, our full-length mirror was a real hit. When I brought it out of the house, a few of them looked at themselves in it and preened, never having seen themselves so clearly before. Soon they called others to come and look at this wonder. Eventually, as more nomads showed up, they also expressed a desire to see inside of our houses. How many other marvels might be hiding there?

We controlled the tours as carefully as we could, only allowing a few into the houses at a time so they wouldn't help themselves freely to our belongings.

Now, instead of the group of nomads sitting at the edge of our clearing each day, they had begun coming into camp to sit behind the houses where our Yuquí coworkers from Chimoré were staying, near the river on the southeast end of our camp. We put up a corrugated tin-roofed shelter to give protection from the sun and rain so we could sit around the fire there as we cooked corn and rice. As the group sat around,

Group of Yuquí visiting our Víbora River camp.

chatting, Slim and I went to the other end of camp so he could check for eggs in my henhouse. While there, he spotted one of my domestic pigs in the jungle area Felix and I had fenced off. He got very excited and posed in a hunting stance, thinking it was a wild pig, although he had no weapon with him to shoot it.

I explained to him that it was my pet and took him over so he could see all four of them. The pigs were trained to come when I called, so I called them over, and they came up to us so Slim could see them close up. Soon we went back to where the main group of people were sitting, and he animatedly told them about the pet pigs. Now the whole group got excited and had to go see this phenomenon. On the way down, I filled the slop bucket with ripe bananas for the pigs. We reached the enclosure, but the pigs were long gone, nowhere in sight. As I called and banged the slop bucket, the pigs came galloping up to see us, and I went into the pen to talk to the pigs and scratch them behind the ears, luring them up to the fence where Matador and others could reach through the fence to pinch them and see how fat they were.

Since jungle pigs (peccaries) are very lean, the nomads were impressed with my plump porkers. I explained to them that they weren't for eating now but would grow to be as large as small tapirs. I went on to say that once they were fully grown and the sows were expecting, we would kill one of the males and share the meat with them. The pigs held their attention for a lengthy period of time before we went back to sit behind the house where our Yuquí coworkers were living.

Straight Hair and Wooly Hair had gone hunting across the river, and around 1:30 p.m., they appeared on the far bank carrying four collared peccaries. Once they had crossed the river, everyone sat around, rejoicing over the peccaries as they told us of their hunting expedition. One of the pigs was given to Matador and one to someone else, and eventually, the nomads headed home for the day carrying an abundance of meat and bananas. Another successful day with the nomads!

It was two days later that we went hunting for the first time with a small group of nomads. Straight Hair and I took three of them—Smiley, Potbelly, and Dick—with us. Smiley only carried one arrow along with his bow, whereas Dick had two arrows. Straight

Hair and I were armed with .22 rifles, and the nomads were counting on us to shoot the game. Potbelly, Dick's slave, was along to carry any game we shot or to retrieve arrows that might lodge in a tree or far out in a swamp.

Off the northeast end of our airstrip lay a swamp, and game could often be found in such a location. On our way to the swamp, we saw a few birds but let them be as we were hoping for larger game, maybe an alligator or two, or possibly a capybara (world's largest rodent). Straight Hair was leading the way, going slowly and pausing frequently to look and listen, hoping to see game before it spotted him. He was also worried about the armed warriors walking behind him, so he stopped more often than he might have otherwise.

Soon Straight Hair spotted a capybara grazing in the swamp grass near the water's edge. It had also seen him and was moving toward a place of safety, the water, when he fired, hitting it in the shoulder. Motioning to me to remain where I was standing, Straight Hair and the three nomads worked their way around to the other side of the swamp where they had last seen the rodent and soon rousted it from where it was hiding in the undergrowth. Straight Hair shot again and missed, although Smiley was able to shoot it with an arrow as it fled back toward the side of the swamp where I was waiting. It hadn't seen me, and as it paused momentarily, I was able to shoot it in the head, killing it. It had gone into the water, hoping to elude us, and now one of the hunters waded in, grabbed it by one foot, and pulled it to shore.

By the time we returned to camp, we had only been gone two hours and yet returned with fifty pounds of game. A good first hunt! While the Yuquí enjoyed capybara roasted over the fire, it was one meat I never developed a taste for as the flesh was somewhat fish-flavored; even so, I ate it whenever they chose to offer me some.

Trading was going better now that the nomads understood that we asked the airplane to bring items and then gave it something in return. It was beyond their current understanding had we explained how someone in a city purchased goods for us with money and then shipped them to us by air. As their worldview included no money or cities, we had to keep the explanation simple. In their minds, their small group and the two bands of Yuquí from which they had split were the center of the universe. Outsiders were thought to be reincarnated spirits of their dead, most of whom would do them harm, so it was safer to shoot them.

In their thinking, the airplane came from the sky where the spirits of their dead lived, which to them meant that in some way, we were able to communicate with those spirits and with Big Father (God), the new and most powerful Spirit about whom we had begun teaching them. For the most part, they seemed to believe that we were their reincarnated ancestors. That was most evident when we saw their response to our Bolivian coworkers with their cinnamon-colored skin.

On this particular day, we traded quite a few items. Matador and Grandma each wanted a kettle. Harry, Slim, and Macho each brought an arrow to trade for kettles. No one complained as they parted with their arrows and walked away with shiny new aluminum cooking pots.

Once again, Slim wanted to check for eggs in my chicken pen; in fact, he had begun checking when they first arrived and again before they left so as not to miss out on any eggs. When I found eggs, I would leave them just so I could watch his excitement as he discovered them. After checking for eggs, we went to sit by the fire, eat rice, and talk. They began telling us about a lady in their camp who was currently in labor and having a difficult time giving birth. We were able to ascertain that the woman was Giggles, slave to *Tä*.

She had now been in labor for three days, and with the cold weather added to the fact that they didn't want to "waste" food on her since they considered her to be of little value, she was weak and might not survive the delivery. We encouraged them to feed her and sent food along designated for her but doubted the food would reach her. We knew she didn't have much life expectancy, as they were sure to kill her when *Tä*, an important person since she was mother to the chief, died. Someone must die!

They reported almost daily that *Tä* had not improved but continued very ill. If only *Tä* were nearby where we could help her medically, but they were camped several kilometers away and rejected our requests to be taken to their camp.

Hunting together soon became a daily event with often more than one mixed group of nomads and missionaries going into different areas of jungle. They had lost their fear of our boats, so we could take them up or downriver before going into expanses of jungle where we hadn't previously hunted, thereby increasing our odds of finding game. None of the nomad hunters wanted to be left out of the exciting hunting trips, and one day, as we headed off downriver in the boat, we heard loud hollering, so we quickly turned around to see what was happening. Macho was running along the riverbank with his bow and arrows, frantic to join the hunting party in the boat. While he had been retrieving some of his arrows, we had left, not knowing he planned to accompany us.

Some hunts were more productive than others, although relationship building was, to us, the most important part. When the hunts resulted in little fish or game, we would wait until they left for the day and then would head out to spend the evening fishing or using a flashlight to spot game along the shore. By the next day, we would usually have fish or game to give them. The gill nets continued to be one of the most productive means of gathering an abundance, although it meant I had to be up and out the door by 4:30 a.m. in order to beat the piranha to the nets.

By 6:30 or 7:00 a.m., I would arrive home, and within thirty to ninety minutes, the nomads would show up. It was exhausting but necessary if we hoped to keep them coming back until we could convince them to settle with the Yuquí band that lived at the Chimoré River base.

Giggles was successful at giving birth, but they let us know they weren't feeding her and made it clear they didn't want to waste food on her since her mistress, *Tä*, appeared near death. Once again, we, both the Yuquí from Chimoré, and I explained to them that Big Father (God) didn't want them to kill anyone to accompany someone who died, but it was evident the custom was too engrained and it was clear our admonition would be ignored. Fear of the dead person's spirit was a powerful motivator, and they were convinced that if they didn't send someone along to serve *Tä* in death, she would punish the group after she was gone. Her spirit would get revenge, so they had to appease it; their well-being depended on it.

Over the next few days, I continued sharing biblical teaching chronologically and covered much of the first lesson. The groups were small each day and listened intently as I told them about God, His angels, and creation. Slim focused intently on what I was telling them and gave occasional feedback through questions and comments, so I knew I had at least one interested listener. The people in the groups that came varied from day-to-day, so much of the teaching had to be repeated not only since some had missed previous teaching, but also as reinforcement for those who had already heard some of what I had to say. Even so, the days seemed to be spiritually profitable, because the groups were small and showed interest.

Now a larger group of nomads showed up, including Matador, the chief. "We're going to travel far away," he announced, and then went on to explain, "*Tä* (mother) is very ill, and we don't want her to die here as this will then be a place of sadness and we won't want to come back. Better that she dies far away."

Straight Hair responded, "Big Father doesn't want you to kill anyone else if your mother dies. He will protect you from her spirit, so don't kill anyone else."

That exhortation didn't set well with Matador, and he mumbled a few words, showing that he wasn't convinced. Knowing that on their trip they were likely to steal from Bolivian farms, I spoke up, "If you need bananas or manioc while you are gone, send someone to get them from us. Don't take them from the enemy (Bolivian) farms as they might shoot you."

While he verbally agreed to send someone to get bananas from us, I knew it was unlikely he would follow through. He and the other adult males were arrogantly confident in their ability to avoid being shot by the farmers. Over the next eight days until they finally left on their trip, we reminded them daily not to kill someone to accompany another in death and not to steal from the farmers, although the odds were low that they would heed either of our admonitions.

Ever since Vickie had given a red cotton smock to one of the women, everyone in the group had been asking for red cloth, so we ordered some inexpensive red cloth to give away. As we began handing out the red cloth, a bit of a tussle began. Tapir wanted all the cloth, and as we gave it to others, she would "pull rank" and take the cloth from them. She looked enough like *Tä* that I suspected she was sister to the chief, so no one resisted as she took the cloth from them. Straight Hair gave a piece of cloth to Jane, Matador's daughter, and told her to give it to her father, but in a few moments, Tapir went over to take the cloth from Jane.

Seeing that, Straight Hair took the cloth back and said to Jane, "I'll give it to your father tomorrow."

Tapir, a woman, grappled with Straight Hair, trying to take the cloth by force, and Smiley joined in, helping his wife, but Straight Hair pinned them both to the ground. Potbelly joined the fray on behalf of his master, and Straight Hair threw him to the ground. Early on, we had established a policy that we wouldn't allow wrestling with the nomads since it tended to get out of hand and could end with eye-gouging and even shootings, but on this occasion, we all just watched as Straight Hair showed them that we wanted to give things to all of them and not allow one person to take what was meant for all.

Fortunately, the situation never got out of hand, and they could see that Straight Hair was standing up for the rights of the nomads themselves against one "high-class" individual. Doubtless, some of them were appreciative, although they didn't dare show it.

Three days later, a group of nomads was at our camp when a supply flight was due to arrive, and we invited them to accompany us to the airstrip, which was across the river and about 300 meters through the jungle. Several of them accompanied us to see for the first time the small Cessna land, unload, and take off again. As we unloaded, they saw axes, machetes, corn, sugar, and other items of interest to them, and they were excited to see all the "goodies," which we promised to share with them.

The night before, Grant and I had gone fishing and came home with three tiger-striped catfish, a forty-seven-pounder, a twenty-pounder and a seventeen-pounder. Now, having seen these fish we caught with hook and line from our boat, Macho asked if we would take him fishing by river. This would be another new experience for him, so after ferrying the others who had gone to the airstrip back to camp, Macho, Slim, Harry, my son, Sam, and I headed down the river to see if these three hunters could catch fish with hook and line. While the fishing expedition produced no fish, we did have a companionable time together.

By now, the missionary team was weary from the continual challenge of finding fish and game and the pressure of interacting daily with nomads whom we knew could quickly turn unreasonably violent. Two supply flights came, taking Straight Hair and his family along with Lorenzo and his family back to the Chimoré for a break and bringing Jaime and his family to help us. After three more contacts with the nomads, my family and I flew to Cochabamba for three weeks of much-needed rest and relaxation.

Five days after we left, the nomads paid their last visit to the Víbora River base before leaving on their extended trip. It was anybody's guess how long they might be gone; even they didn't know as one of the primary reasons for leaving when they did was to allow *Tä* to die far away from our camp. Matador, her son and chief of the group, had commented to us, "We don't want Mother to die here as then it will be a place of sadness and we won't want to return."

Our hearts were heavy knowing that with her death, Giggles, her slave, would also be sent into eternity without Christ and without hope, and Giggles' newborn infant would doubtless be killed as well.

A Heartbreaking Absence

AFTER THREE WEEKS IN COCHABAMBA, our family returned to Rio Víbora, refreshed and ready to get back in the harness. Nothing had been seen of the nomads during that time, but we were optimistic that some of them would return soon whether to stay awhile or just to pick up bananas and other goodies. We were counting on the alarm buzzer to notify us if they came and failed to hoot or whistle to us, so I was rather surprised when I looked out the window and saw that the bananas hanging from the gift rack were gone and the buzzer had not sounded. The battery had run down and needed replacing.

Two of us men went out to the gift rack and found that not only had they taken the hanging bananas, but they had cut three stalks of bananas in our plantation. Evidently, only a few people had come and, for some reason, had chosen not to let us know they were there. We hung a fresh stalk of bananas and replaced the battery for the buzzer. We would need to test the battery and replace it from time to time.

Three months went by, and rainy season arrived in earnest. For several weeks, it would have been impossible for the nomads to visit us as the river came over the bank and flooded our camp. With water all around us, we had to exercise extra care as vipers were also looking for high places where they could get out of the water. One fer-de-lance viper thought the steps leading into our house was the perfect place to wait out the flood, and a sixty-six-inch long bushmaster gave Felix and Juan quite a scare as they were cutting palm boards in a small area of jungle that hadn't flooded.

Another month went by, and the waters receded somewhat, although we were only halfway through the rainy season. With little hope that the nomads could make it through the water to visit us,

I was daydreaming as I napped in the easy chair in the living room when the silence was shattered by the sudden ring of the buzzer. Occasionally, wild animals came to the bananas, and as they climbed around eating them, they would cause bouncing, setting off the buzzer.

Leaping from my chair, I crossed the room to shut off the buzzer but hit the light switch instead of the alarm due to my groggy mind. Finally, I got the buzzer shut off and headed out the door to call to the Indians if it was them and let them know they had been spotted; otherwise, they might disappear into the woods for another few months. As I got far enough out to where I was confident they could see me, I began calling in their language. With no hesitation, they materialized out of the jungle where they had been hiding and approached the edge of our clearing. Loading a stalk of bananas onto my shoulder, I headed out to meet them.

The group of ten who had come was unusual. The first thing that stood out was the absence of key men, the top hunters of the group. None of the principal men were with them! Tom and Dick, the chief's younger brothers, both of whom were in their late teens or early twenties, had come, accompanying a group comprised mostly of women and slaves—Harry, Potbelly, Friday, Sunday, Jane, Grandma, Spooky, and Vera, the chief's wife. As I got closer, I could see that the time away had not gone well for them; some were gaunt shadows of their former selves. Grandma had lost forty or fifty pounds, and we didn't even recognize her at first.

Others were also difficult to recognize as they were malnourished and bedraggled. All of them, but especially the two older women, Grandma and Vera, were emaciated and covered in gray ash, giving the appearance of being in mourning. Vera had always impressed me as one of the more alert and intelligent of the nomads and had responded well in the past to our overtures of friendship, seeming to trust us. Now she seemed so desolate and downcast that she almost couldn't speak. Since her husband, the chief, was conspicuous by his absence, usually having been one of the first to come out on other contacts, I squatted next to her and quietly murmured, "Where is my older brother?"

She started to cry and said something about "the ones along the sky (spirits of the dead)." I wasn't sure of all she said but understood enough to know it was not a good subject to pursue. Immediately, I was suspicious that the chief might have died. Since many of them had been quite sick with coughs and congested chests when they left five months earlier, I was concerned that possibly their sickness had gotten worse after they left; but could that account for so many men being missing?

As we talked with the nomads, they expressed a desire for bananas. Jack Jones and Phil Burns made a few trips to our banana storage area, bringing fruit out for them. Then some of the nomads walked through our plantation with me, and I cut more fruit for them. While doing this, we worked our way toward the houses. They were slightly fearful about coming far from the shelter of the jungle trees, but we were able to coax them along.

After cutting all the mature bananas in sight and giving them all those stored in our banana shed, we went back out to the edge of our clearing where we sat once more and talked with them. I edged over and squatted down next to Grandma and spoke to her in a low voice, "Where are my younger brothers? Why haven't they come to see me?"

She cried a little and answered, much as Vera had done, telling me something about "the ones along the sky."

Once again, death seemed to be what she was talking of, but I felt there must be another explanation since jungle men such as those are so elusive to outsiders, and it was unlikely that several healthy men would die during an absence of only four months.

The chief's younger brothers, Tom and Dick, seemed to be heading up the group and spent most of the contact with me, either getting bananas or sitting by my side, talking with me. Dick was the only one who seemed in good humor and asked for fishing lines to take with them so they could try their hand at that. We had introduced fishhooks during earlier contacts. I gave the two of them five or six handlines for catching small fish.

As they made up their palm leaf backpacks for carrying the bananas, we continued to chat, and after two hours of being together, they headed off into the jungle, each one saying as they left, "Keep yourself warm (their way of saying goodbye)."

We answered, "Keep yourselves warm!"

Five days later, we received word from Bob Garland at the Chimoré that three Bolivian loggers and three nomads had been shot along the Chore River north of us. Could this be the answer as to where the men of this group had gone? Could all the mature men have been killed in an encounter with the *abaa,* the "enemy?" It seemed unlikely that all of them could have been killed; a few maybe, but *all* of them? Is this why the women responded with crying and sadness when I asked about the top hunters in the group?

Before they had departed on their four-month-long trip, we had been praying that God would remove any hindrances to their hearing and accepting the Gospel. Could this be His answer? Removing this many people? Our hearts were saddened by the radio report as all these jungle dwellers were our friends and special to us. While there was no way to confirm the report, it was obvious there must be some truth to it; otherwise, how could we account for the missing nomads? How many more would need to go into eternity without hope? How about other bands of the tribe that no one was even trying to befriend as yet?

Long ago, God asked Isaiah, "Whom shall I send, and who will go for us" (Isaiah 6:8 KJV)? Isaiah responded, "Here I am; send me." Where would God find Christians who cared enough about the Yuquí to respond to God's call on behalf of the nomads?

Three weeks went by before the same group of ten nomads once again showed up at our clearing. As before, there were no mature men among them with Tom being the oldest man in the group. They looked a little better than they had on their last visit and stayed for two hours as we sat and cooked rice for them at the edge of our clearing.

Dick was in a hurry to leave, although the women were more relaxed. Once again, they wanted to fill their palm-leaf backpacks with bananas, but we explained to them that we weren't going to give them as many bananas as last time so that they would come back to see us sooner. They accepted our refusal well enough to convince me that we would soon see them again.

Sure enough, the next day, as I finished lunch and stood to look out the kitchen window, I saw a shadowy form glide into view under the gift rack and materialize into a man. Turning off the buzzer, which hadn't sounded yet, I headed out. We had fished and hunted overnight and had three alligators, a twelve-pound sunfish, three tiger-striped catfish, one red-tailed Amazon catfish, one machete fish, several two-pound silver catfish, and four young ducks. All of it was roasting over a smoke rack behind the house where our Yuquí coworkers from the Chimoré were staying, and we invited the nomads to join us there.

Initially, the group was wary about coming so far into our camp and sent three "expendables," two slaves and Grandma, to verify the truth of what we were telling them. Once they were convinced we hadn't set an ambush for them, they all came in and sat around the smoke rack as we started another fire and began cooking rice and visiting together. Since their last visit, we had been able to fly in two Yuquí families from the Chimoré to help us, and now they interacted with their jungle cousins, giving them choice pieces of smoked meat to eat as we sat and visited.

By the time they left for the day, we had given each of our visitors a live chicken to take with them as well as abundant bananas, manioc, all the smoked meat, and choice pieces of cloth. Spooky, who was only about thirteen years old, was overjoyed to receive a live chicken and let us know she planned to keep it as a pet, although I knew she would soon succumb to the temptation to eat it. We had also discussed the possibility of hunting with them the following day, which resulted in an invitation to meet them at the Chore River and hunt with them there.

The next morning, Jack Jones, Steve Parker, and I left at 4:00 a.m. for the Chore River and were there by 6:10 a.m. but found no one waiting for us. We hooted off and on and, within thirty minutes, received an answering hoot, so we waded into the river to cross. The water was chest deep and flowing with enough force that Jack lost both his calf-length rubber boots, ending up in stocking feet. Once across, we sat in the forest a short distance from the riverbank and visited with the nomads. They seemed in no hurry to hunt and soon began grieving noisily as they cried and chanted to the spirits of their dead.

Soon, both Vera and Grandma turned to me and said, "Kill me, please (life was meaningless now that their men were gone)." Grandma elaborated, "Let Favorite Joven kill me."

"We will take care of you," I promised. "We are the ones who care about you. We will protect and feed you," I assured them, while knowing that their loss was beyond our ability to heal. Before long, it began threatening rain, so by mutual agreement, we canceled our planned hunting trip, shared our lunches with them, and then headed home, but not before telling them, "We'll come back to hunt tomorrow if it isn't raining and we'll bring sugar."

"Come back to us," they replied. "Keep warm by your fires."

Jack made the long walk home along the muddy slippery trail in stocking feet and did amazingly well. Four kilometers in stocking feet would have been too painful for me, but he hardly slowed us down.

During our time visiting with the nomads, we could clearly see that the group lacked leadership. Tom and Dick seemed to be floundering without the guidance of an older man and were looking to Vera for help. I had found that she listened to and considered advice from me, and with their obvious need for direction, I was hopeful they would look to us for counsel so we could convince them to move to the Chimoré and settle with their kinfolk there. The odds of Tom and Dick providing food from the jungle for the whole group seemed impossible; they would need the help which we could provide, but could we persuade them to accept it?

Early the next morning, Jack, Steve, and I were on our way to the Chore River. Steve had brought along an air mattress with which to raft across the river as well as heavy cord he planned to stretch across the river. Once the cord was tied on both ends, he hoped to lay on the mattress and hold onto the string as he went hand over hand across the river. After the string was tied across the river, Vera thought she would try to wade across, holding onto the string to keep her balance, but the river was too deep for her. Jack and I were able to wade across, but the water had risen since the previous day and was neck deep for us and too deep for the nomads.

After spending some time visiting with them, Dick said, "Let's go hunting," and off we went. Potbelly was unarmed and had been brought along to carry game we might shoot, so when he spotted a peccary, he chased it toward those of us who were armed, but the pig slipped by without any of us seeing it. It didn't take long before they tired of hunting and were ready to head back.

Vera, the chief's widow, had accompanied us on the hunt, and now, when they expressed a desire to turn back, I casually commented, "Let's make a circle and return to your camp," wanting to see if their acceptance and trust in us had grown to the point of allowing us in their camp.

"*Op!*" objected Tom (*Op* is an emphatic way to say no).

Vera amplified further, "*Yiti* (the children) will be scared."

While I understood her concern, I suggested, "You need to help your children get used to us and lose their fear of us."

She acknowledged the wisdom of that but didn't follow through on it. As we made a wide circle through the jungle to return to our starting point, we came to a log bridging a waterway covered with a mat of floating grass. The log was narrow and slippery, and I was struggling to cross without falling, but Tom assisted me and seemed concerned that I not fall. His concern for me was encouraging.

We continued until we hit our gift trail on their side of the river and then followed that until we must have been close to their camp, since when they stopped and hooted, other people soon joined us. Once again, we shared our lunch with them before making our way unaccompanied back to the river. It had risen considerably, so we had to swim across, leaving the cord stretched across in case we needed it another day.

We had three excellent visits with the nomads at the Chore River over the next four days, hunted with them, shared our lunches with them, and presented additional biblical truth. Favorite Joven had flown over from the Chimoré to join us and was doing a great job teaching an attentive audience. Rather than hike the four kilometers back to our base at the Víbora River one night, we camped on the opposite side of the Chore from the nomads, planning to hunt howler monkeys with them early the next morning, but the monkeys remained silent, thus sparing their lives.

The water in the Chore had dropped now to where the nomads could cross, so they accompanied us back to our Víbora River base. On the way, they showed us their trail, which was shorter than ours, and went through much better jungle. For them to show us their trail was an encouraging sign as it indicated their confidence in us was growing. We gave them bananas, sugarcane, cloth, and fishlines, and as they were leaving, they promised to return the following day, although we were pretty sure they wouldn't since the Chore was still dangerously high for people who didn't know how to swim.

If they didn't come, we would take a large inner tube from our swamp tractor with us the following day and see if they could cross more safely using that. With their confidence in us building, we were encouraged that God was at work strengthening our friendship with them.

Steve, Jack, Favorite Joven, Chinaman, and I left the Víbora at a leisurely 7:00 a.m. the next morning and arrived at the Chore two hours later. The river had dropped to where we had no difficulty crossing, and after hooting several times for our friends, we looked around and found one of their abandoned camps but no nomads. Our gift trail left the river at a heading of fifty degrees, so we went in that direction, eventually finding a two-day old camp. Then we found their previous night's camp with fires still hot, but again, no people.

Seven or eight minutes farther on, we heard someone, and it turned out to be Tapir with three girls and one boy, all under four years old. She was alone in camp, terrified and trembling, but slowly calmed down and called the others. People were slow in appearing, but eventually, they all came back. Vera seemed to have taken my earlier admonition to heart and brought out her six children, Little Squirrel, and his doppelgänger, a younger sister, Little Turtle (Clubfoot), and two other children. We saw twenty-four people and were pretty sure we had seen all who were still alive.

We were heartbroken to realize that twelve individuals had gone into a Christless eternity during the four-month trip they had earlier taken: what a tragedy! Now they explained that they weren't planning to travel far, just a little ways, hoping to find white-lipped peccary.

Favorite Joven spent a good bit of time talking to them about spiritual things, and Tom showed us a *cuädu* (porcupine) he had killed. Shortly after noon, we let them know that we were going to make a bridge across the Chore River so they could come to us more easily. We went back to the river and felled a tree into the river from each bank, creating a rustic bridge before going on home.

While both bands of Yuquí had lost the art of making pottery, in one of their abandoned camps, we found a small clay vessel which we carried home to send to the Yuquí Museum at the Chimoré. Most likely it wasn't made by them but was something they had stumbled across as they traveled through the jungle. Whether it was made by their ancestors or other groups who once lived in the forest was anyone's guess.

Over the years, I had gathered four or five clay vessels, mostly near the Hediondo River, and eventually donated them to the university museum in Cochabamba. Some of them had originally been underground and became visible as logging road graders dug culverts, exposing burial urns containing human teeth, the clay urns, and enamel teeth being the only things durable enough to have survived years of burial in the tropical soil.

The next day, we waited until noon, hoping they would come to us, and when they didn't show up, we went to the Chore River but decided not to look for their camp as it seemed like they didn't appreciate our going after them. We hooted a few times and then made our way leisurely back home, shooting monkeys and turkeys along the way so that our coworkers from the Chimoré would have meat to eat. Once again, it would be four months before the nomads returned to see us.

Television News

NOW IT WAS MIDYEAR, AND we had flown out to attend the annual mission conference at our boarding school. While there, three different missionaries who had come from Santa Cruz told us of reports they had seen on television about Bolivians being shot by hostile nomads in the Chore River area. Evidently, the nomads were busy retaliating for the loss of twelve of their own. Pilot Joe Kemper had watched as a reporter visited the hospital to interview a man who had been shot, so there was no question as to the veracity of the reports.

Six days later, we were home on the Víbora River, and I was in my study, listening to the Yuquí language on tape, honing up my language skills for the day when the nomads would return. I decided to go down to the kitchen and make some tea so I could be sipping on that as I listened and read through a tape about arrow making. I drew some filtered water, put it on the stove to heat, and then pulled out a teabag.

As I waited for the water to heat, I walked idly over to the window, not thinking of anything in particular, and automatically glanced out the window, checking the gift rack by force of habit. I saw a figure flit by behind the rack, but at first it didn't dawn on me that it might a nomad. I had seen Phil Burns and his visiting in-laws out there the day before, so when I saw the figure glide by, nothing registered until it dawned on me that the individual was not wearing clothing.

I turned to Vickie and said, "Indians. I think I saw an Indian" as I headed out the door, giving no thought to the tea I had started to make. As I got a few feet from the house, I asked Vickie to inform the camp, letting others know. Then I hooted so the nomads would know I had spotted them before calling to Vangie Parker, our next-door neighbor, asking her to alert others as I ambled casually toward the gift rack.

By that time, coworkers had begun showing up, and soon, Steve, Grant, and I were making our way together toward the gift rack. As we neared the rack, the nomads came out to us without any hesitation and, after we had talked briefly together, asked for bananas. Steve and Grant went into camp and brought out a few bananas before informing them that we had an abundance in the room next to my house. They readily followed us to our banana room where we gave them all the bananas we had hanging there before walking through our plantation with them as we cut more bananas and dug manioc for them.

We had decided to be extremely generous, figuring it would be better to have them go away happy and not return for a while then to be stingy and risk them not returning. We wanted them to go away content and desirous of coming back. The atmosphere of the contact seemed to indicate that they planned to return the next day, and soon, we were standing together on the edge of our clearing as they prepared to leave.

As I stood there, preparing to tell them goodbye, Tom, Dick, and one other nomad warrior were standing near me, and I mentioned to them that we had heard that some *abaas* (enemies) had been shot. While I didn't accuse them of doing the shooting, their response seemed to confirm it had been them. They asked two questions of interest. "Did the *abaas* die?" And they followed up with, "What kind of feathers were on the arrow?"

It seemed they wanted to identify whose arrow had done the damage and whether or not they had accomplished their murderous intention. I was left with little doubt that they had done the shootings.

About two months previously, my two sows had given birth, so during the contact, we took the nomads down to the pigpen and showed them the piglets. I asked Tom if he would like one, and he chose a large, white, male shoat. Then I offered piglets to Dick and to Tapir. All of them chose white piglets, preferring them to the black and white Hampshires.

We gave them flour sacks to bag the piglets and carry them home, but soon they removed the piglets from the bags and let them forage around the fire as we sat cooking and eating rice as well as an old rooster we were boiling up to share with the nomads. The piglets snuffled happily about, eating cinders, banana peels and, in general, cleaning up edible trash in the area around the fire.

The next morning, I began planting a small vegetable garden behind my house and stopped briefly to chat with Grant when he came by. We had told the nomads the previous day to hoot when they came and that we wouldn't be hanging any gifts for them. We heard a hoot-like sound but thought someone in our camp had made the noise: even so, we looked at each other and listened intently. Soon, another hoot sounded, louder than the first one. It sounded like it might be coming from the woods, but we couldn't see anyone out around the gift rack. Then we heard a real loud hoot and hooted loudly back in response.

By this time, everyone in our camp had heard the nomads calling and, in a moment, Big Tummy and Chinaman, who had flown in from the Chimoré along with their families the day before, came over carrying sugarcane and joined us as we headed out to see our visitors. Both Big Tummy and Chinaman had been slaves when the Chimoré group had been befriended, and the family resemblance to the slaves at the Víbora was evident.

Before we reached the edge of the clearing, the nomads emerged from the jungle foliage and advanced right on into our camp to the house where our Yuquí coworkers were staying. Their smoke rack was provisioned with a small alligator, several piranha, a twelve-pound pacú sunfish, and a tiger-striped catfish. Our helpers had also reserved some monkeys for their own consumption but had hidden those in the house so as not to have to give all their meat away.

With the exception of the monkeys, all their meat was smoking on the green-pole rack, so most of us squatted down around the fire to visit and talk.

Now a commotion erupted on the west end of our camp. It turned out that Vera who wasn't allowed to be seen by men since she was "behind leaves (time of the month)" had come into camp accompanied by Jane, who was her attendant. The two of them were trying to find someone like Vangie or Vickie to give them clothing. The two missionary wives didn't realize that Vera was taboo to the group and had encouraged Jane and Vera to come over toward the main group.

The nomad women were embarrassed to be visible to the group, so they hid themselves behind palm branches as they followed closely behind Vickie, trotting along on her heels as she took them to the Mayer's house where we stored used clothing. After Vickie gave them some cloth, sugar, and sugarcane, Vera and Jane were content and went to hide themselves once again from the main group.

The atmosphere of the contact was generally good, although Big Tummy, who came from the slave-class at Chimoré, but was now his own man, came on a little strong with the nomads and was unwise in things he said. He was trying to come across to the nomads as self-important, so Steve and I had to keep a close eye on him and calm him down several times as his words and actions were threatening to damage our relationship with the nomads. They could see that he belonged to the slave-class, although he was acting as if he came from the upper-class and was attempting to boss people around. This was the first time he had come to help us, and we decided it would be the last.

As the nomad women visited with the Yuquí women from Chimoré, they let Carmiña, Chinaman's wife, know that all their husbands were dead, although they believed their fathers were still surviving. Knowing that they had split from another group that roamed east of us, we assumed that their fathers were with that group. With their husbands dead, they were desirous of finding their father's group and rejoining them, although so far, they had been unsuccessful in locating them.

As they were preparing to leave, we asked if they would like us to go along and spend the night so we could hunt monkeys together the next morning, and after some discussion, it was agreed that we would accompany them partway home, hunting as we went, and then return to our camp. The next morning, they would listen for the howler monkeys and try to locate them, then we would join them midmorning and go together to shoot the primates. As we accompanied them along the trail, they pointed out two bee trees and asked if we would bring the chainsaws out in two days to fell the trees for them. Tom reminded me, "Bring fire."

We would need that to "smoke" the bees. I pulled out the Bic lighter I always carried and flicked a flame to show him that I carried fire with me. Although they had seen our lighters many times before, for the first time, he showed an interest and asked, "Can I have it?"

I gave it to him but explained that he shouldn't put it in his campfire as it would explode. I showed him how it worked, and he tested it by lighting some dry palm leaves on fire, pleased with his new treasure, although I didn't tell him that it was almost empty and would run out quickly. I carried a spare lighter in the hollowed-out butt or shoulder stock of my .22 rifle along with other survival gear such as a gauze mosquito net, candle for lighting fires, spare ammunition, and fishline and hooks. Although I had never been a Boy Scout, my motto was, "Be prepared." With fire and a knife, I was confident I could survive in the jungle, although it would also be nice to have a gun.

All the adults in the group as well as most of the older children had come to see us, which left me puzzled as to who was watching their smaller children. I thought perhaps the nomads were camped close to our clearing and had left the children nearby, but when we accompanied them as they left, we went two or three kilometers and never reached their camp.

The oldest children who had not come to see us were Whitey, who was nine or ten years old, and Tapir's oldest boy of a similar age. I found it hard to believe the women would have left all the smaller children and babies in the care of these two young men, but they must have done so as all the adults were with us.

After parting from them, we headed home along their trail, and on the way, Big Tummy and Chinaman spotted fresh dirt where a giant armadillo had just dug a burrow and gone into the ground. We still had plenty of daylight, so they spent the next two hours digging furiously in the soft soil with sharpened sticks until their exhausting efforts were rewarded. The giant armadillo they killed was heavy, about seventy-five pounds, but with the adrenaline rush of killing such a delectable creature, Big Tummy, with a little assistance from Chinaman, hoisted it onto his back and carried it home. The white meat reminded me of turkey breast.

The next day dawned with cold blowing rain from the south, so we didn't meet with the nomads. We all knew that hunting in those conditions would be a waste of time, but the following day, we started off by flashlight at 5:15 a.m., following their trail along the edge of the swamp through several abandoned camps. Once it was light enough, we left our flashlights in one of their camps and continued to the Chore River where we hooted for them and received an immediate reply.

Soon they appeared on the far bank, and although the river had risen some due to the rain, they found a crossing that was only waist deep and came across to join us. With four of them and four of us, we were able to split into two hunting parties. Big Tummy and I went with Tom and Friday, while Steve and Chinaman were with Dick and Potbelly.

My group stayed close to the river while Steve's group paralleled us farther from the river as we worked our way downriver, looking and listening for howler monkeys. Friday scared up a pig, but as a slave, he was unarmed and had no opportunity to shoot it.

Big Tummy found a turtle and shot a macaw, which he gave to them, although he kept the wing feathers for feathering his arrows. Eventually, we turned around and began working our way back the other direction up the river. When we came to some drinkable water, I told Big Tummy, "Let me stop and get a drink. I'm thirsty."

I leaned my gun against a tree, and right then, we heard capuchin monkeys traveling with little yellow squirrel monkeys. I grabbed my gun, ignoring the drink I had been about to get, and off we went to shoot monkeys. I shot three or four with the .22 rifle, and Big Tummy shot one with the shotgun. While we were shooting, Dick came running up. The action was over, and he had missed out on it.

We continued up the river to the place where we had felled trees to make a bridge and stopped there to build a fire and cook rice for them. As we sat, I entertained them by pulling out an empty used shotgun shell and blew across it to make it whistle and then showed them how to blow the shotgun barrel so it sounded like a trumpet. They enjoyed that and kept telling Steve and I to do it over and over.

The loud noise alerted their womenfolk to the fact that we had returned, and soon they showed up on the other side of the river and hollered across to us. The nomad men said quietly, "Tell them it's too deep to cross." They wanted to keep all the rice for themselves.

We answered, "We don't lie. God's children only tell the truth."

So Tom hollered out, "It's too deep, don't cross."

We hollered, "He's lying."

He would holler a lie to them, and then we would holler the truth; this continued for several minutes, and he was somewhat irritated by our honesty. Pretty soon, the women showed up on our side, and after everyone was settled around the fire, I began telling them more about Big Father (God), that He just existed of Himself, that He didn't have a mother or father, that He didn't have a body and was never born but always was. Potbelly thought that one over and soon he said, "Does He have a head?" It was good to see that he was thinking and considering what I was saying.

The next two days continued to advance our friendship with the nomads as they came to our camp each day, and we went on outings together into the jungle to fell honey trees with the chainsaws. On one of those expeditions, I was walking with Dick, the younger of the two leaders, and as we walked, he asked me to have the airplane bring sugarcane. I said, "You should go with me in the airplane over to see 'your other's' camp (the Chimoré base) and cut sugarcane to bring back."

He seemed open to that possibility. I had noticed that when Tom and Dick were separated, they seemed more open to our suggestions, but when they were together, they were more resistant. Dick seemed to be at the point where he would consider going in the airplane and willing to take my offer to heart, while Tom continued more resistant to our suggestions. I also took the opportunity to request of Dick, "When you decide to travel again, let us know you are leaving so we won't be sad, missing you while you are gone."

He assured me that he would let me know.

Big Tummy continued to be a problem. He had come from the Chimoré to help us but, in his desire to "be important" to the nomads, had a mind of his own and wasn't accepting input from our team. He had learned to run a chainsaw and took one after being told not to so he could "show off" to the nomads that he knew how to run the saw. Later, he took a gun that wasn't his and went off hunting when he shouldn't have, once again wanting to impress the nomads with the skills he had learned that they didn't yet have.

As Grant, Steve, and I discussed the problem, we all would have liked to send Big Tummy back to the Chimoré before he damaged our rapport with the nomads by showing off, but at the moment, there was no one else at the Chimoré who was available to help us. We would have to "put up" with Big Tummy for a little longer.

Now the nomads let us know that they were planning to travel. We asked about the possibility of traveling with them, telling them that when they told us to leave and head back, we would. The way it ended up, they said, "Come out and spend the night with us, and we'll go hunting monkeys in the morning before we travel." It seemed they were willing for us to spend the night with them in their current camp, which was a step forward. At 1:30 p.m., they departed with the understanding that we would join them around sundown and spend the night with them.

By 3:20 p.m., we were on our way, and when we reached a log where their camp trail rejoined our trail after going through a series of their old camps, we stopped for a few minutes rest. Along the way, we had been picking up bananas they had dropped and were collecting them in our backpacks. When we stopped, I heard what sounded like voices and mentioned it to the rest of the guys—Grant, Chinaman, and Big Tummy. We listened.

Sure enough, the nomads had found monkeys and were hollering at them, trying to keep them from fleeing so they could shoot them. We yelled to let them know we were nearby and then joined them as they chased a monkey. Grant and I were able to shoot and kill it, but it hung in the crotch of a tall tree and would have been far too much work to get down. Tom said, "Let's go," leaving the monkey.

So we went on to the Chore River. At the river, Tom said, "Let me go across first with younger brother (Dick), and we'll let the people know you are coming."

On our way to the river and before encountering the nomads, Big Tummy had told me, "We're not going to go across and sleep on their side."

I didn't push him but waited a few minutes and then told him in front of his older brother, Chinaman, "You guys need to talk to God and be willing to obey Him, whatever He wants." I didn't tell them what that should be, whether they should go across or not. I didn't really want to force something on them that they didn't want. We got to the river, and Tom and Dick went across to prepare the people for our arrival, leaving Harry with us. A couple minutes or so after they crossed, they hollered back to let us know we could join them.

Into the river we went, carrying our backpacks, although Grant and I each took time to get a drink of water at the river as we had no idea when we might have another opportunity. As we made our way to their camp, Harry kept telling me what to say when we neared the camp, but I didn't understand much of what he was advising me to say, so I mumbled a response. About a hundred yards after we crossed the river, we encountered a large group of nomads, including Tom. I didn't realize that we were already at their camp until Big Tummy announced to them, "We are going to camp here!"

Once again, he was taking charge when I felt that, as visitors, we should defer to them and their desires. Speaking in dialect so the nomads would understand that they had control, I said to him, "Don't *tell* them where we are going to camp but *ask* Tom (the leader of their group) where he would like us to camp." We wanted them to be comfortable with our presence and preferred that they let us know where they would like us to camp.

Tom, just to be ornery, pointed to a dry creek bed, a place where water would drain off the jungle and flood our bed-sites if it rained the worst possible place to camp and said, "Camp right there."

I said, "That won't do."

After my refusal, he led us up right next to their camp to a beautiful little clearing and pointed to it.

I responded, "This would be a beautiful place for someone to camp."

He said, "You can camp there."

We were happy with his choice of locations. We were only ten to fifteen feet from the edge of their camp, and now they began asking where each of us would sleep. We each picked a spot and showed them exactly where we were going to sleep. Camping that close to them, we had little choice in the matter as they would see where we hung our mosquito nets. I knew Big Tummy wouldn't be too happy with them knowing exactly where each of us planned to sleep as he had been on the team when three missionaries were shot in the night in 1980 while lying in their mosquito nets.

As we set up camp with them watching, Vera said, "Well, you need to enclose your camp (They normally screened their camps with a protective camouflage of palm branches, and she was letting us know that we should do that so that they wouldn't see us or be seen by us)."

I said, "We don't want to enclose our camp. If you are afraid, you can enclose your camp."

She set her slave, Friday, to enclosing their camp, and soon it was hemmed in all around with palm leaves.

Now that everyone was ready for bed, they sat with us until darkness began to fall and, as they left to climb in their hammocks, said to us one by one, "Keep yourselves warm."

We responded in the same manner.

Once we were settled in our mosquito nets on the ground, I learned that brothers Big Tummy and Chinaman, who were sleeping under the same net, hadn't brought a flashlight, so I dug out the spare light from the butt of my gun for me to use and gave them my bigger light so they would feel secure in the night and could shine around if they heard any worrisome noise. My little light would be adequate.

Not long after we were settled for the night in our respective camps, Tom called over to us as they joked back and forth about sleeping so close to us and who was going to shoot who. One of them would say, "Now don't you come and shoot me."

And our guys would respond, "Now don't you come and shoot me."

While we hoped they were joking, it was clear there was an air of concern. Pretty soon, Tom said, "I guess we are just going to have to urinate right here in our camp because we can't go out, you are out there. If we walk around in the night, you might shoot us." We hoped it was all just friendly jesting, but with them, we could never know for sure.

Now they asked if we had brought rice to cook, and we answered, "Yes." It was late enough that I didn't want to be cooking in the dark, so I asked our guys, "Are you hungry? Or shall we cook tomorrow?"

They said, "Cook tomorrow."

We all went to bed without supper, but for me, it didn't matter as I'd eaten well before leaving home and wasn't hungry. I suspected, but didn't know for sure, that Chinaman and Big Tummy were carrying smoked meat in their packs and would snack on that. I knew that often they carried something they could eat in the night and would be fine, regardless. That night, a cold wind blew in from the south, and although the night was chilly, I rested well.

It was 4:45 a.m. when I awoke to the sound of my wristwatch alarm and pulled on my trousers and boots to be prepared if we went after the monkeys. With the cold south wind, the howler monkeys were quiet, and I lay in my blanket on the ground until daybreak when the nomads invited us into their camp and let us know there was no sense looking for howler monkeys when they weren't making noise.

Big Tummy and Chinaman had been first to enter the nomad camp, and now the nomads invited Grant and me in too to warm ourselves by their fires. They thought it was hilarious that we had slept with only a blanket to warm ourselves and no fire.

As Grant and I warmed ourselves next to one of their fires, Big Tummy took the liberty to ask one of them if he could sit in their hammock. I squatted close to Tom and Vera's fire, watching and listening intently until after a while, they said, "Let's go." I wasn't sure where we were going but followed along as Tom led the way upriver and then across. The river had dropped, and the crossing was not much more than knee-deep, although you could almost get your crotch wet if you stepped in a deeper spot. We followed the river to the south, and as we went along, they explained that they needed to retrieve arrows they had left there a few days before when they fled from *abaas* (enemies). They had been hunting monkeys and left many arrows up in the trees. When we arrived in the area, most of us sat around and watched as they sent Potbelly, a slave, up tree after tree to retrieve arrows.

Because of the cold weather, I built a fire, and we huddled around it, keeping warm as we watched Potbelly risk his life repeatedly. One arrow was lodged in a large diameter tree that was too big around to shinny straight up, and the main crotch of the tree was over forty feet from the ground. Potbelly tried to climb it, but since he couldn't get his arms around it, he came back down. He then went eight or ten feet away to a thinner sapling, and up it he went.

When he got up about twenty-five feet, the sapling started to sway vigorously from side to side due to the breeze and his weight. To me, it looked like the tree would snap if there were any flaw in it, and down he would come. I wouldn't have stayed up there. He continued his climb up the sapling, and when he got to the highest possible safe height, went up another seven or eight feet. Then, taking hold of a vine that hung from the big tree, he pulled the top of the little tree right over against the big tree and, using lianas, tied the smaller tree over against the larger tree. Now he was able to clamber across from the sapling to the big tree and climb on up the last eight or ten feet to the wide crotch of the tree.

The two large branches extending from the crotch were almost too thick for his arms to reach around, but he grasped one of them and worked his way around it and up into the crotch. While ascending the sapling, he had also carried a long pole with a hook on the end of it, planning to use it to snag the arrow and pull it down. Now that he was up in the crotch of the tree, he saw that he wouldn't need the pole, so he dropped it to the ground as he continued his ascent into the upper branches to where he could shake the smaller branches, unbalancing the arrow and causing it to tumble to the ground. Once the arrow came down, he descended quickly and was soon beside us on the ground, although I didn't watch much of the descent. His feat had been dangerous and impressive, and I was happy I hadn't been born a slave to the Yuquí.

Potbelly retrieved at least three other arrows in that area before we left that spot and moved on. Vera was with us and had been stripping bark from *ïbai* (ambaibo) trees as we went along and then removed the pliant inner bark from the brittle outer bark. She would take it back to camp to dry before shredding it and rolling it to make bark string and rope for their hammocks, bowstrings, or skirts to be used as baby slings.

Now that I had built a fire, Friday carried some of the smoldering sticks along and stoked up a fire each time we stopped to retrieve arrows. Since none of them wore clothing and the day was quite chilly, they often warmed themselves by the fire. We retrieved one more arrow and then came to a tall tree where they pointed out an arrow lying horizontally across the uppermost branches. The arrow had to be seventy-five or eighty feet up and would have been extremely challenging to retrieve, lying as it was on top of the slender branches.

After some discussion, they decided to leave the arrow, commenting that the wind might soon bring it down. They would check another day. I suspect they were afraid to send Potbelly up after the arrow and risk losing their prize slave, and one of the few they had left.

As we went on our way, Vera would stop briefly every so often and strip off a few more pieces of ambaibo bark and then, whenever we stopped for a longer period of time, she would strip the inner bark from the outer bark, leaving the brittle outer bark behind.

On one of the longer stops, something strange occurred. Potbelly took a machete and went over to a low motacú palm that had two heavy stalks of fruit on it, both still green, and proceeded to cut them both off. Then he laughed about it as if he was taking pleasure in destroying something. Why would he cut two stalks of inedible fruit and leave them lying there? Very puzzling!

Other than retrieving arrows and gathering pliable bark from which to make string and rope, we had accomplished very little, but now they turned and headed back to where we had first crossed the river not far from their camp. When we got to the edge of the river near their camp, they began shooting arrows across onto the beach on the other side. Harry shot one, and it went warping its way through the air in a crooked path. Dick shot a couple across as did Tom, and their arrows went nice and straight. The slaves and lower-class had inferior, crooked, poorly made arrows whereas the high-class had nice straight ones.

We crossed the river, gathered up their arrows, and went on to their camp. Big Tummy made himself at home, going over to Vera and Tom's fire where he relaxed in their hammock. Occasionally, he would relinquish it to Tom for a few minutes and squat nearby. We dug rice out of our packs and passed it around, giving some to Dick to cook, some to Tom, and some to Chinaman to cook for us so we could eat too.

Grant spent the time sitting, looking over their campsite, noting which individuals were at which fires, getting a better picture of who belonged to which family group. Grant was sharing his observations with me, and I was writing some down and making mental notes of others. We counted twenty-four people, four main family groups. Vera and Tom were at fire one and had five boys, sons of Matador. The youngest son was Little Turtle (Clubfoot). The oldest two boys were very much lookalikes. We have a picture of the older one riding a motorless go-kart in our camp. Friday, as their slave, completed the group of eight.

At Dick's fire, it appeared that Jane was his sleeping partner. She was sitting right behind him, but it didn't look like they were on speaking terms. She seemed rather upset for some reason, not at all happy. Potbelly was obviously Dick's slave. There were some kids hanging around there. Whitey, for one, seemed to be hanging around that fire. Some of Tapir's children were also hanging around Dick's fire, one of them being Monkey Eyes, a cute little girl six or seven-years-old.

At Tapir's fire, there were boys and girls. She seemed to have five or six children, and her oldest boy was over at Dick's fire near me. Sunday was over by Tapir and seemed to be her oldest daughter. The other fire consisted of Harry, Spooky, Grandma, and Blanca's two orphaned girls, a two-year old and four-year old. Blanca was one of the twelve people missing and presumed dead.

Over where Potbelly's hammock was slung, two hammocks were hanging. Tapir had a hammock, Grandma had a hammock, Dick had a hammock with thick, heavy ropes, Vera had a hammock, and there may have been another. Vera also had a second older hammock lying on the ground by her fire but was using her newer, heavier one.

Potbelly, Dick's slave, seemed to play the role of a dog to his master. Dick sat in the hammock like the king on his throne, eating. He had a piranha and tore the head apart, eating the good and meaty parts out of it before handing the bones with hardly anything left on them to Potbelly, who licked them clean and sucked off the last edible morsel. Dick ate the flesh from the fish before handing the scales to Potbelly who dutifully and hungrily gobbled them down.

Then Dick reached over for his big aluminum kettle with lid that he had traded a bow and arrow for a few days before, opened it up, and removed a few pieces of honeycomb, which he proceeded to stick in his mouth one by one and chew several times, just enough to get the bulk of the honey out, all the good stuff. Then he pulled the chewed wax from his mouth and handed it to Potbelly who chomped on it until the last drop of goodness was gone. That's how the slave was fed.

It appeared to me that he had fully accepted his lot in life and knew this was how he was going to be treated. Potbelly did the work, and Dick enjoyed the fruits of it. Dick was the hunter and shot the game for Potbelly to carry in and prepare it for eating. Dick spotted the bee trees and had his slave chop them down and fight the bees for the honey. We could see that the high-class ruled over the lowly and despised.

Tom and Dick were royalty along with Vera. They were eating well, and the first fruits of everything went to them. It looked like they were also taking care of Tapir, which lead me to believe she must be closely related, possibly an older sister to Tom and Dick. Also, she had several daughters who could eventually become wives for Vera's sons. The family that was being left out and not being taken care of to speak of was Grandma with Harry, Spooky, and Blanca's two children. They were being treated as dirt under the feet of the high-class group.

Sunday also looked on with a sad face as if life was anything but pleasant. Her man, Macho, was among the missing. My heart went out for those who were not in the ruling class and those who had no provider. Theirs was a miserable lot, and it appeared they would be happy to change it; but the high-class, Tom and Dick especially, still enjoyed life in the woods because they had control not only over their own lives but also over the lives of the others.

We had decided by this time not to travel with them, because we were losing their respect due to the way Big Tummy was acting and felt we needed someone from the high-class working with us, someone whom they would respect more, so we decided to return home to our Víbora River base. After we ate and talked with them for a while, we got up to leave and learned that some of them had decided to accompany us, possibly to retrieve the monkey we had shot the day before.

Harry, Grandma, and Spooky came with us, carrying Blanca's youngest child. As we walked the trail together, they let us know that they were coming to spend the night with us at our camp. This small portion of the nomadic band had reached a point where they would likely have been willing to stay with us and be done with the rigors of nomadic life had the rest of the band been so inclined.

We came to where we had shot the monkey the previous day and found it hadn't fallen but was still lodged high up in the tree; by now, it would be inedible. Shortly before reaching that spot, a squirrel ran up a tree. I had my pack on my back and was weary with exhaustion but asked God to guide my bullet as I prepared to fire. The squirrel had run up a high branch on the tree, and I aimed above and to the left, knowing that as I squeezed the trigger, it would pull over onto the squirrel.

The bullet creased it through the neck, and it came toppling down, crashing to the ground. Harry ran to grab it and was thrilled to have the tiny creature.

Along the way, we scared game up a couple more times but didn't have opportunity to shoot until just after we transitioned from their trail to our own trail, when Big Tummy looked up and said, "Howler monkeys!"

We dropped our packs and started running. As I followed Big Tummy at top speed over a fallen log, I got tangled in vines and went sprawling. My gun went barrel first down into the soft soil, plugging the barrel with dirt, so I had to stop, cut a stick, and punch the barrel clean of dirt. This meant unscrewing the barrel from the gun and removing it so I could run a slender stick through it. Once it was clean and reassembled, I went running after Big Tummy again. He had been able to get a monkey stopped high up in a tree and was shooting at it with a short-barreled shotgun.

I had my .22 rifle and joined him in shooting until the monkey was badly wounded and unable to flee. It had gotten into the crotch of a tree, and Big Tummy told me to stop shooting until it moved from there. As soon as it came out of the crotch and started down a branch, I shot it in the head, and it came crashing to the ground. It was a heavy male.

On the other side of the trail, Grandma and Spooky had their eyes on another monkey and called us over to shoot it for them. Chinaman also had one cornered in a tree, so after shooting the one for Grandma and Spooky, we joined Chinaman. I shot that monkey in the head as well, but it locked its tail around a branch and hung there, dead. The nomads said, "It's locked on, it won't come down."

Grant joined us, and he and I began shooting at the tail with our .22 rifles. Grant shot once or twice, and I shot a couple of times before our shots caused the tail-hold to loosen, and the monkey crashed to the ground. God had given us a large monkey for each family group—one for Chinaman, one for Big Tummy, and one for Harry. Our visitors would enjoy their night at our camp!

Our four guests enjoyed their overnight stay in our camp and the royal treatment we gave them. Steve Parker and David (Chinaman's son) took Harry fishing and were able to catch a fifteen-pound tiger-striped catfish for him. We gave them one of our roosters, so they were well-provided with meat as well as an abundance of bananas. By the time they were ready to head home the next morning, they opted to leave many of the bananas behind, telling us, "We're going to get our hammocks and return." The treatment they were getting from us was far better than the treatment they could expect in their camp, and we hoped they could convince the rest of the band to settle down and move to the Chimoré. That was the last we saw of the nomads for almost four months.

Even though we had chosen not to accompany the group on their travels, we could see that God had been at work, guiding in our decision to come home rather than roam with them. Big Tummy had been doing and saying things that were causing us to lose their respect, but God used that to bring us home and to have a family of them come with us. It was a thrill to see God's concern for this despised family, sending howler monkeys we could shoot for them. More than once, we had hunted with the larger group, looking for howler monkeys, but never found them; whereas this time, God sent monkeys to provide for the most despised among the nomads. His care for them was evident.

Within two days, we began getting radio reports that nomads had been stealing crops from a sawmill located twenty-six kilometers east of us, so Felix, Iroquois of the Chimoré Yuquí, and I paid a visit to the mill. The mill, owned by Enrique Hollweg, had an airstrip, so we were able to get pilots Joe Kemper and Tom Bush of South American Mission to fly us over there, a ten-minute flight from takeoff to landing. Once there, the owner and his family served us lunch and gave us firsthand information on the crops that had been stolen and the dates they were taken before taking us out to see for ourselves. The dates the bananas and sugarcane had been taken overlapped with the period of time we had been in contact with the nomads at the Chore River, so it was clear that more than one band of Yuquí roamed between the Yapacaní and the Ichilo River. Could this be the band of nomads to which Vera's father belonged and which they were trying to find?

October 1985, Steve and Felix Shot

It was almost four months before the jungle dwellers finally returned to see us, and when they came back, we sensed an oppression that hadn't been present in the previous set of contacts. As a missionary team, we spent more time in group prayer and looking to God for wisdom as we puzzled over their change in attitude. While the previous set of contacts had been friendly and we had each spent the night in the other's camp, now there were strong "vibes" that they might have hostile intent toward us. They were antagonistic to all mention of God and spiritual things in a way that they had never been before. After only two or three contacts, they left and didn't return.

It seemed the "prince of the power of the air" was doing his utmost to keep this group of Yuquí from learning of the One True God. He had twice before instigated them to shoot the missionaries who were trying to befriend them, with four missionaries injured over the last five years.

Now, after more than fifty encounters with these jungle dwellers and an incipient friendship, the group, who upon initial contact with the missionary team had numbered thirty-six people, was reduced to twenty-four individuals. Along with death from illness, they had suffered deaths from an encounter with Bolivian loggers in which at least three loggers and three nomads died. Others of the Yuquí had been killed by their own people as they followed their cultural practice of killing some of their own to accompany the spirits of their ruling-class dead to the next world. At this rate, the remaining twenty-four nomads would soon cease to exist, and the missionary team was desperate that not happen.

On the previous set of encounters with the missionaries, the much-reduced band of jungle dwellers had come of their own volition to the mission base on the Víbora River where we loaded them down with foodstuffs, bananas, manioc, sugar, lard, rice, and corn. During those contacts, they had been friendlier than ever, but now resistance to us seemed to be growing once again. On the one hand, they seemed appreciative of what we could provide for them, while at the same time, occasionally showing hostile intent. Clearly there were pressures on them that we didn't understand.

Typically, on contacts such as these, we would fly Yuquí believers over from the base at the Chimoré River where the first band of the tribe had settled twenty years earlier. A good rapport had been developing between these two bands of the tribe, and it was hoped that eventually, the Víbora River Yuquí would prove amenable to the idea of moving to the Chimoré River to settle with their kinfolk there.

However, on this set of contacts, none of the Chimoré Yuquí could be brought over to assist since chicken pox was going around there, and we didn't want to expose the Víbora River group to that illness. The good thing about not bringing Yuquí over from the Chimoré was that all the missionaries at the Víbora base became much more involved in building relationships with the Víbora band of Yuquí, and the jungle dwellers had begun accepting "those who wear clothes" much more than they had previously. Several of the missionary families had only arrived in Bolivia in the last few years and had not yet had opportunity to learn the Yuquí language, but now that they needed to interact more with these people, most of them were beginning to pick up a few words and phrases, and their motivation to learn the language was increasing due to the need to communicate, and all of them were doing what they could to show the nomads that they loved and cared for them.

In some ways, the contacts were going well, while at other times, we sensed a desire on the part of the nomads to do harm to us, the missionary team, to set up situations where they might be able to shoot or kill us. One contact was going beautifully, when suddenly, the new leader of the group, the young man we referred to among ourselves as Tom, seemed to have some other "power" come over him, and the look that came on his face was frightening. I could only describe it to my coworkers as "the prince of the power of the air" took hold of him, and I commented to them, "This is…this is not just human." It was the only way I could think to describe it.

One of my coworkers suggested, "Well, he may have just been really angry."

I had seen Tom a few times when he was quite upset, and the look that came across his face, others might have interpreted it differently, but to me, it brought home the spiritual battle that we were in. That night, we—the missionary team, husbands and wives—got together for a time of intense group prayer. All of us who were in close daily proximity to the nomads could sense that they were really enjoying being with us, while at the same time, some of them were trying not to. There was a resistance to us on the part of some while they also wanted what we had to offer, not only the foodstuff and material goods we were providing them with, but also the friendship and love. We were the first "outsiders" to treat them with care and consideration. God was preparing our hearts for what was to come.

As we sensed their resistance to us in some ways and yet saw their desire to have a friendship with us, sometimes having a super-friendly relationship and at other times detecting that they were trying to get us to go into the jungle with them into situations where they could set up an ambush and shoot some of us, I remarked to the missionary team, "I think that in some ways, we might be pushing them too hard. We're getting resistance and need to back off."

What we didn't fully understand was that it had little to do with us but mostly had to do with their loss of the chief and all the leading men. The survivors hadn't been able to adequately appease the spirits of their dead. They knew that "someone must die" to satisfy the demands of their dead or their lives would be impacted in many negative ways. Who could they kill to keep the spirits happy?

As time went on, we learned that the nomads, in their times away from us, were searching for their "real fathers," a group from which they had split shortly before their initial encounters with us. They were also looking for their missing men, leaving us wondering whether they still had hope of finding some of their warriors alive. Tom and Dick, two young men in their late teens or early twenties, were trying to provide for the entire band of twenty-four individuals, a daunting if not impossible task, with only bows and arrows. Tom and Dick were brothers, possibly younger brothers of the missing Chief, Matador.

As poorly as the group was being provided for in the jungle and with the pressure they were feeling to find the bodies of their dead and avenge those deaths, each time the nomads left us for a few weeks or months, we were concerned we might never see them again, so we were feeling pressure to encourage them to stop roaming the jungle and to settle down where we could help them transition from the nomadic life of deadly encounters with farmers, loggers, hunter/trappers, and oilmen to a more sedentary life of peace with the outside world. They, at the same time, were overwhelmed with the pressing need to find the bodies and appease the spirits of their dead.

Now when they returned, it seemed they might have been successful in finding the bodies of their important dead. When their loved ones originally disappeared, the group had heard gunshots but found no bodies and, a few months after their loss, had come to our camp in terrible condition. On one of their visits to our camp, we let them know that we had learned where another group of their people was roaming, and they were really excited to hear that, exclaiming, "We're going to go look for our real fathers," which I took to mean the group they had split from a few years previously. They only stayed around for a few days before leaving to check out that report, but the next time they returned, they informed us, "We haven't found them." The other group was rumored to be roaming in an area about twenty-one miles to the northeast of our base.

The next time they left, they told us that they would be back in two days, and when they didn't return the second day, we had a time of waiting on God in prayer and, as a group, concluded, "We should send a small team, three guys, out to the Chore River and see if the jungle dwellers are camped there. If so, we can camp nearby, but not too close, making ourselves available so they can come to us there as we continue encouraging them to return to our base camp. We can also use the time to hunt with them, improving their diet and, in the quiet hours while we are sitting around camp interacting with them, we can share more of God's truth with them."

We also decided that if we didn't find them camped there near the Chore River, we would leave our options open as to whether to follow their trail and make contact with them in the jungle or return to our home base.

The next day Steve, Felix, and I went out to the Chore River, crossed it, and then hooted loudly to alert the nomads of our arrival. We were in an area where we knew they frequently camped and where we had spent a night with them in their camp. None of us were as adept in the forest as the jungle people, with Felix being the best of the three of us as a tracker. With no response to our hooting, we looked around the area for a time and then set up camp for the night.

The next morning, by God's grace, we found where they had camped and the trail they followed as they left the area. Returning to our campsite, we prayed and discussed what we should do, and then I polled each man. "Felix, what do you think we should do?"

He replied, "Let's go after them."

I asked Steve the same question and received the same response. While I had some hesitation about following them, I was convinced God was speaking through my colleagues and agreed with their decision, which I felt was also consistent with what we as a team had discussed in our last meeting at the Víbora base. Now we just needed to turn on our Stoner transceiver and update our coworkers at the Víbora River base. "We've found where they camped and the trail they left and are planning to follow them. We'll keep you informed as we are able."

"Understood," came the reply, "we'll be praying for you."

After disconnecting the radio gear and distributing the various components among the three of us so no one person's pack would be too heavy, we packed up camp and prepared to track the nomads... if we could follow their trail. Concern for our jungle friends weighed heavily on us, and we were afraid that if we didn't find them and convince them to settle with the Chimoré band of Yuquí, they would all soon be dead, whether at the hands of those who were invading their homeland or from malnutrition.

God led us down nearly invisible paths as we hiked for six long hard hours along Indian trails and, around noon, when we stopped for a brief rest, Steve commented, "This is the most worn-out I've been since several years back when we went searching for them for several days, not knowing where they might be."

Occasionally, we found ourselves in beautiful areas of forest with tall trees and open woodlands, while in other places, the jungle was dense with vines, cat's-claw thorns that tore at your clothing or skin, and terrain that was almost impossible to traverse. The occasional ravine meant sliding or crawling down the steep walls of the gully and then trying to find a way up the other side by holding onto roots, vines, or bushes, all while carrying a fifty-pound backpack with a rifle in one hand and a machete in the other.

By one o'clock, we had all reached our limit, and it was then that we came upon the camp where the nomads had spent the previous night. The coals of their campfires were still hot, so we fanned one back into flames and stopped for a rest and to cook a modest meal. Evidently, they had taken off only a few hours before and couldn't be far ahead of us.

As we rested, we discussed what to do now that we were so close behind them. Steve was quick to suggest, "Why don't we have a good rest and wait until about three o'clock to follow them?"

Felix and I were in agreement as we all knew that by late afternoon, when we found the Indians, they would be setting up their new camp and mostly clustered in one place. We preferred to find them like that rather than spread out as they would be if they were traveling along the trail. Setting up camp, they would be making noise, cutting palm branches to shield their camp, and gathering firewood for the night. Likely, we would hear them before they heard us, and we would be able to call out and let them know that their friends had come. The last thing we needed was to startle them unnecessarily and be greeted by a barrage of arrows.

The plan worked well! After a two-hour time of relaxation and recuperation, we picked up our packs, guns, and machetes and headed off down the trail. During some of the previous contacts, we had given young domestic piglets to the leaders of the group, and the surviving piglets had learned to follow their owners through the jungle, much like a pet dog. At least once when we had trouble spotting the nomad trail, Steve or Felix found the tracks of the piglets, and we were able to follow those until the Yuquí trail became more obvious. Felix was leading the way with me right on his heels, and we hadn't gone more than a few hundred yards when we came to a Y in the trail. The main trail seemed to go roughly north south, but the more recently used trail seemed to be the arm of the Y which headed off to the east.

More and more, we began to see bits and pieces of fresh palm branches they had broken off while weaving palm mats or backpacks as well as fresh ash that had dropped from the burning brands of fire they carried with them.

With all the debris we were now seeing along the trail, we sensed that their camp couldn't be far away. I spoke softly to Felix, "If we get near them, why don't you let me go first?"

He had been leading the way and replied, "I had that in mind."

I would be able to call out to the people in their own language, whereas Felix only spoke Spanish. Also, the people knew me far better than they did Felix as he had spent much less time with them. Shortly after we turned off to the east at the Y in the trail, Felix stopped and motioned for me to go first. We had only gone a few paces farther when we saw a palm-thatched hut like the nomads often make, and while we didn't yet realize it, we were very close to their camp. We would later see that there were two thatch huts, both of them burial shelters, but we didn't realize that until a little later.

We stopped. Felix looked at me, and Steve looked at me, and we looked at each other, not knowing that the Indian camp was just out of sight beyond these burial shelters.

It was then I decided to whistle. Typically, when the Yuquí are returning from a hunt and nearing their camp in the jungle, they will stop and signal by drawing air in as they whistle a tone that ascends from low to high. This notifies the people in camp that one of their own is approaching so no one is unduly startled. Someone in the camp responds to the whistle with two short indrawn whistles also ascending from low to high tone. Now I whistled in case we were within hearing distance of their camp. I was answered immediately by the frightened cry of a woman but no answering whistle. We had caught them unawares, off guard. I quickly called out in the dialect, "It's us! It's us!"

On the last set of contacts we had with them in our camp, they had told me, "If you go over and run into those other Indians and they holler and scream to run, just call out, 'It's me! It's me!'"

At the time, I had pointed out that since I wore clothing, the hostile Yuquí would think I was an *abaa* (an enemy or Bolivian national) and shoot me anyway. Fortunately, this group knew who we were, so I called out again, "It's us! It's us!" and without waiting for a reply, we began moving forward toward the cry we had heard.

Suddenly, we found ourselves in the clearing where the two burial huts stood and were immediately joined by a small group of nomads. On past occasions, when we had met them in the jungle, the men would all show up with bows and arrows and a worried look on their faces. Not this time. They all came up empty-handed, and most of the faces were joyous, happy to see us; some were smiling broadly. There may have been a few who looked a little shook up that we had shown up so unexpectedly, but even so, they came running up to see us, and we read the situation as, "Hey, great to see you!"

In a few moments, the two leaders of the group, Tom and Dick, came up carrying their bundles of bows and arrows, but not in a threatening manner. It appeared more like they'd grabbed them so as not to lose their weapons as they prepared to flee.

Steve was eyeing the two huts and questioned, "I wonder if these are, you know, burial huts?"

I wasn't too sure if they were or not since occasionally, the nomads make tight enclosures when the weather is cold with heavy rain, but the question was answered within an hour or so when Vera (the chief's widow) commented, "That's Papa's house," referring to her deceased husband as she pointed to one of the shelters. Over the next few minutes, she repeated this several times to make sure we understood. Likely, his decaying body was inside the shelter wrapped in woven palm mats and lying on a raised platform, although we weren't so disrespectful as to look or ask to look. They would need to leave the body there until the flesh rotted from the bones, at which time they would repackage the bones in fresh mats and eventually place the bones in a basket that could be carried with them in their wanderings.

We didn't understand until a few days later that we had found them while they were in the process of "renewing the bones," repackaging them, and moving them to new shelters which had already been constructed beyond their camp.

After we visited with them for about thirty minutes, they began encouraging us to set up our camp for the night. They seemed to have no problem with us setting up nearby, although they didn't offer to let us set up in their camp, which we repeatedly suggested they allow us to do. We could see the smoke from their fires just a short distance down the trail but weren't invited there.

We said, "If we're out here and you're over there, you'll be afraid we'll come around in the night, and we'll be afraid you'll come around in the night. We'll all be fearful, and nobody will sleep." We talked back and forth like this a lot because of shootings that had happened in the past and because they knew that we knew how they were. We went back and forth a good bit verbally with the hope that they would invite us to camp with them. Sometimes it would reach a point where some of them would say, "Come on down and camp with us," and then someone else would say, "No." There seemed to be mixed feelings on their part, but it was pretty clear that Tom, the older of the two leaders, didn't want us to camp with them.

We stalled along as the sun continued to go down and we didn't want to be making camp in the dark by flashlight, so finally, Steve removed his tent from his pack and began setting it up. He had a free-standing tent and commented, "If they invite us to set up in their camp, I can pick up the tent and carry it along." More and more, the people were encouraging us to set up where we were standing, so we began preparing our camp for the night.

About the time we were finishing setting up camp, Friday, one of the lower-class slaves, came over and said, "Oh, we lost a knife here. Let's look for that knife." The jungle floor was covered with dry leaves to a depth of six or eight inches, and since it hadn't rained for several weeks, the leaves were exceptionally dry. Soon, Friday was joined by others who started pushing leaves here and there as they searched, ostensibly for a knife. In the process, they were making trails through the dry leaves.

Soon they had two smooth trails cleared of leaves. By now, Steve was lying in his tent, and I was lying in my jungle hammock on the ground while Felix was on the ground in his mosquito net. I hadn't paid much attention to what was going on, but once I climbed into my hammock, my weary mind came alert, and I said to Steve, "Steve, they weren't looking for a knife, they were making trails so they won't tread on dry leaves when they come to shoot us in the night!"

As they were finishing up clearing the dry leaves, one of them asked, "Hey, do you have those things you shine with at tapirs in the night (referring to our flashlights)?"

I replied, "We sure do." It was getting dark by then, and as I replied, we all got our flashlights out and said, "See how bright they shine!"

They watched as we shone our lights around the area, and they also noticed that each of us had a gun in bed with us. They had hunted with us enough to know that we were proficient with our weapons, and now they began to realize that we would be able to see in the dark with our flashlights. Jokingly, we added, "After you all go to bed, we're going to move camp, because we have lights and we're just going to move to where you can't find us."

It would be a dark night, and the moon wouldn't be up until almost morning. Their plans to shoot us in the night were discarded as they realized the advantage would be ours. Now they decided on a new plan, and Dick, Tom's younger brother, came by to let us know what that might be.

"Did you bring your fishing lines?" he probed. Once he was assured that we had lines along, he proposed, "Why don't we go fishing for pacú (large sunfish) tomorrow? The river isn't very far away."

With that, we lay down to get some much needed rest, but not before I asked Felix and Steve, "Shall we set a guard?"

Initially, they both said, "Yes;" but after more discussion, we decided to all remain alert until it got extremely dark, and then when the moon came up in the morning, we'd stay alert until dawn and keep an eye on things. With our lives on the line, none of us had any trouble coming awake before the moon began to light the sky early in the morning.

At first light, the Indians came, suggesting we go fishing, and we agreed to that. Steve removed the radio from his pack, thinking he could carry it along and we could call our wives at the Víbora River base while we were fishing, but when the Indians mentioned that the beach wasn't far away and that we would come back soon, we decided to leave the radio equipment behind and call when we got back from fishing.

We had gone only a short distance down the trail when the nomad warriors changed their minds. Now they decided that fishing wasn't such a good idea, and they suggested that we leave our fishing lines along the trail and hunt instead. However, within minutes, when we heard a troop of monkeys going through the trees near the trail, they had no interest in us shooting the creatures for them. Normally, monkeys were prized and easy to shoot, but the four Indians with us seemed moody, out of sorts, and in a very bad humor.

Each time we would ask how much farther it was to the river, they would comment, "It's not far." At the same time, they seemed to have little interest in hunting or fishing. It seemed as if they had something else on their minds, and as their attitudes worsened, the three of us decided that the best thing to do would be to turn around and go back to our camp and let our coworkers at the Víbora base know where we were and that we were with the nomads.

As we turned back, Felix, who was now leading the way, feigned having difficulty following the trail and suggested that one of the nomads lead the way. They replied angrily, "You lead, we'll tell you if you get off the trail." Felix had little recourse but to continue leading the way as the three of us headed back down the trail to the southeast followed by four armed and sullen warriors.

We hadn't progressed far before the harsh sound of an arrow grating its way across a palm-wood bow put my senses on alert, and

I found I had thrown myself to the ground to the right of where I had been walking. In the process, I had pivoted 180 degrees and was now looking down our back trail as my gun fired four quick shots in the direction of the attackers. Simultaneous with my reaction, I heard the thud of an arrow driving into Steve's body and the sound of air being violently expelled from him along with an agonized groan. In my heightened sense of awareness, I took in the entire scene at a quick glance. Potbelly had a fully drawn bow with an eight-foot arrow and was trying to get a bead on Felix who was crouched over and turning to his right.

With my gun still aimed down the back trail, I threw two quick shots closely over Potbelly. There had been no conscious thought to pull the trigger for my first four shots, but these two shots were fired with an attitude. We had done so much for these jungle dwellers, and now they were repaying our many kindnesses in this manner! My shots startled the attackers, causing them to scream with fright. Two of them dropped their bows and arrows, and all four fled.

As quickly as the attack had begun, it was over. Of the four attackers, the vision that was seared into my mind was that of Potbelly with a fully drawn bow as he tried to follow Felix's movement and get a shot at him. Fortunately, my two shots and Felix's movement had caused that shot to miss.

We three missionaries had been leading the way down the trail on an aborted fishing expedition with nomads we were in the process of befriending. Felix was leading the way, then Steve, then me with the four jungle dwellers following us. We had interacted with them over the course of several years, hunted together in the jungle, and spent at least two nights camped together with them in the jungle. Why, after almost sixty encounters with them, would they turn on us in this way? Why would they try to kill my two colleagues?

Steve lay on the ground where he had fallen. A lance-shaped bleeder-tipped arrow entering low on the right side of his back had driven itself all the way through his body, pierced the tip of the lung, and left the tip of the arrow protruding from his chest. Steve's moaning broke the silence, and then his first words, "Pull it out, brother, it hurts."

While both men had been hit by bleeder-tipped arrows, Felix was only lightly wounded. An arrow had ricocheted off his left shoulder blade, causing a shallow wound. Meanwhile, Steve had an arrow point embedded in his body. The bleeder-tipped arrow had a tip shaped like a lance made of bamboo. The tip itself was two and a half inches wide and roughly eighteen-inches long, and the cupped shape of the bamboo made a wide semicircular incision where it had entered his body. The tip was poking out the front of Steve's chest while the part that had been attached to the arrow shaft protruded from his back.

While I knew he must be in terrible agony, I replied, "I can't pull it out, we need to leave it in to stop the bleeding."

My thoughts went back to my boyhood, growing up in the small jungle town of Todos Santos. Before I was even eighteen, I had seen at least one man die, shot by another band of the same tribe. On one of the shooting occasions, doctors in the city of Cochabamba made the statement, "If the local doctor had left the arrow tip in the wound, this man would have survived. Pulling the arrow tip out of the body did a lot of damage, plus it increased the bleeding." The peasant farmer bled to death.

I had determined back then in my childhood that if I ever faced a similar situation, I wouldn't pull the arrow point out of the wound. Hours later, once radio communications were established, we were able to talk with Dr. Nina Kunkle of World Gospel Mission who confirmed to us that the best thing was to leave the arrow point in the wound until Steve reached medical attention in the city.

Now the three of us were bunched up tightly together in a depression on the forest floor with a fallen log and some trees around us. Felix and I were holding onto our guns as our first thought was that the Indians might return and try to finish us off, so we crouched down, Felix looking in one direction, and me looking the opposite direction, back-to-back, with Steve between us to protect him, watching 180 degrees of jungle each, listening carefully in case of another attack.

After a few short minutes, it became evident that the Indians had fled. At this point, Steve said, "Go get the radio, brother. Call for help." I knew in my heart that the radio equipment would not be at our campsite. It was clear that this attack was premeditated. It had been obvious to us all morning that we were in a dangerous situation. Our normally friendly relationship with the nomads had not been there. All three of us could sense the imminence of an attack, and yet, there was little we could do about it.

Normally, as we hunted together in the jungle, which we had been doing for a number of months, the hunting party would be interspersed as we traveled along the trail—a missionary, a nomadic Yuquí, another missionary, etc. But on this day, they had refused to mingle with us and insisted on walking behind us. We had spent much of our time that morning looking over our shoulders, watching our backs as best we could. Later, Steve made the comment that just moments before he was struck by the arrow, he had committed his back to God, praying, "Lord, I'm going to trust you with my back," fully expecting that God would protect his back. Only seconds later, the Indians attacked with an arrow slicing into Steve's back.

For myself, I had been walking with a live round of ammunition in the chamber of my .22 rifle with the gun off safety, even though the terrain we were traversing was broken, slippery, with many vines, logs to step over, and the possibility of slipping and falling at any time. But I knew the situation warranted taking some risks.

Steve spoke again, "Go for the radio, brother."

Thoroughly disheartened, I responded, "I'll go, but it won't be there. By now, they've stolen all our belongings, but at least I can go back to look and retrieve what is possible to recover. Let's pray first." My knees were shaking and I could hardly stand.

Steve continued to lay where he had fallen. Felix and I were watching the jungle around us very carefully. A quick prayer meeting was held after which I stood to my feet and attempted to head off toward where we had spent the last night camped in the jungle. My legs were trembling and would barely support my weight, and my bowels were threatening to let loose. I realized that in this state, I wouldn't get far. I turned around and said, "Brothers, we need to pray again." We prayed, committing Steve and Felix to the Lord and me to God as I headed back to our previous night's campsite.

Last night's camp lay twenty or thirty minutes to the south, and we had left the radio there when we took off in the morning to hunt and fish with the nomads. I had little hope that any of our belongings were there now. Surely the nomads had taken what they could use and thrown the rest where I would never find it. They knew we would come to at least look for our belongings and would doubtless set an ambush along the trail. Steve could not be left alone in his defenseless state. Felix would have to stay with him. That left me to walk the trail alone…with God.

I repeated the refrain to myself multiple times, "Alone…with God! Alone…with God!" I had serious doubts that I could even find the trail back to our camp as it was a lightly used Indian trail. Steve's condition was critical. I could wait no longer. After the second word of prayer together with the team, I headed out.

I stumbled along through the jungle, losing the trail, finding it again, thanking God each time. The obvious plan would be for the Indians to ambush the trail, knowing that we would return along it to pick up the belongings we had left at our campsite. I headed down the trail, wondering where I would run into the ambush. After so many years in the jungle, I had a keen sense of direction; even so, the trail was practically impossible to follow, just a seasonally traversed Indian trail with the occasional bent or broken twig to mark it.

The leaves on the forest floor were slightly indented from people having walked over them, including our party of seven that had come along it that very morning as we were going on our hunt, but to the untrained eye, the trail didn't exist. Even for me, having spent the last fifteen years in the jungle, the trail was not always visible, but my sense of direction kept me going. Occasionally, when I lost the trail, I would cry out in my heart, "Thank you, Lord. Thank you, Lord."

At least being off the trail would make it difficult for the Indians to ambush me. They wouldn't know where I was any better than I did myself. Then I would find the trail and continue on. It was not a lengthy distance back to where we had camped the night before, but with the great sense of urgency I had on my shoulders, realizing that Steve was critically injured, it seemed much farther. Even while God was encouraging my heart in other ways, there was a sense of depression knowing that the radio equipment would all be gone when I got back to our campsite. We were two days' travel for a healthy man from our base at the Víbora River, and that was the nearest place we could expect to find any kind of help.

There were no Bolivian farmers in this area, no loggers, no oilmen. The Víbora base was the nearest possible point for any help, and there was no way that it could be reached, humanly speaking, without at least an overnight hike.

As I neared the place where we had camped the previous night, the trail improved slightly. The Indians had walked on it more here. Soon I recognized the area I was in and knew that I would see another trail coming in from the right to join the trail I was on. From that point, I knew it was less than a hundred yards to last night's campsite. It was also the most likely point for an ambush. If they were lying in wait, they would expect us to return for our belongings and would likely have some warriors waiting in ambush.

Now that I knew right where the camp was, I decided that the safest way to arrive at it unharmed was by sprinting. The jungle was open here and the trail level and smooth enough to run. I didn't have a pack on my back to hinder me but hoped to have a pack on my back when I returned to Steve and Felix. Would my pack be there? As I came to the Y in the trail, I took off running at full speed. Next to our camp of the previous night was a tall, wide jungle tree with giant fins coming up off the jungle floor. If I could get to that tree, get my back against it with the fins on my right and left sides, I would only have to face an open area of about 120 degrees in front of me. My back and sides would be protected by the tree and fins while I looked the situation over.

The jungle there was not so dense, and attackers wouldn't be able to position themselves too closely. With good visibility, I would have some chance of survival. I sprinted and almost dove into the protection the giant tree afforded. The tree towered at least 120 feet above the jungle floor and gave solid protection to my back. Any attack would have to be from the front or sides.

Events of the previous afternoon began coming back to me now, and suddenly, I began to understand those events with new clarity. When we had been setting up our campsite the night before, the Indians had come and begun scraping leaves aside. Being dry season, the jungle floor was littered quite deeply with six or eight inches of dry leaves. The Indians had said to us, "We lost a knife over in this area. We need to look for it." They began scraping the leaves aside making little trails through the area where we were going to camp. Now I understood for sure what they had been doing. They had been planning to come in quietly along those trails in the night and shoot us while we lay sleeping unsuspectingly in our jungle hammocks and tents on the floor of the forest.

However, around dusk, when they saw us climb into our mosquito nets with our guns and with flashlights, which by this time the Indians understood and knew allowed us to see in the dark, the attack was evidently called off. It had become obvious to them that we could defend ourselves. Now so many things from the previous day began coming clear in my mind, things that I now realized I should have understood in the light of my fifteen-years of Yuquí culture and language study, living and roaming with the Yuquí.

How dense I had been. All my thoughts had been concentrated on helping these people, knowing they were suffering greatly after the recent loss of their chief and all the other principal men in the group. On the last contacts we had when the Indians came to our camp on the Víbora River, the women and children were emaciated. Women who had previously been fat and healthy were just gaunt shadows of their former selves. It had been obvious to us as missionaries that it was urgent to settle these people down before the rest of the group was killed by the peasant farmers who had moved into the area, following oilmen who had made roads into nearby areas of jungle. With only two young men in their late teens or early twenties left as hunters to provide for this now reduced group of about twenty-four nomads, the urgency of their situation had blinded the eyes of us as missionaries to the danger we were facing.

Later we would discover how much more we had failed to understand the day before. One of the things we had seen shortly before arriving at their camp was an area of jungle possibly fifty by fifty feet where the jungle floor was heavily littered with aluminum kettles, many of them smashed, glass bottles, some broken and others in decent condition; things that normally would have value to the Indians, and yet they had obviously destroyed or abandoned these items. We had wondered at the time but now understood clearly that these things had been sacrificed to the spirits of their dead. At the time, we had paid scant attention to the reason behind these items being in this location, although we had suspected it was related to the twelve Yuquí who had died in recent months. However, we failed to attach an adequate level of importance to what we had seen.

My thoughts returned to the task at hand. Steve needed help. He needed help now! No arrows came flying. I tentatively stuck my head out a little farther from the safety of the finned tree. I couldn't waste time watching out for myself; Steve might not survive. I had expected all our belongings to be missing and the majority were gone. Steve's pack had disappeared. Felix's pack was gone, the cooking kettles, the canteens full of water, the machetes—all had been taken. But God, in His goodness, had seen to it that a few things were spared. My pack was still there.

Evidently, the Indians were trying to keep on my good side and had thoughts of being able to come back to the missionary base sometime in the future to trade goods and to have their tools, axes, machetes, and paring knives sharpened. They were trying to keep their options open. Steve had been carrying a portion of the radio equipment in his backpack, and Felix had also been carrying some of it. One of them had carried the transceiver and microphone, one had the antenna, and one of us had been carrying the battery pack. All these items were necessary to be able to transmit a distress call and get the help we so badly needed.

But God was at work! Shortly before leaving camp that morning, we had discussed the possibility of going on the radio, but since the Indians expressed a desire to get off early on the hunt, we decided to wait and go on the radio when we returned from our morning hunt. However, Steve and Felix had each pulled their portion of the radio gear out of their backpacks and set it on the ground. I had not.

Steve's pack was gone, Felix's pack was gone, but their portions of the radio equipment were still sitting where they had placed them. Joy overwhelmed me as I realized that God had preserved all the radio gear. The Indians had no need for that gadgetry. They didn't understand it; they didn't know how to use it. It held no meaning for them.

I opened my pack and pulled out my portion of the radio gear. The dipole antenna, 116 feet long, was tied up in a careful roll. I didn't want to take the time to properly stretch the antenna through the trees. Time was of the essence. Untying one side of the antenna, I flung it out over the bushes as far as I could. It tangled some but was mostly up off the ground. Then I grabbed the other half of the antenna, threw it out in the opposite direction up over the bushes again, somewhat tangled but off the ground. Screwing the connector to the back of the radio, I now had the antenna prepared. Next, the microphone had to be plugged in and its connector screwed tight. Then, removing the Swiss Army knife from my pocket, I set about screwing the battery cables to the back of the radio. That completed, I turned on the radio.

The speaker greeted me with crackling static before I keyed the microphone and called, "Emergency, emergency! This is Chore River with an emergency. Are you there Víbora River?"

Almost immediately, I was greeted by Larry Depue's voice, "What's the problem, Chore River?"

"We've been attacked. Steve is hard hit. We need help immediately."

With only a few more questions about the situation, Larry swung into action, assuring me that he would get to work on finding a helicopter and some airplanes as well as a ground crew who could be dropped in by helicopter to the nearest beach on the Chore River. From there, they would need to cut their way to where Steve lay struggling for his life before carrying him out to the beach. Fortunately, my Vietnam-era army surplus jungle hammock had loops along the side where poles could be inserted so it could be used as a stretcher.

"I'm going to pack up the radio gear and head back to where Steve and Felix are down the trail," I told Larry, "so I won't be on the radio for at least fifteen minutes." With that, I began rolling up the antenna, disconnecting the rest of the radio equipment, putting it all in my backpack, and gathering up any of our other belongings I could carry with me. We might have to spend another night in the jungle and would need all the equipment possible that was left to us.

I quickly rolled up my jungle hammock, which I had been using as a tent on the ground, and took that along so Steve would have some shelter and refuge from the myriad of insects that populated the jungle. Within a few minutes, I was headed back down the trail toward Steve and Felix, content in the knowledge that the rescue mechanism had been put into operation. I knew I could count on Larry and the team of missionaries in Bolivia as well as God's children worldwide. There is a great sense of love and family among God's people and in the mission family. Within minutes, word was going out worldwide by radio, asking for prayer. Our pilot and pilots from other missions were dropping everything to lend a hand as God drew together a team to rescue His wounded children.

My mind continued active as I headed back down the trail to where Steve and Felix were waiting, and my thoughts once again returned to my boyhood, growing up in a nearby jungle village. The Bolivian farmers who were shot by the Yuquí during those years had none of the technical advantages that our missionary team had. The farmers generally lived from twelve to twenty miles by trail from the small jungle village of Todos Santos, which itself offered no adequate medical facility. If the wounded farmer didn't die in the jungle, they might be transported to this town by dugout canoe where a German immigrant doctor, who appeared to be hiding here after World War II, was living.

Among ourselves, we called this doctor "The Butcher." We suspected that it was thanks to his lack of expertise that at least one of the Bolivian farmers had died, although some of the shooting victims would not have survived even had the doctor known what he was doing. The town lacked most basic medical services.

As I headed back toward Steve and Felix, I realized that once again, I was vulnerable along the trail. If the Indians had not already fled the area, they knew the route I must travel back to Steve. They knew that we would come to retrieve our belongings and would then head back to the shooting site. Where might they set an ambush? Would they shoot from in front or from behind? Again, my thoughts returned to my childhood. One expedition of fishermen from the town of Todos Santos had traversed nomad territory and gone to the Chimoré River where the fishing was superb. Giant catfish, weighing well over one hundred pounds, abounded in that river.

While coming back from the Chimoré River to the town of Todos Santos, a distance of possibly fifteen miles, the fishermen were attacked by a band of nomad warriors. A few of the fishermen were hit by arrows as they fled, running down the trail with packs on their backs, but when they got out of the ambush and took stock of the situation, not one of them had a wound. All the arrows had gone into the packs full of fish. I had a pack on my back now, giving a measure of protection from the waist to the neck. The legs shouldn't be too bad to be struck in. I decided that the best thing to do would be to watch carefully ahead and to the sides of the trail, not turning constantly to see if an Indian stepped out from behind to draw a bead on me.

By now, it was a little after eight in the morning, possibly as late as 8:45. I knew that mission aircraft were being scrambled. Someone was trying to find a helicopter that could extract Steve and Felix. Lord willing, by nightfall, Steve would be in surgery.

When I arrived back at the site of the shooting, Steve still lay where he had fallen. As we discussed the situation, Steve told Felix and me how he himself had broken the arrow shaft off from the point after he was hit. The bleeder point is designed to detach itself and remain in the animal or person who is shot. This type of bamboo tip is the most serious weapon the Yuquí use. It's designed for large animals, jaguar and tapir, animals that are hard to bring down. They use it when they are serious about killing, knowing that by the tip remaining in the animal as it runs the movement of the tip in the fleeing animal will increase the bleeding and bring the animal down more quickly.

For smaller game, or when they aren't as serious about killing, the Yuquí use a barb-tipped arrow. Steve had moved very little after being hit. He was still lying where he had initially fallen, and while he had bled, the arrow tip was minimizing the loss of blood. Their intent had been to kill Steve, but God was watching over him, preserving him for His glory.

Felix was doing what he could to make Steve comfortable. There wasn't much else he could be doing. I unrolled the jungle hammock and began setting it up as protection for Steve. Then I proceeded to set up the radio equipment so that we could get back in touch with the rescue team. A South American Mission pilot, Tom Bush, was already in the air, heading out to locate us and to guide the helicopter and rescue team into the area. There was no clearing nearby. The jungle was much like a forest in this location, very tall trees, somewhat open or clear underneath, not nearly as dense as other areas of jungle. It was evident, though, that a helicopter could not be brought in without substantial clearing being done as many of the trees were towering giants.

I stood and walked the few yards down our back trail to where I had seen Potbelly with the drawn bow and discovered that the nomads had dropped two bows and four arrows when they fled the scene. Often, the Yuquí, to show their displeasure, will break someone's arrows or even their bow when they are extremely angry, so that's what I did. I wanted them to know that we were very unhappy about what they had just done. To break the thick bows required finding two trees that were close together, putting one end of a bow between the trees and using them as I levered the tough palm-wood bow until it broke. After destroying the weapons to where they couldn't be repaired, I left them in a pile on the trail. Eventually, they would come to reconnoiter the area and would see that we weren't pleased with how they had treated us, their friends.

The waiting began. There was not much that Steve, Felix, or I could do except wait and listen to the activity on the airwaves. Larry Depue and others of the missionary team were doing a good job organizing the rescue effort. No one wanted to be left out. Their love and concern for the injured was very evident.

In my backpack was a small first aid kit, including a few painkillers and antibiotics. I dug out some Novalgina tablets for Steve as it was the only analgesic I carried. Felix was being attentive to Steve's needs, fanning him, giving him a little extra air, and spent most of the morning, afternoon, and into the night doing that. The fanning also helped somewhat to keep the insects at bay.

While a rescue craft was being sought, Steve lay in pain. Later in the morning, the sound of the helicopter landing on the river beach over a mile away gave Steve the false hope of being rescued before noon. What he didn't know was that he would have to spend a long miserable night in the jungle before the rescue party eventually reached him. The jungle close to the Chore River was such a tangled mass that it would take the ground party one-and-a-half hours to hack out only 150 yards of trail. They were intent on creating a good enough trail that a stretcher could be carried along it, but the jungle growth was an almost impenetrable thicket of vines, brush, and misshapen trees. Once the growth was cleared, the ground was left littered with debris, making walking extremely difficult.

The arrow that had passed into Steve's body was making every breath a struggle. At one point during the morning, he felt that death was imminent, but in spite of his pain, he was overwhelmed with the joy of knowing that his sins were forgiven and that he was going to meet the Lord he loved. He was ready to go, but he wondered what would happen to his wife, Vangie, and their six children.

A helicopter had been found, and by late morning, the rescue team had been deposited on a river beach less than two thousand yards from where Steve lay. Steve, Felix, and I were optimistic; surely the rescuers would be to us by one o'clock. The distance wasn't that great.

Little did we know how dense and impenetrable the jungle was between us and the Chore River. Even with a machete to slash their way, the rescuers were only moving forward a few feet at a time. An hour passed, and with no sign of the rescuers, I went back down the nomad trail to the south to see if the rescuers had crossed the trail in that direction and missed us. With no sign of their passage across that trail, I went north and once again found no indication they had crossed that trail. By now, it was two o'clock, and with the day passing quickly, we decided I should take a compass heading of 280 degrees toward the Chore River with the hope of encountering the rescue team and guiding them more quickly to where the injured lay. Larry Depue and Tom Bush had given me the heading to the river when they flew over earlier in the day.

Steve was breathing a little more easily now and was encouraged with the knowledge that help was coming, but we all wanted that help sooner rather than later. Leaving my pack and flashlight with Steve and Felix in case there was anything there that would be useful to them, I picked up my rifle and headed west toward the Chore River and the rescue team. All our machetes had been stolen when the nomads raided our camp, so all I was carrying was my rifle.

Shortly after leaving Steve and Felix, I crossed a narrow, shallow waterway that wasn't flowing and was able to drink my fill of cool, dark, tannin-laced water. Not too much farther along, I found myself in a vast dry swamp with vegetation so thick, I had to crawl through on my hands and knees. With no machete, I couldn't cut my way and was reduced to kneeling on the ground, pushing the vegetation apart, throwing my gun through the opening, and then crawling through the doorway I had created, only to repeat the process over and over.

Occasionally, I could walk upright a few paces before once again kneeling as I forced my way through the tangle of vines and brush. At one point, I climbed a short tree, hoping to have some indication that I was near the river but could see nothing but swamp for what looked like miles. That was demoralizing! I said to myself, "The river's gotta be there if I keep going west," so I kept pressing forward.

The heat was unbearable; my body was sapped of water, my clothing soaked as if I had dunked in the river. Time after time, I collapsed from exhaustion. By five o'clock, I was completely wrung-out, and when I found where a large tree had fallen with the root system forming a dome-like half-cave, I stopped, gathered what little rotting firewood and dry palm branches I could find nearby, and lit a fire. The warmth of the fire reflecting over me from the back of the wall the tree root system formed began drying my sweat-soaked clothing, and soon I was dry.

As I lay there, too exhausted to travel any farther and with my mouth so dry, I could do little more than whisper. I heard Larry Depue and the rescue team hoot and fire their guns. They were within a hundred yards of me, although with a breeze influencing the direction of sound, I had no idea they were that close by. Now that I had found a comfortable place to spend the night, I wasn't about to leave my nice hideaway to look for them; moreover, I didn't have the strength to travel farther. I was wrung-out and, with my mouth so dry, couldn't hoot back to them, although I tried. They continued cutting trail by flashlight until after 9:00 p.m. with only one flashlight between them.

With the warmth of my fire reflecting from the cave wall and very few mosquitoes to bother me, God pointed out to me the many blessings I had. The only thing I sensed a lack of was water; on the other hand, I was in good health, I was within yelling distance of the rescue party, I had a warm fire, and a gun with fifteen rounds of ammunition left. As I prayed for Steve, I also thanked God for His goodness to us and was confident that He was in control of the situation and that His hand was continually watching over us.

Early in the morning, the rescue team began cutting trail once again, taking turns leading the way so as to speed the process, and when they next hooted, I was able to answer…barely since my mouth was still dry. I also fired my rifle to give them a clearer indication of where I was at since a light breeze was making it difficult to tell which way the sounds were coming from. By the time I joined up with the rescue party, it was six in the morning.

Throughout the day and into the night, Steve had found himself enrolled in the school of faith. When he had asked God to keep his back, he had meant, "Don't let it get hurt." Now he had a broken arrow shaft protruding from it. Was God still the keeper of his back?

Another big problem was that Steve was dehydrated. His throat was dry and sticking together which triggered an uncontrollable desire to heave. He and Felix had no water, but during the night, they could hear raindrops falling around them. He prayed that God would direct some of the drops through a hole in the canopy of leaves above him. He opened his mouth and stuck out his tongue and waited for a few drops of water. Nothing happened! Had God failed him?

Felix, though wounded, found a small measure of relief for Steve by crawling around on his hands and knees with a flashlight, looking for moisture retained in leaves on the forest floor. It was a tedious task, but one droplet would open Steve's throat for about an hour. Several times throughout the night, Steve asked Felix to pray, and God heard those prayers.

The rescue team consisted of Larry Depue, Sam Major, Ron Gouge, two Yuquí from Chimoré, and Jack Jones. When I joined forces with them a little after six in the morning, I told them that we were still a great distance from Steve and would need to follow a heading of one hundred degrees, the reciprocal of what I had traveled to meet them. About then, Tom Bush flew over us in a small Cessna and circled until we built a smoky fire. Once that was done, he flew back over us and gave us a direct heading to where Steve and Felix were waiting, ninety degrees. We hung on ninety degrees, Woolly Hair going first, myself second with the compass as we pushed hard, cutting just enough to get through and hurrying to arrive at Steve and Felix's location.

We had agreed almost immediately when we found each other in the morning that we would need to make a clearing next to Steve and evacuate him by helicopter as the jungle was too rugged for him to survive if we tried to carry him out to the beach. We continued pushing hard toward Steve and Felix, and after we had gone a certain distance, I told the guys, "About that much again, and we ought to be close to Steve and Felix."

We went that far again and half that far again, and then we fired a gun twice; Felix responded by firing his gun. We all grinned at each other, quit cutting trail, and headed for the sound of the gun.

It was 7:30 a.m. when we arrived where Steve lay, and Sam Major, pilot and trained paramedic, evaluated Steve's condition before beginning an IV. Steve found the fluid restorative and his spirits uplifted by the knowledge that he might soon be on his way to the city and medical attention. Sam Major had worked as a paramedic for about four years before coming to Bolivia, so he was a real asset to the team.

As the rescue party was making its way to Steve and Felix, we had discussed Steve's precarious situation. "There is no way he will survive being carried out to the beach over this rough terrain," I stated.

Larry and the others who had spent many hours hacking their way through jungle obstructions the previous day were quick to agree. "We'll need to have the helicopter drop chainsaws to us and make a clearing for him to land," Larry recommended, and all were quick to concur with that sentiment.

Now Larry reached for the microphone to talk to Linda, his wife, who was operating the radio at the Víbora River base. "Sweetheart, we need someone to get two of the chainsaws, mixed gasoline, a file for sharpening the saws, some axes and machetes, and have all of those items lowered to us from the helicopter. We'll need to make a clearing for the helicopter to pick Steve up here. We won't be able to carry him out to the beach, over."

"Roger, Chore River, I copy that. We'll get someone right on that, over," responded Linda.

"Oh, and by the way, they'll need a very long rope for lowering the items to us as the trees are over 120 feet tall, over," continued Larry.

"Affirmative, we copy that," answered Linda. "We'll let you know when the helicopter is ready to head your way. Tom says to make sure you build a smoky fire so the helicopter can find you. He'll be coming with it to lower the items, over."

"Affirmative, over," Larry replied.

Now that Linda was handling things on the Víbora River end, Larry and I and the two Christian Yuquí who were with the rescue team headed back to the campsite where Felix, Steve, and I had spent our night with the hostile Yuquí. What we found was startling!

One aspect of Yuquí culture was that they didn't bury their dead. Instead, they wrapped the bodies in woven palm-leaf baskets and placed them on a raised pole platform inside a palm-leaf shelter. Once the flesh had decayed from the bones, they were "renewed" by being placed in a new basket and new shelter. Later, the bones of an important person might be painted with the red coloring agent, achiote, and carried along in the nomadic wanderings of the tribe. They believed the spirits of the dead influenced their lives in many ways, even causing death, so they treated their bones with great respect.

The most important way in which they appeased the spirits of the dead was by choosing other individuals to be killed and accompany them to the next world. This was also a form of self-protection so that the dead didn't do the choosing. Someone must die! And in this case, they had decided to send two members of the missionary team along to accompany the spirits of their dead warriors.

We had made camp right next to two burial shelters. The area around us was littered with smashed kettles and broken bottles. The Indians had sacrificed these treasures to show their sorrow to the dead. Now, as we went down the trail beyond their abandoned camp, we found a clearing where poles had been tied into place to build new burial shelters. Our guides explained that the hostile nomads had been in the process of "renewing the bones."

In trying to kill Steve and Felix, the Indians had not been rejecting us nor the Gospel message. Instead, they were trying to satisfy the lust of an ancient Satanic belief that says the spirits of their dead need other spirits to accompany them in the next life. Someone must die! With the tribal chief and other prominent men recently killed by loggers, the slaying of the missionaries would have fulfilled their need to appease the spirits of the dead.

After a quick viewing of the area, we four men—Larry, the two Yuquí, and I—headed back to where Steve and the rescue team were awaiting delivery of the chainsaws. While we had been gone, other team members had chosen a spot in the jungle which looked like it might be the easiest to clear, although the jungle canopy was lofty with tall trees. We needed a spot close to where Steve lay, the easiest spot to clear, yet far enough away that none of the trees would fall on him. It wasn't long until the helicopter came to a hover above the treetops and, using a long rope, Tom Bush lowered chainsaws, gasoline, oil, and other necessities for the chainsaws as well as axes and machetes for hacking a clearing in the forest.

Ron Gouge of World Gospel Mission and a member of the rescue team had worked in the lumber industry in Kentucky before coming to Bolivia and was quick to offer his expertise in running a chainsaw. Larry Depue, a brawny fellow, ran the other saw, and the two of them worked tirelessly, felling the massive trees as the rest of us cut and chopped limbs and bushes. Even so, it took several hours before we had sufficient space for the rotors of the helicopter to clear as it lowered its way into the jungle. With the pile of debris we had generated, he wouldn't be able to land but would need to hover three or four feet above the ground while the injured were loaded aboard. There was still one large tree with overhanging limbs that might be in his way, but our saws were dull and not cutting well by this time, and we were hoping the pilot could maneuver around those branches, so we asked him to fly over and see if the clearing was adequate.

Soon he was hovering overhead, looking down and let us know, "That one big tree has to go." With the condition our saws were in, it would've taken quite a bit of time to sharpen the saws and get that last tree down as it was nearly five feet in diameter. Would we even have time to get it down and extract Steve for medical help today? It was doubtful.

Our hearts sank. Steve couldn't possibly survive another night on the forest floor.

As these thoughts raced through our minds, suddenly and unexpectedly, the helicopter began descending into the clearing, rotating from side to side as it lowered so the pilot could see the tree branches around him and avoid them. The next thing we knew, he was hovering over the dense pile of brush we had created. Steve had not yet been transferred to the jungle hammock/stretcher or prepared for evacuation as we hadn't expected the helicopter to come in. Now Tom Bush, accompanying the pilot onboard the chopper, was saying, "Hurry, hurry with Steve!" We had just been told he couldn't land and now, suddenly he was hovering in front of us.

We rushed over to Steve and lifted him onto the stretcher, a very painful procedure with Steve groaning the whole while, but we got him onto the stretcher and slid him crossways into the helicopter. Felix jumped in, Tom hopped back in, and up they went.

Steve Parker being carried to helicopter on jungle hammock stretcher for evacuation.

As the helicopter lifted toward the sky from the tiny clearing in the forest, its rotor blade forcefully impacted one of the large branches of the tree the pilot had wanted us to take down. I was looking up at the departing aircraft and saw and heard the dreadful loud *thud*, and then saw the helicopter begin falling to my left before it once again lifted upward and flew off to our Víbora base with the two injured men.

Later, when the helicopter pilot was talking to one of our missionaries, he commented, "Someone is watching over you, people. The blow we took to the rotor should have brought the helicopter down. My helicopter has carbon rotor blades that didn't snap off, but most helicopters would have crashed with the blow we took."

Once the helicopter with Steve arrived at the Víbora River base, Steve was transferred to the mission-owned twin Piper Aztec aircraft to be transported to a hospital in the city of Santa Cruz, less than an hour away. He would soon be receiving much needed medical attention.

Now Linda called us by radio with bad news. "The helicopter pilot says he won't go back in again. You'll have to hike home, over."

After acknowledging the news, we all rejoiced that the injured had made it out. The rest of us could handle the lengthy hike home, although it would mean sleeping in the jungle at least one night. We gathered all the nonessential gear we didn't want to carry home and piled it on the pool of blood where Steve had lain for the past thirty hours. After pouring the leftover gasoline mixture from the chainsaws over the pile, we lit it. We didn't want the nomad warriors to have the pleasure of seeing the damage they had done.

As we watched the fire burn, we pulled the handles from our axes and threw them in the fire, then went over to a nearby tree that had a big hollow spot in it and dropped the axe-heads deep down into the tree; once again, we didn't want the nomads to have the axe-heads, thus profiting from their treachery. They would never find the axe-heads there. Sad to say, it gave me a great sense of satisfaction to destroy any profit or pleasure the nomads might have hoped to gain from their dastardly deed.

We had almost finished packing our gear when the Piper Aztec twin transporting Steve arrived overhead and began circling our tiny clearing. Larry was quick to understand and commented, "He wants us on the radio." We had packed all the radio gear and now had to dig it back out and assemble it in order to hear the good news.

Chuck Henson, our mission pilot, reported, "If you can be to the beach in two hours, the helicopter will pick you up there."

Linda Depue confirmed what Chuck had told us, and Larry replied to her, "We'll call you from the beach, but it may take us two and a half hours."

Rapidly repacking the radio gear, we took off and hightailed it for the beach. Once again, we were thankful for our Yuquí guides who were able to find their way back through the jungle until we arrived at the wide trail the rescue team had cut the day before. Because of their tracking ability, we made it to the beach in less than two hours. Once the radio was set up at the beach, Linda reported to us, "The helicopter has a blown fuse and won't be able to come until tomorrow."

Bad news, good news, but we all continued to rejoice, because by now, Steve was in the city and would soon have the best medical care the hospital could provide. A few more nights in the jungle mattered little to us at that point.

Most of us had eaten very little as we pushed ourselves to exhaustion, making the clearing for the helicopter and then rushing for the beach. We also had limited food with us, so after setting up camp for the night, we went fishing for some supper. Our fishing expedition was not too successful, and as we crossed the river, heading back to our campsite, we heard the familiar *thump, thump, thump* of a helicopter in the distance—a sound we hadn't expected to hear until the next day. We sprinted madly for camp and arrived just as the helicopter alighted on the beach.

With the machine continuing to run, the pilot held up four fingers, indicating that four men should jump on board, then he spotted a fifth man standing there and said, "Jump in!" We had already loaded most of our gear, although Larry was up in the edge of the jungle, disassembling our campsite. When the pilot saw me, it was clear he planned to have me jump onboard as well, leaving Larry alone in the jungle. I turned my back and ran for the woods so the pilot wouldn't insist on me getting into the helicopter and leave Larry alone. Larry and I didn't take time to untie the ropes holding our tent and tarps up but slashed all the ropes and strings and barely had time to finish tearing down the camp before the helicopter was back, ready to extract us.

The helicopter pilot seemed to really want to help in any way possible and could see that he had saved Steve's life by pulling him out. He had gone the extra mile in taking risks on our behalf. Thank you, Mr. Pilot, whoever you were!

Once he arrived in the city, Steve was in surgery for three hours, and afterward, the doctors commented that it was impossible to drive that large arrow point through Steve's body in that area and not hit an artery or vital organ. All they could say was, "It's a miracle."

Felix, not seriously wounded, returned within a few days to the Víbora River and the contact effort. Steve was in the hospital for eighteen days and had many opportunities to share the Gospel with doctors, nurses, roommates, and others.

A few weeks after the shootings, I received a note from Steve, "Don't expect me back to the Víbora River base for six or eight weeks, but then expect me back."

Daily doctors were drawing infected fluid out of Steve, and he was on antibiotics for that. They also removed countless maggots, which the doctors said were a good thing as they were eating the decaying flesh and lessening the chance of Steve getting gangrene.

In a five-year period, six missionaries had been shot by the nomads as we worked at building friendship with them and settling them down; Steve was the most seriously wounded of the six, and all had survived.

As I settled back into the routine at the Víbora River base, I spent many hours meditating on God's Word, in communion with Him, and found encouragement, especially in Psalms 27:13–14, "I had fainted, unless I had believed to see the goodness of the Lord in the land of the living. Wait (with expectation) on the Lord: be of good courage, and He shall strengthen thine heart: wait (expectantly), I say, on the Lord" (KJV).

I was glad we were all still in "the land of the living" and continued to "wait expectantly" for the good God had in store for us. I knew He wasn't finished with the plans He had for us or for the hostile group of nomads who still needed to learn of His great love for them. To kill or be killed was a way of life to the hostile nomads, and I was confident they would eventually show up once again at the Víbora River base, acting as if nothing had happened, but how long might it be before they returned? Or would they be annihilated by farmers, hunters, oilmen, or loggers before they had opportunity to return? We prayed that God would protect them and bring them back to us and that their hearts would be prepared to be enlightened through His Word.

After the 1985 Shootings

THREE MONTHS LATER, THE MARABOL lumber company contacted our mission office in Santa Cruz to report that they were in "permanent" contact with a group of presumed Yuquí thirty-five kilometers east of us and having trouble communicating with them. Would we be able to help? We were happy to hear that they had a 700-meter-long airstrip which would allow us to fly a team over to evaluate the situation.

By now, Steve Parker had rejoined us at the Víbora River, so he joined Larry Depue and me as pilot Tom Bush flew us over to Arroyote. We also had Bob Garland and three Yuquí believers on alert, ready to join us if the story proved true.

As we flew over Arroyote, we discovered the airstrip to be in very poor condition, not at all like it had been described to us. Trees were leaning in over the runway, and there was barely space between their tops to fit the wings of the small Cessna. The approach to the airstrip had tall trees sticking up in it, and as we approached, Tom had to lift one wing over a tree to avoid hitting it, a maneuver I had never before experienced.

As we finally settled onto the tall uncut grass of the runway, I wondered if we would be able to get back out without doing significant work to the airstrip and approach. Tom taxied the plane toward a thatch-roofed house near the edge of the runway and shut off the engine. Soon we were talking with Lino Mendez, the caretaker of the property, and learned that we were the first airplane ever to land there.

Lino, a talkative storyteller, along with his few companions, were thrilled to have visitors to their isolated location. Two of the men claimed to have seen fleeting glimpses of the nomads but hadn't had any face-to-face contact and were terrified of the "savages," even more so after they saw Steve's recent scar. Whether the nomads they had seen were from the group we had been having contact with or whether they were from a group we had never met, we had no way of knowing, although we suspected it was the latter.

Before departing, we borrowed machetes and worked our way down the center of the airstrip, cutting a swath wide enough that the propeller of the airplane wouldn't be cutting grass as we made our takeoff roll. Tom didn't seem troubled by the condition of the runway, and we chose to trust his judgment; after all, he had been a flight instructor at a Christian college in Michigan before coming to Bolivia, so he likely understood the capabilities of the small plane.

We did lighten the plane by leaving sixty-six pounds of food and cooking utensils behind, thinking we might send a team to begin a contact effort there while also waiting for the nomads to return to our Víbora River base. Although we might find the two groups to be one and the same, we thought it more likely we were dealing with two different bands of Yuquí.

One month later, and only four months after Steve and Felix had been shot, we flew a team over to Arroyote to set up camp. They would improve the airstrip and look the area over for signs of the nomads, beginning a contact effort there. I was the only adult male to remain behind at the Víbora River, although Steve's son, Kerry Parker, was old enough to count as a second man. The two of us would maintain the base and be available for any needs the missionary wives and families might have. I was left behind since I would be able to communicate with the nomads if they returned to us.

After two nights in Arroyote, the men called by radio and gave us a lengthy list of additional supplies they needed. I made my way to the storage shed to prepare the supplies so they could be flown over to them the next time we had a flight. It was 8:00 a.m. As I worked, I heard the women in camp looking for me, and they seemed rather animated. The nomads who shot Steve and Felix had appeared on the edge of our clearing!

While Kerry Parker stayed back near the houses, holding a rifle, I advanced about halfway out toward the gift rack, staying a safe distance from the edge of the jungle, then stopped and said to the nomads, "Come!"

They replied, "You come!"

I answered, "You come! I am the one you can have confidence in (you can trust me)."

Potbelly, an expendable slave, accompanied by two nomad women, left the safety of the forest and approached to within fifteen feet of me.

Seeing that nothing happened to Potbelly or the women, Tom, Dick, Vera, Tapir, Harry, Friday, Spooky, and Whitey now made their way forward—ten nomads in total. I explained to them that Steve and my other companions had gone to look for "your others (the other group of Yuquí)" and went on to explain, "I will have the airplane bring them back tomorrow, and we will give you bananas then. I will not give you any bananas today. Come back tomorrow."

Tom was watching me closely and now commented, "Why are your legs trembling?"

While I was trying to remain calm, I couldn't control my shaking legs. "Your legs would be shaking in the same way if your friends shot at you like you did to us," I remonstrated, and then went on to explain that the young man with the gun was Steve's son and had orders to shoot them in the legs if they touched me in any way. "Big Father (God) took care of Steve and made him well again. He will be here tomorrow. Come back tomorrow and see him. He will give you bananas," I finished.

The contact lasted for thirty minutes, and after I again promised to give them bananas the next day, they disappeared into the jungle. Now we needed to contact a pilot and see if a plane was available to bring Steve, Larry, and the others back from Arroyote before the nomads returned.

At 8:30 a.m. the next morning, I was lying in my hammock, listening to the rain pour down, convinced the nomads wouldn't come due to the terrible weather. Fortunately, the weather had been good the previous day, and we had been able to fly our team and most of their equipment back from Arroyote. Now Steve came by to let me know that we had visitors.

In earlier discussions, we had decided that Steve would not carry a gun as we didn't want the nomads to think he was going to retaliate against them in any way, but the rest of us were armed with either revolvers or carrying rifles. Even so, the nomads came right into our camp with no hesitation and, with no prompting from us, left their bows and arrows behind. Soon we were sitting around the fire, under the shelter where we normally visited with them, cooking and eating rice and bananas together with thirteen nomads.

Previously, the missionary team had met together and agreed on setting certain conditions for the reestablishment of normal relations with the nomads. We would insist they return Steve's pack and specific other stolen items such as our three machetes, three fishlines, kettle, water jug, mosquito net, clothing, and a few other items. Now, when they asked us to sharpen some axes and machetes for them, we explained our conditions, telling them, "We will give you food—bananas, manioc, rice, and corn—but we will not sharpen tools for you or give you any kettles, axes, machetes, clothing, fishlines, or other trade goods until you return the stolen items." Then, so there would be no misunderstanding, we told them exactly what items needed to be returned.

After a time, the rain lightened up, and they wanted to go and see the piglets. I let them know that once the stolen items were returned, I would give them more pigs. Tom selected a white one, Dick a white and brown one, and Tapir requested a big black male. I promised to hold their chosen pigs for them until our conditions were met.

As we continued to visit with them, it wasn't long before we began to sense that they still posed a danger to us. When I suggested, "Move your camp close to us so we can see you more often and feed you;" they responded, "Come to our camp to verify that we have moved in close, and we will give you back the stolen items at the same time."

Judging by the attitude in which it was said, it seemed to be an attempt to get us out into the jungle where they could once again shoot us.

That afternoon, we went on the radio and asked Bob Garland at the Chimoré if Straight Hair and his brother Wooly Hair along with their wives could come over to help us. Having the best possible help could make the difference. Among other things, the Yuquí from the Chimoré could understand everything the nomads might say and would have a better feel for what they might be thinking.

It would be three months before we saw the nomads again. It rained nightly for the next three weeks, culminating in the river flooding our camp. There was no way the nomads could come to us in these conditions. No doubt, they were roaming the high belts of jungle on the far side of the Chore River and would return when the waters receded.

As the waters went down, our hopes went up, and eventually, the day came when I thought I heard a hoot from the edge of our clearing. I was in my work shed, sorting chainsaw accessories, and called to Vickie who was in the house, "Look out and see if the Indians are there."

She looked out the window but saw nothing. Felix had also heard a hoot, and now he called me, and together we made our way out toward the gift rack. As we approached, we could see Steve's backpack hanging from the rack and, in a moment, nomads began to materialize from the surrounding jungle.

After greeting the people and giving warm hugs to several of them, we began asking for other items that had been stolen, and they produced them one by one, not spontaneously, but forcing us to ask for each item. Soon, most of the requested items had been returned, although two fishing lines had not been brought, and they promised to bring them the next day. We had failed to list many of the belongings that had been taken from Steve and Felix's packs but had decided not to make an issue of those since we hadn't mentioned them earlier.

After the nomads headed home for the day, a flight arrived bringing Straight Hair and Wooly Hair along with their wives and families to help out. Now we felt better prepared to interact with the nomads, although in the night, a cold rainy storm blew in from the south, so we had no visitors for the next three days.

When the nomads did show up again, they brought *all* the stolen items we had requested, putting our relationship with them back on a normal footing, with one major change. Once we began trading with the nomads again, Steve was put in charge of all trade goods, and they had to go to him with their requests. If they made a request of one of us who spoke the language, we would say, "Ask Steve" and then accompany them to Steve and translate their request, letting him fulfil it. We were hoping they would come to value him enough to eventually apologize for having shot him.

All of us who spoke the dialect, the Yuquí from Chimoré and me, also talked sternly to the nomads about their having shot Steve and Felix, letting them know that we wouldn't put up with this type of treatment. To this point, they had seemed flippant about the shootings as if they were no big deal, but soon they began to sober up as they saw we were serious about them treating us with respect. When we went fishing together in the boat, we insisted they leave their weapons behind while we carried ours.

After two more contacts, the nomads failed to appear for several days, so Vickie and I flew out to the mission boarding school for the end of school year ceremonies, leaving coworkers to interact with the nomads if they returned. The morning we were to fly back to the Víbora, the nomads reappeared, but since Vickie and I with our family were due to leave for the United States on home assignment in a few days, it was decided that we shouldn't return to the Víbora.

Our missionary coworkers and Yuquí from the Chimoré would continue the effort to see the Víbora Yuquí settled with the Chimoré River group. Only Dick and his small portion of the group came out to the missionaries. It seemed that he and his older brother, Tom, had quarreled, possibly over the pigs we had given to them. During this contact, they were once again encouraged to visit the base at the Chimoré where the other Yuquí lived, and after some discussion and a promise of being able to bring back sugarcane and other goodies, Dick and Potbelly were convinced to take the plane ride to the Chimoré base.

Potbelly, the slave, was a little braver than his master, Dick, who spent the flight time huddled down, crouching on the floor of the plane.

Within a few weeks, Vickie and I were settled in Spokane, Washington, where we spent the first six months of our home assignment but continued to receive regular updates by amateur radio of how things were going at the Víbora River base. Larry Depue was an amateur and made "phone patches" through a radio operator in the United States in order to keep us informed.

Long Distance Updates

ONE DAY, FIVE MONTHS AFTER we had arrived in Spokane, the telephone shattered the stillness with its shrill beeping. Vickie answered. "Will you accept a collect call from Larry?" said the voice on the other end. It took a moment for Vickie to realize that the caller was referring to Larry Depue, missionary to the jungles of Bolivia. The call was being relayed to us through an amateur radio operator Stateside.

As Larry shared with us, we were overjoyed to hear of the most recent happening on their jungle base. The nomadic Yuquí had returned after a three-month absence, and a few days later, Potbelly, Dick's slave, had slipped away from the group and come by himself to see the missionaries. He had visited the Chimoré base a few months earlier and now wanted to leave his group and move over to the Chimoré River where the larger group of Yuquí were settled. Potbelly was in dangerously poor health, and there was some doubt he would survive. Even so, the missionaries had him flown to the Chimoré where they not only nursed him back to health but also ministered to his spiritual need.

Potbelly, whom God used to convince the Víbora River group of Yuquí to settle down with their relatives at the Chimoré River base.

A week later, when the nomads returned to visit the missionaries, they were upset initially that their slave had fled and had been helped by the missionaries but eventually calmed down and left on a friendly note.

Another two months went by before we received further news, this time in the form of a (slightly edited) letter from Steve and Vangie Parker.

A distant "hoot" broke the still quietness of the morning. "Vangie, check the gift rack!"

"Nobody is there," she replied.

Another hoot came from the edge of the clearing. As we ran out back to see better, we saw a few Yuquí hiding behind a tree. What a joy to see them again after waiting for more than two months for their return. Previously we had decided that during the next contact we would bring Potbelly, the slave who had fled to the Chimoré, along with some Yuquí believers and try to get the nomads to join them at the Chimoré camp. After the initial greetings were over and they were settled down beside a big pot of rice we made arrangements for a flight to bring Potbelly, Bob Garland, and some Yuquí believers from the Chimoré camp.

The flight arrived from the Chimoré and discussions began. As always, they made several promises to us, but after two hours decided to leave. We followed them to the edge of the jungle, pleading with them to stay. It appeared that one fellow might stay with us but his wife prevented him from doing so. They all left and we returned to our houses with heavy hearts feeling the weight of their decision.

Two hours later, just before dark, as we were on the radio letting coworkers know about their rejection someone shouted, "They're back with their hammocks and children!"

We joyously ran out to meet them. They soon told us that they desired to spend the night with us and move to the Chimoré camp the next day. Our hearts filled with praise to the Lord. After they set up their camp, we took them hunting and God provided a capybara (large rodent) for them to roast that night. The next morning, Sunday, we gave them blankets and other gifts and sent them by flight to the Chimoré camp.

After the last of the Víbora Yuquí left, on their way to join the group at the Chimoré, we were reflecting back over the last seven years of hoping, believing, and praying, and looked out to see that God had put a beautiful rainbow in sky above us reminding us of His faithfulness to complete His promises. As we go forth to reach a lost world, He goes with us all the way.

Epilogue

THE NEW LIFE WAS NOT without challenges as the two groups of Yuquí merged and learned to live together at the Chimoré River base, but with the assistance of the missionaries and the group of Yuquí who had already been settled for twenty years, the difficulties were surmounted.

Within a year after the Víbora group settled at the Chimoré, a third small band of Yuquí was also befriended and moved to the Chimoré, but as we, the Fosters, had moved on and had no hand in that, someone else will need to tell that story.

Not long after we returned to Bolivia to serve in Cochabamba, there was an encounter in the jungle between loggers and yet another hostile group of the Yuquí tribe. One logger was wounded by an arrow, and a nomad slave was shot in the thigh with a rifle bullet. The slave, being unable to flee, was flown to Cochabamba to have the bullet removed by doctors there and, after recuperating, was moved to the Chimoré base where he integrated with the Yuquí living there. Bob Garland and I had the privilege of accompanying him through surgery in the city as we calmed him in his own language and translated for the doctor who extracted the bullet.

Thirty years of missionary effort were required to preserve fewer than ninety Yuquí from annihilation by the encroaching world. Was it worth the investment of time, money, and physical and mental trauma on the part of the missionary team? I believe that each Yuquí is a treasure to God and well-worth the sacrifices that were involved and know that some of them will be with us as we worship God forever together in heaven. My only sadness is that more of the Yuquí bands could not have been befriended before the encroaching world brought an end to their existence.

About the Author

RAISED BY MISSIONARY PARENTS IN the western Bolivian Amazon, Alan grew up seeing firsthand the challenges involved in making friends with a group of hostile naked nomads whose language was unknown; and as an adult, he and his wife, Vickie, became involved in the effort to befriend a second band of the same tribe his parents had been instrumental in contacting.

The work was not without danger as six of their missionary coworkers were shot by the nomads during a five-year period. The privilege of seeing the Yuquí preserved from annihilation, ministering to their physical needs, and presenting the loving Creator God to them were well-worth the challenges involved.

Later, Alan and Vickie were based in the Andean mountain valley city of Cochabamba where Alan maintained electronic equipment in mission aircraft. Their last eighteen years of missionary service were spent doing computer support for missionaries worldwide. They retired in 2018, after forty-eight years of missionary service.